OVERLORD

Max Hastings has been studying warfare in libraries and on the
battlefield all his life. A scholar at Charterhouse and University
College, Oxford, he has reported for BBC TV and the London
Standard from more than fifty countries, seeing action in the
Middle East, Indochina and the South Atlantic, and earning his
wings with the TA Parachute Regiment. He has been cited three
times in the British Press Awards, most recently as Journalist of
the Year for his Falklands reporting in 1982, for which he was
also named Granada TV's Reporter of the Year. He is the
author of eight previous books, most on military themes, and
won the Somerset Maugham Prize in 1980 for *Bomber
Command*, his study of the strategic air offensive in the Second
World War. *Battle for the Falklands* won the 1983 *Yorkshire Post*
book of the Year Award. Now thirty-nine, he lives in
Northamptonshire with his wife and three children. His
anthology *The Oxford Book of Military Anecdotes* is published
in 1985. He is currently writing a new study of the Korean war.

Max Hastings

OVERLORD

D-Day and the Battle for Normandy

Pan Books London and Sydney

First published in Great Britain 1984 by Michael Joseph Ltd
This edition published 1985 by Pan Books Ltd,
Cavaye Place, London SW10 9PG
9 8 7 6 5 4 3 2 1
© Max Hastings 1984
ISBN 0 330 28691 9

Photoset by Parker Typesetting Service, Leicester
Printed and bound in Great Britain by
Cox & Wyman Ltd, Reading

Contents

List of Illustrations

MAPS

LINE DRAWINGS

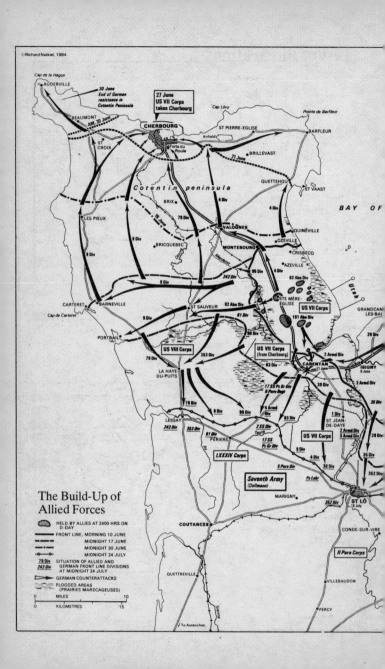

©Richard Natkiel, 1984

Cap de la Hague
AUDERVILLE

30 June
End of German
resistance in
Cotentin Peninsula

AM 30 June

**27 June
US VII Corps
takes Cherbourg**

Cap Lévy

Pointe de Barfleur

BEAUMONT

CHERBOURG

ST PIERRE-EGLISE

BARFLEUR

ST CROIX

Airfield

Forte du
Roule

BRILLEVAST

21 June

Cotentin peninsula

QUETTEHOU

ST VAAST

BRIX

4 Div

4 Div

BAY OF

LES PIEUX

79 Div

79 Div

VALOGNES

QUINÉVILLE

9 Div

BRICQUEBEC

MONTEBOURG

OZEVILLE

CRISBECQ

9 Div

9 Div

9 Div

Merderet

90 Div

4 Div

AZEVILLE

243 Div

82 Abn Div

CARTERET

BARNEVILLE

ST SAUVEUR

82 Abn Div

STE MÈRE-EGLISE

US VII Corps

Cap de Carteret

9 Div

81 Div

101 Abn Div

GRANDCAM
LES-BA

Utah

PORTBAIL

90 Div

Uth

29 Div

US VIII Corps

353 Div

**US VII Corps
(from Cherbourg)**

83 Div

2 Armd Div

CARENTAN

11 Div

ISIGNY
6 June

LA HAYE-
DU-PUITS

17 SS Pz Gr Div
6 Para Regt

38 Div

3 Armd Div

79 Div

8 Div

90 Div

4 Armd
Div

83 Div

1 Div
ST JEAN-
DE-DAYE

35 Div

LESSAY

243 Div

353 Div

81 Div

2 SS
Tout

US VII Corps

2 Armd Div
3 Armd Div

29 Div

PÉRIERS

17 SS
Pz Gr Div

9 Div

4 Div

35 Div

LXXXIV Corps

5 Para Div

30 Div

352 Div

Pz Lehr

**Seventh Army
(Dollmann)**

ST LÔ
18 July

352 Div

MARIGNY

The Build-Up of
Allied Forces

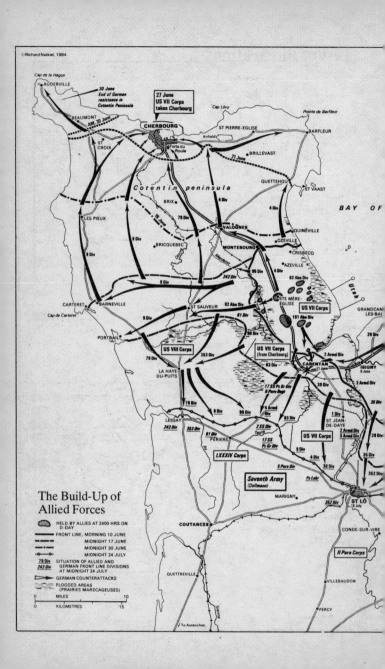

- ▨ HELD BY ALLIES AT 2400 HRS ON
  D-DAY
- ▬▬ FRONT LINE, MORNING 10 JUNE
- ▬▬▬ MIDNIGHT 17 JUNE
- ·–·–· MIDNIGHT 30 JUNE
- ○—○—○ MIDNIGHT 24 JULY
- *79 Div* *243 Div* SITUATION OF ALLIED AND
  GERMAN FRONT LINE DIVISIONS
  AT MIDNIGHT 24 JULY
- ➤ GERMAN COUNTERATTACKS
- ≈≈≈ FLOODED AREAS
  (PRAIRIES MARÉCAGEUSES)

COUTANCES

CONDE-SUR-VIRE

II Para Corps

QUETTREVILLE

VILLEBAUDON

0 ___ MILES ___ 10
0 ___ KILOMETRES ___ 15

To Avranches

Sienne

PERCY

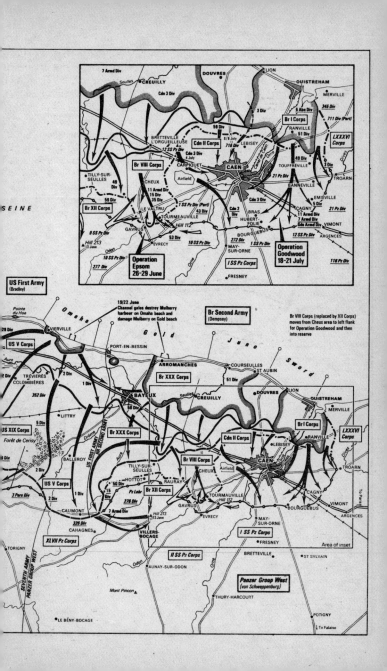

Upper inset map (Operations Epsom and Goodwood):

7 Armd Div

Seulles

CREULLY

DOUVRES

LION

OUISTREHAM

MERVILLE

346 Div

Cdn 3 Div

6 Abn Div

Br I Corps

711 Div (Part)

3 Div

59 Div

RANVILLE

51 Div

LXXXVI Corps

BRETTEVILLE L'ORGUEILLEUSE

12 SS Pz Div

Cdn 3 Div 4 July

Cdn II Corps

9/9 July

716 Div

LEBISEY

49 Div

3 Div

Br VIII Corps

CARPIQUET

CAEN

TOUFFREVILLE

SEINE

TILLY-SUR-SEULLES

CHEUX

Airfield

21 Pz Div

BANNEVILLE

TROARN

49 Div

11 Armd Div
15 Div
35 Div

1 SS Pz Div (Part)

43 Div

EMIEVILLE

5 Div

Br XII Corps

LE VALTRU

Cdn 2 Div

CAGNY

11 Armd Div

21 Pz Div

8 SS Pz Div

GAVRUS

Hill 213
13 June

TOURMEAUVILLE

Hill 112

BRAS
HUBERT-FOLIE

7 Armd Div

VIMONT

53 Div

EVRECY

BOURGUEBUS

272 Div

12 SS Pz Div

ARGENCES

10 SS Pz Div

10 SS Pz Div

MAY-SUR-ORNE

1 SS Pz Div

Operation Epsom 26-29 June

277 Div

Operation Goodwood 18-21 July

116 Pz Div

1 SS Pz Corps

FRESNEY

Lower main map:

US First Army (Bradley)

Pointe du Hoe

Omaha

VIERVILLE

29 Div

US V Corps

Aure

TREVIERES

COLOMBIERES

2 Div

352 Div

US XIX Corps

Forêt de Cerisy

Drôme

BALLEROY

Aure

2 Div

US V Corps

1 Div

3 Para Div

2 Div

326 Div

CAUMONT

CAHAGNES

XLVII Pz Corps

TORIGNY

SEVENTH ARMY PANZER GROUP WEST

LE BÉNY-BOCAGE

Mont Pincon

Odon

AUNAY-SUR-ODON

THURY-HARCOURT

Gold

19/22 June
Channel gales destroy Mulberry harbour on Omaha beach and damage Mulberry on Gold beach

PORT-EN-BESSIN

ARROMANCHES

Br XXX Corps

BAYEUX

56 Div

Seulles

CREULLY

Juno

COURSEULLES

ST AUBIN

51 Div

LITTRY

US FIRST ARMY BR SECOND ARMY

Br XXX Corps

TILLY-SUR-SEULLES

HOTTOT

50 Div

15 Div

RAURAY

Br XII Corps

278 Div

7 Armd Div

Hill 213
13 June

VILLERS-BOCAGE

Pz Lehr

GAVRUS

Br Second Army (Dempsey)

Br VIII Corps (replaced by Br XII Corps) moves from Cheux area to left flank for Operation Goodwood and then into reserve

DOUVRES

LION

OUISTREHAM

MERVILLE

Br I Corps

RANVILLE

LXXXVI Corps

Cdn II Corps

LEBISEY

Br VIII Corps

CHEUX

Airfield

CAEN

TROARN

TOURMAUVILLE

Hill 112

CAGNY

VIMONT

EVRECY

MAY-SUR-ORNE

BOURGUEBUS

ARGENCES

1 SS Pz Corps

FRESNEY

Area of inset

II SS Pz Corps

BRETTEVILLE

ST SYLVAIN

Panzer Group West (von Schweppenburg)

POTIGNY

To Falaise

Foreword

The struggle for Normandy was the decisive western battle of the Second World War, the last moment at which the German army might conceivably have saved Hitler from catastrophe. The post-war generation grew up with the legend of the Allied campaign in 1944–45 as a triumphal progress across Europe, somehow unrelated to the terrible but misty struggle that had taken place in the East. Today, we can recognize that the Russians made a decisive contribution to the western war by destroying the best of the German army, killing some two million men, before the first Allied soldier stepped ashore on 6 June 1944. It is the fact that the battle for Normandy took place against this background which makes the events of June and July so remarkable. Much has been written about the poor quality of the German troops defending the Channel coast. Yet these same men prevented the Allies almost everywhere from gaining their D-Day objectives, and on the American Omaha beach brought them close to defeat, even before the crack units of the SS and the Wehrmacht approached the battlefield. In the weeks that followed, despite the Allies' absolute command of sea and air, their attacks were repeatedly arrested with heavy loss by outnumbered and massively outgunned German units. None of this, of course, masks the essential historical truth that the Allies eventually prevailed. But it makes the campaign seem a far less straightforward affair than chauvinistic post-war platitudes suggested. Captain Basil Liddell Hart suggested in 1952 that the Allies had been strangely reluctant to reflect upon their huge superiority in Normandy and draw some appropriate conclusions about their own performance: "There has been too much glorification of the campaign and too little objective investigation."[1] Even 40 years after the battle, it is astonishing how many books have been published which merely reflect comfortable chauvinistic legends, and how few which seek frankly to examine the record.

It remains an extraordinary feature of the war in the west that,

13

despite the vast weight of technology at the disposal of the Allies, British and American soldiers were called upon to fight the German army in 1944–45 with weapons inferior in every category save that of artillery. Only in the air did the Allies immediately achieve absolute dominance in Normandy. Yet if the massive air forces denied the Germans the hope of victory, their limitations were also revealed. Air power could not provide a magic key to victory without huge exertions by the ground forces.

Post-war study of the campaign has focussed overwhelmingly upon the conduct of the generals, and too little attention has been paid to the respective performance of German, British and American ground troops. How could it be that after the months of preparation for OVERLORD, Allied armoured and infantry tactics in Normandy were found so wanting? The British, to a far greater degree than their commanders confessed even years after the campaign, were haunted by fear of heavy infantry casualties. I believe that Brooke and Montgomery's private perceptions of the campaign – and perhaps those of Bradley, too – were profoundly influenced by the knowledge that the German army was the outstanding fighting force of the Second World War, and that it could be defeated by Allied soldiers only under the most overwhelmingly favourable conditions. In Normandy, the Allies learned the limitations of using explosives as a substitute for ruthless human endeavour. It seems fruitless to consider whether an Allied plan or manoeuvre was sound in abstract terms. The critical question, surely, is whether it was capable of being carried out by the available Allied forces, given their limitations and the extraordinary skill of their enemies.

Few Europeans and Americans of the post-war generation have grasped just how intense were the early OVERLORD battles. In the demands that they made upon the foot soldier, they came closer than any other in the west in the Second World War to matching the horror of the eastern front or of Flanders 30 years earlier. Many British and American infantry units suffered over 100 per cent casualties in the course of the summer, and most German units did so. One American infantryman calculated that by May 1945, 53 lieutenants had passed through his company; few of them left it through transfer or promotion. The commanding officer of the 6th King's Own Scottish Borderers found, when his battalion reached Hamburg in 1945, that an average of five men per rifle company and a total of six officers in the unit were all that remained of those with whom he had landed in Normandy in June 1944. "I was appalled," he said. "I had no idea that it was going to be like that." He, like the Allied nations at large, had been conditioned to believe that industrialized warfare in the 1940s need never match the human cost of the earlier nightmare in France. Yet for those at the tip of the Allied spearhead, it did so.

This, then, is a portrait of a massive and terrible clash of arms redeemed for the Allies, but not for the Germans, by final victory. The early narrative of the background to the landings and their initial stages will be familiar to some readers, but its inclusion seems necessary for the sake of completeness, and it makes such a marvellous tale that it bears retelling. Thereafter, I have tried to examine much less closely studied aspects of the armies' tactics and performance, and to consider some unpalatable truths about what took place in the summer of 1944. Because Normandy was a vast campaign, it is impossible to retrace the history of every battle and every unit in detail, without achieving the tedium and bulk of an official history. By focussing upon the fortunes of a few individuals and units at different moments of the campaign, I hope that I have been able to give an impression of the experiences and difficulties endured by thousands of others. I have described each nation's sectors of the front in separate chapters, even at the cost of some loss of chronology, because only thus can the progress of the armies be considered coherently. Where I have quoted men by name, the ranks given are those that they held at the date concerned. I have adopted American spellings for American units and direct quotations from American personnel. I have made little mention of material that is familiar to every student of war history – Group-Captain Stagg's weather forecasting problems, the commanders' formal statements, the airborne operations on D-Day – which have been exhaustively described in other books. Instead, I have concentrated upon aspects which I hope will be less familiar: the battle inland and the personal experiences of men whose stories have never been told before, above all the Germans. The German army's achievement in Normandy was very great, and I have sought out may of its survivors. I have tried to write dispassionately about the German soldier's experience without reference to the odiousness of the cause for which he fought.

I have interviewed scores of American and British veterans, and corresponded with hundreds more. I am especially indebted to Field-Marshal Lord Carver, Field-Marshal Sir Edwin Bramall, General Sir Charles Richardson, Major-General G. P. B. Roberts, Major-General Sir Brian Wyldbore-Smith, General Elwood R. Quesada, General James Gavin and Brigadier Sir Edgar Williams. I also owe much to the librarians of the London Library, the Royal United Services Institution, the Staff College Camberley and the Public Record Office. For this, as for my earlier books, *Bomber Command* and *Das Reich,* Andrea Whittaker has been a splendid German interpreter and translator. Among the host of relevant literature, I must pay tribute to Nigel Hamilton's latest volume of his official biography of Lord Montgomery, and to Carlo D'Este's important recent study of the strategy of the Normandy campaign, both of which I was able to consult in the later stages of writing this book, and which were invaluable in causing me to consider some issues and some documents which would otherwise have passed me by. As always, I owe a great deal to the patience and forbearance of my wife Tricia who, having endured in recent years my spiritual life in a Lancaster at 20,000 feet and in the midst of occupied France, has now spent many months admidst the ruins of Caen and St Lô. Carlo D'Este and Andrew Wilson MC were kind enough to read the completed manuscript and to make helpful suggestions and corrections, although of course they share no responsibility for the narrative and the judgements, which are entirely my own. I am also greatly indebted to my editor in London, Giles O'Bryen, Philippa Harrison and to Alice Mayhew in New York.

Perhaps I should also avow a debt of gratitude to the British Army and the Royal Navy. One morning early in April 1982, I was sitting at my desk in Northamptonshire seeking to make the leap of imagination that is essential to books of this kind, to conceive what it was like to crouch in a landing craft approaching a hostile shore at dawn on 6 June 1944. By an extraordinary fluke of history, less than two months later I found myself crouched in a British landing craft 8,000 miles away. In the weeks that followed, I had an opportunity to witness an amphibious campaign whose flavour any veteran of June 1944 would immediately have recognized, even to the bren guns, oerlikons and bofors hammering into the sky. I would like to think that the experience taught me a little more about the nature of battles, and about the manner in which men fighting them conduct themselves. It has certainly made me all the more grateful that my generation has never been called upon to endure anything of the scale and ferocity that encompassed the men who fought in Normandy.

Max Hastings
Guilsborough Lodge,
Northamptonshire
October 1983

Prologue

On the night of 9 May 1940, Lieutenant John Warner did not reach his bed until 2.00 a.m. Along with the other officers of the Royal West Kents deployed along the Belgian frontier with the British Expeditionary Force, he had been celebrating in the mess amid the traditional rituals of the British army, with the regimental bands beating retreat in the little town square of Bailleul. It was unusual for all three battalions of a regiment to be campaigning – if the "bore war" in France could be dignified as such – alongside each other, and their party did justice to the occasion.

They were asleep a few hours afterwards when they were forced to take notice of "some enormous banging all over the place".[1] The German offensive in the west had begun. As the West Kents hastily prepared to march that morning of 10 May (caching the band instruments which they would never see again) it is a measure of the British army's collective delusion that they were ordered to advance to the Scheldt and to expect to remain there for some months.

In reality, they occupied their positions on the river for just four days before a trickle, and then a stream, of Allied soldiers began to pass through them towards the rear. Rumours drifted back also that "the French had packed it in down south". Their colonel, Arthur Chitty, hated the enemy with all the fervour of a regular soldier who had been captured in the first weeks of war in 1914 and spent four years behind the wire. Now, he organized the pathetic deployment of their Boyes anti-tank rifles in an anti-aircraft role. Shortly afterwards, the Germans arrived.

The 4th West Kents were deployed along the river bank. For reasons best known to itself, the battalion on their right chose to take up positions some way back from the waterline. As a result, the enemy was quickly able to seize a bridgehead on the British side, threatening the flank of the 4th. John Warner, a 23-year-old solicitor from Canterbury with a Territorial Army commission, claimed that, "as a lawyer, I was a cautious chap who always liked to look round corners before turning them". Yet he found himself leading a succession of headlong charges against the Germans with his bren-gun carrier platoon which resulted in what he later called "a very interesting little battle", and won him the Military Cross. The West Kents held their ground, but they were outflanked and soon forced to withdraw, their rear covered by the Belgians. In the days that followed, driving and marching north-westwards along the dusty roads, they fought one more significant action against the Germans in the forest of Nieppe, but found themselves chiefly confounded by the appalling traffic jams clogging the retreat, refugees and British vehicles entangled upon roads endlessly strafed by the Luftwaffe. Warner and his carrier platoon struck off across country to escape the chaos, which was fortunate, because shortly afterwards the Germans struck the main column, capturing the entire headquarters of the 1st West Kents, just ahead of the 4th. The young officer was dismayed by a brief visit to divisional headquarters, where "control had broken down completely". Morale among his own men remained surprisingly high, but the enemy had achieved absolute psychological dominance of the battlefield. "We thought the Germans were very good. In fact, we overestimated them," said Warner. Like so many others, the West Kents bitterly cursed the absence of the Royal Air Force, and became practised at leaping into ditches at the first glimpse of an aircraft.

When they reached the Dunkirk perimeter, Warner was ordered to abandon his vehicles. But having brought them intact every yard of the way from the Scheldt, he stubbornly drove into the British line, and handed over the carriers to one of the defending battalions. For the next three days, he sat in the sand dunes waiting for rescue, with a motley group of some 60 men who had gathered around him. He thought miserably: "Here I am with an MC in the field, and now I'm going in the bag." On the third day, he wearied of hanging about where he had been told to, and marched his men determinedly onto the Dunkirk mole, where he parleyed them a passage on an Isle of Man pleasure steamer. Thus, sleeping the sleep of utter exhaustion on the sunlit decks, they sailed home to England.

Curiously enough, while senior officers and statesmen were vividly aware that Britain had suffered catastrophe, once the young men of the BEF were home, very few saw their misfortunes in such absolute terms. It is the nature of soldiers to take life as it finds them from day to day. In the months and years that followed Dunkirk, John Warner shared the British army's dramas and anti-climaxes, abrupt moves and lengthy stagnations, leaves and exercises, promotions and changes of equipment. He spent some months defending Romney Marshes, "prepared to do or die". A keen young soldier, he wrote to the legendary apostle of armoured warfare, Captain Basil Liddell Hart, explaining that he had mislaid his copy of the author's *The Future of Infantry* during the goings-on in France. Liddell Hart sent him a new one.

Warner never consciously considered the prospect of going back to fight again against the German army in France until one day in 1942, when he attended an officers' conference in Doncaster addressed by his corps commander, Lieutenant-General Frederick Morgan. Morgan astonished them by expounding upon future landings across the Channel, "talking of how we were going to stream across north-west Europe with huge tank power. For the first time, we did start to think seriously about going back." The conference addressed itself to some tactical problems. An officer inquired how advancing forces would indicate their progress. "They can set fire to the villages they pass through," said Morgan unanswerably. Not only new armies, but also new equipment, would be critical to a landing in Europe: so also would a new spirit.

The chance of war dictated that John Warner did not remain with the 4th West Kents, which was fortunate for him, because the battalion was sent to Burma. If he had gone with it, he would probably have died, like so many others, on the tennis court at Kohima. Instead, he was posted to become second-in-command of 3rd Reconnaissance Regiment, earmarked with its division for north-west Europe. It was with 3rd Recce that in June 1944, Major Warner returned to the battlefield from which he and his comrades had been so ruthlessly ejected four years earlier. Along with a million and a half other Allied soldiers, he went to Normandy.

1 "Much the greatest thing we have ever attempted"

Not the least remarkable aspect of the Second World War was the manner in which the United States, which might have chosen to regard the campaign in Europe as a diversion from the struggle against her principal aggressor, Japan, was persuaded to commit her chief strength in the west. Not only that, but from December 1941 until June 1944 it was the Americans who were passionately impatient to confront the German army on the continent while the British, right up to the eve of D-Day, were haunted by the deepest misgivings about doing so. "Why are we trying to do this?" cried Winston Churchill in a bitter moment of depression about Operation OVERLORD in February 1944,[1] which caused in him a spasm of enthusiasm for an alternative Allied landing in Portugal. "I am very uneasy about the whole operation," wrote the Chief of the Imperial General Staff, Sir Alan Brooke, as late as 5 June 1944. "At the best, it will come very far short of the expectations of the bulk of the people, namely all those who know nothing about its difficulties. At its worst, it may well be the most ghastly disaster of the whole war."[2] Had the United States army been less resolute in its commitment to a landing in Normandy, it is most unlikely that this would have taken place before 1945. Until the very last weeks before OVERLORD was launched, its future was the subject of bitter dissension and debate between the warlords of Britain and America.

For a year following the fall of France in 1940, Britain fought on without any rational prospect of final victory. Only when Hitler invaded Russia in June 1941, the most demented of his strategic decisions, did the first gleam of hope at last present itself to enemies of the Axis. For the remainder of that year, Britain was preoccupied with the struggle to keep open her Atlantic lifeline, to build her bomber offensive into a meaningful menace to Germany, and to keep hopes alive in the only theatre of war where the British army could fight – Africa and the

Middle East. Then, in the dying days of the year, came the miracle of Pearl Harbour. Britain's salvation, the turning point of the war, was confirmed four days later by another remarkable act of German recklessness: Hitler's declaration of war upon the United States.

The outcome of the Second World War was never thereafter in serious doubt. But great delays and difficulties lay ahead in mobilizing America's industrial might for the battlefield, and in determining by what strategy the Axis was to be crushed. To the relief of the British, President Roosevelt and his Chiefs of Staff at once asserted their acceptance of the principle of "Germany first". They acknowledged that her war-making power was by far the most dangerous and that, following her collapse, Japan must soon capitulate. The war in the Pacific became overwhelmingly the concern of the United States navy. The principal weight of the army's ground forces, whch would grow to a strength of eight million men, was to be directed against Germany and Italy. This decision was confirmed at ARCADIA, the first great Anglo-American conference of the war that began in Washington on 31 December 1941. America committed herself to BOLERO, a programme for a vast build-up of her forces in Britain. Churchill, scribbling his own exuberant hopes for the future during the Atlantic passage to that meeting, speculated on a possible landing in Europe by 40 Allied armoured divisions in the following year: "We might hope to win the war at the end of 1943 or 1944."[3]

But in the months after ARCADIA, as the first United States troops and their senior officers crossed to Europe, it was the Americans who began to focus decisively upon an early cross-Channel invasion. The debate that now began, and continued with growing heat through the next 20 months, reflected "an American impatience to get on with direct offensive action as well as a belief, held quite generally in the U.S. War Department, that the war could most efficiently be won by husbanding resources for an all-out attack deliberately planned for a future fixed date. American impatience was opposed by a British note of caution: American faith in an offensive of fixed date was in contrast to British willingness to proceed one step at a time, molding a course of action to the turns of military fortune."[4] Here, in the words of the American official historian, was the root of the growing division between the Combined Chiefs of Staff throughout 1942 and much of 1943.

At first, American thinking was dominated by fear of a rapid Russian collapse unless the western Allies created, at the very least, a powerful diversion on the continent. ROUNDUP was a plan for an early invasion, with whatever forces were available, which the British speedily took pains to crush. Under strong American pressure, Churchill agreed in principle to the notion of executing ROUNDUP with 48 Allied divisions not later than April 1943. But the British – above all Sir Alan Brooke – privately continued to believe that ROUNDUP neither could nor should take place. Despite their assent to the operation, in the name of Allied solidarity, they began a successful struggle to divert resources towards much more modest – and in their view, more realistic – objectives. In the summer of 1942, the Americans reluctantly acceded to GYMNAST, an operation for the invasion of French North Africa. This was allegedly to be undertaken without prejudice to ROUNDUP, because of well-founded British fears that America would shift the weight of her effort to the Pacific if it became obvious that many months must elapse before major action took place in Europe. But as the BOLERO build-up in Britain fell behind schedule, the desert campaign dragged on without decisive result, and the tragic Dieppe raid demonstrated some of the hazards of cross-Channel operations, it became apparent in Washington as well as in London that there could be no campaign in France in 1943. GYMNAST was translated into reality by the TORCH landings of November 1942. It was at Casablanca in January 1943 that the Anglo-American leadership met for their second major conference.

This was to be the last meeting at which, by dint of brilliant military diplomacy, the British gained acceptance of their own ideas about the manner in which the war should be pursued. The Americans reluctantly accepted HUSKY, the invasion of Sicily, with the prospect of further operations in Italy. They also undertook a commitment to an even greater combined bomber offensive against Germany, POINTBLANK, designed to "weaken Germany's war-making capacity to the point to which invasion would become possible".

The American Chiefs of Staff returned to Washington irritably conscious that they had been persuaded to adopt a course they did not favour – the extension of "sideshow" operations in the Mediterranean which they believed were designed chiefly to serve Britain's imperial and diplomatic purposes. But the British had at least acknowledged that north-west Europe must be invaded the following year. Sir Alan Brooke agreed at Casablanca that "we could definitely count on re-entering the continent in 1944 on a large scale". The Americans were determined to countenance no further prevarication. Throughout the remainder of 1943 – while the British argued for extended commitments in the Mediterranean, possible operations in the Balkans, further delays before attempting to broach Hitler's Atlantic Wall – the Americans remained resolute. At the TRIDENT conference in Washington in May, the date for invasion of north-west Europe was provisionally set for 1 May 1944. This commitment was confirmed in August at the QUADRANT conference in Quebec. To the deep dismay of the British, the Americans also pursued most forcefully their intention to execute ANVIL, a landing in southern France simultaneous with OVERLORD, whatever the cost to Allied operations in Italy. This proposal was put to Stalin at the Teheran conference in November 1943; he welcomed it. Thereafter, the Americans argued that, quite apart from their own enthusiasm for OVERLORD and ANVIL, any cancellation or unreasonable postponement of either would constitute a breach of faith with the Russians.

Throughout the autumn and winter of 1943, even as planning and preparation for OVERLORD gathered momentum, the British irked and angered the Americans by displaying their misgivings and fears as if OVERLORD were still a subject of debate, and might be postponed. "I do not doubt our ability in the conditions laid down to get ashore and deploy," Churchill wrote to Roosevelt on 23 October. "I am however deeply concerned with the build-up and with the situation which may arise between the thirtieth and sixtieth days . . . My dear friend, this is much the greatest thing we have ever attempted."[5] The Prime Minister cabled to Marshall in Washington: "We are carrying out our contract, but I pray God it does not cost us dear."[6] On 11 November, the British Chiefs of Staff recorded in an aide-memoire: "We must not . . . regard OVERLORD as the pivot of our whole strategy on which all else turns . . . we firmly believe that OVERLORD (perhaps in the form of RANKIN) will take place next summer. We do not, however, attach vital importance to any particular date or to any particular number of divisions in the assault and follow-up, though naturally the latter should be made as large as possible consistent with the policy stated above."[7]

Remarks of this sort aroused the deepest dismay and suspicion among the Americans. They believed that the British were seeking grounds for further delays because they feared to meet major formations of the German army in France, with the prospect of huge casualties that the battered Empire could so ill afford. A sour memorandum prepared in the U.S. Chiefs of Staffs' office in the autumn declared that, "it is apparent that the British, who have consistently resisted a cross-Channel operation, now feel OVERLORD is no longer necessary. In their view, continued Mediterranean operations, coupled with POINTBLANK and the crushing Russian offensive, will be sufficient to cause the internal collapse of Germany and thus bring about her military defeat without undergoing what they consider an almost certain 'bloodbath'. The conclusion that the forces being built up in the United Kingdom will never be used for a military offensive against western Europe, but are intended as a gigantic deception plan and an occupying force, is inescapable."[8] This document was not a basis for action, but serves to illustrate American suspicion and scepticism at the period.

It was patently true that Britain's strength was waning, her people growing weary: "At the end of 1943, the population of Britain was . . . nearing the limit of capacity to support the Allied offensive,"[9] wrote the British official strategic historian. "The government was therefore faced by the prospect of conducting the main offensive against Germany and Japan over a period when greater casualties and further demands must lead, after a period of uneasy equilibrium, to a reduction in the war effort." By May 1944 the British army would attain the limits of its growth – two and three-quarter million men. Meanwhile, the American army would number five and three-quarter millions, still far short of its potential maximum. British production of ammunition had been falling since late 1942, of vehicles since mid-1943, of artillery and small arms since late 1943. Whereas in 1940 Britain was producing 90.7 per cent of the Commonwealth's munitions, buying 5.6 per cent from America and finding the remainder within the Empire, by 1944 Britain's share of production had fallen to 61.2 per cent, with 8.9 per cent coming from Canada and 28.7 per cent by purchase or Lend-Lease from the U.S. Britain's leaders were more and more despondently conscious of America's dominance of the Grand

Alliance and its strategy. Americans were not slow to point out either at the time or after 1945 that Alamein remained the only major land victory of the war that the British achieved unaided.

Yet the Americans, their minds fixed on the importance of concentrating efforts upon a campaign that they would dominate, often judged British motives and intentions unjustly. For all Churchill's moments of irrationality, quirkiness, senility, his absurd operational proposals and flights of fantasy and depression, his brilliant instinct for the reality of war sparkles through the archives of the Second World War, and often towers over the judgements of his professional service advisers. At root, the Prime Minister never doubted the eventual necessity for a major campaign in Europe. As early as October 1941, dismissing a demand from the Chief of Air Staff for resources which Portal claimed would enable bombers alone to win the war, Churchill looked forward to "the day when Allied armies would conduct simultaneous attacks by armoured forces in many of the conquered countries which were ripe for revolt. Only in this way could a decision certainly be achieved . . . One has to do the best one can, but he is an unwise man who thinks there is any *certain* method of winning this war, or indeed any other war between equals in strength. The only plan is to persevere."[10]

Churchill's uncertainty concerned not whether to invade Europe, but when to do so. Looking back over the strategic debate that took place between 1941 and 1944, it is impossible to acquit America's leadership of naivety, just as it is difficult to deny the inability of Britain's service chiefs to match the American genius for overcoming difficulties. For the Americans, Professor Michael Howard has written, "shortages were not a problem, as for the British, to be lived with indefinitely, but a passing embarrassment which need not affect long term strategy. This view may have led them to underrate not only the problems of organizing production but the difficulties of planning, logistics and tactics which still lay in the way of bringing those resources to bear. But their British Allies were no less prone to regard as insoluble difficulties which American energy and abundance now, for the first time, made it possible to overcome."[11]

In the winter of 1943–44, the British were by no means certain that the moment had come when OVERLORD might be launched on the overwhelmingly favourable terms that they sought. They saw many hazards in haste, and great virtues in delay. The German army had already suffered vast losses in the

28

east, and was being desperately depleted each day by the advancing Russian armies. The air forces believed that strategic bombing was rapidly eroding the ability of Hitler's industries to arm and supply his armies. Operation RANKIN, referred to above in the British Chiefs of Staffs' aide-memoire, was a plan for the occupation of the continent if the bomber offensive or dramatic developments in the east caused German resistance suddenly to collapse. Such a profoundly realistic, even pessimistic, figure as Sir Alan Brooke can never have pinned many hopes on such a remarkable turn of events. But it is a measure of lingering British wishful thinking about the avoidance of a bloody campaign in Europe that, as late as November 1943, the Chiefs of Staff could still refer even to the possibility of implementing RANKIN.

A forceful faction among post-war historians has sought to argue that Germany could have been defeated much earlier had the American strategic view prevailed from the outset and France been invaded in 1943.[12] They suggest that in that year, Allied air supremacy was already overwhelming; that Italy unliberated would have been a drain upon the Axis rather than an asset to it; that the Atlantic Wall and its garrison were visibly weaker in 1943 than the following year; and that the landing craft lacking could readily have been found by reducing the quota for the Pacific and cancelling further amphibious operations in the Mediterranean.

All of this ignores the consideration of the heart of Churchill's and Brooke's fears to the very moment of invasion – their knowledge of the immense and extraordinary fighting power of the German army. Four years of war against the Wehrmacht had convinced Britain's commanders that Allied troops should engage and could defeat their principal enemy only on the most absolutely favourable terms. Throughout the Second World War, where British or American troops met the Germans in anything like equal strength, the Germans almost always prevailed. They possessed an historic reputation as formidable soldiers. Under Hitler their army attained its zenith. Weapon for weapon and tank for tank, even in 1944, its equipment decisively outclassed that of the Allies in every category save artillery and transport.

In four years of war, Churchill had been given ample cause to doubt the ability of British troops to match those of Germany. As late as November 1943, 5,000 British troops on the island of

Leros were defeated by 4,000 German invaders during the ill-fated operations in the Dodecanese. The Germans admittedly possessed strong air support. But in the hands of the British this advantage frequently proved inadequate to ensure victory. Final Allied success in North Africa took months longer than the gloomiest prophet anticipated after Alamein. There was no evidence to suggest that the American soldier was capable of performing any more effectively than the British. Alexander wrote to Brooke from Tunisia about the Americans: "They simply do not know their job as soldiers and this is the case from the highest to the lowest, from the general to the private soldier. Perhaps the weakest link of all is the junior leader, who just does not lead, with the result that their men don't really fight."[13]

This was no fit of chauvinism, but a verdict with which most Americans in North Africa concurred. They learned a great deal in the battles of 1942–43, but there remained no evidence to suggest that they had become the equals of their German opponents. The Italian campaign became a nightmare of frustrated hopes and thwarted ambitions: even with absolute command of sea and air, the Allies proved unable to bring about the collapse of the dogged yet brilliant German fighting retreat up the length of Italy. The Anzio landings of February 1944, designed to outflank the enemy line with dramatic results, came close to ending in a major disaster for the Allies, and provoked one of Churchill's most famous, bitter sallies: "We hoped to land a wild cat that would tear out the bowels of the Boche. Instead we have stranded a vast whale with its tail flopping about in the water."[14]

Most of the German troops in Italy were line formations; only very limited numbers came from elite units. Yet in France the Allies would meet the SS Panzer divisions, the most fanatical and effective battlefield forces of the Second World War. What if the weather should close down, denying the British and Americans the air support that alone could give them a real prospect of victory? An Allied OVERLORD planner reflected in September 1943 upon the difficulties in Sicily where 15 Allied divisions had faced 13 enemy divisions of which just three were German, on a battlefield of 17,000 square miles. In Normandy, he pointed out, 24 Allied divisions would confront at least 17 German formations on a battlefield of 33,000 square miles.[15] These were not, of course, the eventual numbers on the battlefield. But they were estimates which provided food for thought in London in the autumn of 1943.

The revelations since 1974 of Allied success in breaking German codes in the Second World War has created some illusions that Ultra provided a magic key, an open sesame for the Allies on the battlefield. Important as Ultra's contribution was, its supply of information was erratic and incomplete. It provided vital strategic guidance, and its forewarning of German attacks was often of immense importance to the formations seeking to parry these. But Ultra could seldom provide decisive intelligence for Allied troops going into an attack. Only fighting power could gain objectives on the battlefield. It was about this that Churchill and Brooke remained so uncertain in the winter of 1943.

Yet given impetus by American determination, the planning and preparation of OVERLORD now gained pace, and were not to slacken again. Through the winter of 1943 and even into the spring of 1944, other plans and other problems were also occupying and vexing the minds of the British and American high commands. But one by one lesser operations – CULVERIN, BUCCANEER, HERCULES, PIGSTICK – withered on the bough. One of the most divisive Anglo-American quarrels of the war, which continued until high summer of 1944, concerned the diversion of forces from Italy for the ANVIL landings in the south of France. In a moment of strategic fantasy, Roosevelt proposed that ANVIL should precede the landing in Normandy by a month. But inexorably distractions were cast into the wings. The concentration narrowed until it focussed decisively upon OVERLORD. This was an operation for which all paper estimates of strength promised Allied victory. Yet the consequences of failure were so great as to haunt the leaders of the Grand Alliance.

Lieutenant-General Frederick Morgan had been designated Chief of Staff to the Supreme Allied Commander – COSSAC – in April 1943, when there was no appointed Supreme Commander, and for the remainder of the year he and his Anglo-American staff were responsible for the outline planning for OVERLORD. He wrote in his initial report of 15 July: "An operation of the magnitude of Operation OVERLORD has never previously been attempted in history. It is fraught with hazards, both in nature and magnitude, which do not obtain in any other theatre of the present world war. Unless these hazards are squarely faced and adequately overcome, the operation

31

cannot succeed. There is no reason why they should not be overcome, provided the energies of all concerned are bent to the problem."[16]

The COSSAC staff's crippling handicap was that without the authority of a Supreme Commander they were compelled to carry out their task within limitations laid down by the Chiefs of Staff. Morgan was instructed to plan an operation, with a specified and quite inadequate weight of resources, that would put only three divisions ashore in the first landings in France. OVERLORD, even more than any ordinary operation of war, demanded a commander who could decide what forces were necessary for its execution, and then insist that these were provided. It was not until the end of the year that the commanders were appointed; only then was sufficient authority brought to bear upon this issue to enable demands for extra men and ships to be made, and met.

Yet within the limitations of their brief, Morgan and his staff achieved a great deal. They drew upon the fruits of aerial reconnaissance and a canvass of Britain for pre-war holiday photographs of every yard of the coast line of France. The limiting factors for an invasion site were the radius of air cover (effectively the range of a Spitfire, 150 miles); the limits of beach capacity (it was scarcely possible to unload any army beneath steep cliffs); the length of the sea crossing; and the strength of the German defences. For the first three the Pas de Calais, opposite Dover, offered the most obvious advantages. To the end some soldiers, including General Patton, favoured the Pas de Calais as the shortest route to the heart of Germany. Yet Morgan and the Chiefs of Staff easily rejected this choice because of the strength of the German defences. Eyes swung west, towards the broad beaches of Brittany, the Cotentin, Normandy. Brittany lay too far away, beyond the reach of dominant air cover. The Cotentin offered the Germans too simple an opportunity to bottle up the invaders within the peninsula. Very early on, in the spring of 1943, decisive attention concentrated upon the beaches, woods and undulating fields of Normandy. "The Cotentin peninsula and the hinterland behind the Caen beaches are on the whole unsuitable for the use of large armoured forces, coming particularly to the marshy river valleys near the coast and the steep hills and narrow valleys in the Normandy highlands," reported Morgan. "The area N, NW and SE of Caen is good tank country, and in this area the enemy is likely to make best use of his panzer divisions."[17]

Throughout the spring and summer, a constant succession of meetings took place at Norfolk House, COSSAC headquarters in St James's Square. Most were attended by around 40 British and American officers of colonel's rank and above, working painstakingly through every aspect of the invasion. Despite disparaging comments made later by Montgomery and his staff about COSSAC's achievements, the contemporary minutes and memoranda are eloquent testimony to the remarkable range of difficulties they isolated and discussed. "The crux of the operation," wrote Morgan, "is . . . likely to be our ability to drive off the German reserves rather than the initial breaking of the coastal crust."[18] The order of Allied priorities must be Caen, Bayeux and the road to St Lô, followed by the road to Falaise and the port of Cherbourg. There was a danger that if Allied assault divisions pursued overly ambitious objectives inland on D-Day, they would be caught in vulnerable and over-extended positions by the inevitable German counter-attack. COSSAC identified the immense problem of beach exits – the difficulty of pushing vehicles rapidly inland from the landing craft. There were endless staff war games, such as Exercises JANTZEN and HARLEQUIN, testing possible Allied and German movements around the Norman beaches. The planners endured moments of despair. In August, aerial photographs revealed massive German flooding of river areas around Caen, which caused the Operations Division to minute: "The full implications of this have not yet been assessed, but it is quite possible that it will finally 'kill' OVERLORD."[19]

It did not of course do so, and a few days later the staff were considering and rejecting the possibility of a feint invasion: "The feint will be over by D-Day and it will be clear that it was only a feint and the threat to the Pas de Calais will have disappeared, and the enemy may move his reserves. If we are to maintain our threat, we must dispense with the feint. If we are to have the feint, we must dispense with the threat."[20] Here was the germ of FORTITUDE, the brilliant Allied deception operation which would keep the German Fifteenth Army locked in the Pas de Calais deep into July 1944.

While the planners studied beach gradients and the complexities of the French railway system, Roosevelt and Churchill considered leaders. Both Marshall and Brooke were disappointed in their passionate hopes of the Supreme Command,

Marshall because he was indispensable in Washington, Brooke because he was British. On 7 December, Roosevelt was met at Tunis airport by General Dwight Eisenhower. As soon as the two men were side by side in the back of a staff car, the President told him simply: "Well, Ike, you are going to command Overlord." Eisenhower, a 54-year-old Kansan who had risen from colonel to general in three years and who had scarcely heard a shot fired upon a battlefield, was to arouse the scorn of many more brilliant soldiers in the years that followed: "Just a co-ordinator, a good mixer, a champion of inter-Allied co-operation, and in those respects few can hold a candle to him," wrote Brooke. "But is that enough? Or can we not find all the qualities of a Commander in one man?"[21]

Eisenhower was sensitive to the well-founded charge that he was no battlefield commander: "It wearies me to be thought of as timid, when I've had to do things that were so risky as to be almost crazy."[22] But history has thus far remained confident that whatever his shortcomings as a general in the field, he could not have been matched as Supreme Commander. In 1944–45, he revealed a greatness of spirit that escaped Montgomery, perhaps every British general of the Second World War with the exception of Slim. The shortcomings of the Allied high command in north-west Europe in 1944 have provoked close critical study. Most writers have chosen to consider the successes and failures of Eisenhower and his lieutenants in isolation;[23] they have been reluctant to compare them with the collapse of so many other military alliances in other ages, or to reflect upon the vast weight of forces assembled in north-west Europe, which rendered meaningless any comparison with the command methods of Marlborough and Wellington, even those of Grant and Sherman. The most vivid contrast is that of the Allied SHAEF and the German OKW. Alongside the command structure of their enemies, that of the Allied forces was a masterpiece of reason and understanding. Eisenhower understood that in some respects his authority was that of a constitutional monarch: the power that he held was less important than the fact that his possession denied it to others. Eisenhower lacked greatness as a soldier, and tolerated a remarkable number of knaves and mischief-makers in his court at SHAEF. But his behaviour at moments of Anglo-American tension, his extraordinary generosity of spirit to his difficult subordinates, proved his greatness as Supreme Commander. His failures were of omission, seldom of commission. It remains impossible to conceive of any other Allied soldier matching his achievement.

The Americans were irked by the appointment of Englishmen to all three subordinate commands for OVERLORD – Sir Bernard Montgomery on land, Sir Bertram Ramsay at sea, Sir Trafford Leigh-Mallory for air. Yet another Englishman, Air Chief Marshal Sir Arthur Tedder, would serve as Deputy Supreme Commander, a recognition of the critical importance of the air forces to the invasion. Eisenhower quickly realized that his command difficulties with OVERLORD would be much greater than those of TORCH not merely because of the scale of the Normandy invasion, but because in North Africa "we were then engaged in desperate battling and everybody could see the sense of and the necessity for complete unification. The answer also lies partially in the fact that those three men [his deputies in the Mediterranean] were of the broadest possible calibre, while two of my present commanders, although extremely able, are somewhat ritualistic in outlook and require a great deal more of inoculation."[24] He referred to Ramsay and Leigh-Mallory; but he had also wanted Alexander instead of Montgomery as ground commander.

This was the final occasion of the war on which British officers achieved such a measure of authority over Americans, and Americans bowed to British experience and allegedly greater military wisdom. This was ironic, for the invasion was pre-eminently an American design, reflecting an American willingness to confront the enemy head-on in a collision which Britain's leaders had sought for so long to defer. But for the British people far more than for the Americans, the invasion represented a rebirth, a return, a reversal of all the humiliations and defeats that they had endured since 1939. Here, at last, the British army could resume that which it had so disastrously abandoned at Dunkirk: the battle to defeat a major German army in north-west Europe.

2 Preparations

Commanders

General Omar Bradley, Commander designate of the American First Army in north-west Europe, landed in Britain to take up his appointment on a bleak autumn morning in September 1943. Like most Americans, he did not find his spirits exalted by the renewed encounter at a northern airfield with weary, seedy, rationed, wartime Britain: "The waitress, a stocky Scottish girl with a heavy brogue, offered me a choice of two entrées – neither of which I understood. 'Let me have the second,' I replied nonchalantly. She returned with stewed tomatoes. The first choice had been boiled fish. Prestwick taught me to confine my breakfast thereafter to the U.S. army mess."[1] A steady, careful, thoughtful Missourian, like most American professional soldiers Bradley came from modest origins. His father died when he was 14, leaving his mother, a seamstress, to bring him up. He himself worked in a railway workshop until he was able to gain a place at West Point. He served as a soldier for 32 years before seeing action for the first time as a corps commander in Tunisia. Now, just eight months later, he was to bear direct responsibility for the American army's greatest operation of the war thus far. He was 50 years old. If he lacked Patton's driving force and flamboyance, he had proved himself a commander of exceptional stability and discretion, whom men liked and immediately trusted. Bradley could "read" a battle.

He had been plucked from Sicily to Washington for a briefing about his new appointment, seeing Mrs Bradley for the last time before VE Day in her modest temporary home at the Thayer Hotel in West Point. He waited a week for an appointment with General Marshall, at last finding himself squeezed in during the Chief of Staff's journey to Omaha, Nebraska, for an American Legion convention. The President met him, and talked of his fear that the Germans might develop their atomic bomb in time to influence the invasion. Then Bradley flew to Britain, and travelled to London to meet the COSSAC staff and to be briefed about the progress of planning. One morning he walked through Hyde Park and stood amongst the crowd at Speaker's Corner to listen to a soapbox orator bellowing his enthusiasm for the "Second Front Now", a catchphrase of wartime Britain so familiar that it had become a music-hall joke. "I thought of how little comprehension he had of what the 'Second Front' entailed," wrote Bradley, "of the labors that would be required to mount it,"[2] Then he drove to his new headquarters at Bristol to meet the staff with whom he must prepare the American invasion force.

Montgomery arrived in England on 2 January, and immediately began to whip up a whirlwind. He had learned of his own appointment only 10 days earlier, following a protracted period of apprehension that he might be passed over in favour of Alexander, Churchill's favourite general. Having spent the night at Claridges, at 9.00 a.m. the following morning he attended a briefing at his new headquarters, St Paul's School in Hammersmith, where he had once been a pupil. He heard the COSSAC staff outline their plan. Forearmed by a discussion with Eisenhower in Algiers and a glimpse of Churchill's copy in Tunisia a few days earlier, Montgomery found little difficulty in taking the floor when the briefers had finished and demolishing their points one by one in a 20-minute "Monty special". Like Eisenhower and Bedell Smith, he had been immediately convinced that the front was too narrow, the assault lacking in power and depth. He sent the COSSAC staff back to their offices to consider the implications of a far wider assault, perhaps reaching from Dieppe to Brittany. At the second day's session, he accepted the naval arguments against landing west of the Cotentin, but continued to insist upon a line reaching at least as far north as what became Utah beach. On the third day, he crushed formal protests from senior British and American COSSAC officers who insisted that what he wanted could not be done with the resources. The resources must be found, he declared flatly, or another commander appointed to carry out the invasion.

It was a masterly performance – Montgomery at his very best in clarity of purpose and ruthless simplicity. After months of havering among staff officers fatally hampered by lack of authority, he had sketched the design for a feasible operation of war, and begun to exercise his own immense strength of will to ensure that the resources would be found to land five divisions and secure a beachhead large enough to provide fighting room for the Allied armies. He ignored the sensibilities of the existing staff of 21st Army Group, his command for the invasion, by replacing them wholesale with his own tried and tested officers from 8th Army – De Guingand, Williams, Belchem, Richardson and others. One of their first horrified discoveries was that the RAF had begun intensive reconnaisance of the Normandy area. The airmen were hastily persuaded to widen their operations, giving special emphasis to the Pas de Calais.

It was characteristic of Montgomery that, having achieved so much so quickly, having made a forceful and vital initial contribution to OVERLORD, he should also seek to write into history his claim that the new plan was entirely his vision and his conception. In reality, most of the staff in England had been conscious for months of the need to strengthen the attack, but lacked the authority to insist upon it. Eisenhower himself immediately grasped the problem, and had some discussion of it with Montgomery. But throughout his military career, a worm of self-destruction in the austere, awkward little man in the beret caused him to disparage the contribution of his peers, shamelessly to seize the credit for the achievements of others, and rewrite the history of his own battlefield planning to conform with the reality of what took place. These were weaknesses which would come close to destroying him, for they gained him few friends. His staff and subordinates admired and were fascinated by him; few found it possible to like him. "We never lost confidence in him," said one, talking of the Normandy period, "but we would very often say: 'Oh Christ, what's the little bugger doing now?' "[3] The support of one man, the CIGS, Sir Alan Brooke, had carried Montgomery first to the army command in which he gained fame in the desert, and then to the principal British role in OVERLORD. Without Brooke, it is unlikely that Montgomery would ever have gained the chance to display his qualities in the highest commands.

Montgomery's self-esteem, at its most conspicuous in his dealings with Americans, rested upon his faith in himself as a supreme professional, a monkish student of war who understood the conduct of military operations in a way that escaped less dedicated commanders, such as Alexander and Eisenhower, who did not aspire to his summits of military intellectualism. He would never have found himself in the headmaster's chair at St

Paul's in January 1944 had there not been much substance in his claims. In France in 1940, in England until 1942, in the Mediterranean in the 17 months that followed, he had proved himself a consummate trainer and motivator of troops, superb in his choice of subordinate staff and his organization of battles. He commanded immense respect from those who served under him for his willingness to listen to them, his directness and loyalty. Many senior officers in his armies went through the war quite unaware of the dark side of Montgomery's character, the conceit and moments of pettiness, the indifference to truth where it reflected upon himself, the capacity for malice. And perhaps these very vices contributed to Montgomery a quality lacking in many brave and famous British generals – the iron will to prevail. Wavell was an example of an officer much beloved in the British army, of whom it has been said by his best biographer[4] that he possessed the qualities for greatness in almost every sphere of human endeavour save that of high command in war. Alexander was a commander in the tradition of great Anglo-Irish military gentlemen – he lacked the intellect, the ruthless driving force that enables a general to dominate the battlefield. The very qualities that made so many German commanders in the Second World War such unpleasant personalities were also of immense value to them in battle: relentless clarity of purpose, the absolute will to win. For all Montgomery's caution in battle, the passion for "tidiness" that more than once denied him all-embracing victories, this essentially cold, insensitive man was devoted to winning. The outstanding recent American historian of the campaign in north-west Europe has written: "There is every reason to believe in retrospect, as Brooke believed then, that Montgomery not only surpassed Alexander as an operational commander, but was altogether Britain's ablest general of the war."[5]

Eisenhower reached England on 15 January, and on the 21st presided over the first meeting of his staff and commanders at Norfolk House. It was overwhelmingly Montgomery's occasion. He could claim the credit for having immensely refined the simple broad assault discussed earlier with the Supreme Commander, and was able to outline the new plan which in the weeks that followed would be transformed into the operational orders of the Allied armies. The Americans, on the right, would go for Cherbourg, Brest and the Loire ports. It was logical to land them on the western flank, because they would thus be conveniently placed to receive men and supplies arriving direct by sea from the United States. The British and Canadians on the left "would deal with the enemy main body approaching from the east and south-east". Montgomery declared: "In the initial stages, we should concentrate on gaining control quickly of the main centres of road communications. We should then push our armoured formations between and beyond these centres and deploy them on suitable ground. In this way it would be difficult for the enemy to bring up his reserves and get them past three armoured formations."[6] On 23 January, after a final effort by the COSSAC staff to impose some of their own thinking upon Eisenhower, and perhaps also to salvage a little of their deeply bruised self-respect, the Supreme Commander formally accepted Montgomery's proposals. The immense labour began of translating these into operational reality – convincing Washington of the vital need for more landing craft, devising fire plans, air support schemes, loading programmes, engineer inventories, naval escort arrangements.

Two mobile brigade groups were placed on standby in Kent and Sussex lest German commandos seek to land and dislocate the build-up. Work began on printing millions of maps in conditions of absolute secrecy, copying air photographs in their thousands, stockpiling artillery ammunition in hundreds of thousands of rounds. The vast business of marshalling American formations arriving almost weekly from across the Atlantic would continue until ports in France became available. Each armoured division required the equivalent of 40 ships, 386,000 ship tons as against 270,000 tons for an infantry division. Every formation required camps in Britain, trains to move them there, training grounds, rest areas, supplies. Tank crews must test fire their weapons, infantrymen zero their rifles. A proposed scale of one ounce of sweets, two ounces of biscuits and one packet of chewing gum for every man of the assault forces necessitated the distribution of 6,250 pounds of sweets, 12,500 pounds of biscuits and 100,000 packets of gum. Armoured units were reminded that their tanks' mileage before the invasion was to be restricted to 600 (Churchills), 800 (Cromwells and Shermans). The Air Ministry was pressed to get some of its prototype helicopters into service, although the airmen warned that none were likely to be available. Amid serious fears that the Germans might use gas against the invaders, 60 days' supply of gas shells was prepared for retaliatory use, and aircrew were specially trained for gas bombing. Training maps showing real terrain with fictitious names were issued to commanding officers. A staggering weight of orders and schedules was drawn up and sealed, a necessary security risk being taken to brief the naval units some days before the armies knew where they were to sail.

All this was completed in a mere 17 weeks before the newly-revised date for D-Day, 5 June. Its accomplishment remains the greatest organizational achievement of the Second world War, a feat of staff-work that has dazzled history, a monument to the imagination and brilliance of thousands of British and American planners and logisticians which may never be surpassed in war. At Norfolk House, a succession of 12-day courses were held for Allied supply officers, 70 at a time, to study the huge problems of the Q branch. 25 square miles of west Devon between Appledore and Woolacombe were evacuated of their entire civilian population to enable the American assault forces to rehearse with live ammunition. All over Britain exercises were held, christened with characteristic inappropriateness – DUCK I, II, III, BEAVER, FABIUS, TIGER – first for groups of specialists, then for increasingly large bodies of men, until at last entire divisions were engaged. In the assembly areas great tented encampments were created, equipped with water points, field bakeries, bath facilities, post offices, each one camouflaged with the intent of making it indistinguishable from 10,000 feet. The British devised a vehicle waterproofing compound from grease, lime and asbestos fibres. The American initial landing force comprised 130,000 men, with another 1,200,000 to follow by D+90. With them would go 137,000 wheeled and semi-tracked vehicles, 4,217 full-tracked vehicles, 3,500 artillery pieces. Week by week, the transatlantic convoys docked in British ports, unloading new cargoes of artillery shells from Illinois, blood plasma from Tennessee, jeeps from Detroit, K ration cheese from Wisconsin.

The British protested somewhat about the vast allocation of shipping that was proving necessary to provide American troops with their accustomed level of supply. Even the U.S. War Department admitted that its huge support organization was "a factor which produced problems not foreseen . . . the *matériel* needed to provide American soldiers with something corresponding to the American standard of living [caused] a prodigious growth of service and administration units."[7] The British official historian wrote more portentously: "The Americans' belief in their technical supremacy had a significant effect both on strategic thought and on its execution, while their widespread enjoyment of a high standard of living was partly responsible for a quantity of equipment which others might find extravagant, but which, in their case, may have been at the least a stimulant and at the most a necessity."[8] Each American soldier in Normandy received six and a quarter pounds of rations a day, against three and a third pounds for his German enemy. Since only four pounds per man of the American ration was consumed, it was clear that a huge and characteristic waste of shipping was involved. Meanwhile the German small-arms ammunition scale for a rifle company was more than double that of its American equivalent, 56,000 rounds to 21,000.

Throughout this period, 21st Army Group's headquarters was pre-occupied with operational planning. The specialist branches of the American and British forces were responsible for solving the technical and logistical problems of invasion. The huge, bloated staff at SHAEF circulated enormous quantities of paper between their departments – reports, minutes, studies of German reinforcement capability, French railway capacity, German coastal gun range, Allied naval bombardment power. Some of this was extremely valuable, much of it not. But it was Montgomery's staff which bore the overwhelming burden of planning the battle, using very little paper and very long hours of debate and thought. Eisenhower summarized his own preoccupations before OVERLORD as: the French political complications; the allocation of resources; air organization and planning. At 21st Army Group, the staff shared the Supreme Commander's concern about the air problem, but were chiefly haunted during those spring weeks by fear that some breach of security might compromise the landing. If it did so, there was every prospect that the Allies would learn of the enemy's knowledge through Ultra. But until the very morning of D-Day, the possibility that the Germans might secretly be waiting for the Allies in Normandy remained the overriding nightmare of the planners. Only with forewarning did the Germans possess a real prospect of turning back the invaders on the beaches.

It was agreed that gaining a foothold on D-Day was a huge organizational task, but presented no intolerable tactical risks given the weight of Allied resources. All the imponderables, the great dangers, lay in the battle of the build-up. Immense labour was devoted to comparisons of the likely Allied and German strengths. An uncommonly gloomy SHAEF estimate of April 1944 predicted that by D+14 the Germans would have 28 divisions in Normandy against 19⅓ Allied; by D+20: 30 to 24⅔; by D+30: 33 to 28⅔.[9] The differences of opinion between German commanders about the best methods of defending Normandy were known at 21st Army Group through Ultra. But as Montgomery's brilliant intelligence officer, the 31-year-old Brigadier Bill Williams, declared: "All the time we were asking ourselves: To what extent would these chaps make a good showing despite Hitler?"[10] The behaviour of the Führer himself, together with the success or failure of the Allies' FORTITUDE deception plan based upon the fictitious threat to the Pas de Calais posed by General Patton and the "First U.S. Army Group", would determine whether the German build-up attained its immensely dangerous theoretical maximum. The Allies' appreciation in April spotlighted "the grave risk of stabilization" – a euphemism for stalemate– "around D+14 . . . The greatest energy and initiative will be required at this period to ensure that the enemy is not allowed to stabilize his defence."[11]

Afterwards, there would be much discussion about how far the Allied command had anticipated the difficulties of fighting in the close country of the Norman *bocage*. The SHAEF appreciation declared: "Generally speaking the area will not be an easy one for forces to advance through rapidly in the face of determined resistance, but it will likewise be most difficult for the enemy to prevent a slow and steady advance by infiltration . . . Tanks can penetrate most of the hedgerows. It is difficult to judge whether such terrain favours defending or attacking infantry . . . The tactics to be employed in fighting through *bocage* country should be given considerable study by formations to be employed therein."[12] But they were not. The British 7th Armoured Division was prepared for D-Day amidst the flatlands of East Anglia. Most British infantry battalions knew little of the infiltration tactics in which the Germans were so skilled, and relied over-whelmingly upon the straightforward open order advance, two companies forward. Many American formations were training on Dartmoor and Exmoor. As a senior staff officer said afterwards: "We simply did not expect to remain in the *bocage* long enough to justify studying it as a major tactical problem."[13]

There were, however, no delusions among 21st Army Group

about the likely quality of resistance: "The Germans will probably base many of their main and rearguard positions on river obstacles . . . Our formations will be well-trained, but most of them will have little battle experience . . . The enemy . . . will fight fiercely in all encounters, whether major battles or battles simply to gain time for withdrawal . . . An all-out pursuit is considered unlikely until the German army is emphatically beaten in battle, and likely to come only once in the campaign. It will herald the end of the German war."[14]

The landing plan developed at St Paul's called for four corps to feed their men in columns through the five Allied beaches during the period following D-Day. On the right, at Utah beach, the U.S. VII Corps would be led ashore on D-Day by 4th Division; at Omaha, V Corps would be led by 1st and 29th Divisions; at Gold, the British XXX Corps would be led by 50th Division; British I Corps on Juno would be led by 3rd Canadian Division, on Sword by 3rd British Division. Various Ranger and Commando units would land alongside these major formations, but at no phase of the war was the high command's enthusiasm for Special Forces lower than in 1944. There was a strong feeling that these "private armies" had creamed off precious high-quality manpower, and could contribute little to the massive clash on the battlefield that was now to begin. The raiding days were over. With the sole exception of the American Ranger assault on the Pointe du Hoc west of Omaha, and some SAS drops deep inland to work with the Resistance on German lines of communication, the Commandos and other Special Forces were employed for normal infantry tasks on D-Day and for most of the war thereafter.[15]

Montgomery's subsequent attempts to pretend that the Normandy battle developed entirely in accordance with his own plans have distorted what was essentially a clear and simple issue. The evidence of all the planning documents before D-Day about Allied intentions is incontrovertible. The British Second Army and Canadian First Army were to "assault to the west of the R.ORNE and to develop operations to the south and south-east, in order to secure airfield sites and to protect the eastern flank of U.S. First Army while the latter is capturing CHERBOURG. In its subsequent operations the SECOND ARMY will pivot on its left (CAEN) and offer a strong front against enemy movement towards the lodgement area from the east."[16] The U.S. First Army was to capture Cherbourg, and thereafter:

to develop operations southwards towards ST LO in conformity with the advance of Second British Army. After the area CHERBOURG-CAUMONT-VIRE-AVRANCHES has been captured, the Army will be directed southwards with the object of capturing RENNES and then establishing our flank on the R.LOIRE and capturing QUIBERON BAY.[17]

Patton's Third Army was to advance through First Army's front, clearing Brittany, seizing St Nazaire and Nantes, then covering the south flank, "while the First U.S. Army is directed N.E. with a view to operations towards PARIS." From all this, it is obvious that the eventual American movements in Normandy followed the plan created in the spring of 1944 by 21 1st Army Group. Where Montgomery distorted his intentions after the event, and made possible the bitter controversy that has persisted for so many years, was by pretending that the British and Canadians fulfilled their purpose by holding a line north of Caen. Indeed, they did offer a "strong front" to the great weight of German armour. But as Montgomery made abundantly clear before D-Day, he wished that "strong front" to be somewhere in the area of Falaise, which would provide adequate room for build-up and airfield construction between the perimeter and the coast. In the event, the Allies suffered severely from the lack of space within their beachhead as well as the shortage of airfield sites to increase the range of their tactical aircraft. From 6 June until the final Canadian push towards Argentan in August, Montgomery made it plain that he hoped that his troops could surpass his minimum hopes, gain more ground and break through the German front. This they were never able to do, and Montgomery's credibility with his peers and superiors diminished with each letter of intent that he dispatched before Second Army's operations, expressing ambitious hopes which were not fulfilled.

The Commander-in-Chief of 21st Army Group was justified in claiming that nothing which happened in Normandy changed the broad shape of his plan or the intended pattern of the American advance. But all those who knew him and knew the plan – not least the Americans – had a clear idea of what he wanted the British element to accomplish, and were not for a moment deluded by his evasions when these hopes were not fulfilled. Had he himself been more honest and less arrogant about his difficulties on the eastern flank as they took place – above all with

Eisenhower and Tedder – he might have avoided much of the acrimony that descended upon him.

The issue was further confused by the so-called "phase line controversy", the argument surrounding the map, drawn up by the 21st Army Group HQ at St Paul's, showing the perimeters which the Allied armies might expect to hold by given dates following the landings, concluding at the line of the Seine on D+90. Bradley was furious to see this map, and demanded the deletion of the phase lines for the American sector, to which he refused to be committed. In reality, it is difficult to attach much importance to them, or to believe that Montgomery did so either. 21st Army Group expected to fight a measured, stage by stage battle in which the Germans retreated to newly-chosen defensive positions as their front was driven in by successive Allied attacks. Some notion of where the Allies might hope to get to in the weeks after D-Day was desirable. But no general as skilled in the art of war as Montgomery could have intended that a battle lasting many weeks should be conducted *operationally* in accordance with lines on a map. Approximate phase lines were essential *logistically*, for the guidance of the supply planners, because the balance in the armies' relative requirements of ammunition and fuel would vary by many thousands of tons in accordance with their distance from the nearest offloading point, and the speed at which they were advancing. The "phase line controversy" only assumed its subsequent importance because of the tensions within the Alliance, and the willingness of mischief-makers to find a stick with which to belabour Montgomery during the weeks of wrangling that reached a pitch in high summer.

Between 15 January and 5 June – the new target date for invasion after delay became inevitable to provide sufficient landing craft – Montgomery's original concept for the assault was refined, but not altered. Enormous problems of organization and supply were overcome, difficult issues such as the role of de Gaulle and his Free French were painfully resolved[18] It was not, however, the future of the ground battle for Normandy, nor even the political future of France, which lay at the heart of the most bitter struggle within Eisenhower's command in the spring of 1944. This concerned the role and direction of the Allied air forces.

Disagreements, even full-blooded quarrels, between the services were not uncommon either in Britain or America in the Second World War. But none generated more heat and passion or diverted so much attention from the struggle to defeat the Germans than that surrounding the proper use of the Allies' vast air power in 1944.* In the First World War, aircraft were directly controlled by the armies and navies of their respective nations. In April 1918, British airmen successfully escaped the thraldom of the generals and admirals to form the Royal Air Force. In America, air power remained under the direction of the two senior services, but at no time from the 1920s onwards did the nation's leading fliers lose sight of their ambition of independence. It is impossible to escape the conclusion that, between the wars, the air forces of both countries embraced Mitchell, Douhet and Trenchard's theories of strategic air power, which claimed the bomber unsupported to be a war-winning weapon, because of their passionate anxiety to discover a role for themselves beyond that of mere flying eyes and artillery for the older services. Their enthusiasm for stragetic air power critically hampered the development of close air-ground support techniques such as the Luftwaffe took for granted from its inception. Such was the obsession of the RAF with its bomber force that during the rush to re-arm in the last years before war, the Air Ministry would have built far too few fighters to enable the Battle of Britain to be won, had it not been compelled to switch emphasis by civilian politicians more concerned with the defence of their own country than with demonstrating the potential of bombing an enemy.

Yet Britain's inability to strike directly against Germany with her ground forces between 1940 and 1944 thrust upon the RAF the opportunity to play a role of unique strategic importance. The programme for the creation of a vast heavy bomber force, conceived in the days of despair in 1940, had borne full fruit for the airmen by 1944. Each night, up to a thousand British aircraft set off for the industrial cities of Germany, to pour explosives upon them with the aid of the most sophisticated technology that the nation possessed. Air Marshal Sir Arthur Harris, the formidable Commander-in-Chief of Bomber Command, had

---

* For a full account of this debate, see the author's *Bomber Command* (Michael Joseph, London 1979).

become one of the best-known and most fiercely independent war leaders in Britain, waging his campaign with implacable determination, convinced that by this means alone Germany could be beaten, without recourse to a major land campaign. When the Casablanca conference committed the Allied air forces to POINTBLANK, a bombing programme specifically designed to pave the way for the invasion of Europe, Harris paid lip service, but in reality pursued uninterrupted his campaign of "area bombing" against the cities of Germany. "It is my firm belief," he wrote to Portal on 12 August 1943, "that we are on the verge of a final showdown in the bombing war . . . I am certain that given average weather and concentration on the main job, we can push Germany over by bombing this year."[1] In January 1944, almost unbelievably, Harris declared his conviction that, given continued concentration upon his existing policy, Germany could be driven to "a state of devastation in which surrender is inevitable" by 1 April.

By day, meanwhile, the American Fortresses pursued their precision bombing campaign guided by General Carl "Tooey" Spaatz, an airman who disagreed with Harris about the best means of defeating Germany from the air, but made common cause with the Englishman's commitment to independent air power. The American official historians wrote of the USAAF that it was:

young, aggressive, and conscious of its growing power. It was guided by the sense of a special mission to perform. It had to justify the expenditure of billions of dollars and the use of almost a third of the army's manpower. It sought for itself, therefore, both as free a hand as possible to prosecute the air war in accordance with its own ideas, and the maximum credit for its performance.[2]

As the directors of OVERLORD gathered the reins of command into their hands in the first months of 1944, one of their foremost concerns was to ensure that the full weight of Allied air power was available to provide whatever support they felt need of as the campaign unfolded. Eisenhower concluded early on that the "bomber barons' " promise of goodwill would not be sufficient: the lure of their own convictions had often proved too strong in the past. Even more serious, both the British and American bomber chiefs had been proclaiming for months that they considered OVERLORD a vast, gratuitous strategic misjudgement, rendered wholly unnecessary by their own operations. Harris bombarded the Air Ministry with minutes declaring that "clearly the best and indeed the only efficient support which Bomber Command can give to OVERLORD is the intensification of attacks on suitable industrial centres in Germany . . ."[3] Spaatz's diary note of the critical 21 January Supreme Commander's meeting at which the OVERLORD framework was laid down declared only:

Nothing of note from an Air point of view except launching of OVERLORD will result in the calling off of bomber effort on Germany proper from one to two months prior to invasion. If time is as now contemplated, there will be no opportunity to carry out any Air operations of sufficient intensity to justify the theory that Germany can be knocked out by Air power. Operations in connection with OVERLORD will be child's play compared to present operations . . .[4]

As late as April 1944, the minutes of a meeting between Spaatz and General Hoyt Vandenburg, American Deputy Air Commander-in-Chief for OVERLORD, recorded:

General Spaatz stated that he feared that the Allied air forces might be batting their heads against a stone wall in the Overlord operation. If the purpose of Overlord is to seize and hold advanced air bases, this purpose is no longer necessary since the strategic air forces can already reach all vital targets with fighter cover . . . It is of paramount importance the Combined Bomber Offensive continue without interruption and the proposed diversion of the 8th air force to support of Overlord is highly dangerous. Much more effective would be the combined operation on strategic missions under one command of the 8th, 15th and 9th air forces. If this were done, the highly dangerous Overlord operation could be eliminated. It might take somewhat longer, but would be surer, whereas the proposed cross-channel operation is highly dangerous and the outcome is extremely uncertain. A failure of Overlord will have repercussions which may well undo all of the effects of the strategic bombing efforts to date. Another reason that Overlord is no longer necessary is because of the relative success of the use of H_2X [blind bombing radar equipment] operations over or in an overcast . . . Hence, the one heretofore great impediment to the strategic mission (i.e. weather) has been largely overcome and once more is an argument against mounting the Overlord operation.

If I were directing the overall strategic operations, I would go into Norway, where we have a much greater chance of ground force success and where I believe Sweden would come in with us. Why undertake a highly dubious operation in a hurry when there is a surer way to do it as just outlined? It is better to win the war surely than to undertake an operation which has really great risks . . .

In discussing future operations with General Vandenburg, Gen. Spaatz stated that all experience in Africa has indicated the inability of

American troops to cross areas heavily defended by land mines, and that the beaches of Overlord are certain to be more heavily mined than any area in Africa . . . Gen. Vandenburg cited his dissatisfaction with the plans for use of airborne troops. He stated that he has made protest a matter of record in all meetings with the Supreme Commanders [sic].[5]

This document vividly reveals, first, that two months·before D-Day there were still Allied officers in high commands who were deeply sceptical about the entire operation; and, second, the messianic conviction with which the airmen opposed their own participation. It is against the background of opinions such as these that the struggles between the ground and air force commanders in the summer of 1944 must be viewed. It is a tragic reflection of the extent to which strategic bombing doctrine had distorted the thinking of so many senior air force officers in Britain and America that, on the very eve of OVERLORD, they could not grasp that this was the decisive operation of the war in the west, to which every other ambition must be subordinate.

After intense argument between London and Washington, confused by British political reluctance to surrender the independence of Bomber Command, Eisenhower had his way: direction of all the Allied air forces was placed in his hands for as long as the Chiefs of Staff deemed necessary. After a further dispute, aggravated by Churchill's fears about the level of French civilian casualties, the air forces embarked upon the huge programme of transport bombing of French rail junctions and river crossings which was to play such a critical role in restricting the movement of German reinforcements after D-Day. Its scale was intensified by the need to attack targets relating to the entire length of the Channel coast, lest concentration westwards reveal the focus of Allied intentions. Its success was a tribute to the qualities and training of the Allied aircrew, whatever the opinions of their commanders. The cost – 12,000 French and Belgian lives – was substantially lower than Churchill had feared.

Yet if the documents quoted above reveal good reasons for the ground force commanders' mistrust of the airmen, it is ironic that in the spring of 1944 Spaatz achieved one of the decisive victories of the war for the Allies, and embarked upon the course that was to lead him to a second. In fulfilment of POINTBLANK, his Fortresses and Liberators had for months been attacking Germany's aircraft factories, at a cost which compelled the Americans to accept the need for long-range fighter escorts for their daylight operations. By one of the most extraordinary paradoxes of the war, the bombing of the factories achieved only limited impact upon German aircraft production; but the coming of the marvellous Mustang P-51 long-range fighter to the skies over Germany inflicted an irreversible defeat upon the Luftwaffe, unquestionably decisive for OVERLORD. In January 1944 the Germans lost 1,311 aircraft from all causes. This figure rose to 2,121 in February and 2,115 in March. Even more disastrous than lost fighters, the Luftwaffe's trained pilots were being killed far more quickly than they could be replaced, with the direction of the air force in the enfeebled hands of Goering. By March the Americans were consciously attacking targets with the purpose of forcing the Germans to defend them. By June, the Germans no longer possessed sufficient pilots and aircraft to mount more than token resistance to the Allied invasion of France.

In May, Spaatz began attacking Germany's synthetic oil plants. The results of even a limited bombing programme, revealed after the war, were awe-inspiring. Employing only 11.6 per cent of his bomber effort in June, 17 per cent in July, 16.4 per cent in August, he brought about a fall in German oil production from 927,000 tons in March to 715,000 tons in May, and 472,000 tons in June. The Luftwaffe's aviation spirit supply fell from 180,000 tons in April to 50,000 tons in June, and 10,000 tons in August. It seems perfectly possible that had the scale of the German fuel crisis been perceived by the allied chiefs of staff and the American airmen been encouraged to pursue their oil bombing campaign with vigour through the summer of 1944, Germany could have been defeated by the end of the year.

Yet it was Spaatz's tragedy that, by the spring of 1944, his own credibility and that of the other bomber chiefs had fallen low in the eyes of the Allied high command – hardly surprising in the light of their past broken promises and wild declarations of strategic opinion. Claims of Luftwaffe aircraft destroyed had so often proved fantastic that even other leaders of the Allied air forces found it impossible to credit the extent of the Mustang's victory. For that matter, Spaatz himself remained apprehensive about the Luftwaffe's capabilities. Plans were laid for huge forces of fighters to cover the invasion, in expectation of a great battle for air supremacy over the beachhead. SHAEF estimates suggested that the Germans might still be capable of putting as many as 300 fighters and 200 bombers into the air over Normandy in a single operation. Leigh-Mallory feared that the

The American P-51 Mustang fighter made its greatest contribution to Allied victory by winning the battle for air supremacy over Germany before D-Day. In its original form, powered by the Allison engine, the fighter performed disappointingly. But when fitted with the great Rolls-Royce Merlin, it was transformed into one of the most remarkable aircraft of the war, capable of flying to Berlin and back with long-range drop tanks, and outperforming almost every Luftwaffe opponent when it got there. It was also employed over Normandy in interceptor and ground-attack roles. Normally armed with six .5 machine-guns, it possessed a top speed of 475 mph, and a ceiling of 42,000 feet.

Luftwaffe might employ new pathfinder techniques to mount night operations over the British south coast ports. Only on D-Day, when a mere 319 Luftwaffe sorties were flown, was the truth suspected; in the weeks that followed, as enemy air activity over Normandy remained negligible, it was confirmed. The critical air battle had been fought and won by the Americans over Germany weeks before the first Allied soldiers waded ashore.

In the months before the invasion, however, it was the level of mutual dissent between the Allied air chiefs which drove Tedder and Eisenhower to the brink of despair. Beyond the debate about the employment of the bombers, British and American airmen united in their hostility to Leigh-Mallory, the appointed Air Commander-in-Chief for OVERLORD. The bomber commanders flatly declined to accept their orders from him and would acknowledge only the mandate of Tedder. The fighter commanders also made clear their dislike of and lack of respect for the Commander-in-Chief. The American Brereton, an officer of limited abilities commanding IXth Air Force, and the New Zealander "Mary" Coningham, commanding the British 2nd Tactical Air Force, united in their antagonism to Leigh-Mallory, while General Elwood R. "Pete" Quesada, commanding the close-support squadrons under Brereton, was a bewildered spectator of the wrangles: "I just didn't know people at that level behaved like that. Nobody wanted to be under Leigh-Mallory, even the British."[6]

The burly Leigh-Mallory had achieved his eminence, and aroused considerable personal animosity, by intriguing successfully in the wake of the Battle of Britain to supplant its victors, Air Marshals Dowding and Park. He had directed Fighter Command – later curiously rechristened Air Defence of Great Britain – ever since, and retained this post while he acted as Air Commander-in-Chief for OVERLORD. His appointment was clearly an error of judgement by Portal, Chief of Air Staff. To his peers, he seemed gloomy and hesitant. Most of the Americans admired Tedder for his cool brain, incisive wit, and ability to rise above petty issues and work without reservation for the Allied cause. "Trivia were obnoxious to him," said one. "Though an airman, he was also a team player. He understood that war is organized confusion." But they were irked by Leigh-Mallory's pessimism and indecision. "He didn't seem to know what he wanted," said Quesada. "He couldn't get along with people. He seemed more concerned with preserving his forces than with committing them."[7] Brigadier James Gavin of the U.S. 82nd Airborne returned from his division's drop in Sicily to work on the plan for D-Day. "Now, I want you chaps to tell me how you do this airborne business," said Leigh-Mallory indulgently. He listened to them for a time, then said flatly: "I don't think anybody can do that." The exasperated Gavin exploded: "We just got through doing it in Sicily!"[8] At a meeting of the American airmen on 24 March, General Vandenburg asked Spaatz where his personal loyalties were to lie in his role as deputy to Leigh-Mallory. Vandenburg recorded in his diary that: "General Spaatz directed that the number one priority was to be the safeguarding of the interests of the American component and suggested that I make this clear to General Eisenhower and ask for his concurrence."[9]

At a time, therefore, when everywhere else within the Allied forces great and honourable efforts were being made to ensure that Anglo-American unity was a reality, the senior American airmen in Britain were conspiring – in a manner no more nor less dishonourable than that of some of their RAF counterparts – to defend the sectional interests of their own service. It remains an astonishing feature of the invasion that when it was launched the Allied air chiefs were still unwilling to accept Leigh-Mallory's orders, still disputed their proper role and employment, had still devoted only minimal thought or effort to close ground support. Forward air control techniques which had been tried and proven in the desert were not introduced in Normandy until weeks after the landings. On D-Day itself, while the Allied tactical air forces made an important contribution, they lacked forward air controllers with the leading troops ashore, who might have eased the problems of the ground battle considerably. It has become an article of faith in the history of the Normandy campaign to pay tribute to Allied air power, which indeed was critical. Yet we shall see below how many weeks elapsed before the organization – not the technology or the skill of the pilots – reached the point at which aircraft could render closely co-ordinated support to ground troops.

In the spring of 1944, the air chiefs dedicated far too much attention to disputes about their own authority and independence, and not nearly enough to considering how best they could work in harmony with the armies beneath them. The post-OVERLORD report from Montgomery's headquarters declared: "The most difficult single factor during the period of planning from the military point of view, was the delay in deciding and setting up the higher headquarters organization of the Allied air force. It is obvious that this delay was entirely an air force matter, and as such in no way the business of the military planners, but the effect was strongly felt in army planning."[10] To the dismay and near despair of 21st Army Group, the D-Day Air Plan was finally settled only 36 hours before the landings took place.

Invaders

By the spring of 1944, all of southern England and much of the rest of the country had become a vast military encampment. Under the trees beside the roads, protected by corrugated iron, stood dump after dump of artillery ammunition, mines, engineering stores, pierced plank and wire. The soldiers themselves were awed by the tank and vehicle parks in the fields, where Shermans and jeeps, Dodge trucks and artillery pieces stood in ranks reaching to the horizon. Above all, there were the men – 20 American divisions, 14 British, three Canadian, one French, one Polish, and hundreds of thousands of special forces,

54

corps troops, headquarters units, lines of communication personnel. They were packed into Nissen and Quonset huts, tents and requisitioned country houses from Cornwall to Kent and far northwards up the length of the country. Some were homesick, some excited, a few eager to find any means of escape from the terrifying venture in front of them. Most were impatient to end the months or years of training and to begin this thing upon which all their thoughts had been focused for so long.

One of Montgomery's outstanding contributions before D-Day was his careful meshing of experienced veterans from Eighth Army with the keen, green formations that had been training and languishing for so long in England. Major-General G. P. B. "Pip" Roberts found his new headquarters at 11th Armoured Division still operating the routines and mess life of the peacetime British army. Roberts, an old desert hand, rapidly relieved them of such formalities, sacking his senior staff officer – a meticulous guardsman who affected a red light over his office door to indicate that he did not wish to be disturbed.

Lieutenant Andrew Wilson of The Buffs, a flamethrowing Crocodile tank unit of 79th Armoured Division, had watched the Battle of Britain from his home in Kent as a schoolboy, and eagerly hastened to Sandhurst and into the armoured corps at the first opportunity. Thereafter, he and the other young officers of his unit found themselves condemned to months of routine soldiering on the South Downs under the command of ageing senior officers who knew nothing of war, but were expert in the disciplines of mess life. When Wilson, in a flush of enthusiasm for Russian achievements of the kind that was so common at the time, christened his tank "Stalingrad", he was summarily ordered to unchristen it. But at the beginning of 1944, all the senior officers were abruptly removed and replaced by others from a quite different mould, who began training and exercising the regiment to the very limits of its endurance: "We suddenly knew that we were going to be put through the full Monty treatment."[1] For hours and days at a stretch, they shivered in their tanks on the hills through endless mock attacks and deployments. They did not resent this because they felt that they were learning, at last preparing in earnest for what they had to do. The dangers of taking into battle a tank towing a thinly-armoured trailer loaded with flame-throwing fuel did not greatly trouble them: "Any fears were overcome by our excitement at feeling that we were an elite."[2]

Most of the men of that English "battle school army" shared Wilson's enthusiasm. Major Dick Gosling, ex-Eton and Cambridge, commanding a battery of self-propelled 25-pounders of the Essex Yeomanry, had been waiting to see action since 1939: "We were at the very peak of enthusiasm, fitness, training."[3] Major Charles Richardson of the 6th King's Own Scottish Borderers had so far spent the war commanding a tactical school in Edinburgh, attending the Staff College and training troops amid a sense of lingering embarrassment that he had not seen a shot fired in anger, although as he later concluded: "You fight a bloody sight better when you don't know what's coming."[4]

Many of Lieutenant David Priest's men of 5th Duke of Cornwall's Light Infantry spent the weeks before D-Day attempting to master the art of wheeled warfare. They were a bicycle unit, and it was not easy for a soldier to pedal under the weight of full equipment: "the thing would rear up on you".[5] Typically, within hours of their arrival in Normandy, they were ordered to park their transport and never saw the bicycles again. Corporal Chris Portway of the 4th Dorsets claimed to find his experiences in Normandy infinitely less painful than "all those ghastly exercises"[6] which preceded them. During one in which he took part, bitter British animosity towards the French-Canadians, who were acting as the enemy, boiled over into bloodshed near Reading, with men on both sides being killed. Trooper Steve Dyson became so miserably bored with infantry soldiering in England after 1940 that in desperation he volunteered for anything that offered a chance of escape – demolition, paratroops, military police. At last he was accepted for armour, and found himself perfectly happy, for he loved his tank. Private Mick Anniwell, a 30-year-old former shoe-factory worker and scoutmaster, now posted to 2nd Royal Ulster Rifles, quite simply loved the army and everything that happened to him in it. For many working-class civilians, the 1930s had not been a happy time. In the wartime army, not a few found a fulfilment, a comradeship and sense of purpose that they would spend the rest of their post-war lives seeking to recapture.

Other men, not surprisingly, felt more resigned to their part in the invasion than exhilarated by it. Lieutenant Arthur Heal was a bespectacled 28-year-old sapper, who found that throughout his service career, "I never felt like a soldier". Heal was simply "eager to see the end of it all and be able to go home".[7] Private Charles Argent of 2nd King's Own Scottish Borderers was one of those unfortunate men who spent the war being shunted abruptly from posting to posting, each more dismal than the last, after failing to be accepted for the navy or the Parachute Regiment. In the spring of 1944, he was one morning issued with tropical kit, which was promptly withdrawn. The next day he was sent on a mortar course. At last, on the very eve of invasion, he was posted to the Lowland Division where he knew no one, and was conscious of his very un-Scottish origins. Nor, of course, was he detailed as a mortarman.

7th Armoured, 50th Northumbrian and 51st Highland Divisions had been brought home from the Mediterranean, where they had gained great reputations, specifically to provide the stiffening of experience for the British invasion force. From an early stage there were rumours among the men of 50th Division that they were expendable, that they would be used on the battlefield for tasks in which the rate of attrition would be high. Curiously enough, this did not seem greatly to dismay them, and 50th Division's record in Normandy was very good. Among the other veteran formations, however, there was cause for real concern. Lieutenant Edwin Bramall, posted with a draft of eager and untested young officers to the 2nd King's Royal Rifle Corps of 4th Armoured Brigade, found that "as a battalion, they were worn out. They had shot their bolt. Everybody who was any good had been promoted or become a casualty."[8] Many of the men from the Mediterranean, above all the old regular soldiers, were bitter that, after fighting so hard for so long, they were now to be called upon once again to bear the brunt of the battle. A staff officer described the difficulties with one unit recalled from the Mediterranean for the invasion: "The 3rd Royal Tank Regiment were virtually mutinous just before D-Day. They painted the walls of their barracks in Aldershot with such slogans as 'No Second Front', and had it not been for their new commanding officer, David Silvertop – the best C.O. of an armoured regiment that I met during the war – I really think they might have mutinied in fact." Lieutenant-Colonel Michael Carver of 7th Armoured's 1st Royal Tank Regiment found some of his senior NCOs appearing before him to protest about their role, and echoing complaints from their wives, who demanded to know why those who had sat in England for four years and had not "done their bit" could not now take over the burden. It was a sentiment shared by the Prime Minister:

It is a painful reflection [he wrote to the War Office early in 1944], that probably not one in four or five men who wear the King's uniform even hear a bullet whistle, or are likely to hear one. The vast majority run no more risk than the civil population in southern England. It is my unpleasant duty to dwell upon these facts. One set of men are sent back again and again to the front, while the great majority are kept out of all fighting, to their regret.[9]

If the Prime Minister's closing clause can be regarded with scepticism, his earlier remarks were the subject of repeated altercations with his CIGS, who patiently reminded him of the realities of modern war, of the essential need for the vast "tail" behind OVERLORD, and also of the utter exhaustion of Britain's manpower reserves. The British army that landed in Normandy would be the greatest force that Montgomery ever commanded in north-west Europe. Thereafter, as casualties mounted, its numbers must remorselessly decline. This reality was at the forefront of every British commander's mind from the first clash of arms before Caen until the last shots before Luneberg. So too was the knowledge that the early weeks in Europe would be the last of British parity with the Americans in ground-force strength. In July, the American armies would begin to outnumber the British, and thereafter their strength would rise month by month until they dwarfed those of their ally. Already many British servicemen were irked by the extraordinary social dominance the Americans had achieved within Britain, with their staff sergeants receiving the pay of British captains, their vast reservoirs of equipment for themselves, and candy for British children.

From the moment that they boarded their trains at the docks and cursed the narrowness of British carriage doors for a man in full equipment, the fresh Americans found the encounter with the tired British a strange and bewildering experience. "And where do you make your home, Colonel?" Lieutenant Julian Bach heard a newly-arrived Mississipian captain ask a somewhat frigid British officer at their first uneasy meeting over dinner. "Which home do you mean?" inquired the Colonel unhelpfully, "I have three." The Mississipian enjoyed his revenge the next morning when he watched the Englishman's expression as he poured marmalade on his porridge.[10]

Impeccably tailored American officers – and other ranks – crammed the London hotels and restaurants. Corporal Bill Preston of the 743rd Tank Battalion spent his working days practising submarine escapes from the amphibious DD tank in which he would land in Normandy – he and his crew learned that they had 20 seconds in which to get out if the Sherman foundered. But like so many young non-commissioned Americans, he confused the British by the breadth of his social connections, and found it much easier to book a table at the Mirabelle by using the name of his uncle at the U.S. Embassy than by quoting his own. General "Pete" Quesada of IXth Tactical Air Command brought a few of his pilots along whenever business took him to London, and they found no difficulty in making friends. He wrote to his mother in New York asking her to send him a monthly parcel of a box of Montecristos, six boxes of stockings and six lipsticks. Deadpan, for the rest of the war she dispatched regular consignments of men's long socks and vaseline sticks for chapped lips.

Yet if it is easy to focus upon points of friction between the Americans and their hosts, it remains far more remarkable how effectively Allied co-operation worked at every level. Beneath the tensions between governments and army headquarters on matters of high policy, officers of the two nations worked side by side with extraordinary amity in the preparations for OVERLORD. Just as there were boorish Englishmen such as the Colonel who met Julian Bach, so there were Americans of poor quality, such as General "Pinky" Bull, Eisenhower's G-3 at SHAEF, who inspired the disrespect of almost all who worked with him. But most Englishmen were deeply impressed by the energy, the willingness to learn, and the determination to finish the job of their transatlantic allies. The Americans, in their turn, respected the British forces which had been fighting for so long. Much will be said below about differences and jealousies that developed between British and Americans. Reports of these should never mask the co-operation between them, a unity between allies at working level that has seldom, if ever, been matched in war.

If several British formations that went to Normandy were already battle-weary, some of their American counterparts were alarmingly under-prepared and inadequately led for the task that they were to perform. Even though the British divisions were drawn from a citizen army, the British class system and military tradition meant that their men were far more deeply imbued with the manners and habits of regular soldiers than their

American comrades. From the first day of the war to the last, the U.S. Army could never be mistaken for anything other than what it was – a nation of civilians in uniform. Perhaps the greatest of all America's organizational achievements in the Second World War was the expansion of a tiny regular army of 190,000 men into an eight-and-a-half-million-strong host between 1939 and 1945. Even the peacetime cadre had scarcely been an impressive war machine. One cavalry division in the 1940 Louisiana manoeuvres was obliged to rent its horses, and when these poor nags proved useless, to withdraw them by truck to rest areas after the second day.

Even at war, American's ground forces – above all, her corps of infantry – remained something of a cinderella. A 1942 plan to create an army of 334 divisions, 60 of them armoured, shrivelled to a reality of 89 combat divisions by May 1944, 16 of them armoured. These might be compared with Japan's total of 100 divisions, and the Red Army's 300 – albeit smaller – formations. Huge reserves of manpower were drawn off to feed their air corps, service units, and base troops. Where officers made up only 2.86 per cent of the German army, they represented 7 per cent of the U.S. Army, many of whom never approached a front line. By 1944, it was evident to American's commanders that serious errors of judgement had been made in the mobilization of the nation. The most critical, which would markedly influence the campaign in north-west Europe, was that too little emphasis had been placed upon manning the infantry regiments at the very tip of the American spear. The air corps, the specialist branches, and the service staff had been allowed to cream off too high a proportion of the best-educated, fittest recruits. Infantry rifle companies would be called upon to fight Hilter's Wehrmacht, "the most professionally skilful army of modern times,"[11] with men who were, in all too many cases, the least impressive material America had summoned to the colours.

To some extent, this reflected the natural urge of the United States to make the utmost use of technology in fighting the war. But there was also a contrast between the social attitudes of America's "best and brightest" young men towards military service and that of their counterparts in Europe. In America, a military career has never been honourable in the European manner, outside a few thousand "army families". It has traditionally been the route by which impoverished young men – not least Eisenhower and Bradley – can carve out a career for themselves without advantages of birth. George S. Patton was a rare exception. He himself wrote: "It is an unfortunate and, to me, tragic fact that in our attempts to prevent war, we have taught our people to belittle the heroic qualities of the soldier."[12] It is striking to observe that in the Second World War, privileged young Englishmen still gravitated naturally towards rifle and armoured regiments. Their American counterparts by preference sought out exotic postings in the air corps or OSS, or managerial roles on army or diplomatic staffs. It never became fashionable for young Ivy League Americans to serve as front-line officers. This is not to deny that many did so, and fought with gallantry. But it does suggest that the American army's "teeth" elements were severely blunted because they lacked their proper share of the ablest and fittest officers and men. On a tour with General Eisenhower on 4 April, Commander Butcher recorded in his diary: "I am concerned over the absence of toughness and alertness of young American officers whom I saw on this trip. They are as green as growing corn. How will they act in battle and how will they look in three months time?"[13]

In those weeks, hundreds of thousands of young men of Bradley's assault divisions were asking themselves the same question. Private Lindley Higgins was "dumb enough not to feel the slightest trepidation. We really thought that at any moment the whole Reich was going to collapse. We saw what we had, heard what they didn't have. We really thought that we only had to step off that beach and all the krauts would put up their hands."[14] This was a delusion much more common among formations such as the 4th Division, in which Higgins was a rifleman, than among those which had fought in North Africa and Sicily. A shipping clerk from the Bronx – an uncommonly perceptive one – he went to work on 8 December 1941, listened to President Roosevelt's broadcast to the nation, and walked immediately to the army recruiting office in Whitehall Street. His father was delighted: "He thought the army would straighten me out". Higgins himself expected to be home within a few months. Instead, he spent two years practising assault landings on the American east coast, "spending a lot of time fighting the North African campaign – we kept being told that this or that would happen in the desert." The war seemed very remote from them. They felt unable to relate anything in their own experience to what was taking place in Europe and the Pacific. Even in their final pre-invasion exercises in Devon, they concentrated chiefly on the fun of firing the hayricks with tracer bullets: "We were a singularly callous and unfeeling group of young men." But now they burnt their personal papers according to orders, and speculated about where they were going. They were told that it was to be an inundated area, so Higgins said confidently: "I know geography – it's got to be Holland." Their regimental and battalion commanding officers were relieved a few weeks before the landing. At the final briefing their new CO told them that under no circumstances would they turn back after they left the landing craft. It would be a court martial offence to stop or retreat on the beach. At the assembly area outside Plymouth, as they queued for food, Higgins's friend John Schultz peered at his plate and groaned: "Boy, this is the big one. If they're starting to serve steak, we're in trouble." Higgins tried to grasp the reality of what they were about to do: "Me, Lindley Higgins, from Riverdale in the Bronx, was about to invade France. It was a problem that my mind in its then state of maturity couldn't possibly cope with."

Major Harry Herman, executive officer of the 9th Division's 2nd/39th Infantry, had a far shrewder notion of what they faced than most of the invaders. A graduate of Michigan University, his father had been killed in the First World War, his great-grandfather wounded at Gettysburg. As a student, he had read *Mein Kampf* and been a member of an anti-war group. He was earning $18,000 a year with the prosperous family business in January 1940 when, despite his pleas for a deferment, he became the 21st American to be drafted. Like hundreds of thousands of others, he endured the confusion and hardship which marked the first year of the American army's vast expansion, passed out of officer school top in weapons and tactics, bottom in personal appearance, and was shipped to Ireland with his division in October 1942. In January 1943, Herman shared the American army's bitter humiliation in the Kasserine Pass, running for his life amidst men throwing away their arms and equipment, deployed by commanders "who had no idea how to make dispositions for battle. It was awful – there were no supplies, no water, no officer leadership. But then we refitted. we went back, we did better. In a way, the North African campaign was a blessing to American troops."[15] By the time they went into Sicily, they had learned a great deal – about the need to move the ridge lines, instead of the valleys that they had been taught to use in training,[16] about leading from the front, about controlling venereal disease among the men.

Yet when the 1st and 9th Divisions were brought back from Sicily to prepare for OVERLORD, there was bitter resentment among many officers and men that they should be asked to do it all again. They felt that they had done their share, that it was time to go home and reap the glory, leaving the next battlefield to the millions of other men who had thus far endured nothing. Some officers successfully arranged transfers. "Morale was not high," said Herman. Major Frank Colacicci of the 1st Division's 3rd/18th found the same feelings among his own men: "We felt that we'd done our war, we should go home. We kept reading in the papers about the huge increase in U.S. strength."[17]

Bradley wrote: "Much as I disliked subjecting the 1st to still another landing, I felt that as a commander I had no other choice . . . I felt compelled to employ the best troops I had, to minimize the risks and hoist the odds in our favour in any way that I could."[18] Bradley and other American commanders were acutely conscious of the shortcomings of some American formations, above all of their commanders. Marshall wrote in March about the embarrassment of having been compelled to relieve a succession of generals, including two corps commanders: ". . . we couldn't relieve any more without a serious loss of prestige. What seemed to be lacking in each case was aggressive qualities . . ." As the men of the 9th and 1st – now under the command of the forceful Clarence Huebner – began to train in south-west England, as they absorbed the green replacements to fill up their ranks, "we recovered pretty quickly," in the words of one of their officers.[20] That their participation should have been thought essential to the invasion of Europe engendered a sense of pride: "We thought the outcome of the war depended on the 1st and 9th Divisions," said Harry Herman. "We felt it was inevitable that we had to do this thing. There was no way out." Herman himself had become a successful soldier who no longer looked beyond the next battlefield: "I didn't think the war was ever going to end. I thought that for the rest of our lives, we should be fighting one way or another."[21].

Like most Americans, Technical Sergeant Bill Walsh felt no great animosity towards the Germans – he merely regarded the war as a job to be got over before they could all go home. His principal concern was that the waterproofing on his tank should prove secure enough to get him ashore. A dentist's son from

New Jersey, he had joined the Essex Troop of the local National Guard in 1938. They were a mounted unit and in those days of the Depression, Walsh was among thousands of young men for whom the Guard provided a social life to which they could not otherwise have aspired. He took part in the U.S. Army's last review of mounted cavalry, and as they trotted past to the tune of *Old Grey Mare,* most the men were choking back tears. They were among the first units to ship to Europe, where they converted to tanks and began the long two-year wait before the 102nd Cavalry went into action. Walsh and his crew admitted no great apprehension to each other about D-Day: "The movies always show people talking to each other about their problems and fears before action. We never did."[22]

Corporal Dick Raymond of 3rd Canadian Division was in reality an 18-year-old American, the son of an upstate New York chicken farmer who ran away across the border to join the Canadian army – which had a reputation for not asking many questions – in January 1942, when he was 16, "an under-achieving high school drop-out".[23] He was thrown out after a month, but was soon back at Niagara, greeting the recruiting sergeant, a familiar landmark of the place and the period, at the border. To Raymond, who had grown up listening to CBC Radio from Toronto, Canada sounded exciting. The Canadian army seemed full of Americans. When he was sworn in with a detail of other new recruits, they were told that Americans could keep their hands by their sides when the moment came for the oath to the King. Most of the men in the room did so. There were deserters and rejects from the American army, one or two curious fragments of human flotsam from the Spanish Civil War, and the first American negro Raymond had known, a huge, clever man, rumoured to be a lawyer from West Virginia. The young New Yorker found the army tough. When he was foolish enough to reveal that he had some money, it was quickly beaten out of him. He learned to drink and to cheat with some thoroughness. He became cynical about the manner in which the volunteer Canadian forces cleared the military prisons and hospitals in their desperate struggle to fill the ranks before the invasion. He retained a low opinion of most of the officers corps. But he loved their regimental traditions, the pipes and kilts of the Canadian Scottish units. And for all their lack of discipline, he came to admire immensely their behaviour on the battlefield.

In 1927, a 22-year-old Czech named Frank Svboda won a

scholarship to a college in Iowa, where he took a master's degree in theology, was ordained, and subsequently became a presbyterian minister among the Czech community in New York. In 1943, he volunteered to become an army chaplain – he had already done infantry training with the Czech army – and was sent for three months to the chaplain's school at Harvard. He found himself with a Jewish rabbi in the next bunk and a Catholic priest in the one below: the latter remarked cheerfully that he had never expected to find himself bedding down with heretics. Then he was posted to the 79th Division in Arizona and, in March 1944, came with them to England. They were awed by the blitzed streets of Liverpool as they marched through, and touched by the kindness of the local Cheshire families who invited so many men to tea each Sunday afternoon, despite their own desperate shortage of rations. Svboda's invasion equipment comprised a bible and a portable communion set. As a European he understood, in a way that his unblooded division did not, that the Germans would be very difficult to defeat. In the big tent that he used as a chapel before they sailed for France, he listened to men's problems – "mostly about their wives" – and held services for soldiers who filed in carrying their rifles and helmets: "They were going into battle as people go to church, with a sense of reverence. There was no rowdiness or drunkenness."[24]

It was not remarkable that the lofty sentiments about D-Day were chiefly expressed by the senior commanders. "I don't have to tell you what a big show this is, or how important," the commander of the American Western Naval Task Force, Rear-Admiral Alan Kirk, wrote to a friend in Washington on 10 March: "If this is successful the war is won, if this fails it may go on for years. Perhaps too it will settle whether we or Russia dominate the world for a while."[25] Colonel Paddy Flint, the colourful old commander of the 9th Division's 39th Infantry, wrote in a much more homespun spirit to the wife or mother of every officer under his command before D-Day. "We are sort of putting our affairs in order," he said. "Maybe it is just the spring housecleaning that we used to do under Mother's direction when I was a little boy at home. Anyway, I know you will understand. I just wanted to tell you how much we think of your son Harry in the Regiment . . . ."[26]

At St Paul's School on 15 May, Montgomery presented the OVERLORD plan for the last time before the senior officers of the Allied armies, crowded on wooden benches behind the single row of chairs at the front for the King, Churchill, Smuts and Brooke. One of the greatest throngs of commanders in history was gathered in the hall for the briefing: Bradley, whom the British respected and would come to respect more as one of the Americans "who really understood the battle"; General J. Lawton Collins of VII Corps – the nervous, explosive, ambitious "Lightning Joe" who had made his reputation commanding a division on Guadalcanal; Gerow of V Corps, less impressive and untried in action; Corlett of XIX Corps; Middleton of VIII Corps. The British showed consistent concern in north-west Europe about the quality of American command and staffwork at corps and division level. Some senior Americans agreed later that this criticism had some force. There were simply not enough thoroughly trained staff officers to go round their vastly expanded army. But there were also, at St Paul's, some outstanding American divisional commanders – Huebner of 1st Division, Barton of the 4th, Eddy of the 9th.

Sir Miles Dempsey, commanding the British Second Army, was a retiring figure almost unknown to the British public, and said later to have been treated more like a corps than an army commander by Montgomery. But Dempsey was a great professional, a brilliant judge of ground, an utterly reliable agent for the execution of his Commander-in-Chief's wishes. Crocker of 1 Corps was a tough, dependable commander who never caused Montgomery unease in Normandy – unlike Bucknall of XXX Corps, about whom Brooke always had doubts, and who was destined for dismissal. Crerar, who would command the Canadian army when it followed the assault formations into the line, was considered an unimaginative, stolid administrator; Montgomery had tried hard to dispense with him, but political imperatives were too strong. Crerar's senior corps commander, Guy Simonds, was to prove one of the outstanding leaders of the campaign – a dour, direct, clever gunner upon whom Montgomery increasingly relied. For the rest, there were two verterans of the desert, O'Connor of VIII Corps and Ritchie of XII. At divisional level, with brilliant exceptions such as Roberts of 11th Armoured, the British team could better be described as solid than inspired. There were already doubts about 7th Armoured's commander, Major-General W. R. J. "Bobby" Erskine, who had been quite unexpectedly plucked from a staff job to take over the division, and was widely considered to have been promoted above his ceiling. Erskine loved and admired the men of his formation deeply, and here lay the root of much trouble in Normandy: he was too ready to accept the word of his subordinates that they had done all that could be expected of them. He was not a man to drive his command. But in war, as in all human endeavours, there are never sufficient men of a calibre perfectly suited to the demands of the hour. The shortcomings of the Allied command team from OVERLORD were mirrored by those of the Germans on the far shore.

Montgomery's presentation on 15 May, like his earlier briefing on 7 April, was acknowledged even by his critics as a brilliant performance: a display of grip, confidence, absolute mastery of the plan. He had already conducted a long session – Exercise THUNDERCLAP – with his ground force officers before the huge relief model of the battlefield, at which he threw out situations and possible setbacks to test their responses. It was Montgomery's misfortune that his very mastery of advance planning became a source of scepticism to his enemies, following the inevitable imperfections of reality on the battlefield. Throughout the Normandy campaign, Churchill never erased from his memory a paper of Montgomery's of which he received a copy, stressing the need for rapid armoured penetrations after the landings: ". . . I am prepared to accept almost any risk in order to carry out these tactics. I would risk even the total loss of the armoured brigade groups . . . the delay they would cause to the enemy before they could be destroyed would be quite enough to give us time to get our main bodies well ashore and re-organized for strong offensive action."[27] Likewise, Bradley did not forget Montgomery's remarks to him at St Paul's about the prospect of tanks reaching Falaise on D-Day "to knock about a bit down there".[28] Montgomery would have been entirely justified in saying privately to Bradley and Dempsey – above all to Churchill – that whatever exhortations he gave the troops, he did not expect deep penetrations on D-Day from inexperienced troops recovering their land legs. But he did not do so. And thus he paid a price after the event, when the hopes that he had expressed both publicly and privately, to officers both high and low, were disappointed.

In the last weeks before D-Day, the principal dissension within the Allied high command concerned not OVERLORD, but the projected invasion of southern France, ANVIL, to which the Americans were firmly committed and the British bitterly opposed, because this would certainly cripple operations in Italy. Shipping difficulties forced the postponement of ANVIL from a landing simultaneous with OVERLORD to a secondary operation ten weeks later, and the arguments between London and Washington continued until the last days before its launching. This became the first major decision of the war over which the Americans adamantly refused to bow to British pressure, and went their own way. It was an augury of other painful blows to British confidence and pride which lay ahead.

Discussion of the airborne landings in support of OVER-LORD was complicated by the arrival of a delegation of staff officers direct from Marshall, to project the American Chief of Staff's strong view that, having created large and expensive airborne forces, the Allies should employ them for an ambitious envelopment plan. Marshall proposed that they should be dropped near Evreux in the "Orleans Gap" to hold a perimeter and create a major strategic threat in the German rear.[29] Eisenhower was obliged to point out painstakingly to Washington the inability of paratroops to resist armoured forces, their absolute immobility once on the ground, and the difficulties of supplying them with ammunition and heavy weapons.

More disturbingly, German reinforcement of the western Cotentin compelled Bradley to reconsider his existing plan for the American airborne drop on his flank. The two divisions were now to land on the eastern side of the peninsula only. Then it was Leigh-Mallory's turn to create difficulties. In the last days before 6 June, the airman became passionately imbued with the conviction that the American drop was doomed to disaster, with huge casualties in men and aircraft; he impressed this view upon Eisenhower. The Supreme Commander at last overruled him. But the Englishman had added to Eisenhower's huge anxieties and responsibilities at a critical moment, and further diminished confidence in his own nerve and judgement.

It was a remarkable tribute to the power of the image-builders that even among the Americans, in those last weeks before D-Day, nothing did more to boost the confidence of the men of the invasion armies than Montgomery's personal visits. From mid-May until June, he devoted his energies almost entirely to inspecting the troops under his command, whom he would never again have the opportunity to see in such numbers. The measured walk down the ranks; the piercing stare into men's eyes; the order to break ranks and gather around the general on the bonnet of the jeep; the sharp, brittle address – all were studiedly theatrical, yet defy the cynicism of history. "Even Eisenhower with all his engaging ease could never stir American troops to the rapture with which Monty was welcomed by his," wrote Bradley. "Among those men, the legend of Montgomery had become an imperishable fact."[30] Montgomery told them that the enemy had many divisions, but most of these were weak and understrength: "Everything is in the shopwindow. There is nothing 'in the kitty'."[31] He told Americans that "as a British general, I regard it as an honour to serve under American command; General Eisenhower is captain of the team and I am proud to serve under him." Lieutenant Philip Riesler and 12,000 other men of the U.S. 2nd Armored Division gathered to hear Montgomery on the football field at Tidworth camp in Hampshire. "Take off your helmets!" he ordered, and off came every helmet except that of Maurice Rose, beside the jeep. "You, too, general," said Montgomery. He paused and gazed slowly, in silence, round the great mass of men. At last he said: "All right, put them back on. Now next time I see you, I shall know you." It was brilliant stage-management.

There was less enthusiasm from the British government for Montgomery's speeches to factory-workers and railwaymen, which were also a feature of his activities at this time. These smacked too much of the national warlord, arousing the deepest instinctive fears in politicians' hearts. When he drew up a two-page outline, complete with hymns and prayers, for a proposed national service of dedication at Westminster Abbey before the invasion, the plan was speedily squashed. Montgomery would sail for France leaving behind many men who admired his skill and application in bringing the invasion to reality. Not one of his British or American critics could afterwards deny the importance of his contribution to the creation of OVERLORD; no other Allied general could have accomplished so much. But he also left behind a deep reservoir of animosity and bitterness. Morgan, who had laboured so hard and long as COSSAC, would never forgive Montgomery for ruthlessly consigning him to the backwaters of the war after his own arrival in England. Scores of other senior officers who had not belonged to Montgomery's "desert family" were also discarded – some for good reasons, others suffering merely for the misfortune of being unknown to the new Commander-in-Chief. Apart from these, there was an abundance of staff officers at Eisenhower's headquarters ready to poison the ear of the Supreme Commander towards Montgomery. As long as the Englishman remained victorious, he was invulnerable. But should the group campaign falter under his direction, he had provided many powerful hostages to fortune.

Defenders

"If they attack in the west," said Adolf Hitler in December 1943, "that attack will decide the war."[1] Whatever the shortcomings of the Atlantic Wall, Hitler's proclaimed impatience for the Allied invasion was by no means bluff. His armies in Russia were being remorselessly pushed back and destroyed; between July 1943 and May 1944 alone, they lost 41 divisions in the east. Their total manpower had fallen from over three million in July 1943 to 2.6 million in December. Thereafter, between March and May 1944, they suffered a further 341,950 casualties, and lost an additional 150,000 men in the aftermath of the Allied landings in Italy. Germany's sole conceivable chance of escaping catastrophe now lay in the destruction of OVERLORD. "Our only hope is that they come where we can use the army upon them," said General von Thoma to a comrade in captivity.[2] If the Allies could be thrown back into the sea, it was inconceivable that they should mount a new assault for years, if ever. Almost the entire strength of the German army in north-west Europe, 59 divisions, could be transferred east for a fight to the finish against the Russians. Within the year, secret weapons and jet aircraft should be available in quantity. Thereafter, Hitler reasoned, anything was possible. If it was a sketchy scenario, it was not an impossible one – granted only that the Allies could be denied a foothold in France.

In January 1944, Jodl toured the Channel coast and reported grimly on the state of its defences.[3] The perpetual bleeding of manpower from west to east had crippled every division. In the Channel Islands, 319th Division was reduced to 30 per cent of its establishment. Re-equipment was causing chaos – the artillery was armed with 21 types of gun: French, Russian and Czech. Commanders complained that they were being denied time to carry out essential training because their men were continuously employed on building fortifications. The Germans were as preoccupied as the Allies with the need to maintain air superiority over the invasion coast, yet Jodl recognized that ". . . we must not accept battle with the enemy air force".[4] The hapless Commander-in-Chief, von Rundstedt, was never consulted about what forces he deemed necessary to defeat an invasion – he was merely informed of what was to arrive. The bulk of his army was made up of the over-age and medically unfit, convalescents from the east, and an entirely unreliable rabble of Polish, Russian and Italian defectors and forced labourers. Even the majority of the first-line divisions which began to move into France in the spring of 1944, in accordance with Hitler's Directive 51 for the strengthening of the western defences, were formations shattered in the east, which would need massive reinforcement and re-equipment if they were ever to regain their old fighting power. However well Hitler recognized the need to defend against invasion, he was the victim of a remorseless imperative that demanded men and tanks to fight against the present menace in the east, rather than the prospective threat in the west.

If there was a euphoric belief among the western Allies after their victory that they had monopolized the attention and best efforts of Nazi Germany, the figures belie this. In January 1944, Hitler deployed 179 divisions in the east, 26 in south-east Europe, 22 in Italy, 16 in Scandinavia, and 53 in France and the Low Countries. By 6 June, there were 59 in France and the Low Countries – 41 of these north of the Loire – 28 in Italy, but still 165 in the east. There were 24 Panzer divisions in the east and eight elsewhere in January, compared with proportions of 18 to 15 by June. It remains astounding that after three years of devastating losses in the east and the relentless bombing of Hitler's industries, Germany could still produce and equip an army in the west capable of causing the gravest difficulties to the best that Britain and America could throw into the war. "The possibility of Hitler's gaining a victory in France cannot be excluded," wrote Brooke gloomily on 25 January. "The hazards of battle are very great."[5]

Germany's critical weakness on the Channel coast in the spring of 1944 was her blindness. The Luftwaffe had lost not only its strength, but its will. Despite the difficulties posed by Allied command of the air, some measure of air reconnaissance might yet have been possible given real determination by the German airmen. But there was no sign that they recognized the cost of their failure, or of the weakness of their photographic interpreters beside those of the Allies. "That the Luftwaffe did not carry out minimal reconnaissance of the east coast must rank as a miracle of the same dimensions as the destruction of the Armada in 1588," the historian of Allied deception planning has written.[6] The British and Americans were quick to understand the importance of impeding German weather forecasting, and seized enemy stations in Iceland, Greenland, Sptizbergen and Jan Mayen island – actions that were of decisive importance on D-Day.[7] It would have been impossible for an operation of the magnitude of OVERLORD to have sustained its extraordinary level of security had it not been launched from a sealed island. The brilliant British counter-intelligence operations had not only deprived Germany of authentic agents in Britain, but also placed the agents in whom she trusted under the control of the Allied deception planners. The Americans, surprisingly, placed little faith in deception, and showed limited interest in FORTITUDE. Yet it was the Germans' utter uncertainty about where the Allies would land that contributed decisively to their debacle in June.

There has been recent speculation[8] about the possible role of Admiral Canaris himself in Allied deception plans for D-Day. This was prompted by new discussion of the links between the British Secret Intelligence Service and a Polish woman contact of the Abwehr chief. It has been suggested that Canaris was either working actively for British Intelligence, or was at least instrumental in persuading Hitler that the Allies would land in the Pas de Calais. The evidence is overwhelmingly against either of these remarkable notions. Canaris' loyalties wavered, and he certainly leaked some useful information which reached the Allies through the Polish contact; but there is no evidence whatever that he was personally exploited by the British, or that he was privy to the fact that every Abwehr agent in Britain was in the hands of MI5.

The worst charge thus far made against the authors of the British official history of wartime intelligence is dullness. It has not been suggested that they have concealed important elements of the truth, and they have had access to all the relevant documents. They declared flatly in their second volume, published in 1981, that after 1940 the Secret Service possessed no agents whatever in Germany. Professor Hinsley, the senior historian, confirms[9] that there is still no evidence of Canaris' complicity in Allied deception plans, which relied principally on the transmission of false information through Abwehr agents in Britain controlled by MI5. By the spring of 1944, Canaris was discredited in the eyes of Hitler and OKW. In any event, for the admiral or his associates consciously to have assisted Allied deception plans, they would have needed to know the truth about Allied intentions. It is unthinkable that these could have been revealed to them. The British were successfully employing all manner of conduits to channel false information to the Germans without any need of Canaris' direct assistance. The balance of probability remains heavily in favour of the view that Hitler's intelligence departments were incompetent, not treacherous, in their assessments of Allied plans in 1944. No significant historian of the period believes otherwise, and it is only because some recent newspaper reports have insistently suggested Canaris' active involvement in the pre–D-Day deception that it becomes necessary to contradict this delusion at such length.

Many narratives of D-Day have focussed upon the German failure to heed warnings that the invasion was imminent.[10] Yet in truth, while these might have enabled more high commanders to be at their posts when the Allies landed, knowledge of *when* would have been of only the most limited strategic value as long as they remained ignorant of *where*. The confusion of German thinking in the spring of 1944 was astonishing. Hitler's instinct continued to insist that the Allies would come in Normandy. But with uncharacteristic forbearance, he did not pursue his hunch to the point of demanding special emphasis upon Normandy's defences. On 29 April, one report suggested that the Allies were concentrating in western rather than eastern England, but on 15 May "a good Abwehr source" reported the 79th and 83rd U.S. Divisions in Yorkshire and Norfolk, and XX U.S. Corps and 4th Armored around Bury St Edmunds. A report from von Rundstedt's headquarters on 21 May anticipated that the Allies would mount several simultaneous assaults, and use new weapons, including gas – this, of course, was a mirror image of the fear of the invaders. Lieutenant-Colonel Roger Michel of Rommel's intelligence staff predicted that the Allies would land 35 divisions, but Hitler's staff were studying likely figures of 85 or 90 divisions, which was not implausible if America had mobilized the same proportion of manpower for her fighting formations as Germany. Some Allied deception schemes made no impression on the Germans – for instance, the dispatch of an army pay corps lieutenant and former actor to impersonate Montgomery on a tour of the Mediterranean, and the creation of a mythical army in Scotland for the invasion of Norway. But a

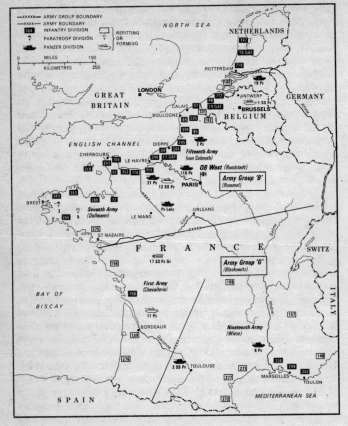

The Disposition of German Forces on D-Day

climate of uncertainty had been masterfully created, which would decisively influence German behaviour until deep into July. Its success reflected poorly both on Hitler's intelligence departments and on the enfeebled self-confidence of his commanders.

Rommel's achievement in galvanizing the building of coastal defences in the spring of 1944 was very real. But he shared the high command's indecision and lack of grip in allowing resources to be wasted building fortifications in all manner of places where it was absurd to imagine that an invasion could occur. All along the 3,000 miles of occupied coastline, bunkers were constructed, positions dug. German perceptions were much blunted by the incompetence of FHW, the western intelligence arm of OKW, the supreme command. While the eastern branch was brilliantly run by Reinhard Gehlen, the western was in the hands of Colonel Baron Alexis von Roenne. Roenne had built his reputation on a confident prediction in 1939 that the French and British armies would not attack in the west while Germany was disposing of Poland, and on his advocacy of the great Sedan thrust in May 1940. But in 1944, he was wrong on almost every vital intelligence issue. Although he never took the bait of an Allied threat to Norway, he was deceived by FORTITUDE's fantasy invasion force for the Pas de Calais. The Allies had placed General Sir Andrew Thorne in command of a fictitious British Fourth Army in Scotland, with wireless traffic to simulate a II Corps based around Stirling and a VII Corps around Dundee. But the central role in the deception operation was that of Patton, commanding the fantasy 1st U.S. Army Group in south-east England, its order of battle greater even than 21st Army Group, with a massive array of dummy landing craft, vehicles, camps and wireless communications provided by the American 3103rd Signals Service Battalion in support. MI5 and the British "XX Committee" were directing the operations of 20 captured or "turned" German agents, nine of these in radio contact with Canaris' controllers in Germany or Portugal, the remainder communicating by secret writing through the mail. The scepticism of many senior American officers about FOR-TITUDE was compounded by their necessary ignorance of the brilliant "XX Committee" operation. But the leading historian of wartime deception has written of "the strange reluctance among the Americans to accept that it was part of modern warfare – all the more strange since the Japanese attack on Pearl Harbor was a successful deceptive operation of the greatest magnitude."[11] Colonel W. A. Harris, the Americans' principal deception expert, was converted to belief in the value of FORTITUDE only after its success. But it is only just to concede that before the triumph of June 1944, Allied deception operations in Europe had been notably less successful than those in the Middle East. In 1943, some elaborate deceptions had been created to delude the enemy about Allied intentions, which caused OKW to move not a single man or tank.

In the wake of Germany's defeat, some bitter German commanders argued that Colonel von Roenne, one of the anti-Hitler plotters, deliberately misled them about Allied intentions. Yet it is too simplistic merely to compare the success of Allied intelligence with the failure of that of Germany, and seek conspiratorial explanations. The Allies' success depended overwhelmingly upon intelligence provided by Ultra, the kind of inspired good fortune that comes to a warring nation seldom in a century. The record of the British Secret Intelligence Service in gaining useful information about Germany from agents was lamentable. For all the nonsense written in recent years about the American wartime OSS and its chief William Donovan, their real profits from agent networks were negligible by comparison with those from decrypts. If the Allies' huge achievement in breaking the Enigma and the Japanese Magic ciphers is set aside, their agent-dependent intelligence operations appear unimpressive. There is no decisive evidence one way or the other about whether the anti-Hitler conspirators deliberately distorted German intelligence analysis. But it remains easier to believe that OKW's men were simply wrong.

Hitler's manic suspicion of his generals and his obsession with dividing authority among them to deny overall power to any one, made for a cumbersome command structure in France. In Paris, the dour, cynical, unbending von Rundstedt presided as Commander-in-Chief. "By this time his arteries were hardening," said Brigadier Williams,[12] Montgomery's principal analyst of the German army, "but they were pretty formidable arteries." At Army Group B's headquarters at La Roche Guyon, Erwin Rommel was to be responsible for directing the battle against the invaders. Yet Rommel was denied direct control of the panzer divisions of OKW reserve, and Hitler was correct in believing that his field-marshal's ability to dominate the battlefield was now deeply flawed by doubt that victory was even possible. Always highly strung, mercurial, that spring Rommel wavered between outbursts of buoyant confidence and deep depression. "If I were doing the invasion," he said laconically to his staff one morning, "I should be at the Rhine in fourteen days."[13] His driving energy was undiminished. His ability to spend hours racing from unit to unit along the coast, designing positions, hastening the erection of beach defences and glider obstacles – "Rommel's asparagus" – still aroused the wonder of his staff. But he was no longer the Desert Fox, the supremely confident Panzer leader of 1941–42. Too many defeats had intervened. Now under his command in northern France were the coastal divisions of Seventh Army in Normandy and Fifteenth Army in the Pas de Calais, together with Geyr von Schweppenburg's Panzer Group West. But while the Allies deliberated about how far Hitler would allow his generals to fight the battle in their own fashion, the Führer had already placed fatal constraints upon them. Rommel was not permitted to deploy the panzer divisions on the coast – a disposition he believed vital in view of the Allied air threat to any movement of forces – and of his armour, only 21st Panzer stood within immediate reach of the beaches, south of Caen. Had Rommel's request to place a second panzer division near St Lo been granted, the consequences for the American landings on D-Day would have been incalculable, conceivably decisive. If the Allies gained a foothold, Rommel's preference was to withdraw to a river line to hold them. Hitler's absolute determination to yield no ground precluded this. Everything would hinge upon the German's ability to halt the Allies upon the beaches. If they failed in this, the generals understood perfectly that their only choice lay between skilful retreat and inexorable destruction.

The men of the German army in France in June 1944 were sustained by a compound of fatalism and blind faith. Above all, perhaps, for most there was a sense of unreality, a comforting impossibility about the notion that their stretch of windswept dunes, their familiar billets and battery positions, should be chosen above all others by the Allies to become one of the great battlefields of history. "It wasn't in our interests to think too much about our feelings," a staff officer of 21st Panzer Division, Captain Eberhard Wagemann, said drily. "We were conscious that neither our men nor our tanks were good enough." The troops of the Division had little confidence in its commander, General Feuchtinger; Rommel still thought well of him, but this opinion was rapidly to change. 21st Panzer retained a core of veterans from its great days in Africa, but had been made up to strength with drafts of very moderate quality, and was equipped with substantial quantities of French and locally-modified equipment. Yet this division, deployed around Caen, would be the first German armoured formation to sustain the shock of the Allied landings.

"We no longer expected total victory," said Sergeant Helmut Gunther of 17th SS Panzergrenadiers, "but we still felt an absolute sense of loyalty. In Russia we had fought men against men. We knew that in Normandy it would be men against machines."[14] A bank trainee before the war, Gunther volunteered in September 1939 at the age of 20, fought across Europe until he was evacuated with frostbite before Moscow, and later served as an infantry instructor before being posted to the Panzergrenadiers in January 1944. Now, as a platoon commander in the reconnaissance battalion, he was training the big draft of 18-year-olds which had reached the unit, many of them conscripts.

One May morning, Rommel visited the 1716th Artillery Regiment in their positions around Ouistreham. He told the assembled circle of battery officers: "If they come, they'll come here."[15] Lieutenant Rudolf Schaaf did not really believe him. Twice wounded in the leg in Russia, Schaaf was one of many officers and men posted to France because they were unfit for further duty in the east – he walked with a pronounced limp. He and most of his comrades were enjoying their time in France, with plenty to eat and drink, all of it cheap. Above all, they were thankful to be out of the east. "The soldiers did as little work as possible," he said, "and we were too busy putting up wire and planting 'Rommel's asparagus' to have much time for training."[16] Private Heinz Walz, a jovial Swabian shopkeeper serving as a signaller with the 266th Artillery in the eastern Cotentin, was dismayed to hear at the beginning of June that there was to be yet another comb-out of his unit for men fit to be transferred to the eastern front. He had already served in Russia with a labour unit, and knew that he would be an obvious candidate for posting. The abrupt arrival of the Allies narrowly saved him from that.

There was a wide gulf between the men of the coastal divisions – at best cynical about their role, at worst opening defeatist – and those of the crack units. Sergeant Hans Stober of 17th SS Panzergrenadiers, a 22-year-old veteran of the East, was sent on an anti-gas course to St Lô, where he found himself alongside men of Seventh Army. The coastal troops distanced themselves from the likes of Stober, although contrary to myth there was no general animosity between soldiers of the SS and the Wehrmacht. The Russians, especially, maintained a stolid silence. Stober was amused to meet one man whom he himself had taken prisoner in 1941. A farmer's son from east Prussia, the sergeant understood that the invasion would be the decisive battle of the war. Like many men on both sides of the Channel, he found that the greatest strain was the interminable waiting for the blow to fall.

Lieutenant Walter Kruger, a signals officer with 12th SS Panzer, was an SS man in the classic mould, asserting his "absolute confidence in victory from first to last".[17] The troops of this, the Hitler Youth division, were to prove the most determined and fanatical opponents facing the Allied armies. "They had received a proper training in the Hitler Youth," said Kruger proudly. "They had a sense of order, discipline. They knew how to sing!" They had practised repeatedly the advance from their camps near Evreux to the Normandy coast. Thinking nothing of the air threat, they confidently expected to be engaged within seven hours of a movement order. Their principal problem was the lack of fuel, which hampered training, and caused such petty restrictions as the divisional mail collection being conducted by horse and cart.

In the last week of May, Kruger was one of 60 officers from his division who found themselves cursorily summoned to divisional headquarters, apprehensive about the cause. To their astonishment, they arrived to find all their wives gathered, brought up from Germany on the orders of General Fritz Witt, their commander. "Since there is going to be no leave for anybody from now on," said Witt, "you can all go to Paris for two days and then say goodbye at the Gare de l'Est." Kruger told his wife Martha that it was obvious that they were "for it". He gave her all his personal possessions to take home to Germany. "They told us that the first five days would be critical. If we could not defeat the landings by then, it would be impossible."

Much depended upon the performance of 12th SS Panzer and the other nine armoured divisions in France. General Guderian, Inspector-General of Armoured Forces, wrote: "All hopes of successful defence were based upon these."[18] Lieutenant-Colonel Kurt Kauffmann, Operations Officer of Panzer Lehr, the finest tank formation in the Wehrmacht, created from the demonstration units of the armoured corps, believed that the invasion could be defeated. Despite Panzer Lehr's lack of opportunity to exercise as a formation, 75 per cent of its men were veterans and it was superbly equipped. Kauffmann's chief worry concerned the performance of its commander, General Fritz

Bayerlein: "He was a very good soldier, but he was worn out. In Normandy he showed himself nervous and weak."[19]

Through those last weeks before 6 June, the men of the coastal units dutifully laid yet more concrete and field telephone wires, pottered between the minefields carrying their little cans of milk from the local farms, hung their washing to dry on the edge of the bunkers, and cherished their hopes that the Tommies and the Americans might come somewhere else. If high morale means the motivation to give everything for a cause or an objective, few of them possessed it. Their senior officers were haunted by the knowledge that they commanded forces inadequate for the task they might face. The highest hope of most of their men was to survive the war. For few was it to be fulfilled.

The mobile formations behind the coast exercised with varying degrees of intensity, their movements watched with deep apprehension by Allied intelligence. The Germans were carrying out their own deception operations, circulating maps showing false positions for their formations through such sources as the Japanese Ambassador to Vichy. In the face of Ultra and incessant reconnaissance, they enjoyed little success. Almost every German formation was accurately plotted on Allied maps. There were only a handful of critical uncertainties. Brigadier Williams suspected that the 352nd Division had been moved forward to the area below the elbow of the American beaches, although the evidence that he circulated proved too uncertain to disturb the American planners. When a maze of tank tracks was photographed in the coastal area of Caen, there were acute fears that 21st Panzer had been moved forward within immediate range of the beaches. In reality, after an exercise, the armour withdrew to its leaguers between Caen and Falaise.

On the afternoon of 5 June, Corporal Werner Kortenhaus, a wireless operator in the division's Panzer Regiment, took his crew's laundry to the local Frenchwoman who had been doing their washing for weeks. Sergeant Heinz Hickmann of the Luftwaffe Parachute Division, stationed outside Nevers, left his base for a relaxed evening in the local army canteen. Colonel Kauffmann of Panzer Lehr was on honeymoon near Stuttgart. Captain Wagemann of 21st Panzer was standing in as duty officer at headquarters in the absence of the division's senior staff officer in Paris, and of the divisional commander on what was believed to be private business with a female friend. Most of

Seventh Army's senior officers were attending war games in Rennes. Sepp Dietrich of 1st SS Panzer Corps was in Brussels. And Rommel had retired to Germany to celebrate his wife's birthday and to importune Hitler for a more realistic attitude to the defence of the Atlantic Wall.

3 To the far shore

The overture

Over the last few days of May and the first of June, vast columns of men and vehicles began to stream south into the assembly areas – the "sausages", as they were known, because of their shapes on the map – where the invaders were briefed and equipped before being loaded aboard the fleet. The trucks and tanks rolled through towns and villages that, to the disappointment of some, paid little heed to their passing, so accustomed had the inhabitants become to mass military movements. Although the coastal areas had supposedly been sealed off to all but local residents, in reality so many exemptions had been granted for weddings, funerals and compassionate cases that the routine of life was very little changed.

Whole divisions of the follow-up waves had been temporarily transferred from training to man the assembly areas, to feed and cosset the assault forces to the utmost extent that the circumstances allowed. The men, crowded into the tiered bunks in the huge tented camps, were issued with seasickness pills and lifejackets, new gas-protective battledress and ODs – which everybody detested because of their extra weight and smell. Each soldier was given a leaflet about getting on with French civilians which urged him to say nothing about 1940 and not to buy up everything in sight at extravagant prices: "Thanks to jokes about 'Gay Paree' etc., there is a fairly widespread belief that the French are a gay, frivolous people with no morals and few convictions. This is especially not true at the present time." More pragmatically, in the "sausages" men were issued with their ammunition and grenades, satchel and pole charges. They worked obsessively to the very last minute upon the waterproofing of their vehicles, conscious of the horror of stalling with a flooded engine under fire in the surf. The plethora of food, fruit and American cigarettes that was thrust upon them made

LAC Norman Phillips of the RAF advance party for Omaha feel "as if we were being fattened like Christmas turkeys". Despite the stringent security precautions which kept the men confined once they had entered the assembly areas, many young British soldiers slipped under the wire for a last glimpse of the pub, the village or their own families. Corporal "Topper" Brown of 5th RTR escaped from his camp near Felixstowe, stripped the unit flashes off his battledress, and travelled all the way home to Tonbridge in Kent.

The tannoy systems in the camps were seldom silent by day or night as groups of men were mustered, loaded into trucks, and driven through meticulously signposted streets to numbered docks where they joined their transports. The concentration and loading operations rank high among the staff achievements of OVERLORD. For once there was little need to motivate men to attend to their tasks: they understood that their lives depended on doing so. Dock officers later commented adversely upon the casual behaviour of the follow-up waves in contrast to that of the troops who embarked for D-Day.

Aboard the ships, each man sought to create his tiny island of privacy amid the mass of humanity crowded below decks. Officers struggled with last-minute loading problems. Lieutenant-Colonel Robin Hastings of the 6th Green Howards was enraged when an officious trade union official counted the lifeboats on his battalion's transport, declared that there were insufficient, and insisted that one vital landing craft should be left behind to make room for an extra lifeboat. The unit's chaplain, Captain Henry Lovegrove, conducted a service from the ship's bridge which men crowded onto the foc'sle to hear. Lovegrove was uncommonly respected as a padre, but he had lost some credibility during a rehearsal at sea off Hayling Island several weeks earlier, when he took as his text for morning service "The hour is now come . . .", which many men took to mean that the padre had been chosen to break it to them that they were on their way to France. In the vast anchorages off the south coast in the first days of June, many ships looked curiously unmilitary, with sailors' drying laundry draped along the rails and strung among the upperworks. A REME driver, passionately proud of his vehicle, expostulated furiously with an East End crane driver swinging his workshop's trucks into the hold of a transport, crushing wings and fenders against the hatch. "You'll be f---ing lucky if that's the worst that happens to your lot over there!" said the docker succinctly, continuing as before.

One of Montgomery's few undoubted errors of judgement during the mounting of OVERLORD was his support for a landing on 5 June despite the adverse weather forecast. Given the difficulties much less severe weather caused on the 6th, there is little doubt that a landing on the previous day would have found itself in deep trouble. For all the scorn that Montgomery later heaped upon Eisenhower's qualities as a military commander, at no single period did the Supreme Commander distinguish himself more than by his judgement and decision during the D-Day launching conferences of 3–4 June. Having unhesitatingly overridden Montgomery to postpone for the 5th, at 9.45 p.m. on the 4th Eisenhower equally firmly brushed aside Leigh-Mallory and ignored Tedder's uncertainty to confirm the decision to go for the 6th: "I'm quite positive we must give the order," he said, "I don't like it, but there it is . . . I don't see how we can possibly do anything else."[1]

The postponement much increased the mental strain and physical pressure on the men crowded in the ships. They played cards incessantly, chatted quietly, in many cases simply lay silent on their bunks, gazing up at the bulkheads. Private James Gimbert and a cluster of other RAOC men of 50th Division brewed up on a little primus stove perched atop the vast stack of ammunition cases loaded on their LST. Brigadier-General Norman "Dutch" Cota assembled his staff of the advanced headquarters group of 29th Division, of which he was deputy commander, in the aft wardroom of the U.S.S. *Carroll*. An officer of legendary forcefulness, somewhat old for his rank at 51, Cota could claim exceptional expertise in amphibious operations. He had taken part in the TORCH landings and subsequently served with Lord Mountbatten's Combined Operations HQ. Now, he addressed his team for the last time:

This is different from any other exercises that you've had so far. The little discrepancies that we tried to correct on Slapton Sands are going to be magnified and are going to give way to incidents that you might at first view as chaotic. The air and naval bombardment are reassuring. But you're going to find confusion. The landing craft aren't going in on schedule, and people are going to be landed in the wrong place. Some won't be landed at all. The enemy will try, and will have some success, in preventing our gaining "lodgement". But we must improvise, carry on, not lose our heads.[2]

Cota and his men were to land on Omaha. On all the ships, officers and NCOs pored over the maps and photographs of their landing areas that they had at last been ordered to strip from the sealed packages: it remains one of the minor miracles of OVER-LORD that although hundreds of men and women had been involved in making and printing them, there was no security leak. On every ship, some or most passengers were seasick. Apart from the assault troops, there was an extraordinary ragbag of men from all manner of units aboard the invasion fleet. On many of the transports crewed by the merchant navy, there were spcially-trained civilian aircraft recognition teams from the Royal Observer Corps. The Sicilian landings had been marred by the alarming quantity of Allied aircraft shot down by reckless ships' gun crews. Now, at the AA positions, men stood in their helmets and flash capes drinking interminable mugs of "kye" – cocoa – and peering out fascinated at the shadowy shapes of the great fleet around them in the darkness. While the soldiers below were more sombrely preoccupied by the task that awaited them on the morrow, most of the sailors felt a strong, conscious sense of pride that they were taking part in the greatest amphibious operation of all time.

One of the most curious spectators of the great invasion fleet's movement to France was an airman named Eric Crofts, seated in a caravan mounted on a turntable on a clifftop in south Devon. Crofts manned one of the RAF's centimetric radar posts, and all spring he and his colleagues had intently scanned the progress of the invasion rehearsals on their screen. Now he arrived on watch a little before midnight on 5 June to find the duty crew clustered round the set: "Large convoys of ships were creeping southward to the top of the radar screen, and small groups were coming from left to right to join the tail. Off to the east, beyond Port-land, other convoys were on the move. Desperate for the relief of seeing everything pass from our range, our interest was seized later that long night by aircraft away to the east, circling but moving slowly away from us. Each dot was in a hazy cloud. We guessed, as others joined or left the group, that they were dropping metal strips of 'Window' to simulate an invasion fleet heading for the Pas de Calais. It was an anti-climax at last to see our tube empty, yet sobering to know that so many men in the ships were heading for a hell ahead of them."[3] The Germans, partly as a result of their own failures of technology, but chiefly because of damage caused by Allied bombing, possessed no sets on the Channel coast capable of showing such an accurate picture that night.

On the later afternoon of 5 June, when the men of the seaborne assault divisions had already been at sea for many hours – in some cases for days – Private Fayette Richardson of the 82nd Airborne Division was still in camp in England. He was lying on his bunk with his hands clasped behind his head, gazing up at the whitewashed ceiling and trying to exorcize from his mind the nagging beat of Tommy Dorsey's *What Is This Thing Called Love?* that had echoed out of the recreation hut every evening for weeks as the men walked to chow. A short, wiry 20-year-old from a small town near Buffalo, New York, Richardson had left home at 17 to drive an old jalopy to the west coast. He was in Seattle when Pearl Harbor was bombed, and enlisted at once "because everybody else was".[4] Like so many others, he wanted to be a pilot and was dismayed to be rejected for poor eyesight. Instead, he joined the Airborne and shipped to Northern Ireland with the 508th Regiment. There he volunteered to become a pathfinder, a decision he did not regret, because his group lived a far more independent and relaxed life than the rifle companies, spared KP and guard duties, free to come and go pretty much as they pleased after completing their special training in handling the Eureka beacon. Now, in his hut in Nottinghamshire, he stood among the rest of the team joking self-consciously with each other as they struggled to stow a mountain of personal equipment about their bodies. A 32-pound radar set was strapped below the reserve parachute on his stomach; fragmentation grenades were hooked on his harness; gammon bombs and a phosphorus grenade, chocolate D rations, fighting knife, water-bottle, anti-tank mine, a morphia syrette and an armed forces paperback edition of *Oliver Twist* were stowed about his body. Richardson, as platoon guinea pig for a morphia demonstration a few weeks earlier, had plunged the tiny needle into his leg and fallen promptly asleep, to dream in brilliant colours of sailing boats against a sunset sky, green tropical islands, flowers, rainbows.

On top of all the kit, the New Yorker was expected to carry a rifle. He decided to leave this and make do with a .45 pistol strapped to his high paratroop boot, where he could reach it easily. The pressure of the pistol belt, the tightly laced boots and equipment made him feel oddly secure, as if he was wearing armour. When the trucks came for them, the paratroopers tottered forward, floundering like men in diving suits, boosted aboard by the cooks and maintenance men who were being left behind. When the shouted messages of good luck faded away, the men in the back of the truck sat silent, scarcely able to recognize each other beneath the layer of burnt cork on their faces. Then they lay beside the fuselage of an olive-drab Dakota in the summer evening silence for almost an hour, drinking coffee and posing for an army photographer. Richardson found himself wanting to stay close to his own friends, reluctant to be alone. They were no longer excited, merely tense and thoughtful. Soon after darkness fell, they were airborne.

Jammed together in the belly of the plane, they could only talk to their neighbours by yelling over the noise of the aircraft, could see out of the windows only by squirming round inside their great clumsy burdens. Lamareux, alongside Richardson, nudged him and pointed down to the moonlight shining on the water. It seemed to the paratrooper to be frozen in smooth, unmoving ripples. The crew chief clambered down the aircraft to the rear and pulled off the door. Richardson saw a flash of light in the sky outside and understood, after a moment of puzzlement, that it was anti-aircraft fire. Then, on the shouted command, they pulled themselves clumsily to their feet and hooked static lines to the overhead cable. Now they could see streams of flashing lights coming up from the ground, making a harmless popping noise around them, like Roman candles being hosed into the sky. Each soldier felt the pressure of the man behind leaning into his pack. Then the green light came, and they began the familiar rush to the door in the paratroop one-step shuffle that they had practised so many times, at last pivoting abruptly before they hurled themselves into the slipstream and the sudden silence that followed.

At the moment "Rich" Richardson jumped over the fields of the Cotentin soon after 1.30 a.m., thousands of other Allied paratroopers were already on the ground ahead of him. Men of the British 6th Airborne Division seized the bridges over the Caen Canal and across the Orne at Ranville a few minutes after midnight. The American 101st Division began to drop at 1.30 a.m., the 82nd following at 2.30, and the bulk of the 6th Airborne – 4,800 parachutists – shortly before 1.00 a.m. A total of 8,000 British and 16,000 American airborne troops were to land by parachute and glider. The drops were marred by the poor performance of many of the Allied Dakota pilots who, by a combination of unsteady navigation and extravagant reaction to German flak, released their parachutists with near-criminal carelessness. Over both the British and American zones that night, extraordinary and undignified scenes took place in some aircraft, with paratroopers cursing the pilots as they were thrown to the floor by the frenzied weaving of their planes, officers and NCOs demanding – in several recorded instances, at gunpoint – that the airmen should resume their course and proceed with the drop rather than abort. The loss of only 30 Allied transport aircraft proved that the flak was not severe.

The glider pilots, by contrast, performed miracles of determination to crash their frail craft on their objectives, above all making possible the seizure of the British bridges after brief battles. 71 of the 196 glider pilots who landed east of the Orne on D-Day became casualties; among the Americans the proportion was even higher. The costly battle to gain the Merville Battery by the British 9th Para was a fine feat of arms, rendered anticlimatic by the discovery that the casemates mounted only 75 mm guns with slight capacity to harass the beaches. The inability of air photographs to distinguish the weapons mounted in many bunkers and casemates was a chronic problem for the planners before 6 June, and the suppression of positions such as the Merville Battery was a vital piece of insurance. The bulk of 6th Airborne struggled through the darkness and the first hours of daylight to concentrate its units, dispose of German patrols and strongpoints and create a firm perimeter east of the Orne from which to resist the powerful counter-attacks that would inevitably follow.

The American 82nd and 101st Airborne suffered even more seriously than the British from scattered dropping, and with far more deadly consequences amid the swamps and floods of the Cotentin, which drowned hundreds of men before they could even escape their harnesses. The 82nd gained one of its principal objectives, the village of St Mère Eglise, and fought to retain it against fierce German pressure. But it proved impossible immediately to secure the causeways across the Merderet. The airborne operations of D-Day emphasized painfully for the Allies the cost and difficulty inseparable from massed drops even before paratroopers could engage the enemy, and the limitations of lightly-armed formations without armoured support. Thousands of young Americans found themselves struggling, alone or with little clusters of other lonely figures, to find a path through the hedges and swamps to a rendezvous many miles from where they had been so mistakenly "given the green". It was a remarkable tribute to the 82nd and the 101st that while thousands of the men found themselves miles from their units and their objectives that night, they engaged the Germans wherever they encountered them. The great achievement of the American airborne forces on 6 June was to bring confusion and uncertainty to the Germans across the whole breadth of the Cherbourg peninsula.

Private Richardson felt a moment of pain on the inside of his thighs from his harness as the canopy jerked open, and his head and neck were jerked so sharply that he suffered a brief headache. Then he was floating rapidly down towards an orchard amid a rattle of fire from the ground. He let go the front risers of his parachute, just missed a tree, and slammed into the ground. Ears ringing, he grabbed his pistol and used his spare hand to struggle out of his harness. Then he walked cautiously towards the sound of the little metal crickets that American soldiers were snapping all over the Cotentin that night as a recognition signal. Through the darkness other men moved in to join them. They struggled to free one of the group whose parachute was caught in the top of a tree, and at last cut him down. Then they counted heads. Around half the team – including almost all the men equipped with beacon lights to back up the radar sets – were missing. These had jumped last and landed beyond a road on which the Germans were already audible, driving hither and thither searching for parachutists. Lamareux, the lead radar operator, switched on his beacon. To Richardson's chagrin, having lugged his own set so far with such sweat, he was now obliged to watch the other man pull the internal detonator to destroy it – only one set was necessary. Then the Americans dispersed hastily across the field. The one remaining tripod-mounted light was switched on. The other men pointed their torches towards the sky. Not many minutes had passed before somebody shouted, "Here they come!" They saw a new sparkle of anti-aircraft fire, moving closer and closer to them as the planes approached and local guns opened up. Then, as the first parachutes became dimly visible against the sky, the pathfinders below broke into muted but ecstatic cheers.

Hundreds of Americans who jumped that night found themselves plunged into action immediately they reached the ground, or were shot dead before they did so. After that brief moment of euphoria when the first wave over Richardson's landing zone jumped as planned, they were dismayed to see the second wave approach their signal on the same course, then drone on past the desperately flashing lights without dropping a single man. Only one plane came close to them. Flames were pouring from its starboard engine and the pilot was revving desperately as he lost height; the windows were clearly visible three or four hundred feet above them. A pathfinder sobbed desperately: "Those are our guys." Then the plane disappeared over the horizon and there was silence in the field again. The stillness persisted, for the expected third wave of aircraft never came. Instead of a powerful paratroop unit at the assembly point, there were only a few dozen men.

Richardson decided that the moment had come to make good his lack of a weapon. He picked up a machine-gun from the bundle attached to a collapsed parachute. Then another man ran over and said curtly, "That's our gun." They argued for a few moments. Richardson lost. His own company was among those which had failed to arrive, so he simply joined the nearest group of men digging slit trenches. When he had made his own foxhole, he dropped into it and fell asleep.

The German sluggishness in responding to the first Allied movements of D-Day had passed into the legend of the war. Montgomery had told his commanders: "By dusk on D-1 day the enemy will be certain that the NEPTUNE [or OVERLORD] area is to be assaulted in strength . . ."[5] Yet the astounding truth remains that even in the early hours of 6 June, the Germans were still in a condition of bewildered uncertainty. The German navy had failed to station patrols in the Channel because of its conviction that the weather was unfit for an invasion. Fifteenth Army's interception of the known BBC codeword for the French Resistance to begin their D-Day tasks was ignored. It is doubtful whether SHAEF would ever have agreed to the transmission of the BBC message on the night of 5 June, given the overwhelming probability that its significance was already compromised somewhere in France, had it not seemed inevitable that the invasion fleet would by that hour be detected.

The failures of the German navy and air force were obviously central to the defenders' lack of warning of the invasion. They had not even noticed the concentration of minesweepers operating off the Normandy coast at last light on 5 June. The lack of action following interception of the BBC message is more comprehensible, for it must be considered against the background of repeated false alarms all that spring, which had exasperated and wearied the coastal units. Neither the Germans nor SHAEF had ever taken the French Resistance entirely seriously, regarding it as a nuisance force rather than a central feature of Allied military operations. It is also important to notice that the message to the Resistance gave no hint of *where* the invasion was to take place. There was some discussion within Allied Special Forces HQ and SOE about the possibility of mobilizing only relevant sections of the Resistance, in order to reduce the possibility of bitter reprisals and long delays before liberation came to groups far from the front. But it was quickly agreed that, on grounds of security, it was vital to mobilize all *résistants* to avoid giving any clues to the Germans as to the whereabouts of the point of assault. There have been suggestions in some recent books[6] that, properly used, the BBC message could have told OKW that the Allies were going to Normandy. This notion is unfounded.

But the absence from headquarters of so many vital senior German commanders was a misfortune of critical importance. The whereabouts of General Edgar Feuchtinger of 21st Panzer have never been confirmed, but it was widely believed by his own men that he was *incommunicado* with a female friend. Rommel, of course, was in Germany, and Dollman of Seventh Army at the Rennes war games. On the night of 5 June, exploiting Rommel's absence, his Chief of Staff, General Hans Speidel, invited several of his fellow anti-Hitler conspirators to join him for drinks at the château at La Roche Guyon. It was here, after they had all dined together, that Speidel was telephone by Fifteenth Army headquarters at Turcoing and informed of the intercepted BBC message. Fifteenth Army had been placed on alert. A staff officer telephoned von Rundstedt's headquarters for a decision on whether Seventh Army should also be alerted. It was decided that it should not. Von Rundstedt's staff confined themselves to a general warning to all units that the BBC message might presage a widespread outbreak of terrorist sabotage.

Seventh Army was finally alerted at 1.35 a.m. Half an hour earlier, General Marcks had called out his own LXXXIV Corps, in the wake of the reported paratroop landings. The confusion was compounded by the Allied drop of thousands of dummies and six uncommonly brave SAS soldiers to divert the defenders inland. The discovery of the dummies doubled the Germans' uncertainty about a possible bluff. General Max Pemsel, Dollman's Chief of Staff, telephoned Rommel's headquarters and spoke to Speidel repeatedly during the night, insisting that a major Allied operation was taking place. At 3.00 a.m., von Rundstedt's headquarters reported to OKW that large-scale air landings were under way. At 4.00 a.m., General Kraiss of 352nd Division sent a regiment on bicycles in pursuit of paratroopers at a location where in reality only dummies had landed. At 6.00 a.m., Blumentritt from von Rundstedt's headquarters told OKW that a major invasion appeared to be taking place, and asked for the release of the armoured reserve, I SS Panzer Corps outside Paris. With Hitler asleep, the request was denied. It was not finally granted until ten hours later. At 6.15 a.m., Pemsel told Speidel of the opening of a massive naval bombardment and air assault on the coastal defences. At 6.45 a.m., Pemsel telephoned Fifteenth Army and told them that his forces expected to be able to cope with the situation from their own resources. Von Salmuth, Commander-in-Chief of Fifteenth Army, thereupon went to bed. So did Speidel and most of the staff at La Roche Guyon. It was after 10.30 a.m., over an hour after Allied radio had formally announced the coming of the invasion, when Rommel left his home in Herrlingen to drive headlong for his headquarters. It was almost 12 hours before he reached La Roche Guyon.

It was an impressive tribute to the success of the Allied deception plans that every key German commander greeted the news of operations in Normandy as evidence of *an* invasion, not of *the* invasion. Rommel's personal presence and energy might have galvanized the local formations to react with vigour. Most recent writers[7] have suggested that it would have availed the Germans nothing to wake Hitler in order to obtain authorization for the release of the OKW armoured reserves, because Allied air power would have prevented their movement in daylight on 6 June. This is patently untrue, since other formations, including 21st Panzer, were able to drive to the battlefield, albeit with some difficulty. The fighter-bombers and naval guns would certainly have hit hard at any German concentration of armour around the beachhead. But on 6 June forward air control and gunnery direction were not operating efficiently. The balance of probability remains that the Allies could have gained their beachhead against any German reaction on D-Day. But the early release of the armour would have made matters incomparably more dangerous for them. It was fortunate that the senior staff officers of all the major German formations behaved with a lassitude that verged upon utter incompetence.

Some subordinate German commanders, such as General Richter of 716th Division, responded more forcefully to the spectacle of enemy paratroopers dropping around them. Richter directed a battalion of infantry with an anti-tank gun and self-propelled artillery support towards Benouville to recapture the Orne and Caen Canal bridges in the early hours of the morning. But when their leading light tank was knocked out by a British PIAT and the paratroopers opened heavy fire on the counter-attacking force, the Germans contented themselves with occupying Benouville and exchanging fire with the British. 716th Division's operations were conducted with nothing like the determination that could have been expected from a top-class formation.

"You could see that the Germans were really frightened because they started being so nasty," said Nicole Ferté,[8] one of the local inhabitants of Hérouville, three miles south of the Orne bridge. "They had always been so courteous in the past." Madamoiselle Ferté, the 20-year-old daughter of a local garage owner, had lain on the floor during the bombing, sheltering her eight-year-old sister and listening spellbound to the sound of the glider tugs and transport aircraft overhead before midnight. Suddenly there was a knock at their door, and the local teacher stood outside. A wounded British soldier was in the school. Could Nicole come and interpret? Together they hurried back down the road and, in a mixture of half-remembered English, French, and even German, began to talk to the airborne soldier, lying in great pain with a broken leg. They had just given him tea when German soldiers burst in. The civilians were busquely sent to their homes, the British soldier taken away. Most of the local inhabitants hastily fled from the village, but the Fertés stayed through a week when the fighting raged to within a few hundred yards of their door, "because we were certain that liberation must come at any moment. The only other people who stayed were the girls who had been sleeping with Germans." After a week, the Germans abruptly ordered all the remaining occupants to leave Hérouville, and they

93

endured many weeks of fear and privation before they saw the village again.

At 21st Panzer's headquarters, although two companies of infantry exercising north of Caen reported the British glider landings immediately, in the absence of General Feuchtinger and his senior staff officer the only action that could be taken was the immediate removal of divisional headquarters to its operational location. Corporal Werner Kortenhaus, wireless operator in one of the division's 127 Mk IV tanks, was out on picket with two other men when they heard the massive air activity overhead – the sound of aircraft descending, and then climbing once more as the glider tugs loosed their tows. As the panzer crew approached their platoon harbour in the darkness, they could see the shadows of men already clambering over the tanks, preparing to move off. While his own crew hastily unloaded their drill rounds and filled the turret with armour-piercing ammunition, Kortenhaus ran to the house of the Frenchwoman who did their laundry to collect their clean clothes. By 2.00 a.m., the crews were in the tanks and ready to move. Yet it was 8.00 a.m. before the 1st Tank Battalion under Captain von Gottberg began to roll north from its harbour up the long, straight road north to Caen. The 2nd Battalion under Major Vierzig did not start to move until 9.00 a.m., although that officer had held his tanks on standby since 2.20 a.m. No order had been given to them and for this failure responsibility must be shared between Speidel and Feuchtinger, who at the very least displayed an astounding lack of initiative when he arrived at his headquarters some time between 6.00 and 7.00 a.m.

Lieutenant Rudolf Schaaf, commanding a self-propelled battery of the 1716th Artillery, was telephoned at 3.00 a.m. and ordered to take his guns to join the counter-attack against the British airborne bridgehead. Yet he had driven only a few miles across country when he received a radio message recalling them to their original positions. It was clear by dawn that the seaborne menace would have to be met by every infantryman and gun that the defenders possessed.

Shortly before H-Hour, Allied bombers struck the station at Caen and soon afterwards fighter-bombers began to strafe German installations and barracks. A loudspeaker vehicle toured the streets, ordering civilians to stay in their houses. Throughout the day there were intermittent Allied air attacks. By mid-morning the first truckloads of British prisoners were being driven through the streets. The first of more than 80 ruthless executions of French civilians alleged to have assisted the invaders were taking place at the barracks. Early reports of the airborne landings and the fleet offshore were as confused as those reaching German headquarters. The overwhelming sensation among the French was terror that a landing might fail. The memory of Dieppe, the possibility that all the suffering, destruction and death might be in vain, hung heavy over Caen and all Normandy that morning and through the days that followed. A local historian described the events of the dawn of D-Day: "Thus Caen, like other towns in Normandy, passed the night of 6–7 June in fire and blood, while elsewhere in France they celebrated the invasion by drinking champagne and dancing to the gramophone."[9]

Before dawn, the invasion coast was lit by flares and flashes as the naval guns pounded the defences, explosions of every hue rippling up and down the shoreline as hundreds of launches and landing craft scuttled amid the dim silhouettes of the battleships and cruisers, transports and rocket ships a few miles out to sea. No man who saw it ever forgot either the spectacle of the vast invasion fleet crowding the Channel at first light on the morning of D-Day, or the roar of the guns rolling across the sea, or the tearing rasp of the rocket batteries firing over the heads of the men in the landing craft. Nine battleships, 23 cruisers, 104 destroyers and 71 corvettes dominated the 6,483-strong assembly of converted liners, merchantmen and tank landing craft now shaking out into their positions a few miles offshore. 4,000 landing ships – craft and barges of all sizes – would carry the troops ashore. Alongside the transports, overburdened men clambered clumsily down the scrambling nets into the pitching assault craft below. For many, this was among the most alarming experiences of the day. Thousands of men tossing upon the swell strained to make their eyes focus through binoculars upon the coastline ahead. Captain Hendrie Bruce of the Royal Artillery wrote in his notebook: "The villages of La Breche and Lion-sur-Mer are smothered with bursts, and enormous dirty clouds of smoke and brick dust rise from the target area and drift out to sea, completely obscuring our target for a time and enveloping many craft in a veritable 'fog of war'."[10] Gunnery observation

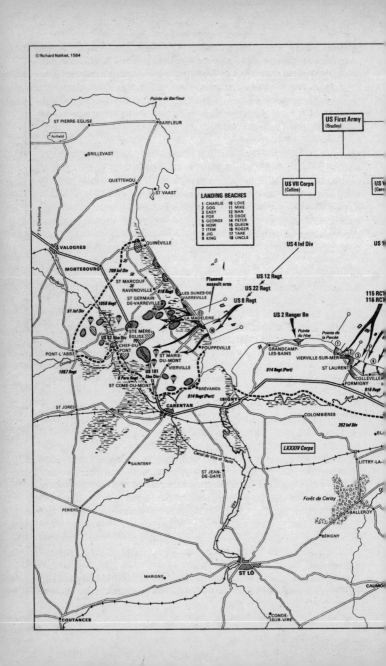

© Richard Natkiel, 1984

Pointe de Barfleur

ST PIERRE-EGLISE • BARFLEUR

Airfield

• BRILLEVAST

QUETTEHOU
ST VAAST

LANDING BEACHES

1 CHARLIE	10 LOVE
2 DOG	11 MIKE
3 EASY	12 NAN
4 FOX	13 OBOE
5 GEORGE	14 PETER
6 HOW	15 QUEEN
7 ITEM	16 ROGER
8 JIG	17 TARE
9 KING	18 UNCLE

US First Army
(Bradley)

US VII Corps
(Collins)

US V
(Ger

US 4 Inf Div

US 1

VALOGNES

MONTEBOURG   709 Inf Div

ST MARCOUF
RAVENOVILLE   919 Regt

ST GERMAIN-
DE-VARREVILLE

91 Inf Div   1058 Regt

Planned
assault area

LES DUNES-DE-
VARREVILLE

LA MADELEINE

US 12 Regt

US 22 Regt

US 8 Regt

US 2 Ranger Bn

115 RCT
116 RCT

STE MÈRE-
EGLISE

US 82 Abn Div CHEF-DU-
PONT

PONT-L'ABBÉ   Douve

1057 Regt

ST MARIE-
DU-MONT

POUPPEVILLE

Pointe
du Hoe   Pointe de
la Percée

GRANDCAMP-
LES-BAINS

VIERVILLE-SUR-MER

VIERVILLE   914 Regt (Part)   ST LAURENT

US 101
Abn Div

6 Para Regt

ST CÔME-DU-MONT   BRÉVANDS

914 Regt (Part)

ST JORES   CARENTAN   ISIGNY

COLLEVILLE
FORMIGNY

916 Regt

Aure

COLOMBIÈRES

352 Inf Div   BLA

• SAINTENY

Canal de Vire et Taute

ST JEAN-
DE-DAYE   LXXXIV Corps   LITTRY-LA-

Taute

PÉRIERS

Forêt de Cerisy   Dr

BALLEROY

• BÉRIGNY

MARIGNY •

ST LÔ   CAUMO

• COUTANCES   • CONDÉ-
SUR-VIRE

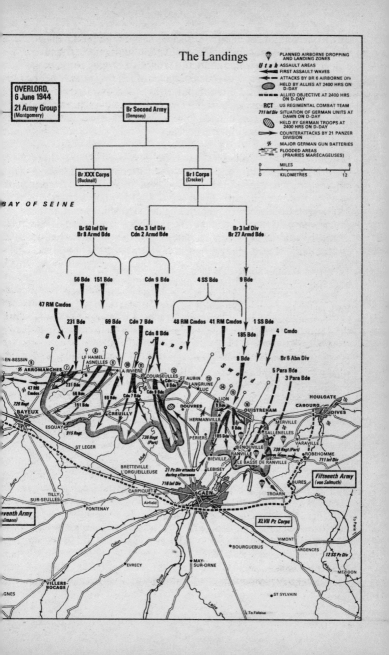

The Landings

PLANNED AIRBORNE DROPPING AND LANDING ZONES
Utah ASSAULT AREAS
FIRST ASSAULT WAVES
ATTACKS BY BR 6 AIRBORNE DIV
HELD BY ALLIES AT 2400 HRS ON D-DAY
ALLIED OBJECTIVE AT 2400 HRS ON D-DAY
RCT US REGIMENTAL COMBAT TEAM
711 Inf Div SITUATION OF GERMAN UNITS AT DAWN ON D-DAY
HELD BY GERMAN TROOPS AT 2400 HRS D-DAY
COUNTERATTACKS BY 21 PANZER DIVISION
MAJOR GERMAN GUN BATTERIES
FLOODED AREAS (PRAIRIES MARÉCAGEUSES)

0   MILES   8
0   KILOMÈTRES   12

OVERLORD, 6 June 1944
21 Army Group (Montgomery)

Br Second Army (Dempsey)

Br XXX Corps (Bucknall)

Br I Corps (Crocker)

BAY OF SEINE

Br 50 Inf Div
Br 8 Armd Bde

Cdn 3 Inf Div
Cdn 2 Armd Bde

Br 3 Inf Div
Br 27 Armd Bde

56 Bde   151 Bde   Cdn 9 Bde   4 SS Bde   9 Bde

47 RM Cmdos   231 Bde   69 Bde   Cdn 7 Bde   48 RM Cmdos   41 RM Cmdos   1 SS Bde
Cdn 8 Bde   185 Bde   4 Cmdo

Gold   *Juno*   *Sword*   Br 6 Abn Div

5 Para Bde
3 Para Bde

-EN-BESSIN   LE HAMEL   ASNELLES   LA RIVIÈRE   COURSEULLES   ST AUBIN   LUC   LANGRUNE   HOULGATE   CABOURG

ARROMANCHES   231 Bde   56 Bde   151 Bde   69 Bde   Cdn 7 Bde   Cdn 9 Bde   8 Bde   OUISTREHAM   DIVES

47 RM Cmdos   *915 Regt*   8 Bde   185 Bde   MERVILLE

BAYEUX   *726 Regt*   CRÉULLY   Seulles   DOUVRES   HERMANVILLE   LION   VARAVILLE   ROBEHOMME   *711 Inf Div*

ESQUAY   *736 Regt (Port)*   PÉRIERS   185 Bde   GALLENELLES

ST LÉGER   BÉNOUVILLE   RANVILLE   LE BASSE DE RANVILLE   *736 Regt (Part)*   Fifteenth Army (von Salmuth)

BRETTEVILLE L'ORGUEILLEUSE   BIÉVILLE   LÉBISEY   BURES   TROARN

Aure   *21 Pz Div attacks during afternoon*   *716 Inf Div*

TILLY-SUR-SEULLES   CARPIQUET   Airfield   CAEN   XLVII Pz Corps

-eventh Army (-timan)   FONTENAY

Odon   VIMONT   ARGENCES

BOURGUEBUS   *12 SS Pz Div*   MEZIDON

EVRECY   MAY-SUR-ORNE   Orne

VILLERS-BOCAGE   Laize   ST SYLVAIN   To Para

-GNES   To Falaise

was to be one of the least satisfactory aspects of the landings, with scores of ships compelled to waste ammunition on harassing objectives selected from the map, for lack of targets pinpointed by forward observers. As the first waves of landing craft headed for the shore, the guns lifted their barrage precisely according to the time schedule. As a result, with so many craft running minutes late, the German defences enjoyed a precious pause before the first infantry hit the beaches.

Probably the first Allied vessel to be destroyed by the shore batteries was PC 1261, one of the American patrol craft leading landing craft towards Utah beach. Lieutenant Halsey Barrett was concentrating intently upon the task of holding a course of 236 degrees true when the quartermaster stepped down into the chartroom and reported that the batteries ashore had just straddled the craft. Seconds later, just 58 minutes before H-Hour at 5.34 a.m., they were hit.

There was a crash – not terribly loud – a lunge – a crash of glass, a rumble of gear falling around the decks – an immediate, yes immediate, 50° list to starboard – all lights darkened and the dawn's early light coming through the pilot house door which had been blown open. The Executive Officer immediately said: "That's it", with finality and threw down his chart pencil. I felt blood covering my face and a gash over my left eye around the eyebrow.[11]

While most of the crew took to the liferafts as the craft turned turtle, Barrett and a cluster of others clung to the upturned hull, watching the great procession of landing craft driving on past them towards the shore.

A landing craft LCVP with thirty or so men aboard was blown a hundred feet in the air in pieces. Shore batteries flashed, splashes appeared sporadically around the bay. Planes were flying in reasonable formation over the beach. One transpired into a huge streaming flame and no trace of the plane remained. Aft of us an LCT lay belly skyward no trace of survivors around it. The USS battleship *Nevada* a mile off to the north-west of us was using her 14-inch guns rapidly and with huge gushes of black smoke and flame extending yards and yards from her broadside . . . There was a beautiful sunrise commencing . . . A small British ML picked up with difficulty one of our men shrieking for help while hanging on a marker buoy. His childish yells for help despite his life jacket and secure buoy was the only disgraceful and unmanly incident which I saw . . .[12]

Most men, even those who had suffered as savage a shock as the crew of PC 1261, felt reassured by the sense of the Allied armada's dominance of the sea. Barrett and the other survivors knew that somebody would pick them up as soon as they had time to spare, as indeed they did. For the men of the British and American navies, there was an overwhelming sense of relief that they faced no sudden, devastating attack from the Luftwaffe as some, despite all the reassurance of the intelligence reports, had feared they might. 'We were all more or less expecting bombs, shells, blood etc.'' wrote a British sailor on the corvette *Gentian*. "Dive bombers were expected to be attacking continually, backed by high-level bombing. But no, nothing like that . . . Instead, a calm, peaceful scene . . . The Luftwaffe is obviously smashed."[13]

In England early that morning, only a few thousand people knew with certainty what was happening across the Channel, and only some thousands more guessed. *The Times* news pages were dominated by the latest reports from Italy, with the Fifth Army past Rome; there was a mention of Allied bombing of Calais and Boulogne. The daily weather bulletin recorded dull conditions in the Channel on 5 June, with a south-west wind becoming very strong in the middle of the day: "Towards dusk the wind had dropped a little, and the sea was less choppy. The outlook was a little more favourable at nightfall."

Outside Portsmouth, at 21st Army Group headquarters, Montgomery's Chief of Staff, Major-General Francis de Guingand, turned to Brigadier Bill Williams and recalled the beginning of other, desert battles. "My God, I wish we had 9th Australian Division with us this morning, don't you?" he said wryly.[14] Some of the British officers at SHAEF were taken aback to discover their American counterparts reporting for duty that morning wearing helmets and sidearms, an earnest of their identification with the men across the water. Brooke described in his diary how he walked in the sunshine of St James's Park: "A most unreal day during which I felt as if I were in a trance entirely detached from the war."[15]

In his foxhole in the Cotentin, Private Richardson of the 82nd Airborne was woken by daylight, and the overhead roar of an Allied fighter-bomber. Hungry and thirsty, he munched a chocolate bar until the word came to move out. Richardson picked up a stray bazooka without enthusiasm, because he had only the barest idea of how to use it. Among a long file of men, all of them unknown to him, he began to march across the Norman fields, ignorant of where they were going. They reached a hedge by a road and halted, while at the front of the column two officers pored over a map and discussed which way to go. Suddenly everybody was signalled to lie flat. A car was approaching. They lay frozen as it approached. Richardson and the others could see the heads of its three German occupants passing the top of the ledge like targets in a shooting gallery. It seemed that no one would move against them, each American privately expecting another to be the first to act. Then one man stood up and emptied a burst of Browning automatic rifle fire at the car. It swerved off the road into a ditch, where somebody shouted, "Finish 'em!" and tossed a grenade. But the Germans were already dead. One of them was Lieutenant-General Wilhelm Falley, commanding the German 91st Division, on his way back to his headquarters from the ill-fated war games in Rennes.

Like Richardson, many of the paratroopers had never seen a man killed before, least of all on a peaceful summer morning in the midst of the countryside. They found the experience rather shocking. Leaving the Germans where they had fallen, they marched on through the meadows and wild flowers, disturbed by nothing more intrusive than the buzzing insects. They encountered another group from the 508th, presiding over 30 German prisoners, arranged in ranks by the roadside as if for a parade. Most were Poles or oriental Russians. One American threw a scene about shooting them: "The Japs killed my brother!" He was dissuaded at the time, but Richardson heard later that the whole group had been killed.

The New Yorker felt better now, because among the new group of paratroopers was one of his closest friends, a tall Oklahoman named Earl Williams, the sergeant commanding 3 Platoon. They sat and talked about money. Williams had changed $100 into francs before take-off. Richardson could not see the point of money at this stage, but Williams insisted upon giving him some. They lay in the grass chatting for what seemed a long time, conscious of the war only because of spasmodic shells falling a few hundred yards away. Finally they wrapped themselves in parachute silk, and once again fell asleep.

Richardson's experience was scarcely universal. While his group were making their way across country with little interference, many other American paratroopers were engaged in desperate battles around the causeways and hamlets of the eastern Cotentin, while the British 6th Airborne was already under fierce German pressure north-east of Caen. But the young New Yorker's story catches the dreamlike quality, the curious sense of detachment that so many men felt in those first hours after being wrenched from the peace of the English summer, and thrust onto an alien battlefield. As the days went by, the battlefield became the reality, until there came a time when they scarcely remembered that another world existed. For thousands of men, it was only when OVERLORD was behind them that they could grasp the magnitude of the events in which they had taken part. While the great drama was unfolding, it seemed a fantasy into which they had somehow slipped as spectators.

As they approached Sword beach, Lieutenant Charles Mundy's men did their best to dull their sensations with the rum rations which they had saved and bottled for three months in anticipation of this moment. They were still over a mile offshore, gazing like eager tourists towards the beach ahead, when a shell smashed through the side of their landing craft and the entire troop were ordered to close down in the tanks. Their Sherman minesweeping flails of 22nd Dragoon Guards were to lead the landing on the eastern flank. Mundy, a 31-year-old Londoner, was impressed to see that the shoreline ahead conformed precisely to the photographs that he and his men had studied so earnestly.

Some men reacted theatrically to their parts. A bugler of the East Yorkshire regiment sounded the General Salute as his landing craft passed the British command ship. Commander Angus Mackenzie, aboard the destroyer *Undaunted,* stood in his Highlander's bonnet playing the bagpipes from his bridge as the LCAs, crammed with seated infantry, ploughed by his ship towards the beach.

Private John Hein of the American 1st Division "felt a little queasy. But I trusted this vast organization – everything was so organized, so programmed that there seemed little scope for individual fear."[16] Hein was born in Germany, the son of a Jewish doctor. He and his family fled in 1936, when he was 15, and adopted their new country with the enthusiasm that only immigrants can achieve. Now, as the former music student headed towards Omaha beach, he felt only intense pride to be wearing an American uniform.

Chaplain Henry Lovegrove of the Green Howards was relieved to find that he was experienced enough not to behave as he had when, in action for the first time in North Africa, he had scrambled panic-stricken under mortar fire, crying, "Where's my helmet? Where's my helmet?" On 6 June, it was a vast reassurance to every soldier who had been in battle before to know that he was capable of doing what was asked of him. This was a consolation denied to many thousands of the men now crouched in the landing craft, bucketing towards the beaches with spray drenching themselves and their weapons.

The American beaches

Many of the defenders of Utah beach, the most westerly of the Allied landing zones just above the elbow of the Cotentin peninsula, were still helplessly stunned by the bombardment or demoralized by the spectacle before them as the first landing craft closed in. In strongpoint W 5, at the very centre of the sea wall where the 4th Division was approaching, the men of 3 Company, 919th Regiment, had lain shaking, hands pressed to their ears as 360 Marauder medium bombers attacked their positions, followed by a naval bombardment which poured down explosives around them with remarkable accuracy, destroying all the position's 50 mm guns, its 75 mm anti-tank gun and many of its bunkers. An elderly mess orderly ran out as the shelling died down, shouting desperately to his commanding officer: "Everything's wrecked! Everything's wrecked! We've got to surrender!"[1] The company commander, a 23-year-old veteran named Lieutenant Arthur Jahnke, who had won the Knight's Cross in Russia before his wounds caused him to be posted to France, pulled his garrison back into their positions. But he understood, with a sense of desperation, that he was now compelled to defend his sector of beach with only a single 88 mm gun, an old Renault tank turret dug into the sands, and a handful of machine-guns and mortars. Above all, he was shocked to gaze out at the vast armada offshore and perceive that they were attacking at low water. Every gun, every bunker had been sited to match Rommel's certain anticipation that "the Amies" would come with the high tide.

Yet now the Germans in W 5 and its adjoining positions were bewildered to see armour, Sherman tanks, rising directly from the sea and opening fire upon them. In the Renault turret, Lance-Corporal Friedrich peered through his pebble spectacles and began firing long machine-gun bursts in the direction of the waterline. A few minutes later, a direct hit from an American 75 mm tank gun destroyed his weapon and shattered his leg. W 5's 88 mm gun, damaged in the bombing, fired one round before jamming permanently. Jahnke's other positions remained in action for only a few minutes before tank fire began to focus upon them. A sudden explosion buried him in sand. He collapsed into unconsciousness, and awoke to find himself staring up the rifle barrel of an American soldier. Together with the survivors of his company, he was herded away towards imprisonment, suffering the final misery, a few moments later, of being wounded by a belated shell from the German battery inland which had been supporting his position.

Although the current off Utah swept the American landing craft 2,000 yards south of the area designated by the plan, in every other respect VII Corps' operations conformed more nearly to the timetable than those of any other Allied formation that day. 28 of the 32 amphibious DD tanks launched reached the sands. At 6.30 a.m., the three regimental combat teams of 4th Division began to come ashore under very light enemy fire. The Germans had thought it most unlikely that Allied troops would land immediately in front of the wide flooded areas beyond the beach. The navigational error caused by the current had brought the men of 4th Division into the most lightly defended sector of the entire Normandy front. As the forward infantry mopped up beach defences, the engineers began to blow up beach obstacles under only sporadic artillery fire. Vehicles and follow-up units poured in as the Americans discovered one undefended beach exit across the inundations, and the 101st Airborne secured four others at the western end. Most of the lone defending regiment of the German 709th Division surrendered as soon as the Americans came to close quarters with them.

Private Lindley Higgins waded through three feet of water to the shore in a manner that made his own invasion seem more farcical than lethal. He and other men of the 12th Regiment could hear only distant firing, but suddenly they were ordered to lie down among the organized chaos of vehicles and stores on the sand: "They're sending in artillery!" somebody shouted. As he hit the ground, Higgins felt himself being squeezed in half by an agonizing pressure at his waist. He yelled: "Aid man!" Then he saw that he had accidentally hit the release of his life jacket, which was inflating. Furious and embarrassed, he pulled his bayonet off his rifle and hacked the life jacket into submission. Then, in long straggling files, his company began to move inland.

Almost all the Americans' difficulties on Utah that day began as they left the beach. The units dispatched northwards to secure the area where the 4th Division would have landed, but for the diversion caused by the current, ran into strong resistance. When 12th Regiment and other forces striking inland clambered over the high, sandy bank looking out over the sea and began to plunge through the flat, flooded fields behind the dunes, their movement became agonizingly slow.

Captain John McGirr of the 65th Armored Field Artillery was under orders to advance with the leading elements inland, and commence acting with the 101st Airborne as a forward observer at the earliest opportunity. But he found himself lying behind the sea wall for more than two hours while waiting for his infantry unit to move off; the monotony was relieved only by a fire in an ammunition truck hit by a stray shell which he helped to fight. The guns of his battery were already coming ashore before McGirr was off the beach.

To Higgins and his companions of Company L, struggling under their impossibly heavy loads of weapons and equipment, the swamps seemed endless. Shorter men found themselves stumbling into concealed ditches that almost drowned them, and from which they had to be painfully extracted. They waded between the white tapes laid ahead of them by the engineers, rifles held high above their heads to keep dry. Higgins was carrying an entire carton of Lucky Strikes in his invasion jacket, but by evening the only smoke he managed to salvage was in the pack in his helmet. They came upon a crashed glider with a jeep still trapped inside it, which the company commander ordered them to retrieve. They hacked at the fuselage until the jeep was almost free, when suddenly a senior officer appeared and furiously ordered them to leave the vehicle and continue their advance.

All along the line, time was already slipping. The chronic problem was to maintain momentum. Yet the landing of 23,000 men on Utah, at a cost of only 197 casualties on the first day, was an almost miraculous piece of good fortune and good judgement. It seemed all the more so in contrast with the events that were unfolding that morning a few miles to the east. While the 4th Division was streaming ashore with fewer casualties than in their last exercise on Slapton Sands, on Omaha beach, where two-thirds of the entire American D-Day effort was concentrated, the 1st and 29th Divisions were enduring ten times as many losses as the 4th's, and very many times their fear and confusion.

Lieutenant Jahnke's company had been stunned and disorganized by the Utah bombardment, but the Germans manning the defences around Vierville and St Laurent had escaped almost totally unscathed. Attacking blind through cloud, the Liberator heavy bombing inevitably lacked precision. In their anxiety to avoid the risk of bombing short onto the approaching invasion fleet, the Allied aircraft poured hundreds of tons of high explosive onto the fields behind the forward defences. Here too, the Germans were defending the strongest natural positions facing the entire assault – hills and cliffs rising steeply up to 200 feet from the beach and the sea wall above it. Brigadier Williams' worst fears were confirmed. In addition to the regiment of the 716th Division defending the Omaha sector, there were strong elements of the much more formidable 352nd. The Americans below the bluffs faced by far the greatest concentration of German fire on the entire invasion front.

A little after 7.00 a.m., a 21-year-old farm boy from Metzingen named Lance-Corporal Hein Severloh had borrowed the binoculars of his battery commander, Lieutenant Frerking. He peered in fascination over the thick concrete parapet at the spectacle unfolding out to sea: "The big one is still hove to, not moving . . . More ships coming up now . . ."[2] Severloh was one of the forward observation team of 1 Battery, 352 Artillery Regiment. When the alert was called, he and the others had driven hastily to the coast from their billets in the battery position at Houteville. Now the gunners were reporting by field telephone, having suffered no hits from the bombing, "perhaps they weren't really after us . . ." Severloh began his running commentary again: "The big one's moving inshore . . . Landing craft on our left, off Vierville, making for the beach." Sergeant Krone said: "They must be crazy. Are they going to swim ashore? Right under our muzzles?" He was one of the 19 men of the 726th Grenadiers sharing position WN 62 – *Wilderstandsnes-ten*, "resistance nest", 62 – with the gunner OP. The telephone buzzed from regimental HQ with an order to withhold fire until the enemy touched the shore. Severloh laid aside the glasses and took up his own position at an MG 42. Frerking began telephoning fire orders to his guns: "Target Dora, all guns, range Four Eight Five Zero, basic direction Twenty Plus, impact fuse." Now there was a long, violent pause, as the naval bombardment plastering the sand and scrub around the pillboxes reached a crescendo, deafening even men behind five feet of concrete. Yet although the blasts filled the bunkers with dust, shook fragments of masonry from the ceilings, fired the scrub along the hillside at intervals above the 6,000 yards of beach where the Americans were to land, the naval shelling did no more than the bombing to reduce the fighting power of the defences. These had been constructed to be almost immune to direct fire from the sea. Now, 47 minutes after it began, the bombardment lifted as a black smoke signal curled into the sky from the command ship. There was a brief moment of silence. The grey shoals of landing craft bumped through the four-foot waves breaking onto the shore. There was only one casualty thus far in WN 62 – an NCO wounded by a shrapnel splinter tearing through a firing slit. Then the first boat dropped its ramp a few yards short of the beach and the overburdened Americans within it began to pour forward, splashing into the surf. The Germans in WN 62 and every position along the Omaha front opened fire, their machine-guns traversing steadily to and fro across the waterline, arcs of fire interlocking, occasional ricochets shrieking off the steel of the beach obstacles. Frerking called into his handset: "Target Dora – Fire!"

There is no more demanding task for infantry than to press home an attack across open ground under heavy fire, amid heavy casualties. The American assault on Omaha beach came as close as the experience of any western Allied soldiers in the Second World War to the kind of headlong encounters between flesh and fire that were a dreadful commonplace in the battles of 30 years before, and which were so grimly familiar on the eastern front. V Corps' plan for Omaha eschewed tactical subtleties, the use of British specialized armour, and any attempt to seize the five vital beach exits by manoeuvre. Instead, General Gerow committed his men to hurling themselves frontally against the most strongly defended areas in the assault zone. This was an act of *hubris* compounded by the collapse, amidst the rough weather, of all the elaborate timetables for the landing.

Whipped by a 10-knot north-westerly wind, the seas swamped at least 10 LCVPs during the run-in, drowning many of their infantry. The attempt to land artillery from amphibious DUKWs failed disastrously, and in all 26 guns from elements of five regiments were lost. The supporting rocket ships opened fire at extreme range from the shore, and most of their projectiles fell short, some landing among the assault craft. Under the impact of the waves, the flimsy canvas walls on most of the amphibious DD tanks collapsed immediately. A special kind of sacrificial heroism was demanded of the DD crews that morning when, by a serious error of judgement, 32 were launched 6,000 yards from the beach. Each one, as it dropped off the ramp of the landing craft, plunged like a stone to the bottom of the sea, leaving pitifully few survivors struggling in the swell. Yet the following crews drove on into the water undeterred by ghastly example. One commander – a certain Sergeant Sertell – insisted upon launching even after his canvas screen had been gashed open before he left the craft. Just five of this wave of DDs reached the shore. The infantry were thus called upon to storm the beach without the benefit of vital supporting armour which was intended to shoot open the way ashore. Those tanks which reached Omaha did so behind, rather than ahead of, the leading wave of eight companies – 1,450 men in 36 landing craft.

Most of the young Americans plunging into the surf had been crouched in their landing craft for some three hours, having been transferred from the transports 12 miles out from the beach rather than the seven miles the British decided upon. Many had quickly thrown up their breakfasts, and then crouched miserably in the bucketing boats, drenched in spray, paddling in vomit, as darkness gave way to the first light of dawn. Each man was grotesquely heavily loaded with gas mask, grenades, half -pound blocks of TNT, pole or satchel charges, two bandoliers of rifle ammunition, rations and waterbottle – 68 pounds in total. Now, in an instant, they were compelled to rouse themselves from the cramped, crowded stagnation of the landing craft and stumble forward into the hail of machine-gun and mortar fire from the German defences, which killed and wounded many before they even reached dry ground. Others, still groggy with seasickness, their clothes and equipment stiff and matted with salt, desperately sought cover among the beach obstacles or lay paralyzed amid the harvest of wreckage that quickly gathered on the shoreline. Early in the assault the beach was clogged with grounded and damaged landing craft, some hulks being swept broadside onto the German obstacles to create a logjam which the next wave could not pass. A flamethrower operator on one vessel suffered a direct hit on his weapon: the explosion catapulted his dying body into the sea, spewing blazing fuel over the decks. The landing craft caught fire and burnt for the next 18 hours, amid constant detonations from its 20 mm oerlikon ammunition.

The plan demanded that 270 specially-trained demolition men would follow the lead infantry onto the beach and immediately begin to blow the German obstacles, clearing the way for the great rolling succession of follow-up units before the tide covered the mines. 25,000 more men and 4,000 vehicles were due on Omaha with the second tide of the day. In the event, under the intense fire, which killed or wounded more than 40 per cent of the engineers, and the chaos of soldiers wounded or terrified behind the steel hedgehogs, only a handful of obstacles were exploded that morning. The path to the beach was forced open principally by the hulls of landing craft that rammed obstacles by accident or intent, often triggering the mines and adding more hulks to the debris on the waterline. Of 16 armoured bulldozers sent ashore, only six arrived and three of these were quickly destroyed. Among the infantry, command quickly approached collapse. Three-quarters of the 116th Regiment's radio sets were destroyed or rendered unworkable, and the unit's forward headquarters was effectively wiped out by a direct hit. Many men were confused to discover that they had been landed far from the sector for which they had been briefed and trained. Americans lay prone in the shallow water seeking cover, or dragged themselves painfully up the sand with wounds suffered before they were even out of the landing craft. Hundreds huddled beneath the sea wall at the head of the beach, seizing the only shelter Omaha offered that day, although some companies' survivors took 45 minutes to struggle even that far from the waterline. Hundreds of men were already dying or dead – there would be more than 2,000 casualties on the beach that day.

Among the living, an overwhelming paralysis set in. Much of what takes place on every battlefield is decided by example, men being driven to act in noble or ignoble fashion by the behaviour of those around them. On Omaha that morning, the inexperience of many American junior leaders made itself felt. The confused nature of the landings, with men landing by half-platoons often many yards from the boats carrying their own officers and comrades, destroyed unit cohesion. To the great majority of infantrymen looking for an example to follow out of the apparent collapse of purpose on Omaha that morning, it seemed most prudent merely to seek what shelter they could, and cling to it.

Aboard the cruiser *Augusta* offshore, General Bradley watched the events unfolding on the beaches frustrated by the paucity of communications. A steel command cabin had been built for him on deck, 20 feet by 10, the walls dominated by Michelin motoring maps of France, a few pin-ups and large-scale maps of Normandy. A row of clerks sat at typewriters along one wall, while Bradley and his personal staff clustered around the big plotting table in the centre. Much of that morning, however, the general was on the bridge, standing beside the Task Force commander, Admiral Kirk, watching through binoculars the distant smoke shrouding the shore, his ears plugged with cotton to muffle the blast of the *Augusta*'s guns, his nose swathed in plaster over an embarrassing boil that had been troubling him for days. Photographers were kept away from First Army's commander on 6 June.

The day had begun with a series of minor alarms: the sight of the swell that they knew at once would imperil the DD tanks; the report of 15 E-boats putting out from Cherbourg, sinking the Norwegian destroyer *Svenner* before they were put to flight: "As the morning lengthened," Bradley wrote, "my worries deepened over the alarming and fragmentary reports we picked up on the navy net. From those messages we could piece together only an incoherent account of sinkings, swampings, heavy enemy fire and chaos on the beaches. Though we could see it dimly through the haze and hear the echo of its guns, the battle belonged that morning to the thin, wet line of khaki that dragged itself ashore on the Channel coast of France."[3] By mid-morning the apparent collapse of the landing plan, both on and offshore, had plunged V Corps' staff into the deepest dismay. Colonel Benjamin Talley, cruising in a DUKW a few hundred yards from the beach to report directly to Gerow, told of LCTs milling around the smoke-shrouded sands "like a stampeding herd of cattle".

Bradley "gained the impression that our forces had suffered an irreversible catastrophe".[4] A situation was unfolding that came nearer than any that day to matching the terrible fears of Churchill, Brooke and Eisenhower.

Ranger Mike Rehm of C Company, 5th Battalion, landed in Dog Green sector shortly after H-Hour with 10 men, two of whom were killed and three wounded in the first hundred yards between the sea and the base of the hill. Rehm huddled for shelter behind a knocked-out DD tank, finding himself beside a Ranger whom he did not recognize, smoking a cigar. Suddenly they discovered that the tank was not knocked out, for its engine sprang into life and it began to move. The two men ran hastily towards the sea wall. After a few paces Rehm glanced around and saw that his companion lay covered in blood from the waist down. He reached the wall alone. There he lay through the two hours which followed, amidst a huddle of infantry and other Rangers representing almost every unit on the beach that morning.

A, B and C Companies of 2nd Ranger Battalion had lain offshore awaiting a signal from their commanding officer, Colonel Rudder, to land and advance through the positions of the landing force on Pointe du Hoc, if this successfully gained its objectives. But even after delaying 15 minutes beyond the appointed radio rendezvous, the men tossing in the boats had heard nothing. They were obliged to assume that the Pointe du Hoc landing had failed. They were ordered in to the western flank of Omaha beach. One LCA struck a mine as it approached, blowing off the door of the craft, killing the sea-man manning it and stunning the Ranger platoon commander. His 34 men floundered out of the sinking vessel and struck out for the shore. The next platoon commander, Lieutenant Brice, waded onto the beach and turned to shout "Let's go!" to his men before falling dead in front of them. Meanwhile, A Company's craft had grounded 75 yards offshore, and many of its men died in the water under machine-gun fire. When Gerard Rotthof's mother heard that her son was to become a radio-man, she said: "Well at least he won't have to carry a rifle any more." But now Rotthof lay trapped on the beach beneath the weight of his 60-pound SCR 284 set, wounded by mortar frag-ments in the face and back. He received the last rites twice, but somehow survived terrible internal injuries. Only 35 men of A Company and 27 from B of the 2nd Rangers reached the sea wall, out of 130 who launched from the transports before dawn.

200 yards out from the beach, Lieutenant Sid Salomon and 1 Platoon of C Company still supposed that the whole thing looked a pushover: not a single shell or small-arms round had come close to them. Then the ramp dropped and they were exposed to the full fury of the defences. An immensely tall 31-year-old graduate of New York University who enlisted in March 1942, Salomon had ordered his men to go all-out for the cliff base, under no circumstances pausing for a casualty. Yet within seconds one of his sergeants, Oliver Reed, was hit and fell beneath the ramp. Salomon could not stop himself from seizing the wounded man and dragging him through the waist-high water to the beach. Some of the platoon overtook him as he floundered, and now he passed four already dead from a mortar burst. He himself fell hit in the shoulder. Convinced that he was finished, he called to his platoon sergeant, Bob Kennedy. Reaching into his field jacket, he said: "I'm dead. Take the maps." But then a machine-gun began to kick up sand in front of them, and Salomon found that he was not only alive, but could run. At the base of the cliff he counted nine survivors of his platoon, out of 30 who left the landing craft. His old sergeant, who had left the platoon on promotion, insisted upon joining them for the assault. Salomon had placed him last out of the boat to give him the best chance of making it. But Sergeant Goales was already among the dead. All told, some two-thirds of the company were casualties.

It was a tribute to the quality of the Rangers that despite losses on a scale that stopped many infantry units in their tracks on Omaha that morning, the survivors of C Company pressed on to climb the cliffs west of the beach with bayonets and toggle ropes, clearing German positions one by one in a succession of fierce close-quarter actions with tommy guns and phosphorus grenades. Sergeant Julius Belcher charged head-long against one pillbox, tossed in a grenade and then shot down the garrison as they staggered out of the entrance. In their own area, they found later that they had killed some 60 Germans on 6 June. Yet they lacked the strength and the heavy weapons to press on westwards towards Pointe du Hoc. Towards the end of morning, Salomon stood in a captured German position, gazing down on the chaos below. "I was of the opinion that the invasion had been a failure," he said

111

laconically.[5] He reflected that it was going to be a long swim home.

Corporal Bill Preston's DD crew of the 743rd Tank Battalion watched five of their unit's Shermans sink on launching offshore before it became obvious to the officer commanding their group of eight LCTs that the conditions were impossible. The remainder of the tanks were brought to within 250 yards of the beach before leaving the craft, very late. They glimpsed the cliffs shrouded in thick clouds of smoke as they ran in, then they were crawling out of the water among huddles of isolated infantrymen under intense small-arms fire. The tank commander, a Minnesotan farmer named Ted Geske, pressed the button to collapse their canvas screens, but nothing happened. He clambered out of the turret to do the job manually. At that moment, the waterproofing fell, and Geske was left cursing at his own vulnerability, perched on the hull in the midst of the battlefield. They saw that their tank was well to the right of its objective. They could see dead engineers floating beyond the beach obstacles, where so many wounded men also died as the tide came in over them. They later discovered to their dismay that they had run over one man, for they found his clothing jammed in their tracks. Then they saw the neighbouring platoon of Shermans brew up briskly one by one as an anti-tank gun caught them. Their battalion commander was hit in the shoulder as he stood on the sand, seeking to direct a tankdozer to clear a path for the armour through one of the beach exits.

It was obvious that something was very wrong. 21 of the unit's 51 tanks were destroyed on Omaha, and the neighbouring battalion fared even worse. Preston's crew simply took up position just above the high-water mark, and began to fire at such German positions as they could identify. These were not very many, for the tank fired only about a third of its ammunition before dusk. The 743rd remained on the beach for the next 12 hours.

Some unhappy men ended up on Omaha who should never have been there at all under such circumstances. Sergeant Andy Hertz, the Boston-bred son of a Dutch Jewish father and British mother, had been building airfields in England for almost two years with the 922nd Aviation Engineer Regiment when, somewhat to their bewilderment, he and his unit were issued with carbines, mines, bazookas and combat equipment, and loaded onto invasion transports to build airstrips in France. Aboard his liberty ship offshore, Hertz was in the galley listening to radio reports of the fall of Rome when the engineers were piped on deck. They saw the burning shore before them. A landing craft came alongside. Its skipper asked if the ship could provide any coffee, and announced that he could take in 90 men. A Ranger commanding officer sharing the ship with them declined to send his men ashore at that moment. The major responsible for the engineers shouted that they would go. Lacking assault training, they found the most frightening experience of the morning to be the descent of the scrambling nets into the pitching craft. Then, as they pulled away from the side, they saw their major waving farewell from the upper deck. He had decided to leave Hertz and the others to explore Omaha alone that day, and they never saw him again. An hour or so later, they struggled through five feet of water to the beach.

Few men or vehicles seemed to be moving. Hertz met a very frightened young 18-year-old from the 29th Division who said that he was the only survivor of his squad. The man in front of Hertz, Sergeant Valducci, suddenly fell down, screaming: "I'm shot!" A beachmaster ran to the group and demanded: "Who are you people?" Engineers, they said. "Sounds good," he replied, "we've got wire to clear here. You got bangalores?" No, they said. They were aviation engineers. "Who the hell sent you in?" They shrugged: "Some sonofabitch." And so they joined the clusters of stranded Americans on Omaha, lying behind such shelter as they could find through the hours that followed.[6]

Leading Aircraftsman Norman Phillips was one of a party of 158 British RAF personnel who were landed on Omaha: "We could see a shambles ahead of us on the beach – burning tanks, jeeps, abandoned vehicles, a terrific crossfire."[7] The captain of their LCT ordered them to offload anyway. The first vehicles found themselves driving into eight feet of water. The men struggled to the shore and formed a human chain to assist the non-swimmers. They landed on a sandspit crowded with wounded soldiers who lacked any medical attention. The British officers organized their men into salvage parties to rescue all the equipment that they could, but most had lost everything. Two RAF men were seized and taken prisoner by nervous Americans who could not identify their uniforms. By nightfall, the air force party had lost eight killed, 35 wounded, and 28 of their 35 vehicles. It was 33 days before they were issued with fresh clothing, 108 days before their lost arms and ammunition were replaced.

The reports that reached V Corps and General Bradley from Omaha that morning were not merely gloomy, but at times almost panic-stricken. Bradley's personal aide and Admiral Kirk's gunnery officer cruised close inshore aboard a PT boat and returned soaked and grim. Bradley considered halting all landings on the eastern beach and diverting the follow-up waves to Utah. A monstrous traffic jam had developed off the beach. By a serious flaw in the timetable, soft-skinned vehicles were beginning to arrive to offload in the middle of the battle. Among many naval crews who displayed exemplary courage, there were others whose lack of experience and determination magnified the confusion. The sailors manning a huge rhino raft loaded with vehicles simply abandoned it, 700 yards out, and the drivers and cargo drifted out of control until the rising tide brought them ashore. The Rangers had developed an early scepticism about naval efficiency when the officer in charge of one of their landing craft rammed a breakwater before getting out of his English harbour, and the skipper of another spent the cross-Channel voyage prostrate with seasickness. Now, one group of Rangers found themselves left to bring their landing craft in to the beach unaided. Its crew simply took to their dinghy and deserted them. In contrast to these episodes, the sailors manning two LCTs with immense courage rammed the beach obstacles head-on, and remained in position using every gun to support the infantry in their plight.

Lieutenant-Colonel John Williamson, commanding the 2nd/18th Infantry of the 1st Division, led his men into their LCVPs soon after 8.00 a.m., more than an hour late. When some craft began to swamp as they circled waiting for word that the beach was clear, the crews of others sought to begin rescue operations. After some forceful urging from Williamson, the craft began their run-in. They approached the shore not in an orderly wave, line abreast, but in a column, a queue, jostling for position on the sands. "The beach was loaded with men, tanks, DUKWs," said Williamson. "I was surprised that nobody had moved off." Major Frank Colacicco, executive officer of the 3rd/18th, stood among his men on the deck of an LCI, watching the spectacle ashore in utter bewilderment: "It was like a theatre. We could see it all, we knew that something was knocking the tanks out, but we kept asking, 'Why don't they clear the beach? Why aren't our people getting off?' " When at last their own turn came to approach the sands, Colacicco's LCI struck an obstacle whose mine blew up. Some men were hurled into the water by the blast, others found themselves struggling in the surf moments later as the craft settled. At last someone on the beach got a lifeline out to them, and the soaking men dragged themselves ashore. The major was told that Brigadier Wyman, the assistant divisional commander, wanted to see him. He reached the command post after being knocked off his feet by a mortar blast. He was told to take over the objectives of the 1st/16th, and returned to his men lying below the sea wall to point out to them, unanswerably: "We can't stay here." Slowly they began to work up the hillside, crawling over the immobile figures of men of the 116th Infantry: "They were too green to know that the closer you are to the enemy, the better off you will be." Colacicco tore a strip off one man he saw firing apparently recklessly along the hillside: "Just settle down," said the major soothingly. "That's our men over there." "But sir, they have overcoats on," insisted the soldier. Indeed they were German riflemen.

Yet although the defenders possessed the capability to maul the American landing on Omaha seriously, to impede and to disorganize it, they lacked the power to halt it absolutely. Despite the near total destruction of the first wave of invaders landing on the western flank below Vierville, despite the casualties and the terror inflicted upon thousands of green troops, a great many men survived to reach the sea wall alive – enough, finally, to swamp the vastly outnumbered German defenders. General Marcks' LXXXIV Corps reserve, the 915th Regiment, had set off in pursuit of the mythical paratroop force of Allied dummies at 4.00 a.m. on 6 June. It was hours after the seaborne landing before the 915th could be reached by dispatch rider, regrouped, and brought back from the Carentan–Isigny area on foot and by commandeered vehicle. The defenders thus lacked any force capable of mounting a co-ordinated counter-attack either against the attackers of Omaha, or against the British threat to Bayeux, further east. At Omaha, the Americans found themselves facing Germans of the 352nd Division as well as the 716th – eight battalions instead of four. The defenders possessed the strength and determination to fight doggedly from fixed positions. But where the Americans, inch by inch, gained ground, they were able to keep it. The toeholds prised out of the heights above the beach that day by a few brave men of the

Rangers, the 1st and 29th Divisions could never normally have been held against the quick local counter-attacks at which the German army excelled. But such movements did not develop. Like a trickling stream slipping between pebbles, a handful of courageous leaders and small groups of men found their way around the German strongpoints covering the beach exits, and forced a path for the American army off Omaha beach. The Corps plan for the attack was a failure. But the men on the hillside, spurred by their own desperation, found their own means to gain the high ground.

The principal problem in almost every attack on every battle-field is to maintain momentum. Every instinct, especially among inexperienced soldiers, is to take cover under fire. Instinct is reinforced when the bodies of others who have failed to do so lie all around. It requires a considerable act of will to persuade limbs to act which have suddenly acquired an immobility of their own. Inexperienced troops find it notoriously difficult to assess the extent of resistance and risk. On some occasions this can be to their advantage – or rather, that of their commanders – because it leads them to perform acts that more seasoned soldiers would not be so foolhardy as to attempt. But on Omaha the 29th Division, in its first experience of combat, deprived in the first hours of many of its officers, dismayed by its losses and confused by its predicament, became dangerously paralyzed. The veteran 1st Division, on its left, performed significantly better – indeed, most Americans later agreed that without "The Big Red One" the battle would have been lost.

It was individuals, not divisions, who determined the outcome of the day. It is arguable that as early as mid-morning, when Bradley and Gerow were still receiving deeply gloomy reports from Omaha, the real situation was much more encouraging than the view of the beach from the ships led the commanders to believe. Barely two hours after H-Hour, when the formidable network of German wire and machine-guns was still blocking all movement up the five valleys offering vehicle access from the beach, small groups of Americans had already reached the high ground to threaten the German flanks. The survivors of the 2nd Rangers' A and B Companies reached the sea wall at 7.45 a.m., and immediately began to work up the heights. Staff Sergeant William Courtney and Private First Class William Braher of A Company's 1 Platoon were probably the first Americans to reach the top of the cliff, around 8.30 a.m. When the Rangers gained the summit, they were too few in number to achieve a decisive success, although they sent word to a company of the 116th Infantry below to follow them up, and one boat section did so. But in the next two hours, a succession of similar small-scale actions took place all along the Omaha front, driving vital wedges into the German defences. 23 men of E Company, 2/16th Infantry, under Lieutenant John Spalding gained the hill and began to attack the German strongpoint which covered the east side of the St Laurent exit from the rear. After two hours of dogged fighting within the network of pillboxes and communicating trenches, the Americans cornered an officer and 20 men and forced their surrender.

Brigadier-General Norman Cota and his 29th Division command group reached the beach at 7.30 a.m. with the 116th Regiment's headquarters. The general began to move among the bewildered tangle of infantrymen, Rangers, naval beach maintenance parties and gunner forward observers. He saw one man who attempted to move up the hill shot down. The soldier lay in front of the American positions crying: "Medico, I'm hit!" repeatedly for several minutes. Then he moaned "Mama" and cried for a few moments before he died. Two of the headquarters group were killed within three feet of Cota when he established his first command post, while his signaller was hurled 20 feet up the bluff by blast. But the fiery, inexhaustible brigadier began pushing officers, urging men, seeking routes by which to break the bloody deadlock by the sea wall.

Mike Rehm of the 5th Rangers had been huddled beneath the shingle bank for two hours or more with a group of men when Cota appeared. In one of his legendary encounters of the day, the general demanded to know who they were. Rangers, he was told. "Then, godammit, if you're Rangers get up and lead the way!" exploded Cota.[8] The men began to thrust four-foot lengths of bangalore torpedo beneath the wire ahead, locking them together until they could blow a gap. In front, the entire hillside was wreathed in smoke from the blazing undergrowth. Coughing and choking, the Rangers realized that they could not run through it, but at last they pulled on their gas masks and groped forward. Some 35 men reached the metalled road at the top of the hill. Covered by 60 mm mortars firing at such short range that the tubes were almost vertical, they began to work slowly westwards. There were now Americans behind some of the most dangerous German positions covering the beach.

By 11.00 a.m., Vierville was in American hands. When Cota himself reached a house on the edge of the village, he found 70 men sheltering against the wall who shouted "Sniper! Sniper!" as he approached. The brigadier impatiently ordered them to clear the way. They closed in on the German, who threw a stick grenade down the hill towards them before being killed seconds later. Cota began to move back down the draw towards the beach. He met one of his own staff officers, Major William Bretton, clutching a briefcase and looking exceedingly angry. "Dammit, I can't get these people to move," complained Bretton. Cota called a young infantry captain and told him to get his men going off the beach. Hesitantly, they began to obey. Then Cota spotted an abandoned bulldozer loaded with TNT, desperately needed to blow obstacles down the beach. He shouted to the men lying around it for a volunteer to drive the explosives to the engineers. At last a red-headed soldier stood up and said, "I'll do it," and climbed on the vehicle. Yard by yard, the beach was unsticking.[9] At 1.30 p.m., Gerow signalled to Bradley: "Troops formerly pinned down on beaches . . . advancing up heights behind beaches."

The German strongpoints were being knocked out either by superbly vigorous gunfire from the destroyers steaming as close as 800 yards offshore, or by determined action from Rangers or infantry. Hein Severloh's battery had long since been reduced to firing single rounds in place of salvoes, for several weeks earlier half its ammunition reserve had been moved further inland as an intended precautionary measure against a direct hit. Now the gunners had no means of bringing shells forward and the only truck driver who attempted to do so was blown up on the journey by an Allied aircraft attack. By noon, Severloh himself had fired 12,000 rounds from his machine-gun, and was reduced to shooting tracer. This was helpful to his aim, for the gun's sights had been shot off by a stray bullet, but deadly in revealing his position to American spotters. WN 59 and 61 – the neighbouring "resistance nests" – had fallen silent. WN 62 had no field of fire on its west side, where the invaders were already working up to the rear. When their battery had fired all its ammunition, the gunners blew up their pieces and retreated southwards on their horsedrawn limbers. Severloh and the men in the strongpoint decided that enough was enough. They ran crouching from the entrance had began to work their way up the hill towards the rear, and safety. Only Severloh and one signaller escaped alive.

All that afternoon, Brigadier Cota moved relentlessly up and down the hillside, urging on the men clambering in sluggish files through the minefields and over the bodies of the dead. There were still perilously few heavy weapons on the higher ground to support the infantry now beginning to fight through the first hedges and fields of the *bocage*. When he found a group of Rangers claiming to be pinned down beyond Vierville, Cota himself walked ahead of them across the open ground to demonstrate that a man could move and survive. Many soldiers who attempted to set this sort of example on 6 June and in the weeks that followed were killed instantly. But Cota lived and the Rangers moved forward. Although persistent shellfire was still falling on the beach behind them, most of the Germans defending the hillside were dead or captured, and their gunnery OPs had been destroyed, removing the batteries' vital eyes. Medical corpsmen were moving among the wounded, looking out for those who had died so that they might give their blankets to men who were still living, but shivering. One of Cota's staff marvelled at the spectacle of a group of engineers sitting on the sand eating their K rations, apparently oblivious of the dead and wounded all around them. A dog, which had evidently been the pet of one of the German strongpoints, fell upon men of the 1st Division moving up the bluff with impressive enthusiasm, and had to be driven off with carbine fire. At 4.30 p.m., a staff officer of the 29th Division noted in his diary: "Prayed for the fourth time today, asking God – 'Why do these things have to be visited upon men?' " Brigadier Cota and his aide saw a soldier who appeared to be frozen with terror, praying on his knees in the scrub above the beach. But when they reached him, they saw that he was dead.[10]

On the high ground, Lieutenant-Colonel Williamson and the 2nd/18th had advanced to within a mile of their designated D-Day objectives. Like every American soldier above Omaha that day, he and his men were cursing the hedges of the *bocage*, which provided such perfect cover for snipers and were already inflicting interminable delays upon advancing units. Men sought cover whenever firing sounded nearby. Crossing a gap, the young soldier in front of Williamson was shot. The colonel put a Browning automatic rifle on top of the hedge and raked the area with fire. They moved onwards a little way without further casualties, then took up positions for the night just short of Colville. The Omaha beachhead had been secured. The Germans lacked the power and mobility to reverse the verdict of the afternoon. By nightfall, the Americans controlled a perimeter up to a mile deep beyond Omaha, while the 4th Division on Utah had linked up with General Maxwell Taylor and his men of the 82nd Airborne Division west of the causeways from the beach. Gerow of V Corps had not planned to establish his headquarters ashore until the following day. But Bradley, conscious of the urgent need to get a grip on the situation from the beach, told him to get his corps staff offloaded immediately. All the plans for a rapid supply build-up were to be sacrificed to the need to get more men onto the ground. 90 amphibious DUKWs, preloaded with ammunition, provided the vital minimum supply to sustain the forces ashore overnight. Some landing craft crews, utterly exhausted, dropped their anchors when darkness fell. Naval officers in launches hastened among them, urging the crews back into motion. That night Montgomery discussed with Dempsey the possibility of landing all further troops planned for Omaha on the British beaches. The suggestion was never pursued, but in view of the immensely dangerous gulf that such a change of plan would have exposed in the middle of the Allied line, it is a measure of the alarm surrounding the Omaha situation that it was ever discussed.

While the Utah landing had gone as nearly in accordance with planning as any commander could have expected, on Omaha the failures and errors of judgement by the staff had only been redeemed by the men on the sand. Many officers, including Brigadier Cota, believed that the American landings would have proved far easier had they been made in darkness, a possibility rejected by the navy and air force, who insisted upon the need for daylight to make best use of their bombardment power. Had elite infantry such as the Rangers led the way ashore before dawn, it is indeed likely that they would have been able to get off the beach and work in among the German positions with or without the bombardment. The events of D-Day emphasized the limited ability of high explosives to destroy strong defensive positions. But the follow-up waves and armour would have suffered immense problems attempting to get ashore under heavy fire before dawn. The timing of the landing was probably sound, although the troops could have profited immensely from continuing support fire until the moment they reached the beach, and from better gunnery forward observation thereafter. American naval reports spoke of the frustration of ships cruising silently offshore, unable to fire because of lack of identified targets.

The Americans refused to employ British-designed specialized armour – tanks throwing flame and explosive charges, and flail mineclearers. These would certainly have made a significant impact on Omaha. But they were not a magic formula for success. Given the formidable weight of German firepower concentrated against the five critical beach exits, it is likely that much of the specialized armour would have been knocked out on the beach in the same fashion as so many gun Shermans, merely contributing to the logjam of wreckage that did so much to hamper movement of vehicles and landing craft.

Chester Wilmot and others have seized upon the example of Omaha to demonstrate the supposed shortcomings of the American soldier.[12] In the weeks that followed, some American commanders, including Bradley, were to be seriously worried by the performance of some infantry units. On D-Day, there proved to be sufficient outstanding individual American soldiers and enough elite units such as the Rangers and Airborne to gain the day. Casualties on each of the Allied beaches, including Omaha, were almost exactly in proportion to the weight of unsuppressed enemy fire that the invaders met. The Americans suffered 4,649 casualties among their seaborne landing force to put ashore 55,000 men on D-Day. If the American line at midnight on 6 June was still tenuous, and fell some distance short of its planned objectives, V and VII Corps had achieved their vital strategic purposes merely by establishing themselves ashore.

It was on the British front on D-Day, where so much rested upon fast and ruthless progress inland from the beaches, that far more dramatic strategic hopes were at stake.

The British beaches

At 7.25 a.m., an hour after the Americans began landing on Omaha, the minesweeping flail tanks of the 22nd Dragoon Guards touched Sword beach at the eastern end of the Allied line, precisely on schedule. Lieutenant Charles Munday in *Leander I* drove ashore into the mortar and machine-gun fire with the hatch open as usual because of his haunting fear of fire. Some of the sappers disembarking with them were hit immediately.

Corporal Charles Baldwin watched the same instant fate befall the engineers who led his flail of the Westminster Dragoons: "They were flung about as German machine-gun fire hit them, clutching various parts of their bodies, jolting like rag dolls, then sinking out of sight into the water. I often wondered if any of those unfortunate men survived the landing. Even slightly wounded, the weight of their equipment dragged them under."[1]

Mundy's column of five Shermans clattered forward out of the landing craft and took up echelon formation to begin flailing, thrashing the sand with their great proboscos of chains, creeping forward astonishingly unscathed to the metalled road, where they switched off the equipment and began engaging the German defences with their 75 mm guns. Mundy could hear screams from defensive positions above the beach as a Crocodile flame-thrower puffed its terrible jet of fire towards them. 34 of the 40 Sherman DD amphibious tanks launched against Sword also arrived as planned, ahead of the infantry, cleared the beach successfully and became heavily engaged in the dunes beyond. A few minutes later, the 20 landing craft carrying the first wave of the 1st South Lancashires and 2nd East Yorkshires dropped their ramps and launched the lead companies, followed 20 minutes later by the second wave. These point battalions suffered less severely crossing the beach than those which followed. The East Yorkshires immediately began moving off towards Ouistreham, with men of 4 and 10 Commandos. 41 Commando, which took heavy casualties in their landing, headed for Lion-sur-Mer. By 9.00 a.m. the South Lancashires were between one and one and a half miles inland, at Hermanville. Vehicles and supporting units were pouring ashore, clogging the beaches. From the outset, the Sword landing was a remarkable success. Lieutenant Arthur Heal, commanding the sapper platoon attached to the 1st Suffolks, was still congratulating himself on completing his first trip in a landing craft without feeling seasick when the order came, "Ramp down! All out!" A few moments later, having passed through the infantry on the beach and regrouped for the battalion's advance to its objectives inland, Heal was enjoying a moment of anti-climax and relief. There had been powerful rumours within the unit before D-Day that they would pay for the honour of leading the assault by accepting withering losses.

The British landing plan for each brigade front called for four LCTs carrying four DD tanks apiece to put these ashore at H−5 minutes, followed at H-Hour by four LCTs carrying the specialized armour – flails, Crocodiles, Petards and the like – with sapper groups to begin work on the obstacles. Behind them at H+7 came eight assault landing craft bearing the two leading infantry companies; at H+20 another eight LCAs followed with two more infantry companies, and at H+25 came two LCAs with the men of the beach group. At H+35 bulldozers and more specialized armour rolled ashore; at H+60 nine LCTs with self-propelled guns; at H+90 10 LCTs with a full squadron of tanks. The tenth wave, behind all these, carried more gunners and 21 amphibious DUKWs loaded with stores and ammunition. COSSAC had predicted the loss of 10 per cent of the landing craft, with a further 20 per cent damaged. In the event, the losses were less severe, but it was not remarkable that, with a landing plan of such complexity, in many places the schedule collapsed in the first half-hour and successive waves reached the shore helplessly entangled with each other – creating a great jumble of men, vehicles, landing craft and wreckage on the waterline.

Even on Sword, where the losses were slight in relation to the scale of the assault, some men paid a speedy price for the success of the 3rd Division. Two LCTs ran off course and rammed two DD tanks, which sank with merciless immediacy. The seizure of the La Breche strongpoint covering the beach took three hours, during which troops coming ashore had to struggle through fierce fire. Some men reaching the beach in Queen White sector were touched to see a lone French girl struggling in the shallows to help wounded men out of the water. Shell and mortar fire from inland continued to harass the beach for most of 6 June and the days which followed it. The South Lancashires, who bore the brunt of the La Breche battle, lost 11 officers and 96 other ranks on D-Day; the East Yorkshires about the same.

Private Len Ainslie was an anti-tank gunner of the King's Regiment, which was to provide local defence for the beach area. A regular soldier who had been in the army since 1938, if Ainslie had had his way he would have landed by glider, for he had asked for a transfer to airborne forces. But his colonel refused to forward the request because Ainslie was a battalion bugler. Now, 100 yards offshore, his landing craft was struck amidships on the starboard side by a shell. Ainslie was appalled by the trail of devastation immediately in front of him. A big cook's head vanished, the company commander's batman lost his legs. A jumble of other broken bodies drifted amid the rush of water pouring through the side. A naval officer called abruptly: "Come on, all out!" Men began to struggle over the side of the sinking hulk. Ainslie tried for a moment to help a young soldier, who remarked flatly as he lay, "I can't do anything now, can I?" Then the officer shouted to Ainslie: "Leave him." Somebody ashore hurled them a line. The survivors swam and stumbled through the dead and the wounded in the water to the beach, where they saw the battalion's commanding officer killed a few minutes later. They were all soaking wet, their battledress and boots and equipment stiff with salt for days. But Ainslie and most of his comrades felt less a sense of shock than elation at their own achievement in survival, in having made it.

Some of the fire falling upon Sword beach during the morning came from the four 150 mm self-propelled guns of 3 Battery, 1716th Artillery Regiment, firing from a position at Plumetot, 3,000 yards inland from the coast. After standing by since midnight, at dawn its commander, Lieutenant Rudolf Schaaf, walked forward a little way until he could see the great invasion fleet stretched out before him off the coast. He found the spectacle impressive rather than frightening – it all seemed somehow detached from himself. "Well," he wondered thoughtfully, "what do we do now?" Contact with the battery's forward observer in a "resistance nest" on the beach was lost soon after first light. Thereafter, the guns fired on predetermined DFs – Defensive Fire targets – measured many weeks before. Around midmorning, Schaaf was suddenly ordered to take his guns immediately north to the coast, and counter-attack towards Lion-sur-Mer with infantry of the 3rd Battalion of 736th Regiment.

It was a pathetic episode. The first man of the battery to be killed was a taxi-driver from Leipzig who had been posted back to Germany several days earlier, but lingered in order to buy food and presents to take home. Now he died driving forward a truck loaded with ammunition. The German infantry were middle-aged men. They were strafed intermittently from the air as they advanced in open order down the gentle decline to the sea, and soon found themselves under fierce gun and small-arms fire. Schaaf's guns, astonishingly, approached Lion intact at around 10.30 a.m., and the Germans watched British infantrymen scuttling for cover, lacking heavy weapons or tanks to deal with them. As they fired into the buildings over open sights, little clusters of invaders emerged with their hands up,

124

and were hustled to the rear. But the weight of British fire rapidly overwhelmed the infantry. When the Germans at last despaired and began to pull back, only 20 men of the 3rd/736th remained with the guns when they reached the old battery position. They examined their prisoners, and were awed by their superb maps, food and equipment. Schaaf ordered them to be herded into a shell hole. In great agitation, a German-speaking British officer produced a copy of the Geneva Convention which he waved at the artilleryman, declaring forcefully that it was illegal to shoot them. "Nobody is going to be shot," said Schaaf brusquely. A few minutes later, he was telephoned by the excitable Major Hof, his battalion commander, and ordered to advance immediately to regimental HQ, two miles away on Hill 61, and attempt to extricate them from heavy attack. Schaaf abandoned his prisoners in their shell hole, and departed southeastwards.

On Juno beach, a few miles west of Sword, the Canadians had also broken through the coastal crust, but at heavier cost. The local naval commanders delayed H-Hour from 7.35 to 7.45 a.m., and even then many craft were late. As a result, the fast incoming tide covered an offshore reef which it had been feared would prove a serious hazard, and the first units found themselves landing right in amid the German beach obstacles. As the landing craft went astern after unloading, the coxswains could do nothing to prevent themselves from becoming helplessly entangled in mines and twisted steel. 20 of the leading 24 vessels were lost or damaged, among a total of 90 out of 306 employed on Juno that morning. Close artillery support for all the British landings was to be provided by Royal Marines manning obsolete Centaur tanks mounting 95 mm howitzers, but these proved lethally unseaworthy in landing craft. Scores capsized and were lost. Only six of 40 intended to support the Canadians reached the shore. Most of the DD tanks made it, but arrived behind the leading infantry rather than in time to provide suppressive fire ahead of them. Tanks and infantry moved inland together, becoming entangled in heavy street fighting in Courseulles that lasted well into the afternoon. The capture of St Aubin took three hours. The enemy in Bernières, where the assault company landing below the village lost fifty per cent of its strength in 100 yards, fought hard until they were outflanked. But in accordance with the plan, the Canadian follow-up units passed through the assault troops still mopping up around the beaches, ignored the snipers, who continued in action until nightfall, and pressed on towards their objectives inland.

The 50th Division attacking Gold, the most westerly of the three British beaches, ran into their first serious difficulty in front of the fortified German positions at Le Hamel. The 1st Hampshires and 1st Dorsets landed under furious fire from bunkers scarcely scarred by the bombardment, manned by Germans of 716th Division's 1st Battalion. The British supporting tanks arrived too late to give the infantry immediate support and, as on Juno, very few of the Royal Marine Centaurs arrived at all. Corporal Chris Portway, who landed with 231st Brigade HQ, was impressed above all by the sense of "noise, noise, noise", the continuous roar of gunfire, much of it from the Allied bombardment ships. Major Dick Gosling, the artillery battery commander, who landed with the Hampshires' battalion headquarters, was pleasantly surprised in his first moments ashore to find that the beach "was not the raging inferno some people had feared". Then he saw ripples of sand being pitched up all around him, and heard a noise like a swarm of angry bees over his head – his first encounter with enemy fire in six years of soldiering. Nelson-Smith, the Hampshires' fire-eating CO, who had insisted upon leading his headquarters in with the first wave, called to the others to lie down. Gosling, hopeful that the colonel knew more than he did about what to do next, dutifully prostrated himself in a foot of water. Then they all sprang to their feet and began to run for the shelter of the dunes. A blast close at hand killed a man beside Gosling, and suddenly he found that he could not walk. A mortar fragment had struck him in the leg. Somehow he reached the dunes, where he found Nelson-Smith, also wounded. Gosling began desperately scraping a hole for his head with an entrenching tool. Most of the Hampshires' wireless sets had been knocked out by the blast in the midst of the headquarters group, and the gunner found his own set so hopelessly clogged with ships' morse and other units' communications that he was unable to send a single radio message that morning to his own guns offshore. A rifleman nearby craned his head briefly to look over the rim of the dune and immediately fell back dead. Gosling looked up cautiously, and was astounded to glimpse a German only 10 yards away. He pulled out his revolver and fired a shot which discouraged the enemy soldier – no doubt as shocked as the gunner himself – from appearing again.

The sound of intense small-arms fire now seemed more distant. Gosling assumed that the Hampshires were making progress. He had been lying immobile for some time when he glimpsed the first of his own self-propelled guns coming ashore, led by his second-in-command, Vere Broke, standing proudly upright in his half-track. Gosling yelled: "Vere – get your head down, you'll get shot!" Broke studiedly tilted his helmet an inch forward on his head.

Gunner Charles Wilson, also of the 147th Field Regiment, spent most of the run-in to the beach seeking shelter from the devastating noise of four 25-pounders firing alongside each other in the landing craft. Wilson was stripped to vest, pants and gym shoes for the invasion, for he was one of a group detailed to tow ashore and release one of the huge "roly-poly" mats over which the guns would drive up the beach:

We hit two mines going in [wrote Wilson] – bottle mines on stakes. They didn't stop us, although our ramp was damaged and an officer standing on it was killed. We grounded on a sandbank. The first man off was a commando sergeant in full kit. He disappeared like a stone into six feet of water. We grasped the ropes of the "Roly Poly" and plunged down the ramp into the icy water. The mat was quite unmanageable in the rough water and dragged us away towards some mines. We let go the ropes and scrambled ashore. I lost my shoes and vest in the struggle, and had only my PT shorts. Somebody offered cigarettes but they were soaking wet. George in the bren carrier was first vehicle off the LCT. It floated for a moment, drifted onto a mine and sank. George dived overboard and swam ashore. The battery command post half-track got off with me running behind. The beach was strewn with wreckage, a blazing tank, bundles of blankets and kit, bodies and bits of bodies. One bloke near me was blown in half by a shell and his lower part collapsed in a bloody heap in the sand. The half-track stopped and I managed to struggle into my clothes.[2]

Major Gosling eventually managed to hobble down to a German pillbox on the beach, where he sat among other casualties waiting for evacuation. The occupants had clearly been disturbed over breakfast – coffee and sausage lay on the table, a picture of Hitler on the wall. Gosling found a letter from a French girl named Madeleine, obviously addressed to one of the garrison, promising to meet him on the evening of 6 June.

It is only for commanders and historians that it is possible to say that a battle proved a great deal easier than expected, and that casualties were remarkably light. For the men taking part in the D-Day landings, there were moments of violent intensity and horror on the British beaches as shattering as anything that happened on Omaha. It would have availed them little to know that their experience was much less terrible in scale than that of the Americans, for in kind it was equally deadly. Three of the five landing craft bringing 47 Commando ashore struck mines. When the survivors who swam to the beach regrouped to begin their advance towards Port-en-Bessin, 46 men and almost every wireless set in the unit had been lost.

Most of the men of 73rd Field Company, Royal Engineers, shared a common sensation of relief on reaching a shore – even a hostile shore – after three days imprisoned on their landing craft. When the first of their LCTs lowered its ramp off Le Hamel, the leading Petard AVRE tank tipped forward into the water and jammed itself half in, half out. The craft swung slowly round with the tide until a mine exploded against its stern. With the bridge and engine badly damaged, and fire from the shore raking the crippled vessel, it lay helpless on the waterline until it could be unloaded at the next low tide at 1.00 p.m. Of the engineers aboard it, two were killed and several more wounded, including one young officer who had somehow escaped from the debacle at Singapore in 1942. A second LCT hit a mine and began to settle 300 yards offshore. One section of men was rescued by an LCT leaving the beach which, to their fury, insisted upon carrying them back to England. Another group was threatened with the same fate but, after furious protests from its NCO in charge, had themselves trans-shipped to yet another craft heading into the beach. Captain James Smith and his team had been working desperately on the beach obstacles for almost an hour when he ran to his company commander to report progress, and was killed by machine-gun fire as he reached him. For any of those ignorant of war who believed that army engineers merely built roads or bridges, 6 June revealed how the sappers were required to bear the very brunt of the battle, and the price that they paid for doing so.

The flail tanks of the Westminster Dragoons were modified to wade rather than to swim the last yards to the beach. As they tipped over the LCT ramps, the drivers saw the view through their periscopes turn dark green, then progressively lighten until the sky appeared once more and water poured off the hulls as they crawled up the shore. Captain Roger Bell halted for a moment to check his position below La Rivière. His crew watched three sappers from a neighbouring AVRE Churchill clambering out onto its hull. Then there was a massive explosion, hurling sappers and fragments of tank into the air all around them and a sledgehammer thump on their own tank. For a moment they believed that they themselves had been hit by a shell, until Captain Bell reported that the engine of the exploding Churchill had struck them. They saw another tank explode. Corporal Charlie Baldwin in the co-driver's seat spotted the flash of the German gun and called over the intercom: "Eighty-eight-pillbox-eleven o'clock." They traversed rapidly and fired. "Missed," said Baldwin laconically. Jimmy Smith, the gunner, fired again and once more they assumed a miss. Bell said that they must press on anyway. They only learned later that they had destroyed the German gun. For all the attention focussed since D-Day upon the role of the specialized armour, it is striking to notice that, on the beaches, the "funnies" performing as conventional gun tanks made a markedly greater impact on the course of the battle than they did by using their engineer equipment, although this was obviously also valuable.

They began flailing at the high-water mark, and continued until they reached clear ground, where Bell pulled the pin on the green smoke canister to signal to the infantry that a lane was open. It fell on the floor of the turret, and they gasped and cursed amid the choking fumes until it could be retrieved and tossed out. Bell fought through the days that followed with his hair, face and moustache dyed a brilliant green. They drove on towards Crepon, Baldwin suddenly glimpsing three Germans cowering in a shellhole in the road. As they passed, the tank track slipped sideways into it and, over the roar of the engine, the Englishman caught the sound of the terrible screams beneath them. At their rendezvous in an orchard, they had just begun to boil a kettle when a bullet smacked against the hull beside them. They leapt quickly back into the tank and scanned the scenery. Like so many Allied soldiers in the weeks that followed, they decided that the shot could only have come from a church tower overlooking them. They worked high explosive rounds up and down the building until they were convinced that nothing inside it could have survived. Then the tanks moved on.

The 6th Green Howards, landing 1,000 yards eastwards below the German strongpoint at La Rivière, suffered the common run of small comedies, tragedies and moments of heroism. When the

LCA carrying the battalion HQ group grounded, its stern at once began to swing round towards a mined obstacle. The CO, Robin Hastings, sat on the ramp and dropped his feet cautiously into the water to explore the depth. Hitting bottom when he was only ankle-deep, the colonel paddled ashore. This was not an absurd precaution. Sergeant Hill of 16 Platoon, who had survived the entire North African and Sicilian campaigns, jumped from the ramp of another LCA into a deep shellhole, from which he could not extricate himself before the vessel ran over him.

Sergeant-Major Stan Hollis reached the beach feeling a little foolish, for he was already suffering a self-inflicted wound from a bad burn on the hand. He had carelessly seized the barrel of the bren gun with which he had been firing over the side of the craft as they closed in. His D Company advanced only a few hundred yards inland before they began to take casualties from a position to the right of the road. Major Lofthouse, the company commander, pointed it out to Hollis: "There's a pillbox in there, sergeant-major!" Without hesitating, Hollis sprang to his feet and ran 30 yards to the German position, spraying sten-gun fire as he went, until he reached the weapon slit, where he thrust in the barrel and hosed the interior with fire. Then he climbed on the roof, pulled the pin from a grenade, and leaned over to drop it through the slit. Not content with this, he began to advance alone along the communicating trench to the next pillbox. Its garrison hastily emerged and began to surrender. Hollis returned with 25 prisoners.

The sergeant-major, who performed a succession of feats of this kind in the weeks that followed, was later awarded the Victoria Cross. Every unit in every war needs a handful of men willing to commit acts of sacrificial courage to enable it to gain its objectives, and it is the nature of these that few who carry them out survive. But Hollis did, and lived to keep a Yorkshire pub after the war. Lieutenant-Colonel Hastings described him as a simple, straightforward Yorkshireman keen on horse-racing: "He was absolutely personally dedicated to winning the war – one of the few men I ever met who felt like that."

Austin Baker, wireless operator in an armoured recovery vehicle of the 4th/7th Dragoon Guards, was in an LCT which struck a mine as it manoeuvred inshore, among infantry wading up to their necks in the sea. Baker was hurled forward by the concussion, smashing a tooth on the turret hatch rim, but he managed hastily to close down the lid. The sailor directing the ramp lowering was hurled bodily into the air, and as the leading scout car drove off it was immediately knocked out by a shell. The others drove quickly off the beach, joining a procession of vehicles moving forwards between grassy banks and the skull and crossbones warnings, ACHTUNG MINEN, that were among the most familiar landmarks of every German battlefield. The village of Ver-sur-Mer had been considerably damaged in the bombardment, but a little cluster of French civilians emerged from the ruins to cheer and throw flowers. After losing their way for a time, Baker and his crew reached the inevitable orchard rendezvous. Among the other crews of the squadron, they began to exchange their excited stories of the landing while they drank tea and shared bully beef and biscuits with the crew of their wrecked landing craft, who had followed them ashore. Two tank commanders had already been killed by small-arms fire during the clearing of La Rivière. Two tanks had been swamped on the beach and a third disabled by a mine. A troop commander of B Squadron had met a self-propelled gun almost immediately after landing, and been beaten into action by the German's shot. This took off his leg, killed his operator and wounded the rest of the crew.

Yet nothing could dampen the exhilaration of those who had survived, sitting as wondering sightseers on ground that over four long years had attained for them the alien and mysterious status of the dark side of the moon. Corporal Portway of 231st Brigade thought that "once ashore, it all seemed better organised than most exercises". By 10.30 a.m., the British Second Army had landed fifteen infantry battalions, seven commandos, seven tank regiments, two engineer assault regiments, nine field artillery regiments and detachments of scores of supporting units. There had been setbacks, local failures, severe casualties to certain units, poor performance by some specialist equipment. Yet overall, the plan had succeeded stunningly well. Almost everywhere along the British line, the German coastal positions had been rolled up. It now remained to press forward to complete the second phase of the D-Day operation, to exploit German shock and surprise, ruthlessly to seize the vital ground inland.

Hitler's appointments for the morning of 6 June were not altered by the news of the Allied landings. He himself was in the Berghof at Berchtesgarten. OKW's Chief of Operations, Jodl, was in the little Reichchancellerie. For their usual midday conference that day, both men, along with their principal staff officers, were compelled to drive for an hour to Klessheim Castle, where they were officially receiving a Hungarian state visit. In a room beside the great entrance hall of the castle, Hitler was briefed on the first reports of the invasion. He approached the map of France on the wall, gazed at it for a moment, chuckled and declared in unusually broad Austrian tones: "So, we're off."[1] Then, after a few moments' further conversation with Jodl, he departed to meet the new Hungarian Prime Minister. A junior officer from Jodl's staff was dispatched to von Rundstedt to emphasize that there must be vigorous local counter-attacks against the beachhead.

Corporal Werner Kortenhaus and the rest of his company of 21st Panzer had begun to move up the Falaise–Caen road at 8.00 a.m. They were deeply unhappy, for the road ran perfectly straight and open. Moving in column in broad daylight, they felt utterly vulnerable – as indeed they were. The company was frequently halted to allow other units to speed past them. On the distant horizon, they glimpsed the smoke of the battlefield. Just south of Caen, they spotted an odd little tableau of two British soldiers standing alone in the corn by the road with their hands up, almost certainly men of 6th Airborne who had been dropped hopelessly wide. The panzers had no time to take prisoners, and hastened on. Then they learned that three companies of the regiment had been ordered to swing north-west, to move against the seaborne landings. They themselves were to head up the east bank of the Orne to engage the British airborne troops. As they moved forward, they were repeatedly compelled to pull in by the roadside and scramble beneath their tanks as Allied aircraft roared low overhead. They suffered their first casualty, a very young, half-trained replacement named Rammelkampf, who was killed by a machine-gun bullet from a strafing Typhoon. It remains one of the minor mysteries of D-Day that throughout their long drive up the road to the battlefield that morning, even after the lifting of the cloud that hampered air operations for part of the morning, 21st Panzer suffered little material damage from Allied fighter-bombers. Yet Kortenhaus and his comrades cursed the absence of the Luftwaffe as they watched the enemy overfly them with impunity. Where, they asked, were the thousands of German aircraft that they had been promised would be in the sky to support them on "The Day"?

All that morning and well into the afternoon, 21st Panzer's powerful armoured regiments – 127 Mk IV tanks and 40 assault guns – moved northwards, hampered by checks, delays and changes of orders imposed more as a result of failures of intelligence and the indecision of their own command than by Allied interference. Feuchtinger was impatient to move against the 6th Airborne bridgehead, but was frustrated by the British possession of the only bridge north of Caen by which his troops could cross the Orne. His panzergrenadiers were thus obliged to move through the city itself. The 2nd Battalion of 22nd Panzer Regi-

The Panzer IV was the most numerously-produced German tank of the war, equipping half the German tank units in Normandy. By 1944, it was obsolescent, but in its upgunned version – which the Allies called the Mk IV Special – was still a formidable enough opponent. Weighing 25 tons and moving at up to 25 mph, it carried 80 mm of frontal armour and 30 mm of side armour. Its 75-mm KwK 40 gun could penetrate 99 mm of armour at 100 yards, 92 mm at 500 yards, 84 mm at 1,000 yards. The "skirts" shown surrounding the hull in this version were designed to absorb the impact of hollow-charge projectiles, but all German armoured units in Normandy were exasperated by the manner in which these were torn off during movements among the dense hedges and orchards.

ment, 40 tanks strong, with which Kortenhaus was driving, was already approaching the paratroopers' perimeter when it was halted by orders from General Marcks at LXXXIV Corps. Marcks believed this to be a wasteful use of armour. One company only, the 4th, was left to support operations east of the Orne. The remainder were diverted to join the counter-attack west of Caen. The 1st Battalion, 80 tanks under Captain von Gottberg, was making its best speed to the startline near Lebisey, where the regimental commander, Colonel von Oppeln-Bronikowski, was already waiting with General Marcks. The corps commander had driven in person to oversee the battle. It was around 4.30 in the afternoon before this, the first major German armoured counter-attack upon OVERLORD, was ready to jump off against the British 3rd Division.

At 11.00 a.m. on the morning of 6 June, the three infantry battalions of Brigadier K. Pearce Smith's 185th Brigade were assembled exactly as planned near the village of Hermanville, ready to begin one of the most vital British movements of the day – the advance to and seizure of Caen. The 2nd King's Own Shropshire Light Infantry, who were to lead the advance on the tanks of the Staffordshire Yeomanry, had landed in better order than they did in most exercises. They warmed themselves with self-heating cocoa in an orchard near Lion, and with satisfaction discarded their first sets of maps covering the beach area, turning now to the ones covering the ground ahead, marked, like those of all the invading force, with every known German position. They marched down the road into Hermanville amid the cheers of excited local civilians, and the encouraging spectacle of clusters of German prisoners being herded in the opposite direction. Yet already the brigadier and his unit commanders were deeply concerned by the non-appearance of the tanks that were to provide vital mobility and fire support. The Staffordshires had become embroiled in the vast traffic jam on Sword beach, which was to create critical delays for the next phase of the assault. The strong onshore winds had caused an unprecedently high tide. Instead of a normal width of 30 yards of sand, that morning the incoming mass of armour and soft-skinned vehicles was attempting to manoeuvre towards the beach exits across a mere 30 feet of beach. The Staffordshires found themselves immobile for an hour before they could even reach the road. Thereafter, their progress was agonizingly slow, nose to tail on the narrow road bordered on either side by uncleared minefields. It is arguable that, if there was a serious flaw in all the Allied landing schedules, it lay in allowing too many non-essential vehicles to clog the path inland in the first hours. Inevitably, among the wreckage and under continuing German shelling, the beach-masters were unable to direct the unloading operations with precision. All along the Normandy shore by the later stages of that morning, the difficulties of getting the spearhead units off the beaches and on their way inland were snowballing into serious delays for the follow-up brigades coming ashore. There was a lull, a period of reorganization, when men were brewing up at their rendezvous, locating their units and checking vehicles and equipment, from which the momentum of the advance never recovered that day. Lieutenant-Colonel F. J. Maurice, commanding the 2nd KSLI, bicycled back to the beach to investigate the plight of the Staffordshires, then pedalled forward once more to report to Brigadier Smith at Hermanville. 185th Brigade was ordered to start its move towards Caen on foot, to be followed by the tanks as speedily as possible. It was now noon.

Meanwhile ahead of them, 8th Brigade was attempting to clear the way by destroying the two key German strongpoints, "Morris" and "Hillman". "Morris's" 65-strong garrison surrendered to B Company of the 1st Suffolks at 1.00 p.m. after a heavy bombardment. But when the battalion's A Company then attempted to seize "Hillman", a network of strongpoints some 600 by 400 yards, they were met by furious fire which caused heavy casualties. The covering wire was breached, but the infantry could not get through under the intense machine-gun fire. A tank of the Staffordshires which sought to silence the position could make no impact with its 75 mm gun. Arthur Heal, the sapper officer attached to the Suffolks, recalled afterwards that the tanks declined to mount a direct assault unless the mines had been cleared in their path. The attackers possessed no heavy artillery support, for the gunnery forward observer had been killed earlier. Heal and a lance-corporal named Bolton crawled forward under cover of smoke, each clutching a mine detector. When the sapper found the first mine, scrabbling bare-handed to uncover it, he could not recognize any known German pattern. After gazing at it apprehensively for a few moments, he pulled it out and identified an aged British Mark II, booty from Dunkirk. He returned to report that there was no threat to the tanks, and late that evening the Suffolks, led by two squadrons of

Shermans, successfully closed on "Hillman" and stormed the position, using 30-pound Beehive charges to blow open the bunkers. In Chester Wilmot's account of this battle, he is severely critical of the Suffolks for their sluggishness in taking a position that it was vital to seize quickly, at almost any cost. The battalion lost only seven killed that day. More recently, Carlo D'Este has argued that it was the fault of the planners, rather than of the infantry, who failed to assess the seriousness of the threat "Hillman" represented. But there also seem to be grounds for believing that the tanks were reluctant to force the issue. Whatever the cause, the delay in seizing the position enabled its defenders to inflict 150 casualties on the 1st Norfolks as they advanced southwards past "Hillman", following the KSLI towards Caen. The stubbornness of a handful of positions behind the coast was remorselessly reducing the strength of the British push inland.

Meanwhile the KSLI had been pressing on alone down the road to Caen, fighting a brisk battle for possession of Hill 61, whence Major Hof had telephoned Schaaf and asked him to bring his self-propelled guns to the aid of regimental HQ. Schaaf duly advanced across the cornfields. He saw the heads of the Shropshires peering at him over the standing corn, rapidly disappearing again when he opened fire. But by now, a squadron of the Staffordshire's Shermans had caught up. When Schaaf spotted these, he determined that for self-propelled guns to engage tanks was beyond the call of duty. He beat a hasty retreat. When he next found a telephone line and tried to contact regimental HQ, an English voice – presumably one of the victorious KSLI – answered the call.

The Shropshires approached Biéville later in the afternoon, having fought a succession of tough little battles against moderate German opposition. They encouraged strong enemy fire from the village. "The civilians refused to evacuate themselves," one of their company commanders, Captain Robert Rylands, wrote later, "and at that early stage we were too soft-hearted to shell their homes – a proceeding which might have facilitated our advance considerably." W Company's commander, Major Slatter, was hit in the shoulder by a sniper, but walked decisively forward to the house from which the shot had come and lobbed a grenade through its window before returning, grinning broadly, to have his wound dressed. The battalion now attacked from the flanks, sending one company forward east of the village, another

136

west. After a fierce firefight in which they suffered heavy casualties, the Shropshire's leading Y Company approached the commanding feature of Lebisey wood. They were told that there was little more opposition ahead. They were just three miles short of Caen.

Yet it was here that the KSLI first met panzergrenadiers of 21st Panzer Division, and here, late on the evening of 6 June, that Allied hopes of reaching Caen finally vanished. Y Company's advance was stopped in its tracks, the company commander killed. At 6.00 p.m., the battalion halted under fierce German fire and the rear companies dug in for the night. Under cover of darkness, Y Company disengaged and retired into the battalion position. "We were not unpleased with ourselves," wrote Captain Rylands of W Company,[2] and indeed, at a cost of 113 men killed and wounded, their achievement had been remarkable. But a single infantry battalion with limited tank and artillery support had not the slightest hope of generating sufficient violence to gain a foothold in Caen.

From the outset, the British 3rd Division's objectives for D-Day were the most ambitious, and their achievement would have had the most far-reaching consequences. 6th Airborne, east of Orne, was expected to gain and hold a perimeter. This it did with immense courage and determination, for in addition to the static German units in their area, they found themselves facing heavy counter-attacks from elements of the 125th and 192nd panzergrenadiers of 21st Panzer. West of the Orne, however, lay the road to Caen, where, above all, Montgomery had demanded dash and determination from his commanders to carry them to the city. The first of 3rd Division's three brigades, the 8th, expended much of its strength and energy in the early operations beyond the beaches, the seizure of "Morris" and "Hillman", and the securing of Hermanville, Coleville and Ouistreham. Among 185th Brigade, which was to play such a critical role in the dash for Caen, the KSLI's advance has already been described. The 1st Norfolks and 2nd Warwicks began to move south only at around 3.00 p.m., on the left of the KSLI, and the Norfolks were severely mauled in their movement past "Hillman". By nightfall on 6 June, they were between Beuville and Bénouville. 9th Brigade, in reserve, came ashore and assembled too slowly to be sent immediately forward with the 185th. By the time they were ready to move Rennie, their divisional commander, concluded that the most urgent priority was to reinforce the bridges across the Orne and Caen canal, which were under heavy German pressure. It is no great exaggeration to say that the sole determined thrust made by 3rd Division against Caen that day was that of the KSLI, with energetic support from the self-propelled guns of 7th Field Regiment RA, and some tanks of the Staffordshire Yeomanry.

The obvious absentees from this roll-call of British units are the remaining units of 27th Armoured Brigade. Each independent armoured brigade contained 190 Shermans and 33 light tanks, giving it a greater tank striking power than many German armoured divisions. It was never realistic to imagine that the British infantry battalions could march through Caen on their feet on the same day they had landed. The only possibility of dramatic success lay in a concentrated, racing armoured thrust by 27th Brigade. Crocker had written before D-Day: "As soon as the beach defences have been penetrated, not a moment must be lost in beginning the advance inland. Armour should be used boldly from the start."[3] Yet two-thirds of 27th Brigade's strength – the tanks of the 13/18th Royal Hussars and the 1st East Riding Yeomanry – were too deeply entangled in the fighting on the beaches and immediately inland to be available for the movement south. The entire burden of the push for Caen therefore lay with the Staffordshire Yeomanry, whose tanks were rapidly dispersed to support British infantry in difficulty against objectives inland. The unit concentrated only towards evening, in the face of the sudden threat from 21st Panzer. If it is true that the British plan underestimated the difficulty of overcoming "Hillman", and failed to take sufficient account of the known presence of panzergrenadier elements north of Caen, neither of these factors alone explains the failure to reach the city. Had the KSLI, by some miracle, reached Caen on D-Day with their few supporting tanks, they would have been crushed within hours by 21st Panzer. There was nothing like enough hitting power in the vanguard of 3rd Division to occupy and organize the defence of a city against strong enemy armour, especially with 12th SS Panzer Division already on its way to reinforce. Once any hope had vanished of spearheading the British advance with strong tank forces, any British infantry who somehow made their way forward must have been pushed back with crippling loss. It is possible to criticize the lack of drive by Rennie and his brigade commanders, and a certain loss of urgency by some units after the landing. But the failure to gain Caen on D-Day was chiefly the fault of over-optimism and sloppy thinking by the planners, together with the immense difficulty of organizing a major all-arms attack in the wake of an amphibious landing.

The last important action on the British left on 6 June was the battle against 21st Panzer's armoured thrust, an action which went entirely the way of the invaders. General Marcks, on his hill above Lebisey, told 22nd Panzer Regiment's commander: "Oppeln, if you don't succeed in throwing the British into the sea, we shall have lost the war."[4] The armoured officer, a former Olympic equestrian champion, saluted and mounted his vehicle. Marcks himself drove forward from the startline with the command group of 1st/192nd Panzergrenadiers. The tanks raced north towards the sea across the open ground, driving headlong into the gap between the British and Canadian perimeters.

British troops reported several tank formations advancing towards their positions. The Germans recoiled westwards on meeting fierce fire. When at last they encountered the heavily-gunned Sherman Fireflies of the Staffordshires on Hill 61, the consequences for the Germans were devastating. 13 tanks were immediately destroyed. Only a handful of 21st Panzer's tanks and infantry reached the surviving strongpoints of the 716th Division around Lion-sur-Mer. By a dramatic coincidence, only minutes after they did so, the fly-in began of 250 gliders of 6th Airborne Division to a landing zone eastwards, around St Aubin, near the Orne bridge. This was too much for the Germans. 21st Panzer was a sound enough formation, but lacked the ruthless driving force of an SS armoured division. Arguing that the glider landings threatened them with encirclement, they withdrew up the hill towards Caen. By nightfall, they were strongly emplaced around the city with the support of their 24 88 mm guns. But they had lost 70 of the 124 tanks with which they had begun the day. For all the dash with which Marcks and von Oppeln urged 22nd Panzer Regiment into action, its belated attack had been pushed home without determination or subtlety. A gesture had been made, no more.

The leading elements of the Canadian assault force on the right of the British 3rd Division almost reached Carpiquet on the evening of D-Day. Two troops of the 1st Hussars, leaving their infantry far behind, pressed on through Bretteville along the Bayeux–Caen road until they found their loneliness too alarming and turned back. They were two miles ahead of the rest of their formation. The Canadians suffered the universal problems of congestion on their beaches, and the need to fight hard to clear isolated strongpoints. But by the night of D-Day, they had established themselves strongly up to five miles inland. Upon the Canadians, in the days that followed, would fall the principal weight of 12th SS Panzer, perhaps the most formidable of all the German units now on their way to Normandy. Having set out from Lisieux, 65 miles from Caen, late in the afternoon, its leading elements were across the Odon, south of Caen, by nightfall, and moving to take up position on the left of 21st Panzer.

50th Division, moving inland from Gold beach, had fought a succession of hard battles against elements of the 352nd Division. By evening, troops of the British 151st Brigade had reached the Bayeux–Caen road, and tanks of the 4th/7th Dragoon Guards were reporting little in front of them. Though the 50th was also short of most of its D-Day objectives, it was solidly established in the Norman hedges and fields, with only limited German forces on its front. Among fields and villages all along the coast, British and American soldiers were settling into positions for the night, mopping up stragglers, herding prisoners to the rear, pausing for the first time to absorb their surroundings. Private John Price of the 2nd Ox & Bucks was one of the men who had landed by glider to join the 6th Airborne that evening. His aircraft bucked and bumped across a field until it came to a stop in high-standing corn within reach of the sea. Price jumped down from the fuselage, and was at once confronted by three ineffectual-looking Germans, who rose at his feet and put up their hands. One had thick pebble glasses, the others looked very young and frightened. He felt somehow disappointed. These men did not look in the least like specimens of the master race. He handed them over to a nearby group of Devonshires, and walked away towards the Orne bridge in search of his own unit, past a dead German lying alone at a crossroads, and a frightened-looking French family craning out of a cottage window.

Private Len Ainslie of the 5th King's had been one of thousands of awed spectators of the airborne landing. He, and the others who had been compelled to swim the last yards to the beach, were now dug in around their anti-tank guns, seeking to dry their boots. Just beyond their position near Hermanville, they found the body of a large German officer. The platoon sergeant said off-handedly: "Just get him out of the way," and

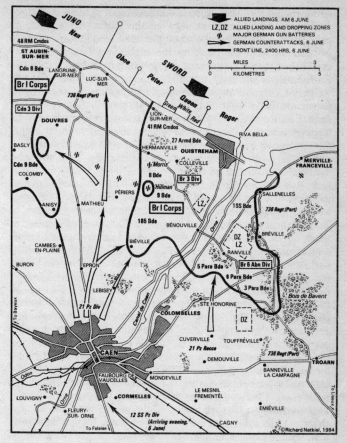

D-Day: the Push for Caen

having had no previous dealings with corpses, they threw him
over a nearby hedge. One man had already been injured seeking
to clean his gun. It exploded beside his face, blackening and
scorching him. As darkness came, all of them began to curse the
plague of mosquitoes. It was the first time that he and many
other men had set foot on foreign soil. They found it very
strange.

James Phillips, one of the American crew of an LCVP which had been shuttling men to and from the fleet off Utah beach all day, was chiefly preoccupied by exhaustion and hunger. Most of the landing craft ran out of rations on D-Day, and their crews had to survive by scrounging and begging from bigger ships. A British minesweeper gave Phillips' craft some stew and a canteen of brandy around midday. But at nightfall, when they closed alongside the vast battleship *Texas*, they were brusquely ordered to get back about their business. For the landing craft crews, there was less glory, more discomfort and more acute danger than for any other men in the seaborne task forces. Even when the battle moved on, the weather and chronic collisions gave them little respite for many weeks.

Private John Hein of the American 1st Division was deeply impressed to find himself bivouacked for the night in the very orchard, by a crossroads above St Laurent-sur-Mer, where he had been briefed to expect to be. Following an afternoon of alarming shelling on Omaha, he moved up the dirt track through the village with his unit, and at last begun to dig in around the divisional CP. The darkness was interrupted by German bombing activity and some shelling of the beach. Hein reassured himself by digging his own foxhole next door to that of the chaplain, where he felt that nothing very serious could happen to him. Whatever acute alarm the events on Omaha had caused to his commanders, Private Hein felt that the plan had worked out pretty well in the end.

Other men endured a much more disturbed night. Major Frank Colacicco of the 3rd/18th Infantry was in the battalion command post when it suffered a sudden night attack by the Germans, in the course of which he was taken prisoner. After a few minutes, he managed to take advantage of the confusion to leap a gully and make his escape. Back among his unit's riflemen, he began to move among them, urging the confused soldiers to bring down fire on the Germans. After 45 minutes the enemy withdrew, taking some American prisoners with them. Some manner of quiet returned to the positions.

The German battalion commander of the 3rd/716th infantry told Lieutenant Schaaf that he had been told to pull back to Caen with his 30 or so surviving men. Without orders since the fall of his regimental headquarters, Schaaf decided to do likewise. Driving south-eastwards, he lost one gun, which threw a track and became bogged down in a ditch. The drive continued without incident, until he glimpsed ahead a crude roadblock of farm implements manned by British soldiers. He ordered his men to take off their helmets, and laid a tarpaulin over the side of the hull to conceal the German black cross. As they roared past the roadblock, they could see that the British had identified them but were too surprised to intervene. They saw no more troops of any nationality until three miles on, at the outskirts of Caen, where they encountered German infantry. A stream of stragglers and survivors, men and vehicles, were making their way back into the perimeter from the coast. When Schaaf reported to the divisional artillery headquarters, he was told that his was the only battery, among 11 in the regiment, to make contact since morning. They pressed him for information about the situation forward, about which there was still terrible confusion. Then he was ordered to take up position near Epron, just north of the city. They remained in action there until, weeks later, ceaseless use had reduced their guns to wrecks.

Along 60 miles of front, men lay over their weapons peering out into the darkness lit up by occasonal flares and tracer, then slept the sleep of utter exhaustion in their foxholes or ruined cottages. Some soldiers of the British and American airborne divisions were still probing warily through the darkness miles from their own lines, wading streams and swamps on the long march from their ill-aimed dropping points. A few thousand men lay dead, others wounded in the field dressing stations or positions from which they could not be evacuated. There were already Allied stragglers and deserters, who had slipped away from their units, skulking in villages the length of the invasion coast.

In England and America, the newspapers were being printed, *The Times* for 7 June carried the headlines: "The Great Assault going well; Allies several miles inland; Battle for town of Caen; Mass attacks by airborne troops". A leading article proclaimed: "Four years after the rescue at Dunkirk of that gallant defeated army without which as a nucleus the forces of liberation could never have been rebuilt, the United Nations returned today with power to the soil of France." D-Day provoked *The Times*, along with many politicians, to a breathless torrent of verbosity. On the Letters page, a Mr R. B. D. Blakeney reminded readers that William the Conqueror had embarked for England from Dives. The *Daily Express,* characteristically, plunged into sensation: there were tales of Allied paratroopers treacherously shot in mid-air, of the glider pilot who cried as he shot up a German staff car: "Remember Dunkirk when you drove me off!" There was a photograph of a triumphant glider pilot carrying a German helmet with the words HE'S DEAD chalked upon it.

Corporal Adolf Hohenstein of the 276th Infantry Division, billeted at Bayonne, many miles from the battlefield, wrote in his diary: "A beautiful day. In the evening we hear the long-expected but still surprising news that the invasion has come. The civilians will have to pay the most dearly, and the French around here have suddenly become very quiet. They will become even quieter when this country has been devastated by Allied bombs and German shells, when they experience the full horror of war."[5]

No disappointment or setback could mask the absolute Allied triumph of establishing themselves ashore on D-Day. But the failure to gain Caen was a substantial strategic misfortune. Bradley wrote: "In subsequent days, after I had had an opportunity to study Dempsey's D-Day operation, I was keenly disappointed."[6] There is overwhelming evidence that with greater drive and energy Second Army could have "staked out claims" deeper inland on 6 June. But with 21st Panzer solidly established around Caen, it is impossible to believe that the British could have reached the city without running into deep trouble. The German coastal defenders may not have been the cream of the Wehrmacht, but they fought extraordinarily well in many places, given their isolation, the poverty of their manpower and the paucity of their equipment. Too little credit has been granted to German garrisons for their struggle with the best that the Allies could throw against them. They achieved all that Rommel could reasonably have expected – a delaying action which deprived the British advance of the momentum that it needed to reach Caen. The city was only a realistic objective for Dempsey's army if the coastal crust crumbled immediately the Allies landed. It did not. Whatever the sluggishness of some British units, Bradley was to discover ample difficulties of this kind among his own divisions in the days to come.

The Allied command of the air was plainly decisive on 6 June: "The Anglo-American air forces did more than facilitate the historic invasion," wrote the American official historians, "they made it possible."[7] The Luftwaffe put less than a hundred fighters into the sky on D-Day, and mounted only 22 sorties against

144

shipping late that evening. Given the difficulties that the invaders suffered against the Atlantic Wall, it is difficult to imagine that they could have pierced it at all had their assault been subject to serious air attack. As it was, they were ashore. But they were still gasping to regain breath after the vast strain of getting there.

4 The British before Caen

Closing the lines

There was never any doubt in the minds of either German or
Allied commanders that, in the immediate weeks of the
invasion, the vital strategic ground lay in the east, where the
British Second Army stood before Caen. Here, for the Germans, the threat was 50 miles closer to the heart of France, and
to Germany. Here, for the British, glittered the opportunity to
break into the open tank country to the south-east, freeing
airfield sites and gaining fighting room before the mass of the
German army could be committed to battle. By securing their
beachhead ashore, the first great Allied hopes for OVERLORD
had been fulfilled. Yet on the Second Army front in the weeks
that followed, their second hopes – their prospects of a quick
breakthrough from Normandy – died stillborn. They did so in a
fashion that raised serious questions about the fighting power of
the British army that had landed in France, and which demonstrated decisively the genius of the German soldier in adversity.

Between 6 June and the end of the month, Montgomery
directed three attempts, first, to seize Caen by direct assault – on
7 and 8 June – and then to envelop it – the Villers-Bocage
operation of 13 June, and EPSOM on 25 June. The initial
operations were merely the continuation of those undertaken on
D-Day. On 7 June, 185th Brigade's renewed attempt to force the
direct route to the town through Lebisey, with powerful fire
support, broke down after heavy casualties. 9th Brigade's battle
for Cambes was at last successful after the Royal Ulster Rifles
had fought their way across 1,000 yards of open ground under
punishing enemy fire. But they could go no further. When the
3rd Canadian Division began to push forward, its men encountered the leading elements of 12th SS Panzer, newly arrived on
the battlefield, and bent upon breaking through to the sea.
Colonel Kurt "Panzer" Meyer, commanding the division's

armoured regiment, directed his tanks' first actions from a superb vantage point in the tower of the Ardenne Abbey on the western edge of Caen. To cope with the immense difficulties of moving forward adequate supplies of fuel, Meyer organized a shuttle of jerry cans loaded aboard Volkswagen field cars. Throughout the 7th and 8th, the Canadians and the fanatical teenagers of the SS Hitler Jugend fought some of the fiercest actions of the campaign, with heavy loss to both sides. Lieutenant Rudolf Schaaf of the 1716th Artillery was at Corps headquarters in a mineshaft outside Caen when a swaggering colonel from 12th SS Panzer arrived to announce his intention not to halt anywhere before the sea. This, of course was the legendary Meyer, who assumed command of the division a few days later. Only 33 years old, tall and stiffly handsome, he was the archetype of the Nazi fanatic. Even as a prisoner in 1945, he told his interrogator: "You will hear a lot against Adolf Hitler in this camp, but you will never hear it from me. As far as I am concerned he was and still is the greatest thing that ever happened to Germany."[1]

"The SS showed that they believed that thus far, everybody had been fighting like milkmaids," said Schaaf.[2] He watched the bleak young men of the Hitler Jugend Division riding forward into their attack, and saw some of them return that night, utterly spent, crying tears of frustration for their failure to reach their objective. "It was a very sad chapter for them." But it had also been less than happy for the Canadian 3rd Division. By the night of 7 June, as their official historian described the situation, when the Division's forward elements had been pushed back up to two miles:

The 9th Canadian Infantry Brigade Group had fought its first battle with courage and spirit, but somewhat clumsily. Encountering an unusually efficient German force of about its own strength, it had come off secondbest. Its advance guard had been caught off balance and defeated in detail.[3]

This was scarcely an encouraging omen for rapid progress inland. While the Germans co-ordinated armour, infantry and artillery superbly, the Canadians did not. While 9th Brigade was facing 12th SS Panzer, 8th Brigade spent the day preoccupied with mopping up strongpoints in the rear which had not been taken on D-Day. The following morning, 8 June, 7th Brigade came under heavy attack; the positions of the Royal Winnipeg

Rifles were overrun, and the Canadian Scottish were compelled to mount a major counter-attack to recover the lost ground, at a cost of 125 casualties. That night, Panthers of 12th SS Panzer, led personally by Kurt Meyer on his customary motor-cycle, hit the Canadian 7th Brigade yet again. As fires and flares lit up the area, the Regina Rifles at one stage reported 22 Panthers around their own battalion headquarters. In the confusion of the night battle, the Germans began to believe that they had broken through. A panzer officer halted a Volkswagen field car immediately outside the Reginas' command post, which was blown up seconds later by a PIAT bomb. The Canadians lost contact with all but one of their companies. "It is hard to picture the confusion which existed," said their commanding officer.[4] Six Panthers were destroyed by the Canadian anti-tank guns and PIATs before Meyer broke off the attack, and his armour squealed and clattered away into the darkness.

The Canadians were unbowed, but shaken. Corporal Dick Raymond and a draft of replacements for their 3rd Division closed on Juno beach late in the afternoon of 7 June. The landing craft dropped its ramp a hundred yards offshore, at which point the replacements flatly refused to disembark. At last, after an absurd argument, the officer in charge jumped into the chest-high water, and the men straggled ashore after him. The beach was quiet, littered with wreckage, stinking of oil. When the group had marched a little way inland, Raymond found himself suffering pains and, with his accustomed independence, fell out by the roadside. He found two drunken Canadian engineers, and joined them by a vast wine cask in a cellar. Then a half-track took the other men away, and Raymond was alone again. Having slept where he lay beside the wine cask, the next morning he met a Scottish major who had been on the landing craft with him. He learned that a random bomb from a Luftwaffe nuisance raider during the night had landed in the midst of his group of replacements, killing some 20 and wounding as many again. Still alone, he walked forward until he encountered a field artillery battery, shooting furiously in support of two infantry battalions locked in the struggle against 12th SS Panzer. Raymond spent the remainder of that day helping a gun team. At last the gunners told him to go and report to his own unit. Late that night, near Les Buissons, he found his Vickers machine-gun platoon, supporting a battalion of the Stormont,

Dundas and Glengarry Highlanders. They were utterly exhausted after the battles of the day. No questions were asked about his movements – he was simply given a shovel and told that he was with C Company. That night, the battalion was reduced to some 200 men, although more straggled in later. The next morning, Raymond found himself plunged into the bitter struggle that persisted through the days that followed: "It was just a straight shoot-out, both sides blasting at each other day and night. We used to joke about 'last man, last round'. Watching infantry advancing across those open corn fields may not have been quite as terrible as the battle of the Somme, but at times it seemed to come pretty close to it."[5] Raymond was touched by the courage of the Royal Naval gunfire forward observers, declining to wear steel helmets, being steadily killed: "They seemed to have the David Niven touch." But he was even more surprised and impressed by the performance of the Canadians. In months past, he had often been scornful of their indiscipline and doubtful of their quality, above all sceptical about their leadership: "But the strength of that Canadian army was as close-in fighters. They went at it like hockey players."

In the first six days ashore, the Canadians lost 196 officers and 2,635 other ranks, 72 and 945 of these, respectively, being killed. After the 9th, the Germans broke off their attacks for some days. The Canadians were able to consolidate their positions and plug the gaps in their line; they could draw satisfaction from beating off 12th SS Panzer's attacks. Yet if the Germans were dismayed by their failure to break through to the sea, the Canadians had also proved unable to maintain the momentum of D-Day. Meyer's panzers had successfully thrown them off balance: they now concentrated chiefly upon holding the ground that they possessed, and were most cautious about launching any attacks without secure flanks and powerful gun and tank support. They found themselves unable to advance beyond Authie.

On 7 June the British 50th Division, on the right, occupied Bayeux, which the Germans had evacuated on D-Day, and pushed forward more than three miles towards Tilly-sur-Seulles, Sully, and Longues. Yet when Montgomery himself came ashore to establish his tactical headquarters in the grounds of the château at Creully on 8 June, the leading assault units, which had landed on D-Day and been continuously in contact with the enemy ever since, were visibly weary. The prospect of breaking through the line held by 12th SS Panzer and 21st Panzer in front of Caen was very small. "The Germans are doing everything they can to hold onto Caen," Montgomery wrote to the Military Secretary at the War Office that day. "I have decided not to have a lot of casualties by butting against the place. So I have ordered Second Army to keep up a good pressure at and to make its main effort towards Villers-Bocage and Evrecy, and thence south-east towards Falaise."[6] Despite the worsening weather, which had restricted air support and delayed the progress of unloading, it is impossible now to forget Montgomery's parting address to his commanders before they sailed for Normandy:

Great energy and "drive" will be required from all senior officers and commanders. I consider that once the beaches are in our possession, success will depend largely on our ability to be able to concentrate our armour and push fairly strong armoured columns rapidly inland to secure important ground or communications centres. Such columns will form *firm bases in enemy territory* [emphasis in original] from which to develop offensive action in all directions.[7]

For all Montgomery's declarations of willingness to regard the independent armoured brigades, with their formidable tank strength, as "expendable" in pursuit of these objectives, they had scarcely been attempted, far less attained. Second Army's efforts had been entirely absorbed by the struggle to create and hold a narrow perimeter; and this despite the overwhelming success of the FORTITUDE deception plan, and a rate of build-up by Rommel's forces as slow as the most optimistic Allied planner could have hoped for. In these first days, as much as at any phase of the campaign, the Allies felt their lack of an armoured infantry carrier capable of moving men rapidly on the battlefield alongside the tanks. From first to last, infantry in Normandy marched rather than rode, sometimes 10 or 15 miles in a day. Too many tired soldiers were asked to march far as well as fight hard. It took days for some units to re-adjust themselves after the huge psychological effort and surge of relief attached to getting ashore. In the training of paratroops, great emphasis is laid upon the fact that the act of jumping is a beginning, not an end in itself, and that their task commences only when they have discarded their harness on the ground. Yet throughout the months of preparation in England, the thoughts of the armies were concentrated overwhelmingly upon the narrow strip of fire-swept sand that they had been obliged to cross and hold on D-Day. Brigadier Williams of 21st Army Group said: "There was a slight feeling of a lack of cutting edge about operations at the very beginning after the landing."[8] A less tactful critic might have expressed the issue more forcefully, and compared the ruthlessness with which 12th SS Panzer and Panzer Lehr threw themselves into the battle with the sluggishness of Allied movements in those first, vital days before the mass of the German army reached the battlefield. The loss of momentum in the days after 6 June provided the Germans with a critical opportunity to organize a coherent defence and to bring forward reinforcements to contain the beachhead. The huge tactical advantage of surprise had already been lost.

On the evening of 9 June, Bayerlein's superb Panzer Lehr Division moved into the line on the left of 12th SS Panzer after a 90-mile drive to the front from Chartres, during which they were fiercely harassed and strafed by the Allied air force. The formation had lost 130 trucks, five tanks and 84 self-propelled guns and other armoured vehicles. But the delay and dismay it had suffered were more serious than the material damage to its fighting power, since its total complement of tanks and vehicles was around 3,000. The three panzer divisions – 21st, 12th SS and Panzer Lehr – now formed the principal German shield around Caen, supported by the remains of the various static divisions that had been manning the sector on D-Day. 21st Panzer's poor performance and reluctance to press home attacks were a source of constant complaint by Meyer's Hitler Jugend, who claimed that in several battles already they had been let down by Feuchtinger's units. But Panzer Lehr, for all their misfortunes on the road, were fighting superbly to hold the ruins of Tilly, the little town in a valley south-east of Caen which was to be the scene of some of the most bitter fighting of the campaign. Their panzergrenadier half-tracks had been sent to the rear, for they did not expect to move far or fast in any direction. Instead, the infantry were deployed in ditches and ruined houses alongside tanks employed as mobile strongpoints, meticulously camouflaged and emplaced to present only a foot or two of turret to attacking Allied armour. The tracks that they made approaching their positions were painstakingly swept away or concealed before daylight brought the spotter planes. Caked in dust, unwashed and often unfed, in the appalling heat and stink of their steel coffins, the tank crews fought through days and nights of attack and counter-attack, artillery and naval bombardment, mortaring and Allied tank fire. The panzergrenadiers found the Tilly battle

151

especially painful because it was difficult to dig deep in the stony ground, and at times of heavy bombardment their officers had difficulty holding even Bayerlein's men from headlong flight.

For the British 50th Division also, the lyrical name of Tilly-sur-Seulles became a synonym for fear and endless death. The little fields of cowslips and buttercups, innocent squares of rural peace, became loathsome for the mortal dangers that each ditch and hedgerow concealed. The guidebook prettiness of the woods and valleys, so like those of Dorset and Devon, mocked their straining nerves and ears, cocked for the first round of mortar fire or the sniper's bullet. For the tank crews, there was the certain knowledge that a hit from a German Tiger, Panther or 88 mm gun would be fatal. The same was not true the other way around.

The tension before a set-piece attack was appalling [wrote a young Churchill Crocodile troop commander, Andrew Wilson]. When Crocodiles were used, they were generally in the lead . . . You wondered if

The Crocodile flame-throwing tank was among the best-known of the British 79th Armoured Division's "Funnies", the specialized tanks which were the brain-children of General Sir Percy Hobart. Almost all were modified Churchills – slow infantry tanks capable of only 15 mph, five tons heavier than the Sherman, 10 tons heavier than the Cromwell. Some were modified to carry bridge-laying or ditch-filling equipment, others to lay steel track or to throw a heavy bunker-busting bomb. The Crocodile, with which two British armoured regiments were equipped, carried flame fuel in a towed trailer, and could effectively incinerate men in its path at a range of 40–50 yards. Crocodiles were normally employed in small detachments to support Allied attacks against strongly dug-in German infantry.

you'd done the reconnaissance properly; if you'd again recognise those small landmarks, the isolated bush, the dip in the ground, which showed you where to cross the start-line. You wondered if in the smoke and murk of the half-light battle, with your forehead pressed to the periscope pad, you'd ever pick out the target. And all the while you saw in your imagination the muzzle of an eighty-eight behind each leaf.

Then the bombardment grew louder, and the order came: "Advance" . . . There was the run with the blurred shape of the copse at the end. Spandaus were firing, but you couldn't see them. A Sherman officer was telling his troop to close up. The distance shortened. The Crocodiles began to speed up, firing their Besas. The objective took on detail. Individual trees stood out, and beneath them a mass of undergrowth. Something slammed through the air.[9]

He knew at once that it was an anti-tank gun. But there was nothing he could do about it. The troop ran in, pouring in the flame. Once he thought he heard a scream, but it might have been the creak of the tracks on the track guides. Suddenly it was all over. The infantry came up and ran in through the smoke. The flame-gunners put on their safety-switches, and from inside the copse came the rasp of machine-guns. A little later, when he drove back to refuel, he saw that the field was littered with dead infantry and that one of the Shermans had been hit through the turret.

Villers-Bocage

It was at this stage that Montgomery determined to commit his two veteran divisions of the old Eighth Army, 51st Highland and 7th Armoured. "You don't send your best batsman in first," he had said crisply before D-Day when one of a group of 7th Armoured officers asked – in a spirit that might not have been shared by some of his colleagues – why the formation was not to take part in the initial landings.[1] Now, he proposed to use his "best batsmen" in two major flank attacks around Caen: 51st Highland would pass through the 6th Airborne bridgehead east of the Orne; 7th Armoured would hook to the south-west. The landings of the 7th Armoured and 51st Highland had been delayed by the weather, which was also causing serious artillery ammunition shortages. Beach organization and traffic control remained a chronic problem – on Gold alone, the engineers had been compelled to deal with 2,500 obstacles, many of them mined, comprising a total of 900 tons of steel and concrete.

Nuisance night raids by up to 50 Luftwaffe aircraft constituted no major threat to the beachhead, but still compounded delays and difficulties. Sword beach continued to be plagued by incoming shellfire.

Throughout these days, the German army mounted no major counter-attack. A desperate plan contrived by General Geyr von Schweppenburg of Panzer Group West was aborted by Rommel on 10 June – insufficient forces were concentrated. The following day, Geyr's headquarters were pinpointed by Allied Ultra decrypts, and put out of action by air strikes. Yet the local counter-attacks mounted by German forces in the line, above all against the paratroopers east of the Orne, were so formidable as to inflict devastating casualties upon the British paratroopers, and finally to crush 51st Highland's attack within hours of its inception on 11 June. The Germans had now deployed their 346th and 711th Divisions alongside elements of 21st Panzer and 716th on this right flank. 5th Black Watch, advancing into their first action at 4.30 a.m. that morning, suffered 200 casualties in an attempt to reach Bréville. "Every man of the leading platoon died with his face to the foe," recorded the divisional history proudly.[2] Yet General Gale, commanding 6th Airborne, concluded that it was essential to seize the village to close a dangerous gap in his own perimeter. The next night, the 12th Battalion, Parachute Regiment, in a brilliant sacrificial battle, gained Bréville at a cost of 141 casualties among the 160 men with which the unit advanced. The German 3rd/858th Regiment, which was defending the village, was reduced from 564 men to 146 in three days of fighting. Between the 11th and the 13th, other elements of 51st Highland Division sought to push southwards towards Sainte Honorine. But after a bitter series of to-and-fro actions in which every temporary gain was met by fierce German counter-attack, the British attack east of Caen petered out. The lightly-armed parachute battalions were exhausted and drained of men and ammunition. 51st Highland was unable to make progress.

"The fact must be faced," declared the divisional history, "that at this period the normally very high morale of the Division fell temporarily to a very low ebb . . . A kind of claustrophobia affected the troops, and the continual shelling and mortaring from an unseen enemy in relatively great strength were certainly very trying . . ."[3]

For the enemy also, the struggle east of the Orne remained an appalling memory. Corporal Werner Kortenhaus of 21st Panzer

154

saw four of his company's 10 tanks brewed up in five minutes during the attack on the château at Escoville on 9 June. Again and again the Mk IVs crawled forward, supporting infantry huddled behind the protection of their hulls as they advanced into the furious British mortar and shellfire. But when the tanks reversed they were often unable to see behind them, and rolled over the terrible screams of the injured or sheltering men who lay in their path. A wounded panzergrenadier cried for his mother from no man's land all one night in front of their position. Kortenhaus, trying to sleep beneath his tank, woke in the morning to find the tunic that he had laid on the hull when he dismounted was shredded by shell fragments. The bombardment seldom seemed to pause.

On 13 June, his company lost four more tanks in the struggle against 51st Highland Division. They saved the driver and gunner of one panzer, who ran from their burning vehicle, by cramming them somehow into their own turret as they accelerated away in retreat through the cornfields. Their company commander, Lieutenant Neumann, leapt down from his own tank and led the infantry in a desperate counter-attack against the Black Watch, firing a Schmeisser. He survived, only to be hit as he climbed back into his own turret. "We became very depressed," said Kortenhaus. "We had given up any hope of victory after repeated failures in attack."[4] Yet the Germans held their ground east of the Orne despite the overwhelming superiority of the Allies in fire support.

Montgomery's 8 June concept for the envelopment of Caen included a plan to drop 1st Airborne Division behind the town when 51st Highland and 7th Armoured had made sufficient progress on the flanks. To his bitter anger, this was decisively vetoed by Leigh-Mallory, always a sceptic about parachute operations. Yet the disappointment that now attended the push by 7th Armoured on Second Army's western flank made discussion of ambitious objectives beyond Caen almost immediately irrelevant.

On 10 June, when the division moved through 50th Division's positions west of Caen, its commander Major-General Erskine could report that he "never felt serious difficulty in beating down enemy resistance". Only four tanks were lost. It thus seemed all the more remarkable that the Desert Rats made little progress, and fared no better on 11 June. British infantry who penetrated Tilly were unable to secure the town for lack of tank support.

But as opposition stiffened in front of them, Dempsey and Bucknall – XXX Corps' commander – perceived a weakness on the enemy's left – a yawning hole in the German line between Caumont and Villers-Bocage. On 12 June, they swung 7th Armoured westwards to launch a new attack on this south-easterly axis. This advance began at 3 p.m., led by the 8th Hussars, and progressed intoxicatingly well for some hours. "On arrival at Cahagnolles we meet a U.S. patrol in armoured cars and jeeps looking very dusty and excited," the Hussars CO, Lieutenant-Colonel Cuthbert Goulburn, recorded in his diary. "We are all beginning to think we have obtained a complete breakthrough." But then, at the approach to Livry, the Hussars leading tank was knocked out by a panzerfaust. In the close country, they could find no means of bypassing the village, and the motor company of the Rifle Brigade had to be called forward to clear the German outpost defending it. Meanwhile, Brigadier "Loony" Hinde, commanding 22nd Armoured Brigade, ordered Goulburn's regiment to swing east and reconnoitre a possible alternative line of advance via the village of La Croix Des Landes. "A direct advance up the road is the only way," wrote the Colonel. "So I say OK to Guy [Thirdfall] and off go Talbot Harvey's troop. After two or three minutes we hear an anti-tank gun fire about three shots. Harvey goes 'off the air' and Guy gets no reply. Shortly afterwards, Harvey's troop corporal returns in his tank, very shaken and in tears, to say that both leading tanks have been 'brewed up'." Livry was by now cleared, but with darkness falling, the advance was halted. It was well into the small hours before the supply vehicles could find their way forward among the great jam of British armour clogging the narrow road to refuel and re-arm the lead squadrons. The day's events had demonstrated how readily even small numbers of Germans could hamper the movement of a British armoured division in country where it was enormously difficult to present more than one small unit at a time to the enemy.

After reveille at 4.30 a.m. on the 13th, 7th Armoured renewed their advance towards Villers-Bocage through Livry, now led by 4th County of London Yeomanry under Lieutenant-Colonel Lord Cranley. The British column clattered up the winding road among the great chestnut trees before Villers, and into the town at about 8 a.m. without meeting opposition. The bulk of the regiment halted and its crews dismounted while Cranley, with one squadron of tanks, two command vehicles, and the Rifle Brigade motor company, moved on to their objective, the high ground of Point 213, one-and-a-half miles east of the town. They passed the tantalising concrete signpost with its bald legend: CAEN 24. Cranley deployed most of his A Squadron in the fields straddling the road, facing eastwards. The balance of the tanks, followed by the half-tracks of the Rifle Brigade, halted in a long column by the roadside down the long, straight slope yards behind them. The riflemen dismounted while their officers went forward for further orders. Montgomery signalled the news to De Guingand at his main headquarters in England: "So my pincer movement to get Caen is taking good shape, and there are distinct possibilities that the enemy divisions may not find it too easy to escape; especially Panzer Lehr . . ."

Yet already nemesis was approaching every British hope around Villers, in the form of a Tiger tank commanded by Captain Michael Wittman, leader of a group of five from the 501st SS Heavy Tank Battalion. His company had left Beauvais on 7 June, and after suffering severely from an air attack near Versailles on the 8th, had travelled only in darkness to reach their present position on 12 June. They had planned to spend the 13th making repairs and urgent maintenance on their tanks. But now Wittman stood in his turret studying the halted British column beyond Villers. The Germans were some 250 yards south of the road, well behind Cranley's forward screen. "They're acting as if they've won the war already," muttered his gunner, Corporal Woll. Wittman, already celebrated on the Eastern Front as the greatest panzer ace of the war, said calmly: "We're going to prove them wrong." At about 9.05 a.m. his Tiger, two more behind it, roared forward in line ahead, parallel to the Rifle Brigade column. A horrified British dispatch rider spotted the threat: "I called to Mr de Pass and told him, and he said something like it being one of ours. At this point I decided to tell Major Wright. He calmly informed me that he knew and that they were all round us." The Tigers swung towards the British line. The rear two halted and opened fire, while Wittman himself charged forward up a farm track towards the road, to begin one of the most devastating single-handed actions of the war.

His first 88 mm shell destroyed the rearmost of 4th CLY's Cromwells, while his second hit a Sherman Firefly in front of it. Then the Tiger reached the road, swerved left towards Villers, and roared down the hill machine-gunning the Rifle Brigade and their half-tracks at point-blank range. Lieutenant de Pass jumped up saying, "We must get the PIAT," and was killed instantly as he sought to clamber on to his vehicle. A few riflemen attempted to engage the Tigers with their 6pdr anti-tank guns before being shot down. Others ran desperately for open country as machine-gun fire raked the ditch in which they had taken refuge. "Looking back down the road towards the town," wrote a British officer, "it was possible to see a long column of blazing tanks and half-tracks, which had been hopelessly surprised by the unexpected attack – a 'school solution' ambush."

Having effectively written off the motor company, Wittman reached the top of the narrow high street of Villers, where the remainder of 4th CLY's Cromwells lay wholly unawares. Here, he destroyed three tanks of the HQ group, then that of Major Carr, the 2i/c whose driver frantically reversed into a garden, unable to fire more than three rounds because his loader was dismounted. Sergeant Stan Lockwood, a 30-year-old Londoner commanding a Sherman Firefly leading B Squadron, heard shooting start nearby, then saw a scout car race around the corner towards him, the driver waving his arms in frantic warning. Lockwood's Sherman nosed cautiously around a building to see before it, 200 yards away with its turret broadside on, Wittman's Tiger apparently firing up a sidestreet. Lockwood's gunner slammed four 17-pounder shots at the Tiger, one of which caused smoke and flame to appear on the hull. Then a shot from Wittman brought half the building above the Sherman down on to its hull, and before the British had extricated themselves from the debris, the German was gone. Only superficially damaged, Wittman's tank was able to demolish a last Cromwell before reversing away. Its commander, Captain Pat Dyas, escaped with the help of a local French girl to another tank of B Squadron, from which he radioed his commanding officer Lord Cranley with a report on the disastrous events in Villers. The Colonel could only reply that he knew the situation was desperate, but that he himself, along with the tanks of A Squadron, was at that moment being engaged by other Tigers. It was the regiment's last contact with him. At 10.30 a.m. he spoke for the last time to Brigadier Hinde, then his signals to brigade ceased. The surviving tanks of 4th CLY remained in their positions with a handful of riflemen amid intermittent shellfire, hoping for rescue. The officer commanding A Squadron had been killed by shellfire. An attempt by one Cromwell to probe an escape route up a track north-eastwards was terminated abruptly by German tank fire. Thereafter, there was little movement at

Point 213 for more than two hours. Brigade assumed that the British force was already destroyed. In reality, only at 1 p.m. did new German armour reach the scene, taking prisoner almost all the British survivors, including Lord Cranley. Captain Christopher Milner of the Rifle Brigade escaped alone on foot, to rejoin his formation the next day.

Meanwhile, in the town of Villers, a day of desperate fighting had begun. Infantry of the 1/7th Queens arriving to support 4th CLY encountered a German staff car and two motor-cycle combinations head on at the western approach of the town. They staged a brisk firefight with the survivors. They then planned to advance to the relief of Point 213. Cranley vetoed this by radio. A lull ensued until about 2 p.m., when a new German armoured and infantry attack on Villers developed, and the Queens hastily deployed among the houses to meet it. This time, with PIATs and anti-tank guns, the Germans were beaten off with the loss of seven tanks, including that of Wittman, although all the German crews escaped. Brigadier Hinde sent orders that the town must be held at all costs. Yet the Germans were also desperate to destroy the threat to their line. Lieutenant-Colonel Kurt Kauffman, Operations Officer of Panzer Lehr, personally assembled two 88 mm guns, three field guns and a ragtag of rear area troops and led them into the street fighting in Villers, while infantry of 2 Panzer moved up from the south. Intermittent fierce rain showers added to the trials of the combatants. Lieutenant Cotton of the CLY, finding his 95 mm-gunned tank useless in a battle of this kind, tidily disposed of it in a nearby garage and fought on foot, clutching an umbrella. Yet as evening approached, with the Queens' battalion headquarters pinned down and his men under constant heavy shellfire, their CO reported that he could halt German infantry infiltration only with reinforcements. These were not forthcoming. Throughout 7th Armoured's sector, its units were sending back to Hinde and Erskine disturbing reports of pressure and casualties from all points of the compass. "News trickled back," wrote a British scout car commander of 1st RTR, Sergeant Peter Roach:

The leading regiment . . . had run into real trouble . . . Regiment two was sitting dangerously tight while Jerry was making his way down the flanks . . . Chalky and I sat in the shelter of our hedge and watched. Someone was reporting a man moving towards him. Was it a civilian? Perhaps it was! No, it wasn't! It must be a German infantryman.

Suddenly the colonel's voice, with a touch of weariness and exasperation, "Besa the bugger then." . . . We were all refreshed; we knew what to do and were back in reality.

"We are in a corridor with enemy on both sides", wrote Lieutenant-Colonel Goulburn of the 8th Hussars, although his German opponents were simultaneously reporting to Army Group B the acute threat presented to their front by the British penetration. Around 6 p.m. that evening, with German reinforcements still concentrating around Villers, the surviving British forces were withdrawn to positions around Tracy-Bocage, two miles west, where Hinde had created a "brigade box". The surviving tanks of the City of London Yeomanry had been warned to time their retirement precisely, for as they departed a massive bombardment was to fall on Villers-Bocage to cover them, with American support from the west. Sergeant Lockwood's Sherman moved only a few yards across the square of Villers-Bocage before it stalled. The driver reported with horror: "I can't start the bloody thing!" Then, to their enormous relief, Sergeant Bill Moore jumped down from the turret of his following tank amidst the fierce sniping and machine-gun fire, shackled his cable to their hull, and towed them out of the town minutes before the barrage erupted. "We felt bad about getting out," said Lockwood. "It made it seem as if it had been such a waste." The day's fighting had cost 7th Armoured 25 tanks and 28 other armoured vehicles.

The following morning, further east, XXX Corps launched a new series of attacks by 50th Division against 901 Panzer-grenadiers in Tilly. The British were supported by 11 squadrons of fighter-bombers in an attempt to push back Panzer Lehr's units and generate sufficient pressure to enable 7th Armoured to renew its own offensive. But two brigades attacking on a 4000-yard front failed to gain ground. The Germans considered that the day was decided by the new *Panzerfaust*, the superb hand-held infantry anti-tank weapon which they were able to use to formidable effect against Allied tanks advancing in the close country. For reasons that will never be known, General Bucknall failed to ask Second Army for infantry reinforcements to provide direct support for the cut-off tanks of 7th Armoured. 1/7th Queens, which had fought so hard for Villers the previous day, had by now lost 8 officers and 120 other ranks. A massive artillery bombardment by American guns around Caumont broke up an attack on the British tank positions by 2 Panzer, but the 'brigade box' was now threatened with a serious risk of encirclement. Brigadier "Looney" Hinde drove up to his tank positions in a scout car, and began to give his officers their night orders for withdrawal, covered by the exhausted infantry of the Queens. Hinde had won his nickname in the desert both for courage and eccentricity. Now, he suddenly broke off in mid-sentence and peered fascinated at the ground. "Anybody got a matchbox?" he demanded in excitement. Amidst the acute strain of the battle, Lieutenant-Colonel Carver of 1st RTR suggested that this might not be a good moment to worry about nature. "Don't be such a bloody fool, Mike!" exploded Hinde. "You can fight a battle every day of your life, but you might not see a caterpillar like that in fifteen years!"

At the divisional commander's briefing for the withdrawal,

The Villers-Bocage battle: 11–14 June

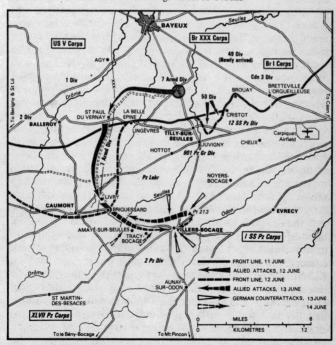

Lieutenant-Colonel Goulburn recorded the reasons given: "Firstly, 50 Div attack towards Longreves-Tilly, which commenced this morning, has made very little progress. Secondly, 2 Panzer Division has been identified on our front and it would appear that unless we can form a firm base back on our centre line with at least an infantry brigade (which we haven't got), he could cut off our communications, work round us and attack us from any direction." Early on the evening of the 14th, a heavy German attack on 22nd Armoured Brigade's "box" at Tracy-Bocage was repulsed. In its aftermath, the Germans were unable to impede 7th Armoured's disengagement and retreat under cover of darkness. They withdrew four miles to positions east of Caumont, their supporting infantry slumbering exhausted on the hulls of the Cromwells, in many cases too far gone to waken or to dismount even when they reached the safety of their new harbours.

By any measure, Villers-Bocage had been a wretched episode for the British, a great opportunity lost as the Germans now closed the gap in their line. As Second Army reviewed the events of the past four days, it was apparent that the Germans had handled a dangerous situation superbly, while XXX Corps and 7th Armoured division had notably failed to meet the responsibilities that had been thrust upon them. On 10/11 June, the division had begun its attack led by tanks widely separated from their supporting infantry. When they encountered snipers and pockets of resistance manned by only handfuls of Germans, the entire advance was blocked for lack of infantry close at hand to deal with them. High explosive shells fired by tanks possessed negligible ability to dislodge well dug-in troops, although invaluable in suppressing enemy fire to cover an infantry advance. When tanks met infantry in defensive positions supported by anti-tank weapons, their best and often only possible tactic was to push forward their own infantry within a matter of minutes to clear them, supported by mortars. Yet again and again in Normandy, British tanks outran their infantry, leaving themselves exposed to German anti-tank screens, and the foot soldiers without cover for their own movement under fire. The suspicion was also born at 21st Army Group, hardening rapidly in the weeks which followed, that 7th Armoured Division now seriously lacked the spirit and determination which made it so formidable a formation in the desert. Many of its veterans felt strongly that they had done their share of fighting in the

Mediterranean, and had become wary and cunning in the reduction of risk. They lacked the tight discipline which is even more critical on the battlefield than off it. The Tiger tank was incomparably a more formidable weapon of war than the Cromwell, but the shambles created by Wittman and his tiny force in Villers-Bocage scarcely reflected well upon the vigilance or tactics of a seasoned British armoured formation. Responsibility for the paralysis of purpose which overcame XXX Corps when 7th Armoured's tanks lay isolated at Tracy-Bocage after their initial withdrawal had to rest with its commander, General Bucknall, an officer henceforth treated with suspicion by Dempsey and Montgomery. Dempsey said:

This attack by 7th Armoured Division should have succeeded. My feeling that Bucknall and Erskine would have to go started with that failure. Early on the morning of 12 June I went down to see Erskine – gave him his orders and told him to get moving . . . If he had carried out my orders he would not have been kicked out of Villers-Bocage but by this time 7th Armoured Division was living on its reputation and the whole handling of that battle was a disgrace.

Yet the men of 7th Armoured Division bitterly resented any suggestion that, in the Villers battle, they had given less than their best. It was enormously difficult to adjust their tactics and outlook overnight to the new conditions of Normandy after years of fighting in the desert. They were newly-equipped with the inadequate Cromwell, which many of their gunners had scarcely test-fired, after fighting with Shermans in North Africa. There had been spectacular acts of individual heroism, many of which cost men their lives. The 1/7th Queens, especially, had fought desperately to hold the town. For those at the forefront of 22nd Armoured's battle, it was intolerable to suggest that somehow an easy opportunity had been thrown away through any fault of theirs. The German achievement on 13/14 June had been that, while heavily outnumbered in the sector as a whole, they successfully kept the British everywhere feeling insecure and off-balance, while concentrating sufficient forces to dominate the decisive points. The British, in their turn, failed to bring sufficient forces to bear upon these. It seems likely that Brigadier Hinde, while a superbly courageous exponent of "leading from the front", did not handle the large brigade group under his command as imaginatively as might have been possible, and higher formations failed to give him the support he needed. It is remarkable to reflect that the men on the spot believed a single extra infantry brigade could have been decisive in turning the scale at Villers, yet this was not forthcoming. Some 7th Armoured veterans later argued that Montgomery and Dempsey should have taken a much closer personal interest in a battle of such critical importance. For whatever reasons, the only conclusion must be that the British failed to concentrate forces that were available on the battlefield at a vital point at a critical moment of the campaign.

A sour sense, not of defeat, but of fumbled failure overlay the British operation on the western flank. On 11 June, while 7th Armoured was probing hesitantly south, on its left flank the 69th Brigade of 50th Division was hastily ordered forward to exploit what was believed to be another gap in the German line, around the village of Cristot. Lieutenant-Colonel Robin Hastings of the 6th Green Howards was mistrustful of the reported lack of opposition – he anyway lacked confidence in his elderly brigadier – and was no more sanguine after his battalion had waited three hours for transport to its start-line. When the Green Howards moved off, two companies up, they were quickly outdistanced by their supporting tanks of the 4th/7th Dragoon Guards, who raced forward along through the orchards. They failed to observe the hidden positions of panzergrenadiers of 12th SS Panzer, who had been rushed forward to secure the Cristot line in the hours since the British reconnaissance. Lying mute after the passage of the tanks, the SS poured a devastating fire on the Green Howards advancing through the corn, while anti-tank guns disposed of the British armour from their rear. Only two of the nine Shermans escaped, and the advancing infantry suffered appallingly.

With one company commander dead and the other wounded, Hastings' B and C Companies were pinned down. He ordered A to move up on the right and attempt to outflank the enemy. When he himself began to go forward to sort out B and C, his battalion headquarters came under such heavy fire that he was compelled to call up D Company, his last reserve, to clear the way ahead. CSM Stan Hollis, whose courage had done so much for the battalion on D-Day, was now commanding a platoon of D. As they advanced up a sunken lane edged with trees towards the enemy, they came under fierce fire from a German machine-gun. Hollis reached in his pouch for a grenade and found only a shaving brush. Demanding a grenade from the man behind, he tossed it before he realized, to his chagrin, that the had failed to pull the pin. A second later, he concluded that the Germans would not know that and charged them, firing his sten gun while they were taking cover from the expected explosion.

Hastings found that A and B Companies had joined up amid the burning British tanks, one turning out of control in continuous circles between the trees. They gathered the German prisoners and pressed on. Then A Company commander was killed, and the attack was again pinned down. The Green Howards had lost 24 officers and suffered a total of 250 casualties. "I think there's a lot of work for you to do, padre," said Hastings wearily to Captain Henry Lovegrove, who won a Military Cross that day. The padre searched the hedges and ditches around Cristot for hours. He became a smoker for the first time in his life after a few horrific burials. Lacking armoured support and an artillery fire plan, the Green Howards could not hold their ground against German counter-attacks. Bitterly, Hastings ordered a withdrawal. The SS immediately retook possession and by nightfall were counter-attacking towards the British startline on Hill 103.

Hastings remained bitter about the losses his men had sustained in an attack that he believed was misconceived – that was simply "not on" – a fragment of British army shorthand which carried especial weight when used at any level in the ordering of war. Before every attack, most battalion commanders made a private decision about whether its objectives were "on", and thereby decided whether its purpose justified an all-out effort, regardless of casualties, or merely sufficient movement to conform and to satisfy the higher formation. Among most of the units which landed in Normandy, there was a great initial reservoir of willingness to try, to give of their best in attack, and this was exploited to the full in the first weeks of the campaign. Thereafter, following bloody losses and failures, many battalion commanders determined privately that they would husband the lives of their men when they were ordered into attack, making personal judgements about an operation's value. The war had been in progress for a long time; now, the possibility of surviving it was in distant view. The longer men had been fighting, the more appealing that chance appeared. As the campaign progressed, as the infantry casualty lists rose, it became a more and more serious problem for the army commanders to persuade their battalions that the next ridge, tomorrow's map reference, deserved of their utmost. Hastings was among those who believed that an unnecessary amount of unit determination and will for sacrifice was expended in minor operations for limited objectives too early in the campaign. The problem of "non-trying" units was to become a thorn in the side of every division and corps commander, distinct from the normal demands of morale and leadership, although naturally associated with them.

EPSOM

The debacle at Villers-Bocage marked, for the British, the end of the scramble for ground that had continued since D-Day. The Germans had plugged the last vital hole in their line. Henceforward, for almost all the men who fought in Normandy, the principal memory would be of hard, painful fighting over narrow strips of wood and meadow; of weeks on end when they contested the same battered grid squares, the same ruined villages; of a battle of attrition which was at last to break down Rommel's divisions, but which seemed at the time to be causing equal loss and grief to the men of Dempsey's and Bradley's armies.

In the days following Villers-Bocage, unloading on the beaches fell seriously behind schedule in the wake of the "great storm" of 19/23 June, which cost the armies 140,000 tons of scheduled stores and ammunition. Montgomery considered and rejected a plan for a new offensive east of the Orne. With the remorseless build-up of opposing forces on the Allied perimeter, it was no longer sufficient to commit a single division in the hope of gaining significant ground. When Second Army began its third attempt to gain Caen by envelopment, Operation EPSOM, the entire VIII Corps was committed to attack on a four-mile front between Carpiquet and Rauray towards the thickly-wooded banks of the river Odon. Three of the finest divisions in the British Army – 15th Scottish, 11th Armoured and 43rd Wessex – were to take part, under the command of Lieutenant-General Sir Richard O'Connor, who had made a brilliant reputation for himself leading the first British campaign in the western desert. A personal friend of Montgomery since their days as Staff College instructors together in the 1920s, O'Connor had been captured and spent two years languishing in an Italian prisoner-of-war camp. This was to be his first battle since Beda Fomm in 1941. Early on the morning of 26 June, 60,000 men and more than 600 tanks, supported by over 700 guns on land and sea, embarked on the great new offensive: "The minute hand touched 7.30," wrote a young platoon commander of the King's Own Scottish Borderers:

Concealed guns opened from fields, hedges and farms in every direction around us, almost as if arranged in tiers. During short pauses between salvoes more guns could be heard, and right away, further guns, filling and reverberating the very atmosphere with a sustained, muffled hammering. It was like rolls of thunder, only it never slackened. Then the guns nearby battered out again with loud, vicious, strangely mournful repercussions. Little rashes of goose-flesh ran over the skin. One was hot and cold, and very moved. All this "stuff" in support of us! . . . So down a small winding road, with the absurd feeling that this was just another exercise.[1]

In the first hours, VIII Corps achieved penetrations on a three-mile frontage. But then, from out of the hedges and hamlets, fierce German resistance developed. Some of the great Scottish regiments of the British army – Gordons, Seaforths, Cameronians – began to pour out their best blood for every yard of ground gained. Lieutenant Edwin Bramall of the 2nd KRRC, later to become professional head of the British army, observed that a battalion of the Argylls which infiltrated forward in small groups by use of cover reached their objectives with modest casualties. But the great mass of the British advance moved forward in classic infantry formation: "It was pretty unimaginative, all the things that we had learned to do at battle school. A straightforward infantry bash."[2] That evening, the young platoon commander of the KOSB wrote again:

Rifle fire from the village periodically flared up. We were in bewildering ignorance of what was happening. The rain dripped and trickled into our slits, and there had been no hot food since before dawn. The big shells banging away on the T-roads jarred us, while the faces of the three dead Fusiliers could still be seen there as pale blobs through the gloom and rain, motionless among the shells, with their ghastly whiteness. And this, and those savage crashes, and the great spreadeagled hounds, and the grim churchyard across the wall, evoked a dull weight of depression such as one could never have dreamed. All the elation of the morning had ebbed away. It seemed there was no hope or sanity left, but only this appalling unknown and unseen, in which life was so precious where all rooted, and where all was loneliness and rain.[3]

The prose of Passchendaele seemed born again. A new experience very terrible in kind was being created in Normandy – that of the infantry soldier locked in battle of an intensity few men of

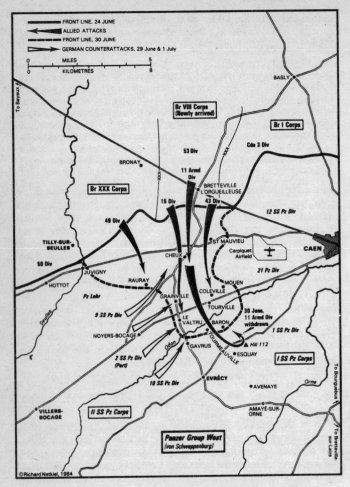

FRONT LINE, 24 JUNE
ALLIED ATTACKS
FRONT LINE, 30 JUNE
GERMAN COUNTERATTACKS, 29 June & 1 July

MILES 0 — 5
KILOMETRES 0 — 8

To Bayeux

BASLY

Br VIII Corps
(Newly arrived)

Br I Corps

53 Div

Cdn 3 Div

BRONAY

11 Armd
Div

BRETTEVILLE
L'ORGUEILLEUSE

Br XXX Corps

15 Div

43 Div

12 SS Pz Div

49 Div

ST MAUVIEU

TILLY-SUR-
SEULLES

Carpiquet
Airfield

CAEN

50 Div

CHEUX

JUVIGNY

21 Pz Div

HOTTOT

RAURAY

Pz Lehr

MOUEN

COLEVILLE

Seulles

GRAINVILLE

TOURVILLE

9 SS Pz Div

LE
VALTRU

30 June,
11 Armd Div
withdraws

BARON

1 SS Pz Div

NOYERS-BOCAGE

GAVRUS

TOURMAUVILLE

Odon

▲ Hill 112

ESQUAY

I SS Pz Corps

2 SS Pz Div
(Part)

EVRECY

10 SS Pz Div

AVENAYE

Orne

To Bourguébus

VILLERS-
BOCAGE

AMAYE-SUR-
ORNE

II SS Pz Corps

Panzer Group West
(von Schweppenburg)

To Bretteville-
sur-Laize

©Richard Natkiel, 1984

Operation EPSOM: 26 June–1 July

the Allied armies had ever envisaged at their battle schools in
Britain. Nor was the struggle much less painful for the crews of
the armoured units. A tank wireless-operator of the 4th/7th
Dragoon Guards on the British left flank recorded in his diary

the fortunes of his squadron on the morning of 26 June:

The whole squadron was now in the field, with the tanks scattered around by the hedges. We soon discovered from the wireless that we were in a trap. There appeared to be Tigers and Panthers all around us – there were about six on the high ground ahead, four in the edge of the wood just across the field to our left. Between them they covered every gap. The hours dragged by. In our tank we sat without saying much, listening intently to what was going on over the wireless. I was eating boiled sweets by the dozen and the others were smoking furiously. I didn't know how long we'd been sitting there when the tank behind us was hit. It was Joe Davis's. I saw a spout of earth shoot up near it as a shot ricochetéd through it. Some smoke curled up from the turret, but it didn't actually brew up. We did not know till after that the whole turret crew had been killed. Brian Sutton and his co-driver baled out, but I didn't see them. That made six of the squadron killed already that day. In Lilly's crew Fairman had been killed inside the tank and Digger James had been blown apart by a mortar bomb as he jumped off the turret. Charrison was badly burnt and George Varley was rumoured to be dead. One of Thompson's crew, Jackie Birch, had been shot through the head by a King's Royal Rifle Corps man who mistook him for a Jerry after he baled out . . .

The Tyneside Scottish came back across the field in single file, led by a piper who was playing what sounded like a lament. I felt lucky to be alive.[4]

A German counter-attack was repulsed on 27 June. The next day, in mud and rain, tanks of 11th Armoured at last poured across the bloody stream of the Odon to gain the heights of Hill 112 on 29 June. Now, at the desperate bidding of General Dollman of Seventh Army, who committed suicide a day later, General Hausser of II SS Panzer Corps launched a major counter-attack. 9th and 10th SS Panzer Divisions, newly arrived from the east, were hurled against VIII Corps – and driven back. It was a fine fighting achievement by the British divisions and their air support, marred by the tragedy that, at this moment, General Dempsey misread the balance of advantage. Still expecting a greater effort from Hausser's Panthers, he concluded that O'Connor's exhausted men were dangerously exposed east of the Odon. On 29 June, he ordered the withdrawal of 11th Armoured to the west bank. The next day, Hill 112 was lost. Montgomery ordered that EPSOM should be closed down. VIII Corps had lost 4,020 men, 2,331 from 15th Scottish Division, 1,256 from 11th Armoured and 43rd Division.

Major Charles Richardson of 6th KOSB came out of EPSOM,

his first battle, overcome with horror and disgust after seeing his battalion lose 150 casualties. "We were one big family. I knew every man."[5] He remembered a briefing from a psychiatrist before leaving England, who said that if men wanted to talk about a terrible experience they had endured, it was essential to let them do so rather than to stifle it in their minds. Talk they now did, about the spectacle of the Royal Scots Fusiliers cresting a hill to find the Germans dug in on the reverse slope, "something we had never envisaged"; about the Germans who shot it out until the Borderers were within yards of their positions and then raised their hands, "much good it did them"; about the vital importance of keeping pace with the rolling barrage of the guns.

One of the most remarkable features of EPSOM, like almost all the Normandy battles, was that its failure provoked no widespread loss of confidence by the troops in their commanders generally, or Montgomery in particular, the one general familiar to them all. Senior officers criticized and cursed errors of tactics and judgement. The men fighting the battles became more cautious in action, more reluctant to sacrifice their own lives when told for the third, fourth, fifth time that a given operation was to be decisive. But at no time did their faith in the direction of the campaign falter. "We thought the senior officers were marvellous," said Trooper Stephen Dyson: "They had all the responsibility, didn't they?"[6] Lieutenant Andrew Wilson of The Buffs ". . . found it increasingly difficult to see how we should get out of all this – it seemed an absolute deadlock. There was some effect on morale, and places got a bad name, like Caumont. But when Montgomery passed us one day in his staff car all my crew stood up in the tank and cheered."[7] Lieutenant David Priest of 5th DCLI said: "I though it was going alright, but it might take years. We didn't seem to move very much."[8]

After the war, Montgomery said:

Of course we would have liked to get Caen on the first day and I was never happy about the left flank until we had got Caen. But the important thing on the flank was to maintain our strength so that we could not only avoid any setback, but could keep the initiative by attacking whenever we liked. On this flank ground was of no importance at all. I had learnt from the last war the senseless sacrifice that can be made by sentimental attachment to a piece of ground. All I asked Dempsey to do was to keep German armour tied down on this flank so that my breakout with the Americans could go more easily. Ground did not matter so long as the German divisions stayed on this flank. If I had attacked Caen in early June I might have wrecked the whole plan.[9]

It was in consequence of nonsense such as this that a great professional soldier caused so much of the controversy about the Normandy campaign to focus upon his own actions. By his determination to reap the maximum personal credit for victory and to distort history to conform with his own advance planning, he also heaped upon himself the lion's share of responsibility for much that went wrong in Normandy. No sane commander could have mounted British attacks of the kind that took place in June and were to follow in July without every hope of breaking through the German defences, or at least of causing the enemy to make substantial withdrawals. Part of Montgomery's exceptional quality as a commander lay in his ability to retain an atmosphere of poise, balance and security within his armies when a less self-disciplined general could have allowed dismay and disappointment to seep through the ranks. Montgomery served his own interests and those of his men very well by maintaining his insistence to his subordinates that all was going to plan. But he did himself a great disservice by making the same assertions in private to Eisenhower, Churchill, Tedder and even his unshakeable patron, Brooke.

Even Montgomery's admirers concede the lack of concern for truth in his make-up.[10] Like Sherlock Holmes' silent dog, an interesting sidelight on the general's character is revealed by the episode of the salmon before D-Day. Visiting troops in Scotland, he cast a fly on the Spey with signal lack of success. On his return, he sent a fish to his close friends the Reynolds, who ran a school, with a note: "I have just got back from Scotland and I send you a salmon – a magnificent fish of some 18 lb. I hope it will feed the whole school."[11] It would be a natural assumption of anyone receiving such a note and such a gift to assume that the donor had caught it himself. Many men would have inserted a jesting line to explain that this was not the case. It seems typical of Montgomery that, while not positively asserting that the salmon was his own prize, he was perfectly content to leave such an assumption in the minds of the Reynolds.

Montgomery's version of the fiasco at Villers-Bocage on 12/13 June was given in an equally characteristic letter to Brooke on the 14th:

When 2nd Panzer division suddenly appeared in the Villers-Bocage–Caumont area, it plugged the hole through which I had broken. I think it had been meant for offensive action against I Corps in the Caen area. So long as Rommel uses his strategic reserves to plug holes, that is good.

Anyhow, I had to think again, and I have got to be careful not to get off balance.[12]

Montgomery was perfectly justified in telling Brooke that the German commitment of armour to create a defensive perimeter was in the long-term interests of the Allies. But it was, of course, preposterous to assert that 7th Armoured Division had "broken through" anything before it encountered Captain Wittman's Tiger tank. Only the leading elements of 2nd Panzer were deployed in the area in time to influence Erskine's withdrawal. It must be to Montgomery's credit that, while he accepted any available glory for his army's achievements, he did not seek to burden it with blame for failures. But it was rash to expect shrewd and thoroughly informed officers at the War Office and SHAEF to accept indefinitely and at face value such travesties of reality as the account above. As Villers-Bocage was followed by EPSOM, and EPSOM by GOODWOOD, it was not the doings of Second Army, but Montgomery's version of them, that became more and more difficult for his peers and critics to swallow. As early as 15 June, Leigh-Mallory recorded his reservations about the handling of the ground campaign in a fashion that was widely echoed among the other airmen, and Montgomery's enemies:

As an airman I look at the battle from a totally different point of view. I have never waited to be told by the army what to do in the air, and my view is not bounded, as seems to be the case with the army, by the nearest hedge or stream. I said as much, though in different words, to Monty and tried to describe the wider aspects of this battle as I see them, particularly stressing the number of divisions which he might have had to fight had they not been prevented from appearing on the scene by air action. He was profoundly uninterested. The fact of the matter is, however, that we have reduced the enemy's opposition considerably and the efficiency of their troops and armour even more so. In spite of this, the army just won't get on . . . The fact remains that the great advantage originally gained by the achievement of surprise in the attack has now been lost.[13]

Much attention has been focussed since the war upon the issue of whether Montgomery's strategy in Normandy did or did not work as he had intended. The implicit assumption is that if it did not, his methods were unsound. Yet his initial plan to seize Caen, and his later movements to envelop the town, seem admirably conceived. The failure lay in their execution. The focus of debate about many Allied disappointments in Normandy should not be upon Montgomery or for that matter Rommel, but upon the subordinate commanders and formations who fought the battles. How

172

was it possible that German troops facing overwhelming firepower and air power, often outnumbered, drawn from an army that had been bled of two million dead in three years on the eastern front, could mount such a formidable resistance against the flower of the British and American armies?

The British experience during the June battles gave their commanders little cause for satisfaction about the fighting power of many of their troops, the tactics that they had been taught to employ, or the subordinate commanders at division and corps level by whom they were led. Earlier in the war Brooke wrote gloomily: "Half our corps and divisional commanders are totally unfit for their appointments. If I were to sack them, I could find no better! They lack character, drive and power of leadership. The reason for this state of affairs is to be found in the losses we sustained in the last war of all our best officers who should now be our senior officers."[14] Even in 1944, it was striking to compare the very high quality of Montgomery's staff at 21st Army Group with the moderate talents revealed by many field commanders of corps and divisions. Bucknall was already suspect as a leader of large forces. Some of those working most closely with O'Connor believed that he too fell short of the qualities needed for corps command in Europe in 1944. Much as he was liked by his staff, many of his officers believed that he had been out of the war too long now to take a grip on a vast new battlefield. At divisional level, confidence had been lost in Erskine. There were doubts about G. I. Thomas of 43rd Division – "the butcher" as he was known – one of the most detested generals in the British army. The performance and leadership of 51st Highland was the subject of deep disappointment.

Regret to report it is considered opinion Crocker, Dempsey and myself that 51st Division is at present not – NOT – battleworthy [Montgomery cabled to Brooke in July]. It does not fight with determination and has failed in every operation it has been given to do. It cannot fight the Germans successfully; I consider the divisional commander is to blame and I am removing him from command.[15]

After paying tribute to the manner in which the Canadian 3rd Division performed on D-Day, General Crocker of 1 Corps wrote to Dempsey early in July expressing dismay about its failure in a new attempt to gain Carpiquet airfield, and deploring the manner in which since 6 June:

Once the excitement of the initial phase passed, however, the Div lapsed into a very nervy state . . . Exaggerated reports of enemy activity and of their own difficulties were rife; everyone was far too quick on the trigger, and a general attitude of despondency prevailed . . . The state of the Div was a reflection of the state of its commander. He was obviously not standing up to the strain and showing signs of fatigue and nervousness (one might almost say fright) which were patent for all to see.[16]

Early reports from Normandy about the tactical performance of British troops dwelt upon their sluggishness in attack, their lack of the flexibility and initiative which – in defiance of all the caricatures of propaganda – were such a remarkable characteristic of German operations at every level. The close country overwhelmingly favoured defence, as the Allies discovered to their advantage whenever the Germans embarked upon counterattacks. But throughout the Normandy campaign, the strategic onus of movement lay upon the Allies, and thus their weakness in armoured-infantry co-operation told severely against them. "Armoured divisions have been slow to appreciate the importance of infantry in this type of fighting," declared an early War Office report circulated to all commanding officers.[17]

It is quite clear from even a short experience of fighting in this type of country that the tanks require a great deal more infantry than the motor battalion can provide . . . This co-operation works very well if the tank and infantry commanders of corresponding formations see the picture from the same angle and have a good knowledge of each other's role, in fact "muck in". But where such co-operation is lacking, then valuable time is wasted while higher authority is asked to adjudicate.[18]

A reasonable level of understanding between infantry and tank commanders on the battlefield was often absent. The infantry elements of British armoured divisions seldom, if ever, achieved the vital integration with their tanks that was fundamental to the German panzergrenadiers, who were also equipped with an exceptionally good armoured half-track vehicle to carry them across the battlefield. This must partly be attributed to the parochialism inseparable from the British regimental system. An immense source of strength in sustaining pride and morale, on a vast battlefield such as that of Normandy the regimental system could also become a handicap. German loyalties were to the division as a whole, and absolute mutual support within the division was bred as second nature into the German soldier. There remained a tendency among British battalions to concern themselves almost exclusively with their own affairs in battle.

The Panzer Mk V, or Panther, was the outstanding German tank of the campaign in north-west Europe, less heavily gunned but more mobile and reliable than the Tiger. One of the two tank regiments in almost every German armoured division was equipped with the Panther, which weighed 45 tons, could move at 34 mph, and carried 100 mm of frontal armour, 45 mm of side armour. Its 75 mm KwK 42 gun had a muzzle velocity of 3060 fps, and its 14-pound shell could penetrate 138 mm of armour at 100 yards, 128 mm at 500 yards, 118 mm at 1,000 yards. Its only serious weaknesses against the Sherman were indifferent periscope optics and slow turret traverse.

The infantry and armoured brigade commanders of one elite British armoured division were scarcely on speaking terms with each other in Normandy. Lieutenant-Colonel Hay of the 5th/7th Gordons was exasperated when he climbed on a young troop commander's tank during one of the desperate battles in the Orne bridgehead, and was unable to persuade the officer to advance in support because he considered the risk to his tanks too great. Conversely, following the EPSOM battle, the infantry brigade commander and two battalion COs of one British armoured division had to be sacked. Their divisional commander spoke furiously of the brigadier, "who dug a slit trench at the beginning of the battle and never left it".[19]

The SHAEF appreciation of the Normandy battlefield in April had correctly assessed the *bocage* as country in which, "it will

. . . be most difficult for the enemy to prevent a slow and steady advance by infiltration".[20] The Germans were masters of this art, working small parties behind Allied positions and forcing the defenders out by showing that their flanks were turned. Allied infantry seldom employed the technique, and thus denied themselves an important means of progress in close country. Their commanders relied almost invariably upon the setpiece battalion attack, with two companies forward. This tactic was far too rigid and predictable to defeat a determined defence. In a circular to commanding officers late in June, Montgomery made a vain effort to urge units to show more flexibility. He deplored the habit of preparing troops to fight "the normal battle". He wrote: "This tendency is highly dangerous, as there is no such thing as 'the normal battle'. Leaders at all levels must adapt their actions to the particular problems confronting them."[21] The problem had been succinctly analysed a few weeks earlier by a British corps commander in Italy:

The destruction of the enemy was most easily achieved when we managed to keep him tired and in a state of disorganisation, which resulted in unco-ordinated defence and lack of food, petrol and ammunition. We were undoubtedly too inelastic in our methods when faced with changing conditions. After six weeks of mobile fighting, during which the enemy never launched anything bigger than weak company counter-attacks, we still talked too much about "firm bases" and "exposed flanks".[22]

It is interesting to turn to German intelligence reports of this period, such as one from Panzer Lehr which declared it "a successful break-in by the enemy was seldom exploited to pursuit. If our own troops were ready near the front for a local counter-attack, the ground was immediately regained. Enemy infantry offensive action by night is limited to small reconnaissance patrols." The Germans quickly developed the technique of holding their front line with only observation posts and a thin defensive screen, holding the bulk of their forces further back, to move forward when the huge Allied bombardments died away: "It is better to attack the English, who are very sensitive to close combat and flank attack, at their weakest moment – that is, when they have to fight without their artillery."[23] A German report from Italy at about this time is also worth quoting, for it reflects similar criticisms made by Rommel's officers in Normandy:

The conduct of the battle by the Americans and English was, taken all round, once again very methodical. Local successes were seldom exploited . . . British attacking formations were split up into large numbers of assault squads commanded by officers. NCOs were rarely in the "big picture", so that if the officer became a casualty, they were unable to act in accordance with the main plan. The result was that in a quickly changing situation, *the junior commanders showed insufficient flexibility*. For instance, when an objective was reached, the enemy would neglect to exploit and dig in for defence. The conclusion is: as far as possible *go for the enemy officers*. Then seize the initiative yourself.[24] [Emphases in original.]

Another German report, captured in north-west Europe, was circulated to British senior officers: "The British infantryman," it declared, "is distinguished more by physical endurance than by special bravery. The impetuous attack, executed with dash, is foreign to him. He is sensitive to energetic counter-attack."[25] It is natural that most histories of the Normandy campaign have focussed upon the many acts of courage by British troops, and said less about the occasions on which whole units collapsed under pressure. By this stage of the war, the British Army found that it never possessed as many first-rate officer's and NCOs as it wished, and the performance of some units caused deep dismay at Twenty-First Army Group. The consequence was that the best formations had to be thrust forward again and again in the heart of the battle, while others were considered too unreliable to be entrusted with a vital role in operations. On 30 June, the commanding officer of a battalion suffering serious problems in Normandy, 49th Division's 6th Duke of Wellington's Regiment, wrote a report which bears quoting in full, because it portrays so vividly the strain that the battle thrust upon units which lacked the outstanding qualities of, for instance, 6th Airborne or 15th Scottish:

1. I arrived at 6 DWR on the evening of 26 June. From am 27 June until am 30 June we have been in contact with the enemy and under moderately heavy mortar and shell fire.

2. The following facts make it clear that this report makes no reflection on the state of 6 DWR when they left UK:
   a) In 14 days there have been some 23 officer and 350 OR casualties.
   b) Only 12 of the original officers remain and they are all junior. The CO and every rank above Cpl (except for 2 Lts) in battalion HQ have gone, all company commanders have gone. One company has lost every officer, another has only one left.
   c) Since I took over I have lost two second-in-commands in successive days and a company commander the third day.

d) Majority of transport, all documents, records and a large amount of equipment was lost.

3. *State of Men*

a) 75% of the men react adversely to enemy shelling and are "jumpy".

b) 5 cases in 3 days of self-inflicted wounds – more possible cases.

c) Each time men are killed or wounded a number of men become casualties through shell shock or hysteria.

d) In addition to genuine hysteria a large number of men have left their positions after shelling on one pretext or another and gone to the rear until sent back by the M.O. or myself.

e) the new drafts have been affected, and 3 young soldiers became casualties with hysteria after hearing our own guns.

f) The situation has got worse each day as more key personnel have become casualties.

4. *Discipline and Leadership*

a) State of discipline is bad, although the men are a cheerful, pleasant type normally.

b) NCOs do not wear stripes and some officers have no badges of rank. This makes the situation impossible when 50% of the battalion do not know each other.

c) NCO leadership is weak in most cases and the newly drafted officers are in consequence having to expose themselves unduly to try to get anything done. It is difficult for the new officers (60%) to lead the men under fire as they do not know them.

Conclusion

a) 6 DWR is not fit to take its place in the line.

b) Even excluding the question of nerves and morale 6 DWR will not be fit to go back into the line until it is remobilised, reorganised, and to an extent retrained. It is no longer a battalion but a collection of individuals. There is naturally no esprit de corps for those who are frightened (as we all are to one degree or another) to fall back on. I have twice had to stand at the end of a track and draw my revolver on retreating men.

Recommendation

If it is not possible to withdraw the battalion to the base or UK to re-equip, reorganise and train, then it should be disbanded and split among other units.

If it is not possible to do either of the above and if it is essential that the battalion should return to the line, I request that I may be relieved of my command and I suggest that a CO with 2 or 3 years experience should relieve me, and that he should bring his adjutant and a signals officer with him.

Being a regular officer I realise the seriousness of this request and its effect on my career. On the other hand I have the lives of the new officer personnel (which is excellent) to consider. Three days running a major has been killed or seriously wounded because I have ordered him to in effect stop them running during mortar concentrations. Unless withdrawn from the division I do not think I can get the battalion fit to fight normally and this waste of life would continue. My honest opinion is that if you continue to throw new officer and other rank replacements into 6 DWR as casualties occur, you are throwing good money after bad.

I know my opinion is shared by two other commanding officers who know the full circumstances.

In the field
30 June 1944   (Sgd)_____, Lt-Col., Commanding, 6 DWR[27]

If the difficulties of 6th DWR were exceptional, it is seldom that the plight of a moderate unit under pressure on the battlefield is so precisely chronicled. Montgomery, on whose desk this report finally arrived, was furious. He wrote to the Secretary of State for War, P. J. Grigg, saying that he had withdrawn 6th DWR from the 49th Division, and castigating its commanding officer: "I consider that the CO displays a defeatist mentality and is not a 'proper chap'."[28] The unit was disbanded. The Commander-in-Chief perhaps had no other option but to adopt a ruthless attitude to any manifestation of failing will at this juncture in the battle. If some divisions had proved capable of extraordinary exertions and sacrifices, in a struggle of such magnitude it was the overall quality of the army, rather than of a small number of outstanding units within it, which would determine its outcome. It was because of problems such as these that Montgomery found it necessary to keep elite formations, such as 6th Airborne, in action long after their casualties and exhaustion made them deserving candidates for relief. It must also be said that even average German formations proved capable of continuing to fight effectively when reduced to 25 per cent of their strength. None of the German formations transferred from the eastern front to Normandy were found wanting by their commanders because they had been over-exposed to action, as 7th Armoured and 51st Highland were. When the war was over that most astringent of military critics, Captain Basil Liddell Hart, made his own comments upon the performance of British units in Normandy:

Time after time they were checked or even induced to withdraw by boldly handled pockets of Germans of greatly inferior strength. But for our air superiority, which hampered the Germans at every turn, the results would have been much worse. Our forces seem to have had too

179

little initiative in infiltration, and also too little determination – with certain exceptions. Repeatedly one finds that big opportunities were forfeited because crucial attacks were stopped after suffering trifling casualties. That was particularly marked with the armoured formations.[29]

Montgomery's massive conceit masked the extent to which his own generalship in Normandy fell victim to the inability of his army to match the performance of their opponents on the battlefield. After all the months of meticulous training and preparation for OVERLORD, British tactics were shown to be not only unimaginative, but also inadequate to cope with the conditions of Normandy. Battalion and brigade commanders seemed capable of little beyond the conventional setpiece assault "by the book". It may be argued that it was Montgomery's business to adjust his plans to the limitations of his forces. But it was enormously difficult, indeed all but impossible, to retrain an army, to change the entire tactical thinking of a generation, in mid-campaign. Montgomery was uncommonly skilled in making the most of the units he had, discerning the qualities that suited a certain division to a certain role. It was he himself who declared that the British are a martial, not a military people. There was nothing cowardly about the performance of the British army in Normandy. But it proved too much to ask a citizen army in the fifth year of war, with the certainty of victory in the distance, to display the same sacrificial courage as Hitler's legions, faced with the collapse of everything that in the perversion of Nazism they held dear. Brigadier Williams said: "We were always very aware of the doctrine, 'Let metal do it rather than flesh'. The morale of our troops depended upon this. We always said: 'Waste all the ammunition you like, but not lives.' "[30]

But in Normandy, the Allied armies discovered the limits of what metal alone could achieve. Individual Allied soldiers proved capable of immense sacrifice and bravery; men who felt – like Sergeant-Major Hollis of the Green Howards or Corporal Kelly of the 314th Infantry at Cherbourg – that winning the war was their personal responsibility. But the British failure to gain Caen in June 1944 revealed a weakness of fighting power and tactics within the British army much more than a failure of generalship by Sir Bernard Montgomery.

5 The Americans before Cherbourg

The bocage

Something between a week and a month of intense action suffices to transform most infantryman from novices – unable to discern the source of firing, uncertain of the scale of danger, unconvinced of the need to dig deep – into veterans or casualties. In the days following 6 June, the American forces in Normandy faced few German opponents of the quality and determination of those who were already moving into battle against the British Second Army. But for the men of Bradley's divisions, fighting first to unite their beachheads, then to expand these and secure Cherbourg and the Contentin Peninsula, the first encounters with the enemy in the close confinement of the Norman *bocage* proved a testing experience. "Although there had been some talk in the U.K. before D-Day about the hedgerows," wrote Gavin of the 82nd Airborne, "none of us had really anticipated how difficult they would be."[1] The huge earthen walls, thickly woven with tree and brush roots, that bordered every field were impenetrable to tanks; each one was a natural line of fortification. In the Cotentin, the difficulties of the ground were compounded by wide areas of reclaimed marshland likewise impassable to armour, which was thus restricted to the roads. Gerow's V Corps, which had endured so much to secure Omaha beach, was fortunate during the next phase of their advance inland in meeting few German reinforcements – only the 30th Mobile Brigade began to arrive on 7 June to support the badly mauled 352nd Division. The American 29th Division, which had revealed its lack of experience on D-Day, made slow work of its move westward to link up with the survivors of the Ranger companies still holding out on Pointe du Hoc.

"Those goddam Bosch just won't stop fighting," Huebner of 1st Division complained to Bradley, when the latter hitched a lift ashore in a DUKW on the morning of the 7th.[2] But the 18th and

181

26th Regiments of 1st Division pushed forward to link up with the British XXX Corps across the river Drome on 8 June, and Isigny was cleared on the night of 7/8 June. The redoubtable Brigadier-General Cota of 29th Division was one of the first men into the ruined town, where the Americans found only the acrid smell of burning and the crackle of flames from buildings ignited by shells and bombs lighting up the darkness:

"Hell, they didn't even blow the bridge", Cota yelled to Co. Gill as he walked across the sturdy stone span [related the divisional after-action narrative]. Everyone was on edge waiting for sniper fire, and it was fortunate for the few prisoners that dribbled out of the ruins that they did not get shot. One of them offered to lead our men to a place where 14 of his comrades were hiding. He said they'd give up but were afraid to come out. A patrol was hastily organised, and under the prisoner's direction, rounded up his fellow soldiers.[3]

Cota dispatched a liaison officer, Lieutenant Delcazel, to report to the division that Isigny was clear. Less than a mile along the road to the division CP, his jeep was surrounded by armed men who disarmed the lieutenant and his driver and took them back to their positions. It emerged that these were not Germans, but a hodgepodge of Poles, Serbs and Russians whose officers and NCOs had fled, and who were chiefly concerned to find the means to surrender safely. They were mortally frightened of being intercepted by nearby German troops, who would shoot them at once if their intentions became apparent. After much discussion with the captured Americans, on the morning of 10 June they marched fully armed down the road towards Maisy until they encountered an astonished American half-track driver. Delcazel ran forward shouting, "Don't shoot! Don't shoot! They want to surrender.' 75 men walked forward and laid down their weapons. A squadron of impeccably-attired White Russian cavalrymen in astrakhan hats, who surrendered a few days later, sent forward a deputation to an American reconnaissance troop to demand it strength. They declared that they were eager to give up, but could only do so in the face of a substantial force. The Americans convinced them that they were in sufficient strength for honour to be served. In those first days after the landings, First Army found the quality of their opposition extraordinarily uneven: at one moment a handful of GIs were receiving wholesale enemy surrenders; at the next, an entire division was being held up by the stubborn resistance of a company of Germans with a detachment of anti-tank guns.

182

Following the capture of Isigny and the link-up of Omaha and Utah, the eastern American flank gave the Allied high command little anxiety in the aftermath of its troubled landings. All attention was focussed north-westwards, upon the struggle of General Collins' VII Corps to secure the Cotentin. Montgomery was eager that V Corps should press on southwards while Collins moved west and north, but Bradley told his commanders: "Nobody's going anywhere until Joe gets Cherbourg. I want to see Pete and Gee dug in solidly on their fronts. The other fellow might still hit them, and we're not going to risk his busting through to Omaha beach . . ."[4]

The German forces in the peninsula lacked the mobility and cohesion to mount a large-scale counter-attack against the Utah beachhead. But they could still defend the hedgerows and causeways with bitter tenacity, and launch a succession of local assaults in battalion or regimental strength which, at times, caused the American command much anxiety. 7 June found the airborne divisions still fighting hard to concentrate their scattered companies, and to gain the elusive passages through the floods which alone could promise Collins' corps a breakout from the beaches. Bradley told Collins to pour all the air power he wished onto Carentan, "and take the city apart. Then rush it and you'll get in."[5] It quickly emerged that by no means all the American units coming ashore could match the paratroopers' determination or skill on the battlefield. Jittery leading elements of the 90th Division moving forward from Utah encountered an approaching column of German prisoners, and opened fire upon them with every weapon they possessed. When the 325th Gliderborne Infantry were shown by Gavin and his tired soldiers where they were to make their attack, their battalion commander declared that he did not feel well, and had to be relieved. When the unit finally advanced in the face of German fire, on this first encounter with the enemy, they halted and could not be persuaded to move. Gavin was compelled to signal his paratroopers to pass through and seize the objective themselves. The airborne divisions had expected early relief after carrying out their D-Day missions – withdrawal to England to prepare for a new parachute operation. Yet because of a serious shortage of determined and competent American infantry, they were now to be called upon to fight through to the end of the battle for the Cotentin. Their experience and their achievement, lightly armed and having borne the brunt of the first fighting for the peninsula without armoured support, proved that an elite American force could match the troops of any army in Normandy. But those of them who had experienced little action before found the process of learning as painful as any line infantryman.

Private Richardson of the 82nd Airborne – who unlike most of his comrades had not seen action – was last seen asleep in a field in the midst of the Cotentin on the evening of 6 June. By the night of the 7th, he was dug into a hedgerow looking out across a field to a wood, amid the machine-gun platoon of his battalion:

Someplace far off in the distance beyond the woods I began to hear a squeaking noise. It was the sound of a rusty wheel that needed grease, the sound of an old farm wagon I'd often heard around my farming village home. Some French farmer hauling goods? That seemed unlikely with two armies poised with uneasy fingers on the triggers of a thousand guns. Germans? That too seemed unlikely. If the Germans were moving through territory where we might be, wouldn't they be silent? Wouldn't they creep practically on tiptoe? I dismissed the idea that this distance noise meant anything dangerous, or tried to. The trouble was the noise, the only noise in the whole night around me, was coming our way. For a time there was a silence, then I heard someone shout "HALT!" and immediately a burst of fire – sub-machine gun, German. What was happening? Why wasn't the machine-gun platoon doing something? Finally there was firing from one of our machine-guns, the slower dat-dat-dat, tracer bullets though instead of being aimed were going up into the sky in a crazy wavering arc. I finally woke Johnson up and we sat there staring at the tracers flying around the sky. When the shooting stopped we could hear the Germans running around yelling and gradually moving back towards the road near the house. Then the house was on fire, and after a time the vehicle that made the squeaking noise started up again, but this time it headed down the road away from us.[6]

The Germans resumed their attack on the paratroopers' position early the following afternoon. Richardson fired only one round from the MI rifle he had picked up before it jammed, and he understood why its original owner had thrown it away. Feeling helpless and nervous, he began to shoot single rounds towards the woods from which the enemy fire seemed to be coming, pausing after each shot to ram home the sticking bolt. As a small boy, he had read a series of splendid children's adventure stories entitled *American Boys Over There*, which had planted a vivid image in his mind of big-bellied, heavy-booted "huns" or "bosch" charging across a field in spiked helmets against American doughboys, who eventually prevailed. Now, at each warning of a new German assault, he saw this picture more clearly. And at last, it became a reality. A solitary tank began to rattle slowly across the field towards the Americans, who could confront it only with fierce machine-gun fire. To their astonishment and delight, suddenly it halted. A plume of smoke rose from its turret. This was no Panther or Tiger, but some French-built makeweight. The paratroopers cheered, "like kids at a football game when their team scores". The tank turned about and lumbered away into the woods. But the defenders' exhilaration was stillborn. Moments later, very accurate mortar fire began to fall among them. "Men I had just lain shoulder to shoulder with began screaming in pain, screaming for help, hysterical helpless screams that made my stomach tighten. Because of the apparent protection of the hedgerow and our greenness, we had not realized the necessity of digging in and few of us had holes which would have saved us from all but a direct hit."[7]

Richardson remembered vividly a photograph that he had seen in a magazine, of a Russian soldier who was captioned as the only survivor of his company. Now, the young American felt that he shared the man's sensation. When his unit, and the other survivors of the airborne divisions, were withdrawn from the battle at the beginning of July, after 33 days in action, his company numbered 19 men. His division had suffered 46 per cent casualties. Lieutenant Sidney Eichen of the 30th Division's 120th Infantry was one of the men who relieved the 82nd Airborne. The green, unblooded newcomers gazed in shock and awe at the paratroopers they were to succeed:

We asked them: "Where are your officers?", and they answered: "All dead." We asked: "Who's in charge, then?", and some sergeant said: "I am." I looked at the unshaven, red-eyed GIs, the dirty clothes and the droop in their walk, and I wondered: is this how we are going to look after a few days of combat?[8]

The 29th Division's difficulties continued throughout the first weeks in Normandy. They called for all the leadership and driving power of Brigadier Cota and a handful of other officers to keep the men moving on their push south from the beaches. In the early hours of 10 June, Cota was at the command post of the 175th Regiment in a field at Lison, when three soldiers walked in from the east and announced they were from the 2nd Battalion, which had been surrounded and wiped out. Despite the Brigadier's scepticism and efforts to calm them, the sergeant with them insisted that they were the only survivors.

We'd just gotten into our bivouac area when it all started [the sergeant described their collapse in the after-action narrative]. All of a sudden flares went up and burp guns started to fire into the big field where most of the battalion was located. We could hear the Germans yelling. Sometimes they'd yell "Surrender! Surrender!" in English. We We tried to fight back but we didn't have any firing positions. Every time we tried to move the Germans would see the movement in the bushes for flares lit up the whole field, and they'd let loose with machine gun fire. They kept shooting mortars into the field all the time. There were seven or eight of us in the little group near me. We figured a way to get out, but a couple of the boys were hit as they tried to make it.[9]

In the hours that followed, more stragglers from the battalion, including its chaplain, arrived and confirmed the NCO's story. Later in the day, Cota talked forcefully to some hundred men of the battalion who had now been reassembled.

The members of this group were visibly shaken from their experiences of the night before. One medical aid man called "Skippy" just kept repeating over and over, "That bayonet charge, that goddam bayonet charge." Cota told the group that they were under the wrong impression – that the battalion had by no means been wiped out. General Gerhardt had already appointed Lieutenant-Colonel Arthur Sheppe, who had been acting as regimental executive, to take over command. He told them that they would have an opportunity to rest, be re-equipped and would be able to go back and fight the Germans. At the moment this proposition was not accepted too warmly.[10]

The 29th Division's narrative of an action south of Lison on 11 June, when two companies of the 175th Infantry advanced across the Vire, perfectly reflects the experience of scores of units in those painful, bitter weeks in the *bocage* when every yard of ground was gained with such painful slowness:

It was with difficulty that Major Miller managed to get his heavy machine-guns up to a base-of-fire position to sweep the hedges of the suspected road. Radio channels within the company were not functioning, and the "pass-it-back" method of requesting the weapons to come forward was slow. The entire command weight of the company at this point rested upon small unit leadership. Could the sergeant make his men do what he wanted? Was the sergeant a leader? Some exemplified all the finer qualities, about one-third fell down in this respect. All were handicapped by a general lack of understanding of the situation that confronted them. The enemy never presented himself as a target in this phase, and the fire of the company had, seemingly, little effect on him. On Gen. Cota's insistence the other weapon of the infantry – movement – paid off well. Our troops continued to move into the fire by rushes, by creeping, by crawling, by ever moving forward. Result – enemy fire diminished and then stopped.

. . . Cota had advanced only 25 yards when the crisis broke. One or two burp guns, which seemed to be located behind the high hedge that bordered the left side of the road, opened up with their excited chattering. The column on both sides of the road immediately dropped into the ditch – but this ditch was a shallow affair, about 4 or 5 inches deep, and offered no natural concealment of any kind. The suddenness with which the fire started, after the intense quiet of the last 20 minutes, stunned every member of the company. They dropped there and lay still. Several men were hit by the bullets spraying along, ricocheting off the road and nipping the shrubbery. Someone yelled "Return the fire! Shoot back at the bastards!" At intervals men would rise from the ditch and try to escape from the entrapment by either scurrying to the rear, or trying to vault over the hedges. One man attempting to cross the left hedge received a blast of burp gun fire that shoved him crashing back into the road – dead . . . Shea [Cota's aide] worked his way back through the culvert to the road. Gen. Cota was standing in the shelter of a corner of the hedgerow at the road junction opposite the culvert. He was smiling. "What's this, 'Cota's Last Stand'?" he quipped. "One minute I'm surrounded by a rifle company – those birds started to shoot – and I looked around to find myself all alone."[11]

Most or all of the German 243rd, 709th, and 91st Divisions were in the Cotentin, reinforced by the 6th Parachute Regiment, the 206th Panzer Battalion, and the Seventh Army Storm Battalion. Despite the vast weight of Allied air power interdicting communications, the 77th Division was also able to reach the area virtually unscathed, and VII Corps was in consequence obliged to pay dearly to enlarge the Utah perimeter across the swamp-ridden ground northwards. Major Harry Herman, executive officer of the 9th Division's 2nd/39th Infantry, described the struggle to overcome the huge concrete casemates of Fort St Marcouf, even after it had been subjected to heavy air attack:

Not a shot is fired taking our first objective. We walk upright into the bunker through one of the doors of twisted steel, throw in a hand grenade just for luck, and rush in on the ready to be greeted only by dead jerries strewn around inside 20-foot-thick concrete walls like so many loaves of bread – concussion. It feels rather strange and eerie, all very quiet, the sea beyond the fort looking cool and green. Have the Germans pulled out? Where is the 4th division? Where is our heavy weapons company? We worm our way to the top of the bunker, get careless, stand up, loll around, planning the next jump.

While we are discussing this possibility, the entire party is suddenly lifted up and sat down hard by a blast that wounds Colonel Lockett in the head and arm. It is direct frontal fire, amazing because it gives no whistle and you find yourself out in the open with a tight expression around the eyes when the thing hits. At dusk, we open up: a tremendous sight. The entire strip of beach being combed and raked by sixteen cannon, 3 and 4 inch naval guns, 8 mortars, 16 machine-guns for fifteen minutes. Then we jump off, being greeted with very heavy enfilade fire on our 15-foot wide front. The 155 mm barrage had only bounced off the fort. I send G Company on a flanking mission to the left in an effort to either divert or knock out the resistance there which is preventing any forward movement. G reports that they are up to their chests in water and can go no further. We, the remainder of E Company, start forward again after laying in that damn water for a day and a half. We inch up the road along with a tank destroyer while the first battalion is engaged in heavy rifle fire. It seemed that we would finally get to the church which was our first phase line, but sweeping machine-fire tears the road. Men will not move and finally we have to withdraw. We have taken a beating.

Several hours later, we start out again, this time with no barrage. We meet the first battalion which, in spite of mines and heavy fire, is coming up the beach. Walking "at the ready" behind our TDs, they absorb most of the hail of fire that greets us. We get to the first bunker, Sergeant Hickey with a crowbar forces open the vent and we plant a 5 lb TNT block inside, which opens a hole about the size of a man's body. Through this the TD fires 5 rounds of HE. That was that. Like killing flies with a sledgehammer. We have lost only 14 men, but the first battalion is in trouble. They lost Colonel Tinley who was first hit by a rifle bullet in the chest then while being carried on a stretcher, the litter bearers stepped on a mine. So he was buried later at St Mère Eglise. We gain the front part of the church, but jerry has the rear part and the cloisters. It is point-blank firing for a good hour until we have to get out because they got up in the rear and threw potato mashers down the belfry onto the altar where we are entrenched.[12]

The Americans gained the fort at last after blasting their way inch by inch through the defences in the manner described by Herman. The 9th Division found such fighting tolerable after all their experience in North African and Sicily, but already other, greener American formations were proving sluggish in action. Herman and his men watched the first actions of the 79th Division with deep dismay: "They were almost a cruel laugh. They had one regiment attacking through our assembly area whose commander could not read a map, and they lost more men than I've ever seen through damn recruit tricks. It is quite evident that they are not prepared for combat – a shameful waste of good American lives."[13] Major Randall Bryant, executive officer of the 1st Battalion of the 9th Division's 47th Regiment, found his unit summoned into action to relieve the 90th Division, a formation whose record was almost disastrously unsatisfactory throughout the Normandy campaign. ~~Bryant and his men~~ marched past the 90th's infantry, lying by the roadside behind the line: "They looked awful – unshaven, dirty, pitiful.".[14]

Carentan fell only on 12 June, and it was the 13th before the two American beachheads were at last in firm contact across the great flat sweep of wetlands dividing them. That day, Taylor's paratroopers fought off a determined counter-attack by 17th SS Panzergrenadiers. Ultra intercepts had provided Bradley with warning of this German movement. Without explanation, he ordered Gerow immediately to move elements of 2nd Armored Division into the area in time to support the Airborne, and subsequently to push back the SS. In the two weeks that followed, although Gerow's V Corps progressively pushed its perimeter southwards to Caumont, American attention focussed squarely upon the drive for Cherbourg, the critical OVERLORD objective of gaining the Allies a major port. Already, the American commanders were profoundly conscious that time was slipping away, that more and more German forces were arriving on the battlefield, that ground was only slowly being gained. There was concern about the quality of infantry leadership. A forceful directive from First Army reminded all officers that they must wear badges of rank. Many had removed them, for fear of snipers. When on 14 June Gerow of V Corps told General Hodges, with some satisfaction, that his men had achieved all their objectives, Hodges reminded him with a quiet smile: "Gee, the objective of Berlin."[15] Yet the chronic shortage of supplies – above all, of artillery ammunition – was such that First Army could sustain only one major thrust at a time.[16]

Despite Collins' eagerness to strike hard and fast for Cherbourg, Bradley concluded that the risk would be intolerable unless the peninsula was first cut, to isolate the port from German reinforcements. In the first days after 6 June, the American airborne divisions fought their way forward inch by inch to consolidate the tenuous footholds they had gained in their drop, and to defeat dangerous German counter-attacks such as that on 7 June against St Mère Eglise. Then, led by the 9th and 90th Divisions and elements of 82nd Airborne, V Corps launched its drive westward, completed at the little coastal holiday resort of Barneville on 18 June. For many of the Americans, it was an exhilarating dash, infantry clinging to the hulls of the Shermans

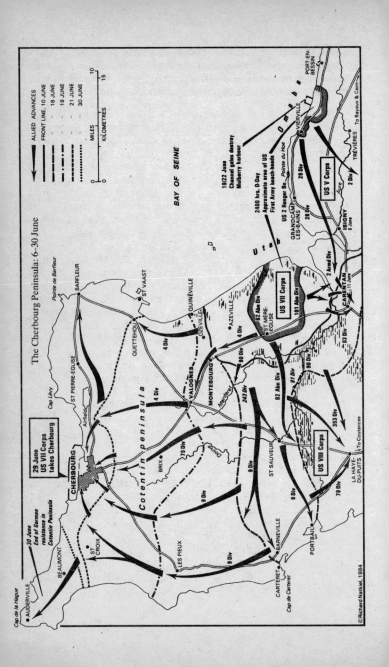

The Cherbourg Peninsula: 6–30 June

ALLIED ADVANCES

FRONT LINE, 10 JUNE
" " 18 JUNE
" " 19 JUNE
" " 21 JUNE
" " 30 JUNE

MILES
KILOMETRES

BAY OF SEINE

19/22 June, D-Day
Channel gales destroy
Mulberry harbour

2400 hrs, D-Day
Approximate area of US
First Army beach-heads

US 2 Ranger Bn.   Pointe du Hoe
PORT-EN-BESSIN
VIERVILLE
To Bayeux & Caen

US V Corps

29 Div
TRÉVIÈRES
2 Div
Aure
ISIGNY
9 June
GRANDCAMP-LES-BAINS
29 Div

Utah

2 Armd Div   CARENTAN
11 June
83 Div
90 Div
101 Abn Div
US VII Corps
82 Abn Div
ST MÈRE-ÉGLISE

QUINÉVILLE
4 Div
OZEVILLE
AZEVILLE
4 Div
90 Div
82 Abn Div
353 Div
91 Div

243 Div
MONTEBOURG
VALOGNES
Merderet
4 Div

QUETTEHOU
Pointe de Barfleur
BARFLEUR
ST VAAST

ST PIERRE-ÉGLISE
Cap Lévy
Airfield
4 Div

Cotentin peninsula

CHERBOURG
29 June
US VII Corps
takes Cherbourg

BRIX
70 Div
Douve
9 Div

ST SAUVEUR
9 Div
90 Div
9 Div
US VIII Corps
79 Div
LA HAYE-DU-PUITS
To Coutances

30 June
End of German
resistance in
Cotentin Peninsula

Cap de la Hague
AUDERVILLE
BEAUMONT
ST CROIX
9 Div
LES PIEUX
9 Div

BARNEVILLE
PORTBAIL
CARTERET
Cap de Carteret

© Richard Natkiel, 1984

and tank destroyers as they bucketed across the countryside, meeting only isolated pockets of resistance. Parties of fugitive Germans or half-hearted counter-attacks on American positions were ruthlessly cut down, although 1,500 men of the German 77th Division were able to escape southwards across country, surprising men of the 90th Division guarding a bridge over the river Olande, and taking more than 100 prisoners. The 77th was one of the few formations of reasonable quality in the Cotentin. Most of the German static units were undertrained, poorly-equipped, demoralized. Hodges' First Army diary for 16 June recorded that, "the Boche artillery extremely weak, and G-2 [intelligence] reports an increasing demoralisation because of lack of ammunition and supply." Such tanks as the Germans possessed were almost invariably captured French or Czech models. "We knew that we were not facing the top panzers," said Corporal Preston of the 743rd Tank Battalion.[17] The German units proved capable of stubborn resistance when defending prepared positions against direct assault, but lacked the will or the means to interfere with major American units manoeuvring in open country.

There was a legendary exchange between Bradley and Collins at this time, when the First Army commander received a characteristic signal from Montgomery declaring loftily that "Caen is really the key to Cherbourg." Collins exploded: "Brad, let's wire him to send us the key!"[18] Yet while the Americans interpreted Montgomery's words both as an excuse for British difficulties around Caen, and an attempt to diminish that which they themselves were seeking to accomplish in the Cotentin, Montgomery was correct. Almost every single German formation of quality was fighting against the British. There could be no comparison between the difficulty of facing 12th SS Panzer or Panzer Lehr, and that of rolling up the weak enemy divisions falling back on Cherbourg.

Not that this diminishes the qualities of speed and energy which VII Corps displayed in reaching the great port. Collins was already revealing himself as one of the outstanding personalities of the campaign. The tenth child of a Louisiana Irish family, he was 48 years old. Like so many other American career soldiers, he had spent years between the wars gaining age and enduring stagnation, seemingly without hope of glory or professional fulfilment. In 1920, when he found himself demoted to captain in the general post-war rundown of the services, he considered resignation. He was 44 before he attained a lieutenant-colonelcy, and it was January 1943 before he saw action for the first time, as a divisional commander in the Pacific. As a young man, he had considered becoming a lawyer, and possessed uncommonly catholic tastes for a soldier. He had travelled widely in Europe and the Far East, was a fine shot and an opera lover. A ruthless driver of men, he unhesitatingly sacked officers of any rank who failed to match his standards. Beyond the various divisional and regimental commanders whom he dismissed in the weeks after D-Day, he disposed of an operations officer who persisted with the fatal American army pre-war doctrine of placing unit boundaries on high ground, and an artillery commander who seemed unable to understand the vital importance of forward observation. Intolerant of excuses, he had a superb eye for an opportunity on the battlefield: American – and British – forces in Normandy sorely needed more commanders out of his mould.

Just 22 hours after gaining Barneville, having achieved an astonishingly rapid change of axis through 90 degrees, Collins' men began to push north for the port. Middleton's VIII Corps, newly operational, accepted responsibility for securing the American east-west line while VII Corps drove for the port. Collins was already agitating for a leading role in the push south when Cherbourg fell. Bradley told him: "Troy [Middleton of VIII Corps] likes to fight, too."

General Bradley also had some definite words to say about divisions and commanders who appeared to be fighting the war for newspaper headlines alone [reported Hodges' diary]. This competition for publicity, he told General Collins, will have to cease.[19]

The intensity of rivalry between senior officers in battle is often difficult for civilians to grasp. But it is a simple fact of life that for professional soldiers, war offers the same opportunities and fulfilments as great sales drives offer corporation presidents. This is not a moral judgement, but a reality as old as war itself. All that was new in the Second World War was that unique opportunities were available to commanders on the battlefield to ingratiate themselves with newspaper correspondents, and thus to make themselves national figures. In the British Army, only an officer of Montgomery's rank could exploit this. But within the American forces in Normandy, many divisional commanders competed ferociously for publicity for themselves and their formations, and there was bitter jealousy, for instance, of the fame of "The Big Red One".

The Battle For Cherbourg

At 2.00 p.m. on 22 June, preceded by a massive air bombardment, the Americans opened their attack against the three ridge lines on which the German outer defence of Cherbourg was centred. "The combat efficiency of all the [defending] troops was extremely low," admitted a German writer later.[1] Cherbourg's defences had been designed principally to meet an attack from the sea, and in an exercise early in May, General Marcks had demonstrated their vulnerability to landward assault by breaking through at exactly the points at which the Americans now attacked. Collins later expressed his astonishment that the Germans failed to make a stand on the outer range of high ground around the city, instead retiring immediately to the inner forts. They appeared to lack not only the numbers, but the will to conduct such a defence. Four German battle-groups had been formed from the remains of the units which had retreated up the Cotentin, and static defence in fortified positions is the least demanding role for poor quality troops. If the Americans were able to mount their attack without enduring forceful counter-attacks, of the kind which were creating such difficulties for the British around Caen, it remained a harrowing task for infantry to advance into the intense machine-gun fire from the huge concrete bunkers.

Major Randall Bryant's battalion had fought a procession of minor skirmishes against pockets of German resistance up the peninsula, in one of which Bryant surprised himself as much as his men by successfully bouncing a bazooka round off a road into the belly of a German tank – the Americans had learned by bitter experience that direct fire would not penetrate its armour. Now, in the streets of Cherbourg, they began two days of nerve-wracking house-to-house fighting on the road to Fort du Roule. They learned by experience the techniques of covering the building opposite while squads leapfrogged forward, paving their path with grenades, for it was a skill in which they had never trained. The enemy's massive network of strongpoints had to be reduced one by one in dogged fighting, the assaulting infantry scaling the open approaches under withering machine-gun fire.

193

We jump off Fort Octeville [wrote Major Herman of the 39th Infantry]. A barrage pins us down initially, but men filter through somehow, running like scared rabbits directly into the fort. We stop our artillery; it falls short on G Company, knocking out a platoon. Everything seems wrong. Our supporting tanks turn tail. With my Sgt. Maachi in tow, we crawl under heavy but high machine-gun fire up to the fort that looms up like Grand Central Station. I don't quite remember what happens from here on, but piecing it together, we got two bazookas up to about sixty yards from the fort when we hit the outpost. I kneeled up to fire my MI and a burst caught me in the right hip, taking my jacket with it. I started to run towards the pillbox, firing. A potato masher tore the gun out of my hands, ripping the forearm muscles of my right arm away, but not touching the bone. My boys said that I rolled down into a ditch, unconscious.[2]

9th Division gained Octeville, and the 314th Infantry stormed Fort du Roule by other examples of the sacrificial courage which alone enables infantry to seize strongly fortified positions. When Corporal John Kelly found his platoon pinned down by machine-gun fire, he crawled forward to fix a pole charge beneath the German firing-slit, but returned to find that it had failed to detonate, and went back with another one. This time, the explosion blew off the protruding gun barrels, enabling the corporal to climb the slope a third time, reach the rear door of

The German *Maschinegewehr* MG 42 – universally known as the Spandau among Allied troops – was a superb general-purpose machine-gun, with a startling 1,200 rpm rate of fire. It could be fed either through boxed belts or – as here – by drum for greater portability. Distributed prodigally among all German units, it contributed decisively to their ability to generate immense defensive fire-power even when positions were manned by only small numbers of men. 750,000 were made before the end of the war, and achieved a remarkable reputation for reliability – the MG 42's barrel could be changed in five seconds during periods of heavy firing.

the pillbox and grenade it into silence. Lieutenant Carlos Ogden cleared the way for his company by knocking out an 88 mm gun with a rifle grenade although already wounded in the head, ignoring a second wound to run forward with grenades and silence the supporting German machine-guns. Both Kelly and Ogden were awarded the Congressional Medal of Honor.

Underground in their tunnels and bunkers, thousands of German personnel lay crowded beneath the bombardment: naval ratings, Luftwaffe ground staff, supply units, clerks – all the rag-tag of a huge base wretchedly conscious of their isolation and disheartened by days amid the stink of their big generator motors, and the dust and cordite fumes filtering through the caverns. On a wall map in General von Schlieben's command post at St Sauveur, on the southern outskirts of the city, his operations officer, Major Forster, marked the remorseless progress of the American advance – Collins' men had unknowingly bypassed the German's switchboard bunker, leaving their communications intact. On 26 June, the unhappy von Schlieben surrendered with 800 of his men when tank destroyers began firing direct into the tunnel entrances above him. Major Randall Bryant was beside Manton Eddy, the divisional commander, when a tall, dignified German officer detached himself from the long file of surrendering defenders emerging from the arsenal and announced formally: "I am von Schlieben." The astonished Eddy showed the general to a jeep and took him away to his command post for lunch. Bradley, however, declined to entertain the German because of his anger that he had protected Cherbourg's defence at such cost in American lives, and had finally refused to order a total surrender of the port after his capture.

Organized resistance in Cherbourg ended only on 27 June, and the 9th Division was obliged to fight hard for several days more to reduce the defences of Cap de la Hague, at the northwest tip of the peninsula. In the city, Eddy led a desperate attempt to control the men of his division as they ran riot among captured stocks of brandy, wine, champagne. At last he retired in despair, declaring, "Okay, everybody take twenty-four hours and get drunk."[3] Hundreds of cases of looted alcohol were loaded aboard captured German vehicles and followed units of VII Corps across Europe. Half a case of champagne was sent to Bradley, who touchingly sent it home to the U.S. to toast his grandson on his return in 1945. Randall Bryant's officers' club was still drinking its share of the proceeds of Cherbourg in Germany in 1946.

Bryant's battalion regretted its excesses on the morning of 28 June, when they began a long foot march towards Cap de La Hague, following the German formation signposts. They reached the entrance to a huge underground bunker without opposition, seized the single enemy sentry guarding it, and advanced warily inside, pistols in hands, towards the sound of voices. They found themselves in a room full of German officers clustered around a table laden with a large ham. Dean Vanderhouf, the battalion commander, rose to the occasion. "Stop!" he called to his astonished audience. He leaned forward to seize the ham: "I'll take that." The Americans were uncommonly lucky. Other units endured hard fights at Cap de la Hague.

In the month of June, VII Corps had captured 39,042 prisoners and achieved the first American objectives of the campaign. General Collins had proved himself an outstandingly energetic and skilful corps commander, just as General Maton Eddy had shown his capabilities at the head of the 9th Division. The reduction of a "fortress" that Hitler had ordered to resist for months gave sufficient exhilaration to the Allies to mask the disappointment of their commanders when they received the first reports from Cherbourg harbour. The port facilities of Naples had become operational just three days after the city fell, and some such new miracle had been looked for at Cherbourg. Instead, Bradley's engineers found the shambles created by one of the most comprehensive demolition programmes in the history of war. The OVERLORD logistics plan called for Cherbourg to discharge 150,000 tons of stores by 25 July. In reality, the port received less than 18,000 tons by that date. In was late September before it approached full operational capacity, by which time almost every harbour in France and Belgium was in the hands of the Allies. The drive for Cherbourg thus failed to achieve its immediate strategic purpose of accelerating and securing the Allied build-up. But of this, little needed to be said in the days of exultation following the most spectacular Allied ground gains since the landings. It was only Eisenhower, Bradley and Montgomery and their staffs who were conscious that the battle for the northern Cotentin had lasted many days longer than they had hoped or planned for and that, while it persisted, little progress was made with the drive to gain fighting room further south. On 27 June, when Everett Hughes brought Eisenhower news of a renewed delay to movement by First Army, the Supreme Commander reflected moodily: "Sometimes I wish I had George Paton over there."[4]

The men who fought the battle for the Cotentin afterwards remembered chiefly the fear and exhaustion of groping their way through the Norman hedgerows with their infantry company or tank platoon – "tiptoeing in a tank", one gunner called it – prickling with the sense of their own nakedness as they crossed each open space, cursing their inability to see the enemy mortaring or machine-gunning their advance, damning the air force, which was already revealing a disturbing inability to avoid strafing American positions. All wars become a matter of small private battles to those who are fighting them. But this was uniquely true of the struggle for Normandy, where it was seldom possible to see more than 100 or 200 yards in any direction, where forward infantry rarely glimpsed their own armour, artillery or higher commanders, where the appalling attrition rate among the rifle companies at the tip of each army's spear rapidly became one of the dominant factors of the campaign.

In this first battle in north-west Europe, the American army was given cause to regret the poor priority that it had given to infantry recruitment since the great mobilization of American manpower began in 1940. All nations in the Second World War diverted some of their fittest and best-educated recruits to the air forces and technical branches. But no other nation allowed the rifle companies of its armies to become a wastebin for men considered unsuitable for any other occupation. The infantry suffered in the services' attempts to allow men to follow specializations of their choice – of the 1942 volunteers, only 5 per cent chose infantry or armour. "By the end of 1943," confessed the official history of the training and procurement of U.S. army ground forces, "the operations of this priority and a number of other factors had reduced to a dangerously low level the number of men allotted to the ground forces who seemed likely to perform effectively in combat."[5] It was discovered that infantrymen were an inch shorter than the army's average height – a fair measure of general physique. Even more disturbing, statistics produced in March 1944 showed that while the infantry made up only 6 per cent of the army – an extraordinarily low proportion by any measure – they had suffered 53 per cent of its

197

total battle casualties. This proportion rose to far more alarming heights in Normandy.

Great efforts began to be made in the spring of 1944 to push men of higher quality into the infantry. In March, 30,000 dismayed aviation cadets found themselves transferred wholesale to the army, almost all to ground forces. Some specialists were hastily diverted to the infantry, and the first of many comb-outs of service units took place, in search of suitable officers and men for infantry duty. But none of this came in time to assist the army that was to fight the first battles for north-west Europe. In Normandy, only 37 per cent of the replacements arriving to make good casualties were rifle-trained. First Army was suffering a desperate shortage of competent officers and NCOs. Wholesale sackings proved necessary in some units. In a situation in which junior leadership was critical, where again and again men were called up to fight beyond the control and eyes of their battalion or even company commanders, such leadership was repeatedly found wanting. The American army had determinedly eschewed the German policy of building elite and low-grade divisions to meet different requirements, and had sought instead to create a force of uniform quality. But in Normandy and after, Bradley's commanders found themselves principally dependent upon a handful of formations which proved exceptionally determined and competent – the 1st, 4th, 9th, 2nd Armored and the airborne divisions. Just as the first weeks of battle in Normandy caused the British to reach disturbing conclusions about their own tactics and about the determination of some of their principal formations, so the Americans found cause for serious concern in the performance of some units. A First Army report on the tactical lessons of Normandy declared:

It is essential that infantry in training be imbued with a bold, aggressive attitude. Many units do not acquire this attitude until long after their entry into combat, and some never acquire it. On the other hand units containing specially selected personnel such as Airborne and Rangers exhibited an aggressive spirit from the start. The average infantry soldier places too much reliance upon the supporting artillery to drive the enemy from positions opposing his advance. He has not been impressed sufficiently with his own potency and the effect of well-aimed, properly distributed rifle and machine-gun fire. The outstanding impression gained from a review of battle experiences is the importance of aggressive action and continuous energetic forward movement in order to gain ground and reduce casualties.[6]

Like the British, the Americans had discovered that their tank-infantry co-operation was woefully inadequate. They lacked the means for rapid communication on the battlefield between the men on the ground and those in the Shermans, battened down inside their steel hulls. They had no telephones mounted on their armour, which later enabled an infantryman to contact a tank commander without clambering up and hammering on his hatch, often under heavy fire. Officers were surprised to discover after an action how few rounds their riflemen had expended. Despite all their training in the importance of "marching fire" to suppress the defences, many infantrymen were instinctively reluctant to shoot when they could see no target, or were too concerned with hugging the earth for protection to reveal themselves and take an aim. A rifle company commander of the 9th Division reported: "The American soldier is too careless in unduly exposing himself when in view of the enemy. Individually he feels that some other 'Joe' will get shot and not he."[7] It may also be relevant to quote a report from General Mark Clark in Italy at about this time: "The infantryman in landing operations, as in other operations, carries the heavy load, suffers the losses, and must have the guts to go forward despite danger and heavy casualties. Without question our training has not yet produced disciplined officers and disciplined men. Leaders up to and including battalion have a tendency to allow their troops to get out of control."[8]

There was interminable private debate in 1944, and there has been a great deal more in the years since, about the respective fighting power of the British and American soldier, and their shortcomings as revealed in Normandy. The truth seems self-evident – that the best British and American units were very good indeed, and perfectly comparable with each other. Each army was at times bemused by the different national approach to war of the other. Gavin wrote of the British: "In many ways they took the war far less seriously than we."[9] The British, in their turn, were sometimes scornful of the theatricality of the American style – of their generals' invariable habit of wearing helmets and personal weapons when no British commander troubled with either, of their enthusiasm for histrionics on the battlefield while the British sought always to understate the moment. But a British officer who saw much of the Americans said later that "if they were sometimes boastful, they would also go to extraordinary lengths to try to make good their boasts".[10] Gavin added to his comment on the British above: "On the other hand, on matters of discipline and combat effectiveness they set very high standards."[11]

It ill became either army in Normandy to seek to harp upon the shortcomings of the other – the British sluggishness in gaining Caen or the poor performance of some American divisions in the *bocage*. Despite the fine performance of Collins' VII Corps in gaining Cherbourg, each army at large had found it difficult to work up the driving power, the killing force, necessary to break through well-positioned German forces on the battlefield. The most important recent American historian of the campaign has written of Normandy: "There the limitations of the American army in generating sustained combat power were further to cripple the drive into the unknown, on battlefields sorely lacking in appropriate ground to apply mobility."[12]

6 The German army: stemming the tide

Soldiers

For every soldier of imagination in the German army, the battle for Normandy was the last struggle of the war which offered a frail chance of final victory. From all over Europe through the month of June, hundreds of thousands of men, thousands of tanks and vehicles, crawled painfully by the devastated rail network, and finally along roads lined with slit trenches to provide ready refuges from the inevitable fighter-bomber attacks, to bolster the precarious German line in Normandy. A 21st Army Group intelligence report of 22 June, based upon captured correspondence, found in Rommel's soldiers:

. . . the same mixture of brash arrogance (chiefly SS), forlorn hope and outright despair that has appeared in similar collections in the past. The reprisal weapon is still the white hope and the German Air Force the main disappointment. The insistence that, despite his heavy equipment, "Tommy is no soldier" is still common.[1]

Corporal Wilhelm Schickner of the reconnaissance battalion of 2nd Panzer Division was a 25-year-old stonemason's son who had been an apprentice printer in Stuttgart when he was conscripted in March 1939 first for work service and then, a year later, for the infantry. Plunged immediately into the battle for France, like so many others he spent the next four years marching the length of Europe – with the German spearhead into Athens, to the gates of Moscow, where he was wounded in September 1942, back to Russia, to be wounded again in July 1943, and at last to join 2nd Panzer at Cambrai when he was once more fit for duty that December. On the night of 5 June, they were alerted in their positions around Amiens, and then stood down, only to be alerted again on 6 June. They moved at last on the afternoon of the 9th, reached Paris at nightfall, and drove through the empty and darkened streets to cross the Seine.

Thereafter, they leaguered all day in woodlands by the line of march, and drove only in darkness to reach Caumont around noon on 12 June. The reconnaissance battalion was immediately deployed to relieve the thin screen of defending troops covering the town. Schickner himself was ordered to take two machine-guns and one section to take over a position commanding the road 200 yards northwards. When his little party reached the spot, they found two men with a weary NCO, who said: "Thank God you're here – we're getting the hell out of it." There was no other German position to their right for some 600 yards, and little enough on their left. For half an hour, they lay patiently in the mist and waited. Then a jeep appeared in front of them, full of Americans. It stopped hesitantly, and retired abruptly when a 2nd Panzer gun crew behind them fired a 37 mm *Pak* round in its direction. Shermans appeared in the distance – Schickner counted 18 of them, and sent a runner back to report. The American tanks stopped, and began to fire HE towards the Germans. A lone GI rounded the corner of the road, helmet tilted back on his head. Behind him, Schickner could see long files of other enemy infantrymen. He sent his runner back again, and told Briese, the machine-gunner beside him, to link his belts for longer continuous fire. Then Jupp, the other gunner, called: "They're coming now," and the Americans moved confidently up the road towards them.

Schickner marvelled, because if the enemy had advanced through the fields on their flanks rather than along the road, "they could have walked into Caumont". Instead, "it was as if they were out for a Sunday stroll". Jupp asked: "Do I start now?" and settled over the butt of his MG 42. The hail of German fire scythed through the files of approaching men. It stopped, quite simply, when the two guns had fired all their available ammunition, and Schickner himself had emptied five magazines from his Schmeisser. In the silence that followed, the defenders could hear wounded Americans screaming for help from the roadside and the ditches. One of their own men, Gross, had been hit in the stomach. He could still walk, and they gave him cover while he stumbled back towards the houses. A young lieutenant appeared, who inspected the situation and declared: "You must launch a counter-attack." "What, with six men?" demanded Schickner. "Then what do you suggest?" asked the officer less confidently. "Stay put here," said the corporal. The officer disappeared, and for half an hour there was silence. The Germans lay on their weapons and smoked.

Darkness fell, and they could see the flash of firing all around them, but there was no movement on their own front. At last they received the order to pull back into the town, where they found the rest of the battalion, along with 75 mm guns of the *panzerjager* battalion, locked in a house-to-house struggle against American attacks already well inside Caumont. Their own company commander, Captain Schultz, ran from position to position telling his men, "We've got to hold the town – it's a Führer-order." After a huge effort, supported by the 50 mm guns of their big Puma half-tracks, they captured some of the lost ground in a counter-attack in the early hours of the morning. But a few hours later, American armour began pressing them relentlessly. The Germans pulled back down the hill south of the town, having suffered appalling casualties. Schickner said: "We were never told to push forward again."[2] The American official history recorded: "The 26th Infantry at the same time got one battalion to the edge of Caumont but there ran into determined resistance from an estimated two companies of Germans, giving the Americans the impression at some points that counter-attacks were in progress. Actions, however, though sometimes sharp were all local and involved few troops. The town was not cleared until the following morning."[3]

For the German soldier in the first weeks of the Normandy battle, actions such as that of 2nd Panzer's *aufklarungsabteilung* at Caumont were commonplace: a rush to the threatened sector; a fierce and expert defence against clumsy Allied tactics; growing casualties as the enemy's massed firepower was brought to bear; and at last, a retreat of a few hundred yards to the next line to be equally doggedly held with fewer men, less weapons, a slowly dwindling supply of hope. "Let's enjoy the war," ran a Wehrmacht catchphrase of the period, "because the peace will be terrible."[4]

On 6 June, the Allies had inflicted a crushing tactical surprise upon the Germans. In the weeks that followed, they maintained the greatest of all strategic deceptions by the FORTITUDE operation, which imprisoned almost the entire Fifteenth Army in the Pas de Calais until late July. Rommel's efforts were dedicated to stemming the Allied tide, throwing into the line every new unit as it reached the battlefront. Above all, he was compelled to employ his armoured forces as links of steel in the sagging chain around the perimeter, and was thus unable to concentrate them in the rear for a major counter-attack. The armoured divisions reached Normandy first, because they possessed far greater mobility than the infantry, many of whom travelled the last 50 or 100 miles to the front on foot. Tanks made immensely effective strongpoints, but were almost invariably lost wherever the Allies gained ground. They could not be replaced. If the Allies were restricted in Normandy by their perceived shortage of infantry, the Germans were much more desperately frustrated by theirs. A report by 2nd Panzer in July discussed at length the tactics the division had found it necessary to employ in holding their sector of the line against the British. It concluded bleakly: "The fact that a modern panzer division with 2 tank battalions and 2 infantry battalions with armoured half-tracks is not necessary for such fighting is another matter . . ."[5] As Bradley accurately observed, "When the tank is employed in lieu of infantry simply to hold a defensive position, it becomes a wasted and uneconomic weapon."[6]

If it is arguable that the British wasted precious time in the first days following the invasion, the Germans did no better. Rommel reached his château headquarters after his dash across France at 10.00 p.m. on 6 June, to spend most of the night trying to get a grip on his command, to learn precisely what was happening across the battle area in spite of a tangle of jammed wireless wavelengths and severed telephone links. His order for an immediate counter-attack on the 7th by 21st Panzer and 12th SS Panzer came to nothing, for Sepp Dietrich's I SS Panzer Corps were quite unable to concentrate the tanks in time. Rommel issued a prompt and formal protest to Hitler's headquarters about the lack of air and naval support for his battle, and warned Jodl that he was still convinced that the main Allied effort was to come elsewhere. It is interesting that Jodl, often a shrewd judge of strategic situation, never shared this view. But at this stage, both Berlin and Rommel were full of optimism about the prospects of throwing the Allies into the sea. Rommel's adjutant Hellmuth Lang wrote home: "There's a marvellous tranquillity shown by all concerned, particularly our chief of staff Speidel."[7] The field-marshal himself began to fight his battle with the same remorseless, restless energy that he had displayed in Africa, spending each day in headlong drives from formation to formation, inquiring, urging, demanding, galvanizing, and only returning to his headquarters at night to plan and to issue orders. It was a divisional, at most a corps commander's, style of direction.

On the afternoon of 8 June, when Rommel arrived at Panzer Group West's headquarters to find 21st Panzer and 12th SS Panzer's counter-attack against the British in serious trouble, he at once ordered Geyr von Schweppenburg to divert a powerful battle-group north-west to try to recapture Bayeux, a thrust which was broken up by massive artillery and naval gunfire. At von Rundstedt's headquarters in Paris, there was deep dismay that all the available German armour was now committed to piecemeal action, and not embarked upon a concentrated thrust. These complaints reflected sound tactical theory but ignored the desperate practical need on the battlefield to halt the enemy wherever he was pushing forward. That night, Colonel Bodo Zimmerman of Rundstedt's staff telephoned Speidel: "Rommel has got to decide whether he's going to get a big success tonight with the forces he already has. Rundstedt does not think he will, he thinks we're going to have to strip other fronts ruthlessly to provide further strength."[8] Jodl also telephoned, reasserting his conviction that the landings were indeed the sole Allied effort. "There's not going to be any second invasion."[9] Rommel dissented, declared that he was concentrating all his efforts upon preventing the link-up of the British and American beachheads, and declined to demand any weakening of Fifteenth Army in the Pas De Calais.

In the days that followed, some of his most serious losses were among corps and divisional commanders. On 12 June, the formidable old General Marcks of LXXXIV Corps set out to drive for the Carentan front when he heard that the town had fallen, and died in a strafing attack when his wooden leg prevented him from leaping from his car quickly enough to take cover. Fritz Witt of 12th SS Panzer died the same day, to be replaced by Kurt Meyer. The commander of the 243rd Infantry was killed on the 17th, that of the 77th mortally wounded on the 18th.

As Rommel strove to gain a grip of the battle, he could draw some satisfaction from the effectiveness with which the Allied thrusts southwards were being checked and even thrown back. But strategically, this was not enough. If he was frustrating the hopes of Montgomery, his own forces were nowhere within sight of the vital breakthrough to the sea. Even the fanatics of 12th SS Panzer expressed their belief that the Allied line could not be broken after their own attempts to smash through the Canadians had failed on 7 and 8 June. On 11 June, Sepp Dietrich of I SS Panzer Corps asserted that the line could be held for only three weeks. On the 14th, he told Rommel: "I am being bled and getting nowhere." Told that he must attack, he demanded: "With what? We need another eight or ten divisions in a day or two, or we are finished."[10] Wehrmacht staff officers were astonished to see Dietrich, the hoary veteran Nazi whose relationship with Hitler had alone thrust him into high command, openly derisive about their hopes of victory. "He was no soldier, but he was a realist," said one.[11]

Rommel found every counter-attack that he contemplated rendered impossible by local tactical difficulties, fuel shortages or enemy fighter-bomber attacks. Each effort to move troops west to meet the threat to Cherbourg was prevented by more urgent needs closer at hand. A sense of desperation began to overcome him. "The invasion is quite likely to start at other places too, soon," he wrote to his wife. "There's simply no answer to it. I reported to the Führer yesterday. Rundstedt is doing the same. It's time for politics to come into play. It will all be over very quickly."[12] Rommel determined on 13 June that any attempt to reinforce the divisions fighting in the Cotentin would fatally weaken the critical front opposite the British Second Army. Despite furious orders from the Berghof to defend every yard of the road to Cherbourg, he successfully extricated useful elements of the 77th Division before the Americans sealed the peninsula. "It appears dubious whether the gravity of the situation is realized up above," he wrote to Frau Rommel on 14 June, "and whether the proper conclusions are being drawn."[13]

Hitler's visit to Soissons on the 17th enabled him to work his customary magnetic spell upon his field-marshal, momentarily arresting the relentless workings of reason. Rommel "cannot escape the Führer's influence," wrote Hellmuth Lang.[14] The Commander-in-Chief of Army Group B allowed himself to be encouraged by news of the V-I offensive on England, and lifted by the promise of yet more dramatic new weapons to follow. He saw the German front stiffening and holding around Caen and Caumont, the panzer formations inflicting heavy casualties upon the Allies and parrying their attacks. Defeat was still some way off. But Rommel scornfully rejected demands from Berlin for counter-attacks in the Contentin, pointing out that he scarcely possessed the forces to hold a line. The fall of Cherbourg made little impact upon him, for he and von Rundstedt had privately written off the port from the moment Carentan was lost. He was dismayed only by the absurd orders continuing to stream forth from Hitler's headquarters, demanding that Cherbourg should be held "to the last round". The principal achievement of Operation EPSOM on the 26th was to forestall a planned counter-attack by 9th and 10th SS Panzer Divisions, newly arrived from the east, and to inflict serious losses upon them when they were belatedly thrown into the battle.

On the 28th, at the height of the struggle around the Odon, Rommel once again saw Hitler in Berlin, at the Führer's behest. Hitler's intention, plainly, was to strengthen the resolve of his commander. He was enraged when Rommel persistently attempted to bring home to him the terrible reality of the situation in Normandy. At last, Rommel said: "*Mein Führer*, I must speak bluntly. I cannot leave here without speaking on the subject of Germany." Hitler said abruptly: "Field-Marshal, be so good as to leave the room. I think it would be better like that."[15] It was their last meeting. Yet once again, the encounter had served to harden Rommel's faltering determination. He returned to Normandy to find that Geyr von Schweppenburg had persuaded Speidel of the vital importance of withdrawing from the Caen bridgehead, out of range of the Allied naval guns. In the early hours of 1 July, Rommel ordered Geyr to continue to hold his ground instead. Yet von Rundstedt had already received Geyr's report, arguing the need to pull back, and had forwarded it to Berlin with his own endorsement. Von Rundstedt had never troubled to conceal his own despair: "If you doubt what we are doing, get up here and take over this shambles yourself," he told Keitel witheringly when the OKW Chief of Staff sought to challenge his judgement by telephone from Germany.[16] Before midnight on 1 July, Hitler's order for Geyr's dismissal had reached the front. He was succeeded in command of Panzer Group West by General Hans Eberbach. Rundstedt himself resigned his command the following morning, after a peremptory hint from Berlin that his health was plainly no longer adequate to his task.

Von Rundstedt was succeeded by Field-Marshal von Kluge, a leathery Prussian veteran of the eastern front, who immediately sought to assert his own authority over Rommel and to re-establish his command's confidence in their own ability to defend

Normandy. Yet by the evening of 12 July, von Kluge was telephoning Jodl in Berlin. "I want to stress once again," he said, "that I am no pessimist. But in my view, the situation could not be grimmer."[17] Even after the removal of every open sceptic, the utmost exercise of the Führer's personal magic and force, and the commitment to battle of some of the most powerful elements of the German army, there was now no senior officer in the entire German high command in France who believed that the battle for Normandy could be won. "The tragedy of our position is this," Rommel told Admiral Ruge on 13 July: "We are obliged to fight on to the very end, but all the time we're convinced that it's far more vital to stop the Russians than the Anglo-Americans from breaking into Germany."[18] He judged, with remarkable accuracy, that the German front in Normandy must collapse within a month. At that point, the relentless attrition of men and weapons would have become intolerable. Since D-Day, he had lost 2,360 officers and over 94,000 men, while receiving only 6,000 replacements. He had lost 225 tanks and received 17, in addition to the new formations arriving at the front. The ammunition position remained critical. Yet every Allied tank and aircraft lost was replaced within a few hours. "Everywhere our troops are fighting heroically," he reported to von Kluge on 15 July, "but the unequal struggle is drawing to its close."[19]

It was at about this date that, for the first time, Rommel began to put out feelers to his commanders – notably Eberbach and Sepp Dietrich – about the possibility of their support should it prove feasible to open some form of negotiations with the Allies. Hellmuth Lang was witness to one conversation at which Dietrich – Hitler's old chauffeur and devoted follower in the Munich days of Nazism – shook Rommel's hand and declared: "You're the boss, *Herr Feldmarschall*. I obey only you – whatever it is you're planning."[20] Then Rommel and his aide climbed back into the big Horch staff car, a corporal in the back acting as the inevitable "looky-looky" for Allied aircraft, and raced away towards his headquarters. On the N179 short of Vimoutiers, at around 6.00 p.m., a British Typhoon caught them, wounding Rommel's driver and sending the car careering into a tree, throwing its passengers into the road. Rommel, terribly injured in the head, had ended his career as a battlefield commander, and would be forced to suicide three months later on the evidence of the 20 July conspirators. The field-marshal had never

Commanders before D-Day: Tedder, Eisenhower and Montgomery (seated); Bradley, Ramsay, Leigh-Mallory and Bedell Smith (standing). *U.S. National Archives*

The air chiefs: Eisenhower with (left to right) Coningham,
Leigh-Mallory, Brereton and Quesada.
General Elwood R. Quesada

Before D-Day: American Airborne pathfinders pose beside
their Dakota. Private

Matériel massed for the invasion.
Imperial War Museum

THE 21ST ARMY
FRONT ROW: Thomas (43 Div.); Bucknall; Crerar;
MIDDLE ROW: Bullen-Smith (51 Div.); Keller (3 Cdn
O'Connor; Barker (49 Div.); Crocker.
BACK ROW: Macmillan (15 Div.); Gale (6 Abn. Div.)

Richardson is third from the right
in the second row, wearing
helmet. *F.O. Richardson*

American soldiers are briefed for D-Day.
Imperial War Museum

GROUP TEAM
Montgomery; Dempsey; Broadhurst; Ritchie.
Div.); Graham (50 Div.); Roberts (11 Armd Div.);

Erskine (7 Armd Div.). *Imperial War Museum*

Montgomery inspects the 5th/7th Gordons
of 51st Highland Division during the
run-up to OVERLORD. Lt-Col. Eric Hay
walks behind the C-in-C.
Lt-Col. Eric Hay

The myth of Rommel as a 'good' German hostile to Nazism prevailed in the west for many years after the war. In reality, the C-in-C of Army Group B remained passionately devoted to Hitler until he became convinced that the war was militarily unwinnable. *U.S. National Archives*

D-Day: on the beach. *Imperial War Museum*

A fascinating glimpse of the Supreme Commander in mid-Channel; caught by the photographer looking far tougher than when pictured with the accommodating grin of the familiar Ike. *U.S. National Archives*

Beach defenders surrender to the Americans. *U.S. Army photograph*

(RIGHT) The build-up: American troops move inshore from the beaches. *U.S. Army photograph*

(BELOW) George Small

(BELOW RIGHT) Phil Reisler (right, in black) with his tank crew.

Norman Cota. *UPI*

Lindley Higgins

Randall Bryant

Harry Herman

Bill Preston

ilhelm Schickner

Hans Stober

Adolf Hohenstein

Rudolf Schaaf

(LEFT) Panzer leaders: Fritz Bayerlein, Kurt Kauffmann, Sepp Dietrich, staff officer.

Imut Gunther

Heinz-Gunther Guderian

Austin Baker

Guy Simonds

Robin Hastings

Chris Portway

Steve Dyson and (TOP) Dick
Raymond.

Henry Lovegrove

(OPPOSITE) Airborne images of the battlefield: (TOP) Norman chalk pitted with
foxholes *Imperial War Museum*; (LEFT) fighter-bomber's eye view of a German
column after attack *U.S. Air Force*; (RIGHT) tank action among the hedges.
Imperial War Museum

(TOP) A characteristic Normandy horizon: infantry advance through the standing corn behind a British tank. *Imperial War Museum*

(LEFT) American infantry dash between the hated hedges. Dead cows were among the most familiar landmarks of the battlefield. *Imperial War Museum*

(RIGHT) British anti-tank screen near Caen, with armoured bridging equipment in the background. *Imperial War Museum*

been party to their plans, but the evidence that they had considered him a suitable figurehead to lead negotiations with the Allies was sufficient to ensure his death sentence. Von Kluge succeeded him, remaining Commander-in-Chief West while also assuming command of Army Group B. He merely moved his own desk from Paris to Rommel's headquarters at La Roche Guyon.

Throughout his tenure of command in Normandy, Rommel directed the defence of the German front to formidable effect, filling the critical gaps and rushing forward units to stem dangerous Allied attacks. But there was no evidence in his handling of the battle of a great commander making brilliant strokes to confound the enemy. "In Normandy, there was no particular sign of Rommel's presence," said Montgomery's intelligence officer Brigadier Williams,[21] who had also watched the German general through the desert campaign. In the summer of 1944, Rommel played the part of the firefighter with all the energy at his command. It is difficult to see how any other commander could have achieved more, given the limitations of his resources and orders. His absence from Normandy on D-Day was unfortunate, but it is hard to believe that it was decisive. 21st Panzer might have intervened earlier had Rommel been present, but unsupported it could not have threatened the survival of Second Army's beachhead. At no stage in the battle did the division show anything like the determination in action of Panzer Lehr or 12th SS Panzer. It remains just possible that Rommel's personal influence would have sufficed to get Meyer and his tanks onto the battlefield on the afternoon of 6 June, in which case the British and Canadians would have been in serious trouble. But the balance of probability remains that Second Army could have established itself ashore against any available German defence. By mid-afternoon of D-Day, the excellent British anti-tank guns were already inland and deployed in strength. Just as the Allied commanders on D-Day were at the mercy of their subordinates' efficiency in executing their plan, so the German Seventh Army could achieve no more than the quality of its forces on the ground and the strength of the Atlantic Wall allowed. With or without Rommel, it lacked the mobility to concentrate for quick counter-attacks. Only the panzer divisions could execute these, and they could arrive no faster than their road speed and the Allied air forces would permit. "You know that it was my phrase

– 'The Longest Day'?" said Rommel's adjutant Hellmuth Lang. "After that day, after June 6, there was no hope of counter-attacks being decisive."[22]

Once the Allies were firmly established ashore, the only sane strategic course open to the Germans was precisely that which Hitler's madness would not allow – a progressive, carefully ordered retirement forcing the Allies to fight hard for every gain. The Germans would have been relieved of one immense handicap if they could have fought beyond the range of Allied naval gunfire. Southern France could have been abandoned, releasing the forces of Army Group G to support the decisive battle in Normandy. Some writers have sought to suggest that if the Allied FORTITUDE deception plan had been less successful, and if powerful elements of Fifteenth Army had been freed early in the campaign to fight for Normandy, the Germans might even have emerged victorious.[23] It is impossible to accept this. With stronger forces the battles would have been much harder, and Allied losses and delays even more severe. But while much has been said above about the shortcomings of British and American forces in attack, there was no doubt of their fighting prowess in defence. Then, all the terrain factors working for the Germans would operate for Montgomery's divisions, and the British army especially would fight in circumstances in which it always excelled. Overwhelming Allied air and firepower would have disposed of even the strongest German counter-attack in Normandy long before it reached the sea, although a thrust in bad weather, of the kind that crippled Allied air support in the Ardennes, could have caused the Allied high command serious concern.

Much speculation has been lavished upon the extent to which the activities of the anti-Hitler plotters, most notably Rommel's Chief of Staff, General Hans Speidel, contributed to the difficulties of the German defence. It is suggested that certain key divisions, including 116th Panzer, were kept back from the battle in the Pas de Calais to support the conspiracy. This debate was clouded by the self-serving post-war testimony of Speidel and others when they were seeking to establish their credentials as anti-Nazis. There can be no doubt of Rommel's sincerity in expecting a second Allied invasion. He devoted precious days to visiting formations of Fifteenth Army, checking their state of readiness, adjusting their deployments. 116th Panzer was edged nearer the coast in two separate moves following visits by

Rommel, which bewildered officers of the unit who expected to be ordered to Normandy, but seem most unlikely to have been related to the machinations of the 20 July plotters. Much more serious than any tampering of this kind was the vacuum in German intelligence. The second most important factor in the German defeat in Normandy, after inferiority of resources, was the blindness of the high command. Almost totally devoid of air reconnaissance, with every agent in Britain under British control, lacking any breakthrough in Allied codes and aided only by the fruits of low-grade wireless interception and prisoner interrogation on the battlefield, Rommel, von Rundstedt and von Kluge knew pathetically little of their enemies' potential strength or plans. Ignorance, plain ignorance, contributed much more to their failure than any possible acts of deliberate deceit by conspirators among the intelligence staffs. A critical contributory factor to this, as to so much else, was the dead hand of Hitler. More than any other aspect of military operations, intelligence must be conducted in an atmosphere unhampered by preconceptions. Yet Hitler's generals, above all in the latter half of the war, were never permitted to assess their predicament freely, and to act in accordance with their findings. Every act of military planning was conducted within the straitjacket of Hitler's manic instructions, which consistently ran counter to reality and logic. In such a climate, in absolute contrast to that surrounding the brilliantly conducted intelligence operations of the Allies, it becomes far less surprising that Rommel and so many of his colleagues were deluded by the fantasy of FUSAG's threat to the Pas de Calais. Their confidence, their flair and imagination, their belief in themselves, were sapped and corroded by years of serving a lunatic who lacked the military ability which served the other great dictator, Stalin, so well. The German generals were conducting a campaign in which, after the first days, they had no faith, by methods wholly inimical to all their instincts and training. It is difficult to believe that anything they might have done, in these circumstances, would significantly have altered the course of events.

The glory of German arms in Normandy – and it was glory, in however evil a cause – was won by the officers and men at divisional level and below who held the line against the Allies under intolerable conditions for more than two months. Colonel Kurt Kauffmann, operations officer of Panzer Lehr, believed

211

that in the first few days a really determined thrust against the Americans could have driven them into the sea. Thereafter, "I realized that the situation was hopeless, with more than 40 per cent of our infantry gone and the tremendous Allied shelling and air activity."[24] Yet it was Kauffman who led the dramatically successful counter-attack into Villers-Bocage on 13 June, and Panzer Lehr which remained one of the formations most respected by their Allied opponents even after it had suffered crippling losses. "Should we win this war, Kruger," the senior signals officer of 12th SS Panzer Division remarked acidly to one of his lieutenants, "I shall write a book about why we should have lost it."[25] Yet no division fought with more fanatical tenacity than the Hitler Jugend, whose soldiers had an average age of 18½. "It was a situation for despair, but there was no alternative but to keep one's nerve," said Colonel Heinz-Gunther Guderian, son of the great panzer leader and senior staff officer of 116th Panzer Division. "One had to hold before one's eyes the memory of Frederick the Great, and perhaps also to think of the words of the American general who said that the man who wins a battle is he who can remain standing until the last five minutes."[26] Brigadier Williams said: "The Germans adjusted much better to new conditions than we did. By and large they were better soldiers than we were. The Germans *liked* soldiering. We didn't."[27] General Quesada of the American IXth Air Force found afterwards that, "One's imagination boggled at what the German army might have done to us without Hitler working so effectively for our side."[28]

Fritz Langangke's Panzer V *abteilung* of 2nd SS Panzer Division was posted at St Sauveur-Lendelin in corps reserve early in July, when it was suddenly ordered forward in a crisis move to meet a new American breakthrough. He himself was directed to take his platoon to a point on the road near St Denis, and block any enemy advance along it. He asked for the position of the HKL – the main battle line – and was told that this was unknown. Late in the evening, he led his five Panthers cautiously forward, each commander straining his eyes and ears above the roar of his engine and squealing of the track for a hint of the enemy. At last there was a rattle of small-arms fire against the hull of Langangke's tank, and he concluded that he had come far enough. The platoon pulled back to deploy on each side of the road, hull down behind a hedge. "It was a pretty tight night," said the

German. The crews sat absolutely silent in their tanks, whispering when it was necessary to report by radio, listening constantly for movement in front of them. At dawn, despite their careful camouflage, one of the ubiquitous American Piper Cubs pinpointed them, and artillery fire began to fall around the position. Towards noon, men of the division's 3rd Der Führer Panzergrenadiers belatedly arrived and began to dig in around them, while the 6th Parachute Regiment deployed on their left. Conventional wisdom demanded that the tanks should fall back at nightfall and leave the infantry to hold the positions. But Langangke understood that there could be no such refinements here, where the tanks were being employed as strongpoints, and their moral support was essential to the infantry, even of an SS division.

The tank platoon held its positions for two weeks, under constant artillery fire, protected by its very proximity to the Americans, which caused the enemy gunners to fire consistently beyond the German line. At night, when the crews risked crawling out of the vehicles for an hour or two of merciful release, they could hear the American convoys moving up with supplies, and hear American voices across the still summer air. Once, the enemy attempted an infantry attack in a fashion which astonished the German veterans. They marched forward in long, leisurely files towards the Panthers' "as if they were going to a carnival". The SS opened a withering fire, and the attack crumpled.

Langangke remembered the next attack well, for it came on his birthday, 15 July. For a time amid the shooting, he himself could see nothing from his position closed down in his tank on the left hand side of the road. At first, he could not understand why the Americans were not attacking in his sector, but he later found that the ground in front was too soft for armour. Then one of his commanders jumped on the hull and shouted: "We've had it – hit in the turret!" Langangke ordered him to pull back, and ran across the road to see for himself. Five Shermans were approaching. He dashed back to his own tank, and told the crew: "We've got to get across that road." They felt that there was only the slimmest chance of survival once they moved from their closely camouflaged position into the open. But they had to try. At full speed, the tank roared from cover and crashed across the road in front of the Americans – "the longest forty metres I travelled in the war," said Langangke. Then the driver was braking the left track to swing to face the enemy. Still undamaged despite some shellfire, they began to engage the Shermans at point-blank range. They glimpsed dead and wounded German infantry around them, and survivors running from their foxholes to shelter in the lee of the Panther. It was obvious that the foot soldiers were close to panic. The crew urged Langangke to fire on the move, but he knew that if they did so, there was little chance of a hit. Most of the Shermans had fired one or even two rounds before the Panther began to shoot, but it was the German tank which now demonstrated its legendary killing power. A few moments later, four Shermans were burning in front of them. The fifth roared backwards into the thick brush. "A thing like that puts you on an unbelievable emotional level," said Langangke. "You feel like Siegfried, that you can dare to do *anything*."

The lieutenant jumped down from his tank, to be joined by one of his other commanders, and they ran forward up the ditch by the roadside to discover what the Americans were now doing. It was common practice among tank officers of all the armies in Normandy to resort frequently to their feet, for it was too hazardous to take a tank forward among the hedges without the kind of forewarning that only ground reconnaissance could provide. The Germans found the surviving Sherman still struggling to reverse over a hedge; engine revving, it staggered backwards and forwards on the rim of the obstacle. They retired to their tanks, Langangke cursing when he tripped over an abandoned infantry *Panzerfaust* that he could have use to good effect had he noticed it on the way forward. Back in the Panther, they fired a few rounds of HE and a long burst of machine-gun fire to clear the foliage obscuring the gunner's view of the Sherman. Then they hit it once in the turret with an armour-piercing shell. The American tank brewed up in the inevitable pillar of oily, black smoke and flame. The surviving German infantry regrouped. The Americans continued shelling the area, but launched no further major attack. Langangke's platoon had fought one among a thousand similar actions in those weeks in Normandy, demonstrating the remarkable tenacity and skill of the panzer crews and, above all, the superiority of their tanks.

Yet it would be absurd to give the impression that the German soldier found Normandy an easy, or even a tolerable battle. While many men said later that it was a less terrible experience

214

than the war in the east, from which most of them had come, even veterans were deeply shaken by the experience of hurling themselves again and again into action against the great steam-roller of Allied resources. 2nd Panzer Division reported in July on the difficulties they faced:

The incredibly heavy artillery and mortar fire of the enemy is something new for seasoned veterans as much as for the new arrivals from rein-forcement units. The assembly of troops is spotted immediately by enemy reconnaissance aircraft and smashed by bombs and artillery direc-ted from the air; and if, nevertheless, the attacking troops go forward, they become involved in such dense artillery and mortar fire that heavy casualties ensue and the attack peters out within the first few hundred metres. The losses suffered by the infantry are then so heavy that the impetus necessary to renew the attack is spent.

Our soldiers enter the battle in low spirits at the thought of the enemy's enormous superiority of *matériel*. The feeling of helplessness against enemy aircraft operating without hindrance has a paralysing effect; and during the barrage the effect on the inexperienced men is literally soul-shattering. The best results have been obtained by platoon and section commanders leaping forward uttering a good old-fashioned yell. We have also revived the practice of bugle calls.[29]

Hitler's armies had always adopted the policy of fashioning some elite divisions to provide the smashing combat power at the tip of their spear, while others – including most of the infantry form-ations – were equipped and manned principally to hold defensive positions between major battles. The 276th Infantry Division was a typical, moderate line formation, stationed at Bayonne on 6 June, made up to strength by combing Germany for over-age men – including many miners, who had hitherto been excused military service. Corporal Adolf Hohenstein had spent much of the war building bridges with a labour unit in Russia until he was transferred to the 276th. A 22-year-old former student mining engineer, he was much younger than most of the men around him. He found the division, "already pretty weak. We spent too much time doing old Prussian exercises rather than field training." On 16 June, they entrained for Le Mans, where they offloaded in pouring rain on the 19th. Thereafter, they marched by night to the front, advancing some 20 miles at a time, passing the days feeding the horses – upon whom they were overwhelm-ingly dependent for transport – among the cornfields where they halted. They loved their horses, and later were deeply depressed by the terrible casualties the animals suffered.

On 2 July, they took over a sector of the front near Villers-

Bocage from 12th SS Panzer, and spent their first days in the line laying mines and attempting to clear up the appalling wreckage of battle around them – dead men of every nationality, abandoned equipment, shattered vehicles. Harassing fire from British artillery taught them very quickly about the Wehrmacht's desperate shortage of medical supplies. Hohenstein watched his friend Heinz Alles bleed to death when an artery was severed by a bullet in the leg: "A man was lucky if he could get an injection. The doctors could only try to do something for those with a chance of life." Some men's nerve cracked very quickly. After 20 July, they convinced themselves that the shortages of supplies and ammunition and the breakdowns of administration were the fruits of treachery within their own army. In reality, of course, the entire creaking logistical machinery sustaining the German forces in Normandy was collapsing under the strain of air attack and attrition. Morale among the soldiers of the 276th ebbed steadily: "The lack of any success at all affected the men very badly. You could feel the sheer fear growing. We would throw ourselves to the ground at the slightest sound, and many men were saying that we should never leave Normandy alive."

It is important to cite the example of formations such as the 276th Infantry, indifferent soldiers, to emphasize that by no means the entire German front in France was in the hands of elite formations. Many German infantrymen were happy to seize an opportunity to be taken prisoner. They developed what they themselves called sardonically "the German look", ever craning upwards into the sky, watchful for fighter-bombers. While the Tommies played brag in their slit trenches, the Germans played "skat" in their foxholes a few hundred yards away, and listened to Lili Marlene on Radio Belgrade. They were as grateful as their Allied counterparts when, for a few days or even weeks, their sector of the front was quiet, and they endured nothing worse than harassing fire and patrols. They prayed for rain and cloud to keep the *jabos* – the *jagd-bombers* – away from them. Their greatest luxury was the capture of a few American soup cubes or tins of coffee. They pored earnestly over the English cooking instructions, and were jealously scornful of the Allies' material riches. Few German soldiers, even of moderate units, felt great respect for the fighting qualities of their enemies. Sergeant Heinz Hickmann of the Luftwaffe Parachute Division said: "We had no respect whatever for the American soldier." Colonel Kauffmann of Panzer Lehr remarked wryly that, "the

Americans started not too early in the morning, they liked a little bit too much comfort." Corporal Hohenstein reported that his men were constantly puzzled by the reluctance of the Americans to exploit their successes: "We felt that they always over-estimated us. We could not understand why they did not break through. The Allied soldier never seemed to be trained as we were, always to try to do more than had been asked of us." Here was one of the keys to German tactical success on the battlefield. Colonel Brian Wyldbore-Smith, GSO I of the British 11th Armoured Division, said: "The Germans were great opportun-ists. They were prepared to act – always."

It is striking to contrast the manner in which Allied units which suffered 40 or 50 per cent losses expected to be pulled out of the line, even disbanded, with their German counterparts, who were merely reassembled into improvised battlegroups – the *Kampf-gruppen* – which were an essential ingredient of so many of the German army's victories, and of its very survival for so many weeks in Normandy. Cooks, signallers, isolated tank platoons, stray Luftwaffe flak units, were all grist to the mill of the *kampf-gruppen*, which proved astonishingly cohesive and effective in action. When Sergeant Hans Stober of 17th SS Panzergrenadiers found the *flakabteilung* in which he served destroyed by air attack, he saw nothing remarkable in being transferred, with his surviving men, to *Kampfgruppe Ullrich*. A few weeks later, after the collapse at Falaise, he was serving with the remnants of 116th Panzer in *Kampfgruppe Fick*. In the middle of the Normandy battle, 116th Panzer's engineer battalion was drafted to fight as infantry and called upon to mount major ground attacks. The U.S. First Army were surprised to discover that one of their German prisoners in mid-July was a pay corps clerk, who had been given a week's infantry training and thrust into the line. No one could suggest that this manner of organizing an army or fighting a battle was a proper substitute for the maintenance of balanced and fully-equipped formations. But it was a critical factor in the German army's ability to avoid utter collapse even when most of its armoured and infantry formations had been battered into ruin.

The American Colonel Trevor Dupuy has conducted a detailed statistical study of German actions in the Second World War. Some of his explanations as to why Hitler's armies per-formed so much more impressively than their enemies seem fanciful. But no critic has challenged his essential finding that on

217

almost every battlefield of the war, including Normandy, the German soldier performed more impressively than his opponents:

On a man for man basis, the German ground soldier consistently inflicted casualties at about a 50% higher rate than they incurred from the opposing British and American troops UNDER ALL CIRCUM- STANCES. [emphasis in original] This was true when they were attacking and when they were defending, when they had a local numerical superiority and when, as was usually the case, they were outnumbered, when they had air superiority and when they did not, when they won and when they lost.[30]

It is undoubtedly true that the Germans were much more efficient than the Americans in making use of available man- power. An American army corps staff contained 55 per cent more officers and 44 per cent fewer other ranks than its German equivalent. In a panzergrenadier division in 1944–45, 89.4 per cent of the men were fighting soldiers, against only 65.56 per cent in an American division. In June 1944, 54.35 per cent of the German army consisted of fighting soldiers, against 38 per cent of the American army. 44.9 per cent of the German army was employed in combat divisions, against 20.8 per cent of the American. While the U.S. army became a huge industrial organ- ization, whose purpose sometimes seemed to be forgotten by those who administered it, the German army was designed solely as a machine for waging war. Even the British, who possessed nothing like the reserves of manpower of the Americans, tradi- tionally employed officers on a far more lavish scale than the German army, which laid particular emphasis upon NCO leadership.

Events on the Normandy battlefield demonstrated that most British or American troops continued a given operation for as long as reasonable men could. Then – when they had fought for many hours, suffered many casualties, or were running low on fuel or ammunition – they disengaged. The story of German operations, however, is landmarked with repeated examples of what could be achieved by soldiers prepared to attempt more than reasonable men could. German troops did not fight uni- formly well. But Corporal Hohenstein's assertion that they were trained always to try to do more than had been asked of them is borne out by history. Again and again, a single tank, a handful of infantry with an 88 mm gun, a hastily-mounted counter-attack, stopped a thoroughly-organized Allied advance dead in its tracks. German leadership at corps level and above was often little better than that of the Allies, and sometimes markedly worse. But at regimental level and below, it was superb. The German army appeared to have access to a bottomless reservoir of brave, able and quick-thinking colonels commanding battlegroups, and of NCOs capable of directing the defence of an entire sector of the front. The fanatical performance of the SS may partly explain the stubborn German defence of Europe in 1944–45. But it cannot wholly do so, any more than the quality of the Allied armies can be measured by the achievements of their airborne forces. The defence of Normandy was sustained for 10 weeks in the face of overwhelming odds by the professionalism and stubborn skills of the entire Wehrmacht, from General of Pioneers Meise, who somehow kept just sufficient road and rail links operational to maintain a thin stream of supplies to the front, to Corporal Hohenstein and his admittedly half-hearted comrades of 276th Infantry.

The German soldier was denied the sustaining force granted to the Allied armies – the certainty of final victory. But Hohenstein claimed that he and others were motivated above all by, "two words – 'unconditional surrender'. If for the rest of my life I was to chop wood in Canada or Siberia, then I would sooner die in Normandy." There is no doubt that President Roosevelt's insistence upon a public declaration of the unconditional surrender doctrine, despite Churchill's deep misgivings, was of immense value to the Nazi propaganda machine: it stifled many Germans' private hopes of some honourable escape from the war. They believed that defeat in Normandy, and beyond that defeat in Europe, would inaugurate a new dark age for Germany, a ghastly destiny for the German people. Their very sense of community with their American and British opponents, coupled with their view of the Russians as barbarians from another planet, compounded their self-delusions. To the bitter end, many German soldiers harboured a sincere belief that they could make common cause with the western Allies against the Russians. To this end, they told themselves that it was essential to sustain a front until some agreement could be achieved.

There is also little doubt of the validity of the traditional view of the German soldier as naturally obedient and dedicated, far more so than most men of the Allied armies. He was a soldier, and therefore he fought. The British had come to terms with this reality over many years, but Americans were still astonished to discover the strength of this apparently unreasoning approach.

Several times during the European campaign. [wrote Bradley] I wondered why German commanders in the field did not give up their senseless resistance. Prolonged resistance could do nothing but aggravate the disaster that had already claimed the Reich. George Patton offered an answer when he visited Army Group early in August just as we tightened our noose around the German Seventh Army. "The Germans are either crazy or they don't know what's going on," I said, "surely the professionals must know by now that the jig is up." George answered by telling the story of a German general that Third Army had captured several days before. He had been asked by G-2 why he had not surrendered before, if only to spare Germany further destruction. "I am a professional," he replied without emotion, "and I obey my orders."[31]

Most of the German army in Normandy followed his example.

Weapons

If the German army was a superb fighting instrument, a decisive factor in its ability to defend Normandy for so long, and to such effect, was the superiority of almost all its weapons in quality, if not in quantity, to those of the Allied ground forces. In the air and at sea, the Allies achieved a large measure of technological as well as numerical dominance in the second half of the Second World War. Yet the industrial resources of Britain and America were never applied to provide their armies with weapons of the same quality as those produced by German industry in the face of the Allies' strategic bombing offensive. In 1942, Albert Speer and his staff took the decision, since they could not hope to match the quantitative superiority of the Allies, to attempt to defeat them by the qualitative superiority of German equipment. Feats on the battlefield, such as Captain Wittman's ravaging of the British armoured column at Villers-Bocage, were only made possible by the extraordinary power of a Tiger tank in among even a regiment of British Cromwells. During the first weeks in Normandy, Allied tank units were dismayed to discover the ease with which their Shermans "brewed up" after a single hit, while their own shells were unable to penetrate a Panther, far less a Tiger tank, unless they struck a vital spot at close range. On 24 June, Montgomery's Chief of Staff, de Guingand, wrote to him:

"If we are not careful, there will be a danger of the troops developing a Tiger and Panther complex . . . P. J. Grigg rang me up last night and said he thought there might be trouble in the Guards Armoured Division as regards 'the inadequacy of our tanks compared with the Germans' . . . Naturally the reports are not being circulated."[1] Montgomery himself quashed a succession of complaints and open expressions of concern.

"I have had to stamp very heavily on reports that began to be circulated about the inadequate quality of our tanks, equipment, etc., as compared with the Germans . . ." he wrote to Brooke. "In cases where adverse comment is made on British equipment such reports are likely to cause a lowering of morale and a lack of confidence among the troops. It will generally be found that when the equipment at our disposal is used properly and the tactics are good, we have no difficulty in defeating the Germans."[2]

Montgomery knew that it was futile, indeed highly dangerous, to allow the shortcomings of Allied weapons to be voiced openly in his armies, for there was no hope of quickly changing them. The battle must be won or lost with the arms that the Allies had to hand. The Americans, characteristically, felt less disposed to keep silence about technical failure. On 3 July, Eisenhower complained formally to the U.S. War Department about the shortcomings of many of his army's weapons, following a meeting in France at which, "from Monty and Brooke E learnt that our AT equipment and our 76 mm in Shermans are not capable of taking on Panthers and Tigers."[3] General James Gavin of the American 82nd Airborne Division described how his men first came to understand these things in Italy:

For years we had been told that our weapons were superior to any that we would encounter. After all, we were soldiers from the most highly industrialised and the richest nation on earth. But that very preoccupation with our advanced technology caused many to assume that technology alone would win battles – more emphasis was placed upon victory through air power than victory through better infantry . . . Our problems stemmed very often from the lack of imagination, if not lack of intelligence, of those responsible for developing infantry weapons.[4]

The Americans indeed possessed an excellent rifle in the semi-automatic Garand, and the British an adequate one in the bolt-action Lee-Enfield. But on the European battlefield, as commanders learned, men seldom fired their rifles. They had little need of accuracy when they did so, for they could rarely distinguish a target. American research showed that, in many regiments, only 15 per cent of riflemen used their weapons in any given action. What mattered was the weight of fire to saturate the battle area. For this, the Germans possessed the supreme weapons in their MG 34 and 42 machine-guns – invariably known among the Allies as Spandaus – with their fabulous rate of fire drowning out the measured hammer of the British bren or the American BAR squad light machine-gun. The MG 42's tearing, rasping 1,200 rounds a minute, against the bren's 500, proved deeply demoralizing to men advancing against it. A German infantry company carried 16 machine-guns, compared to the British 9, and the American 11, although the heavy Vickers and Brownings of the Allied support companies somewhat redressed this balance.

The handle on the German "potato-masher" hand grenade enabled it to be thrown further than its British or American counterparts. The German Schmeisser was a far superior submachine gun to the American "grease gun" or the British sten, which the War Office had ordered in quantity, in an eccentric moment in 1941, although it derived from a German patent sensibly spurned by the Wehrmacht. All the German small arms enjoyed a significant advantage over their American counterparts – in using ammunition with power which produced less flash and smoke. It was markedly easier for a German soldier to pinpoint American fire than *vice versa*, a technological advantage upon which Marshall commented acidly in a post-war report.

The Germans had made themselves masters in the handling of mortars. Their mortar "stonks", landing without warning in the middle of Allied positions, inaudible in transit because of their slow flight, grated the nerves of every British and American unit in Normandy, and were responsible for an extraordinarily high proportion of casualties – 75 per cent for much of the campaign. Every infantry division possessed some 60 81 mm and up to 20 120 mm mortars, which could throw a 35-pound bomb 6,000 yards. The Allies also, of course, possessed mortars, but never mastered the art of concentrating them with the devastating effect that the Germans achieved. Above all, men detested the *Nebelwerfer*, the multi-barrelled projector whose bombs were fitted with a brilliantly conceived siren, causing them to wail as they flew through the air, which had an effect on those who heard them often more penetrating than their explosive power.

222

Nebelwerfers came in three sizes: 150 mm (75-pound bomb, 7,300-yard range); 210 mm (248-pound, 8,600-yard); 300 mm (277-pound, 5,000-yard). Each of the five regiments of these – the bulk of them concentrated in the British sector in Normandy – contained 60 or 70 projectors, some of them track-mounted. German infantry anti-tank weapons were also markedly superior. British battalions were equipped only with a spring-loaded projector named the PIAT, which threw a 2½-pound bomb 115 yards and demanded strong nerves from its aimer, who knew that if he lingered long enough to fire at his target with a chance of success, failure meant probable extinction. Even in short-range tests in England, the PIAT scored only 57 per cent hits. The American bazooka packed a wholly inadequate projectile for penetrating German tank armour. The Germans, meanwhile, were equipped in Normandy with the excellent *Panzerfaust*, the finest infantry anti-tank weapon of the war. Gavin's paratroopers seized and employed as many as they could capture.

At a higher level Allied artillery and anti-tank guns were good and plentiful. Indeed, every army fighting in Normandy singled out the British and American artillery as the outstanding arm of the Allied forces. Artillery was responsible for more than half the casualties inflicted in the Second World War. Normandy was the first campaign in which the British used the new discarding-sabot ammunition[5] for their 6 and 17-pounders, with formidable penetrating effect. But the towed anti-tank gun was of little value to troops in attack, and even very accurate artillery fire proved an uncertain method of destroying enemy troops who were well dug in. The British 25-pounder was a fine gun, out-ranging the American 105 mm by 13,400 yards to 12,200, and was immensely valuable for "keeping heads down". But it lacked killing power against defensive positions. It was essential to bring down medium or heavy artillery fire for decisive effect, and there was never enough of this to go round. Nor did the Allies possess any weapon with the physical and moral effect of the German 88 mm, the very high velocity anit-aircraft gun that had been used against ground targets with dazzling success since the early days of the war. Time after time in Normandy, a screen of 88 mm guns stopped an Allied attack dead. Firing high-explosive airburst shells, it was also formidable against infantry. The unforgettable lightning crack of an 88 mm remained implanted in the memory of every survivor of the campaign. It was a mystery to the Allied armies why their own industries failed to build a direct copy of the 88 mm, the Schmeisser, or the potato-masher.

Yet the greatest failure was that of the tank. How could American and British industries produce a host of superb air-craft, an astonishing variety of radar equipment, the proximity fuse, the DUKW, the jeep, yet still ask their armies to join battle against the Wehrmacht equipped with a range of tanks utterly inferior in armour and killing power? A British tank officer, newly-arrived in France in June 1944, recorded a conversation with his regimental adjutant about the state of the armoured battle:

"What do the Germans have most of?"

"Panthers. The Panther can slice through a Churchill like butter from a mile away."

"And how does a Churchill get a Panther?"

"It creeps up on it. When it reaches close quarters the gunner tries to bounce a shot off the underside of the Panther's gun mantlet. If he's lucky, it goes through a piece of thin armour above the driver's head."

"Has anybody ever done it?"

"Yes. Davis in C Squadron. He's back with headquarters now, trying to recover his nerve."

"How does a Churchill get a Tiger?"

"It's supposed to get within two hundred yards and put a shot through the periscope."

"Has anyone ever done it?"

"No."

If this account[6] bordered upon satire, the reality was little dif-ferent – the product of an extraordinary lack of Allied foresight. A specialist who was intimately concerned in the British tank design programme from its earliest days, Colonel George Mac-leod Ross, suggested after the war that the War Office made a fatal error by separating the development of fighting vehicles from that of tank guns. Ross, and other experts, argued that it was vital to design the right tank gun, and then to build a suitable vehicle to carry it. Instead, throughout the Second World War, a succession of British tanks were produced in isolation from any consideration either of the enemy gun that they must expect to meet, or of the weight of armour that their own gun must expect to penetrate. Tank design was located at Chobham, while gun design was sited at Woolwich. Although the design of the superb British 17-pounder gun was approved and a prototype construc-

The Sherman tank was the principal armoured weapon of the Allied armies, magnificently reliable and mechanically efficient, but critically handicapped by thin armour and lack of an adequate gun, save for the few British 17-pounder-mounted Sherman Fireflies. The Sherman weighed 32 tons and could move at 24 mph. It carried only 76 mm of frontal armour, 51 mm of side armour. The Mk V 75 mm gun with which most models were equipped could penetrate 74 mm of armour at 100 yards, 68 mm at 500 yards, 60 mm at 1,000 yards. Even the upgunned 76 mm and 17-pounder versions suffered problems from the fierce flash when they fired, making it difficult for the crews to observe fall of shot. Note the white star painted on the turret side, the universal identification symbol for all Allied vehicles in Europe.

ted in June 1941, it was not mounted in a tank until the first Sherman Firefly was belatedly produced in August 1943, in too small a quantity to influence OVERLORD decisively. "It is not unfair to say," declared Ross, who served for much of the war as British Technical Liaison officer to the U.S. Army Ordnance in Detroit, "that little of the labour and materials expended on the 25,000 British-built tanks helped to win the war."[7] A visit to Eighth Army in the desert by a temporary technical observer in November 1942 resulted in a disastrous report to the War Office, allegedly approved by Montgomery, asserting that "the 75 mm gun is all we require".[8] This report set the seal upon British tank gun policy for much of the rest of the war, ensuring that

6-pounder and 75 mm-gunned Churchills and Cromwells would form the basis of British tank strength. "None of our authorities seemed to understand as the Germans did", wrote Ross, "the need in war for sustained improvement of weapons."[9]

Yet the decisive force in wartime tank production, as in so much else, was the United States. Russell Weigley, an outstanding American analyst of the U.S. army in the war, has highlighted the failure of its architects to match their end – the application of concentrated power upon the battlefield – to their means: principally, the Sherman tank. Against 24,630 tanks built by the Germans and 24,843 made by the British by the end of 1944, the Americans turned out a staggering 88,410, 25,600 of which were supplied to the British. The great majority were Shermans, first produced in 1942, and dominating all Allied armoured operations in 1944–45. Two-thirds of the tanks employed by British units in Normandy were Shermans, the balance being chiefly Cromwells (7th Armoured Division) and Churchills (79th Division and independent armoured brigades). The Sherman was a superbly reliable piece of machinery, far easier to maintain and with a track life five times longer than its German counterparts. It weighed 33 tons, compared with the 43 tons of the Panther, and 56 tons of the Tiger. Its fast cross-country speed reflected the Americans' doctrinal obsession with pace in armoured operations. It possessed two important advantages over its German opponents: a faster speed of turret traverse to engage the enemy, and a higher rate of fire. Conversely, it suffered two critical weaknesses: first, its readiness to catch fire, which caused soldiers on the battlefield to christen it "the ronson" or "tommy cooker". This was a reflection upon its design and thin armour, rather than (as the U.S. War Department suggested tetchily after early complaints) because its crews were loading too much ammunition into its turret. Second, and more important, it was undergunned. Its original 75 mm gun produced a muzzle velocity of 2,050 feet-per-second against 2,900 f.p.s. of the British 17-pounder and the 3,340 f.p.s. of the German 88 mm. At a range of 200 yards, the British gun had almost thrice the penetration of the 75 mm. A Tiger could knock out a Sherman at a range of 4,000 yards, while the American tank could not penetrate a Tiger's frontal armour at all. Even when the Sherman was up-gunned with a 76 mm, it was compelled to close to within 300 yards of a Tiger to have a chance of knocking it out. "Not only do German Mk V and Mk VI tanks keep out a greater proportion of hits than Shermans," concluded a gloomy SHAEF Operational Research report in 1944, "but also they are *far less likely to brew up when penetrated*" (emphasis in original).[10] Even the much lighter 25-ton German Mk IV tank, which made up about half the tank strength of the panzer divisions, packed a KWK 40 75 mm gun with a muzzle velocity 20 per cent greater than the Sherman's 75 mm. This was capable of penetrating 92 mm of armour at 500 yards against the 68 mm of the Sherman's gun.

The American War Department could not claim ignorance of the enemy's developments in the field of gunnery. As early as May 1942, Major Jarrett of U.S. Army Ordnance shipped a captured 88 mm gun across the Atlantic with a report emphasizing its potency. There were a variety of causes for the American failure to pursue the improvement of the Sherman at once. The designers were pinning most of their hopes upon early production of an entirely new replacement tank. Enormous effort was wasted on a new model, named the T20, whose development spanned three years and seven pilots, but of which only 120 reached the battlefield at the end of the war. General Electric were labouring on a strange white elephant designated the T23. Colonel Ross wrote that "there can be no excuse for the abysmal ignorance of tank tactics generally and tank operations in Europe in particular which prompted this half-hearted attempt to design a worthy successor to the Sherman when the simple answer was to design a better gun, something infinitely easier than a tank."[11] There was undoubtedly chauvinistic resistance in the U.S. to copying either the German 88 mm or, more plausibly, the British 17-pounder. Since the first days of the war, tank design also suffered from the misconceptions of General Lesley McNair, the principal architect of the U.S. army in the Second World War. McNair believed that armoured divisions would chiefly be employed for exploitation and pursuit, and that tanks would seldom be called upon to fight other tanks. He fell victim to the same fallacies that underlay the creation of the battle-cruiser by the admirals of an earlier generation, sacrificing armour to speed only to discover that mere pace in battle is almost meaningless, unless matched by survivability.

Above all, there was a belief at the top of the American armed forces that the Allied armies possessed such a vast numerical superiority of tanks that some technical inferiority was acceptable. Yet when a Sherman tank in Normandy, or even a platoon

227

or battalion of Shermans, found itself confronted by enemy tanks whose armour their guns could not penetrate, numerical advantage seemed to mean little. The apprehension and caution of tank crews were well founded. They knew that if they were hit, they almost certainly burned. If they burned, each crew member had only a 50 per cent statistical prospect of survival. Bradley wrote: "This willingness to expend Shermans offered little comfort to the crews who were forced to expend themselves as well."[12]

We all thought that our tanks were deficient [wrote a British tank officer], and I believe that this had a highly adverse effect on morale. In the end we all became "canny", and would obey orders only to the extent that there appeared a reasonable expectation of successfully carrying them out. There was thus a sort of creeping paralysis in the armoured units; because of the pervading fear of 88s, Panthers, Tigers and Panzerfausts, initiative was losty and squadron commanders tended

The Panzer VI, or Tiger, was the most feared German tank in Normandy, almost impenetrable by frontal Allied tank gunfire, and packing a devastating punch with its 88 mm KwK 36 gun. Muzzle velocity in all guns is chiefly a function of barrel length, and Allied troops were always shocked by their first encounters with the Tiger's gun, "as long as a telegraph pole", as so many men reported. Its 20-pound shell could penetrate 120 mm of armour at 100 yards, 112 mm at 500 yards, 102 mm at 1,000 yards. The Tiger itself carried 100 mm of frontal armour, 80 mm of side armour, weighed 54 tons and had a maximum speed of 23 mph. It was normally employed in independent battalions allocated to German corps or divisions for specific operational purposes. Its principal shortcomings were clumsiness of movement and lack of mechanical reliability.

to go to ground at the first sign of any serious opposition and call up an artillery "stonk". With any luck, as the day wore on, the battle died down and that was at least another day got through.

If the technical detail above seems laboured in a campaign narrative, it has been pursued because no single Allied failure had more important consequences on the European battlefield than the lack of tanks with adequate punch and protection. No weapon, above all no tank, is good or bad in isolation. It must be judged against the enemy weapons which it is expected to fight. Sufficient examples have been given elsewhere in these pages of encounters between German and Allied tanks in which it was not uncommon for the panzer to destroy four, five or even more Shermans before being knocked out itself. The Allies' failure to make forceful judgements about the need to match each new generation of German tanks and the blindness of the General Staffs to the need for bigger tank guns, cost them dearly on the battlefield. Even huge losses of Shermans could be made good. But the knowledge of their own tanks' weakness had a serious effect upon the confidence and aggressiveness of Allied units wherever armour met armour.

Throughout the war, the British authorities were at pains to stifle any public debate about the shortcomings of their tanks, although these were well known throughout the British army. The Labour MP Richard Stokes, who had himself fought gallantly in the First World War, was a thorn in the government's flesh on the issue of tank design, as he was also about strategic bombing, the "unconditional surrender" doctrine, and other embarrassing military matters. Stokes made himself intimately acquainted with every detail of British and German tank performance – thickness of armour, relative muzzle velocities and so on. He became the scourge of the government benches by rehearsing these unwelcome facts at every opportunity. On 30 March 1944, he requested that a Churchill and a captured Tiger tank should be brought to the House of Commons for members to judge for themselves the fighting power of each. The Prime Minister replied:

No sir. I think the trouble and expense involved, though not very great, is still more than is justified to satisfy the spiteful curiosity of my Honourable friend.[13]

Stokes was aided and abetted by a handful of like-minded spirits. On 20 July 1944, Mr Ellis-Smith asked the Prime Minister for details of the relative performance of British and German tanks. Mr Churchill replied:

Before the House rises I shall hope to give a solid report upon the performances of British tanks in the various theatres of war. For the present I rest on my statement of 16 March, as follows: "The next time that the British Army takes the field in country suitable for the use of armour, they will be found to be equipped in a manner at least equal to the forces of any other country in the world."

On 25 July 1944, Stokes asked the Secretary of State for War, "whether he will assure this house that our troops in Normandy are equipped with tanks at least the equal of both the German Tiger and Panther in armour and armament?" As in almost every debate in which this issue was raised, P. J. Grigg dismissed Stokes with the assurance that public discussion of this issue was not in the public interest. The backbencher denounced "the most complete humbug with which this matter is treated". On 2 August 1944, Stokes yet again savaged the government about the shortcomings of British tanks: "Relatively speaking, today, we are just as far behind the Germans as we were in 1940. I submit that this is a disgraceful state of affairs." Another MP, Rear-Admiral Beamish, leapt to the government's defence: "The Honourable member has spent his whole time in doing every-thing he can to lower the prestige of the British army." Stokes rejoined: "My criticisms have been based upon irrefutable facts." Hansard recorded the laughter of the House. "It is all very well for honourable members to laugh," said Stokes, "but these men are dying." He quoted a letter that he had received from a Churchill tank crewman who suggested that the Secretary of State for War should go out and fight "with one of these ruddy things". The Speaker intervened to reproach Stokes for his language: "I have heard bad language from him three times." Stokes declared that he was merely quoting the direct speech of others, from the battlefield. It was self-evident that his informa-tion, and his report on the sentiment of tank crews, were entirely well founded. But he remained a prophet without honour. The government lied systematically, until the very end of the war, about the Allies' tragic failure to produce tanks capable of matching those of the Germans.

Colonel Campbell Clarke, perhaps the foremost British ordnance expert of the war, originator of the 25-pounder and the entire range of successful anti-tank guns, wrote early in 1945:

We here in Britain have some time ago reached the stage where military weapons have developed somewhat beyond the educational capacity of the average soldier to appreciate their functional use; still more so that of the General Staff officer to direct their future lines of development for war. The inevitable consequence has been, and will increasingly be, tactical stagnation and "surprise" by an enemy who is prepared to plan new methods for their use in conjunction with a first-hand knowledge of technical possibilities and limitations.[14]

Any armoured officer fighting in north-west Europe in 1944 would have echoed his sentiments.

7 The battlefield

From the beachhead to the front

By the last days of June, the battle for Normandy had taken on the character that it was to retain for the two months that followed: a struggle involving more than 1,000,000 men pitted against each other on a front of scarcely 100 miles. By August, the numbers would be over 2,000,000. Each morning, while in the fighting areas armoured units ground forward from their night harbours and headquarters staffs plotted the hopeful course of the next battle, thousands of infantrymen lay in their foxholes scratching laconic letters home, overshadowed by a consciousness both of the censor's eye and of the desultory shell and mortar fire around them. "Dear Mum," wrote Private Sid Verrier of the 2nd Ox & Bucks on 27 June:

I'm still feeling rather dirty after living the way I have done since D-Day and I will be very glad to have a good bath, change into civvies and go for a nice walk round the parks at home. Better than a walk would be a couple of days sleep. Still I'm not grumbling, life is too sweet . . .[1]

On the beaches, new columns of men waded ashore from their landing craft, each one awed by the feeling that he was conducting his own personal invasion, no matter how many others had gone before. Bradley, as he came ashore at Omaha on the second day, was puzzled by the sight of a broken tennis racquet and a sodden boxing glove drifting side by side amid the debris in the surf. Ceaseless columns of vehicles bumped across the piers and out of the LCTs beached on the sand, to follow the outstretched gauntlet of a military policeman towards some rendezvous inland. When Trooper Stephen Dyson drove his tank up Juno beach in the last days of June, he jumped down from the hull and filled a matchbox with French sand the moment that the Churchill had cleared the LCT. His squadron harboured alongside tanks of 11th Armoured Division, veterans of some weeks' experience. They chatted together. The 11th Armoured men derided their late appearance on the battlefield. "They told us that the Germans were very, very good."

Every man who approached the French coast that summer was amazed by the panorama of shipping that met his eye, the Rhino ferries shuttling out to the transports with cargoes of dejected German prisoners, the huge caissons and heavily gunned piers of the Mulberry harbours, whose creation had done so much to convince doubters, such as the Prime Minister, that OVER-LORD was feasible. In fact, there will always be grave doubt as to whether the Mulberries justified the enormous cost and effort that was put into them. Their scale fascinated and impressed contemporary servicemen and the first generation of post-war historians, but recent researchers[2] have focussed much more closely upon the American achievement of unloading stores at a greater rate directly across the beaches than had been managed across the Mulberry before the American harbour was wrecked in the "great storm" of 19–23 June. The storm itself, treated by some chroniclers as a veritable cataclysm, has also been the subject of modern dispute. At no time, it has been pointed out, did the winds exceed force six, a moderate blow by nautical standards. The inability of the Mulberries to withstand it – for the British harbour was also severely damaged – seems to reflect more upon the strength of the structures rather than upon the nature of the gales. There was no doubt of the impact of the storm upon the Allied unloading programme, or of its serious effect upon operations at the front. But the surprise of the Allied command about the consequences of the storm was caused chiefly by their expectation that the huge Mulberry programme should have been capable of overcoming any problems of delay. It is likely that Allied unloading operations could have been shielded from the sea just as effectively merely by sinking the screen of blockships and creating a network of piers, rather than by devoting the labour of 45,000 men to building the Mulberries.[3] Some of the same doubts apply to another celebrated innovation, PLUTO – PipeLine Under The Ocean – a device for pumping petrol direct from England to the armies in France. It was 41 days before PLUTO was in position. A few weeks later its submerged couplings gave way and a new line had to be laid from Dungeness to Boulogne. This began to yield 700 tons of fuel a day only in January 1945.[4]

The slow progress inland resulted in a dramatic surplus of

vehicles ashore in the first weks after D-Day – in the first 11 days 81,000 came ashore for the Americans alone. Every GI required 30 pounds of supplies per day to support him in action, compared with 20 pounds per British soldier, and a German quota that sometimes fell to four pounds. The Allied armies demanded 26,000 tons of stores *a day* to sustain them in action. By 25 July, there were 1,450,000 men ashore – 812,000 American, 640,000 British and Canadian. Amid this vast movement of humanity, some simply disappeared into the administrative jungle. General Gerow of the U.S. V Corps was compelled to make a personal visit to England to locate one unit under his command which he was persistently assured was with his corps in Normandy.

Inland from the beaches, newly arriving men gaped at the massive dumps of fuel, ammunition, supplies, the parked ranks of brand-new tanks, vehicles, guns that crowded every field. Uncamouflaged, their safety was a spectacular tribute to the Allies' absolute command of the air. As for so many others, the first impression of Major Charles Richardson of the 6th KOSB was astonishment that the beachhead was so well organized, and bewilderment about where to find a field in which to put anything. Tank tracks scarred the countryside in all directions. Unit signposts and field telephone cables were nailed to every tree by the roadside, or draped along branches and ditches. Patton, when he came, was delighted by the droll spectacle of telephone wires suspended between the crucifixes at every crossroads. The crashed aircraft that lay everywhere reminded him of "dead birds partly eaten by beetles".[5] Soldiers were puzzled, sometimes angered, by the sight of French civilians tending their fields or going about their business with their little carts, apparently indifferent to the claims of their liberators to gratitude. One morning a few days after the landing, Corporal Charles Baldwin of the Westminster Dragoons was sent back to the beaches to bring forward a draft of replacements for his squadron:

Just after leaving Crepon by jeep, in a field on my right I noticed some dead British infantry. There were two civilians there and I pulled up. Another jeep containing a military police lance-corporal pulled up behind me. We walked towards the two men and it became apparent that they had been looting the bodies. Two had had their boots removed. The civilians started to speak quickly in French. But the military policeman simply said: "Bloody bastards" and shot them with his sten gun.[6]

234

Private John Price found most of the French sullen, and was struck by the predominance of the elderly – the young or middle-aged appeared to have fled. But he was touched when a kindly old clockmaker asked for a penny, and worked it into a ring for him. Many of the British, after years of privation at home, were disgusted by the abundance of food in the Norman villages. "The civilians seemed to have eaten well," said Alfred Lee of the Middlesex Regiment. "We saw no skinny ones."[7] There were persistent rumours throughout the beachhead of Fifth Column activities by local Frenchmen spying for the Germans, and these multiplied mistrust. "We almost had the feeling that these people had not been hostile to the Germans," John Hein of the U.S. 1st Division said wonderingly.[8] A captured German of 12th SS Panzer wrote cynically in his diary: "As we are marched through the town towards the port, the French insult us, shake their fists and make throat-cutting gestures. This does not really shock us. We are used to this sort of thing from the French. If it was the other way around, they would be threatening the Tommies . . ."[9] In the British sector, it was found necessary to mount pipeline patrols to prevent civilians from inserting wooden plugs at intervals along them in order to drain off fuel supplies for themselves. Most Normans treated the fighting armies with impartial disdain or occasional kindness. Helmut Gunther of 17th SS Panzergrenadiers once asked an elderly woman why she gave his men cream, and she answered gravely: "Because I have a grandson who is a prisoner in Germany, and I hope that the people there are doing the same for him."[10] It was not remarkable that so many French families were shocked and appalled by the cost of liberation to their own homes, which if anything were looted more thoroughly by the Allied than the German armies. "We have been reproached," wrote a local writer bitterly a few months later, "at least by those who regard the battle of Normandy as a military tattoo, for failing to throw ourselves on the necks of our liberators. Those people have lost sight of the Stations of the Cross that we have passed since 6 June."[11] When it began to rain early in July, the locals told the soldiers that there had not been a summer like it for 50 years. But for this, at least, they did not seek to blame the Allies. They shrugged: "*C'est la guerre.*"

A few overworked Norman prostitutes were already plying their trade. One day General Bradley was astonished to notice a village near Isigny with "Off Limits" signs posted outside it, and drove in with General "Pete" Quesada of IXth Tactical Air Command. He found a house marked "Prophylactic Station", containing three sleeping GIs, none of whom recognized their army commander when he awakened them. He inquired how much business they were doing. The medic shrugged. "Well, yesterday there was just the two for the MPs and one for me and that was it." Characteristically, Bradley moved on without inflicting the trauma of his identity upon them.[12]

It was well into July before facilities for rear-area entertainments began to be established, and few men were withdrawn from the line for long enough to enjoy them. But in the *mairie* of Balleroy, where the U.S. 1st Division had its civil affairs office issuing *laissez-passers* to civilians and supervising the blackout, a group of local inhabitants one day requested permission to hold a concert. On 2 July, a few score civilians and GIs crowded into the little auditorium for what they billed proudly as "the first cultural event in liberated France". The mayor's daughter sang a song, a succession of other local talents performed their little acts, and Leslie Bertal, a Hungarian concert pianist of some pre-war celebrity who was now serving as a prisoner-of-war interrogator, played in the oddest setting of his career. He was killed a week later, when a shell exploded in the tree above him as he was questioning a German soldier.

For most of the men fighting in France, beyond a passing curiosity about alien sights and a foreign language, life revolved around the battle and the cocoon of their units. Each squad or platoon carried its little island of east London or westside New York across Europe, the average GI only communicating with the world outside for long enough to imitate a chicken before a bewildered Frenchwoman, in an effort to persuade her to sell him eggs. They had little eye for the beauty of the creeper-clad farmhouses, the white apple and pear blossom, the golden walls of the châteaux. Most Tommies were bemused by their officer's enthusiasm for the sticky, smelly local cheese – camembert. Sergeant Andy Hertz, an American aviation engineer, was once asked to dinner by a French refugee family, fellow Jews. He said that it was his first inkling of what the Germans were doing to his people. As a souvenir, his hosts gave him one of the yellow Stars of David that they had been compelled to wear. He kept it all his life.

The rear areas were littered with signs – divisional symbols and direction markers, cautionary KEEP TO SWEPT PATH, or roughly daubed FRONT LINE NO VEHICLES FORWARD OF HERE, or simply DUST MEANS DEATH. Except when rain and the vast columns of tracked vehicles had chewed the roads into muddy ruins, one of the greatest perils was the dust thrown up by speeding convoys, bringing down a deadly rain of German artillery fire. Infantry cursed the proximity of their own tanks or artillery for the same reason, and took pains to avoid occupying positions near a major signals unit, for fear of German radio locators and the fire that they could call down. Every German signaller testified to the carelessness of Allied soldiers on the air, especially the Canadians and some American units whose easy chatter provided priceless intelligence.

Among the fighting soldiers, there was little to do between battles except stroll among the fields or visit a nearby village to buy milk or eggs; they could write home; drown themselves in the universal calvados and cider; play cards; or talk interminably. Padre Lovegrove of the Green Howards tried to get his men to speak about their civilian jobs and homes, to preserve some grip upon the world beyond the battlefield. Among themselves many men, inevitably, talked about women. But deep in their hearts most soldiers on the battlefield would readily trade a night with a woman for a hot bath, a home-cooked meal, and a safe bed in which they could merely sleep. Some found solace in religion. Frank Svboda, a presbyterian chaplain with the U.S. 79th Division, was moved by the manner in which his services were attended by Protestants, Jews, and Catholic soldiers clutching their rosaries. Before battle, he found himself administering communion of crackers and squeezed raisin juice to little clusters of 15 or 20 sombre young men in a hedgerow a few hundred yards behind the front. Good chaplains were greatly prized by their units, but bad ones – of whom there were many in the Allied armies – were detested and avoided for the hypocrisy with which they offered their blessings from the rear echelon. Frank Svboda felt that the best aid he possessed in cementing relations with his men was a little axe he had bought in England, and which they found invaluable for hacking off the stubborn hedgerow roots as they dug foxholes. "Chaplain, pass the hatchet!" became a unit catchphrase.

The Americans lived chiefly off 5-pound cartons of C rations, or the more popular three-meal K ration – 60,000,000 of them were shipped to Normandy in the first three weeks of operations. Everybody detested the powdered lemon juice, but otherwise it was the monotony of the food that men cursed, rather than its quality. One night, John Hein found himself called upon to feed four German prisoners seized by a patrol. The men wolfed their first American rations, one of them declaring courteously: "This is first-rate." British soldiers were astonished by the sheer quantity of American supplies, and by the ice cream-making machines that soon appeared in rear areas. But their own rations were of substantially higher quality than the food on which the British civilian population at home was being fed. Augmented by occasional cuts from freshly-dead cattle and produce bought or thieved from the Normans, it was tolerable enough. Almost every man smoked. The armies supplied the troops with cigarettes in prodigal profusion, as the readiest means of sustaining morale, the most portable comfort available to a soldier. For the first weeks ashore in France, their greatest craving was bread. There was none to be had until field bakeries were established in the beachhead, and as they chewed day after day on tasteless hard tack biscuits, soft white bread came to seem an unimaginable luxury.

To almost every man of the Allied armies, the predominant memory of the campaign, beyond the horror of the battle, was the astounding efficiency of the supply services. The Americans had always justly prided themselves upon their organization. But for young British soldiers, who had grown up with the legend of the War Office's chronic bungling, and of the Crimea and the Boer War, Second Army's administration in Normandy seemed a miracle. "We were all very agreeably surprised by the efficiency," said Major John Warner of 3rd Reece Regiment. "We always knew that we would receive ammunition, letters, petrol, food." Curiously enough, whatever the command shortcomings of the British Army in France in the First World War, its administration had been a supreme achievement. So it was now, and this contributed enormously to men's faith in their commanders and in final victory. "There was so much *matériel* at the back," said Alf Lee of the Middlesex Regiment. "Whenever you went to the rear and saw fields packed with petrol tins as high as a house, rows of guns in their canvas covers waiting to come up, huge dumps of shells, you couldn't doubt that we could do it. We would often fire 25,000 rounds from a Vickers gun in a single shoot. Yet we were never short of ammunition."

Few men on the battlefield read anything more demanding than comics. Private Richardson of the 82nd Airborne self-consciously carried around his U.S. army paperback edition of *Oliver Twist* until his unit was withdrawn from action, but he never looked at it. Padre Lovegrove read Housman's *A Shropshire Lad*, and some men clung to their bibles. But most merely glanced at their own unit's weekly duplicated news-sheets – if there was time for headquarters to produce such refinements – or, in the American army, leafed through *Stars and Stripes*. To Lieutenant Floyd Ratliff of the 30th Artillery, this at least "made it seem that there was some design, some grand strategy to what we were doing". Unless a man had access to radio news or headquarters gossip, he lived entirely in the tiny private world of his unit, cut off from both the successes and failures of others, and from the army of which he was a part. The sheer enormity of the forces deployed in Normandy destroyed the sense of personality, the feeling of identity which had been so strong, for instance, in the Eighth Army in the desert. The campaign in north-west Europe was industrialized warfare on a vast scale. For that reason, veterans of earlier campaigns found this one less congenial – dirty and sordid in a fashion unknown in the desert. Many responded by focussing their own loyalties exclusively upon their own squad or company. One of the chronic command difficulties of the campaign was that of overcoming the conviction of many men that another unit or another division's difficulties were entirely its own affair. The sense of detachment was inevitably strongest among the hundreds of thousands of men serving in the rear areas or on the gunlines:

We would suddenly find ourselves put with a different army [said Ratliff of his 155 mm battery], and we would more likely hear about it on the grapevine than from orders. Much of our firing was blind or at night, and we often wondered what we were shooting at. Nobody would say down the telephone: "I can see this village and people running out." We would just hear "50 short" or "50 over" called to the Fire Control Centre. We didn't enjoy the job. It was simply something we had to do, and there was no way out except to finish it. Nobody felt much animosity towards the Germans except a couple of German-speaking Jews in our unit. What hatred there was was generated by propaganda, and didn't go deep. We didn't really know anything about the Germans, or even about their army. Most of our men were bewildered by the whole thing. They didn't understand what it was all about, although they felt that it was a just cause because of Pearl Harbor. Wherever they went they would around and say: "This isn't the way we do things at home."[13]

For the gunners, the greatest strain lay in the shattering noise of their own pieces, and the physical sweat of shifting 95-pound

155 mm projectiles day after day, stripped to the waist and working like automatons through the bombardment before a big attack. Their risk of death or mutilation was small – very small by comparison with that of the infantry. In Ratliff's battalion in Normandy, one observation officer was lost when his Piper Cub was shot down, and a switchboard operator and his assistant were wounded by an incoming shell exploding in a tree above their foxhole. That was all.

Much the most hazardous gunnery task was that of forward observer, either working with the infantry, spotting from the steel towers erected around Caen, or flying an American Piper or British Auster. The pilots droned slowly up and down the line at 120 mph, normally 1,000 feet up and 1,000 yards behind the front. They seldom glimpsed men below, more often the quick flash of German guns or a brief movement of vehicles. Then the pilot called his battery: "Hello Foxtrot 3, I have a Mike target for you." When the guns warned him that they were ready, he called the firing order and watched the ground below for the explosions. Then he radioed "All north 400," or whatever correction was necessary until shells were bracketing the target. The aircraft was often jolted by the passage of shells through the sky around it. "But it was a very disembodied business," said a British spotter pilot, Captain Geoffrey Ivon-Jones.[14] One day he was puzzled by piles of logs lying beside a road, until he saw that they were dead Germans. He developed a personal affection for some of the batteries for which he spotted, above all the 79th Scottish Horse, which prided itself on its smartness. Circling above them in action, the pilot could see the tiny figure of the gun position officer standing with his battery, giving the signal to fire with a sweep of his white silk handkerchief.

Tragic accidents were part of the small change of the battle. One day, spotting for a warship, Ivon-Jones found that the naval gunners were reading the directional "clock" messages upside down, and shelling British positions. An Auster crew watched in horror as bombers rained explosives on friendly forces, and swung alongside to signal frantically by Aldis lamp: WRONG TARGET. On the ground, the pilots lived in foxholes beside the pits bulldozed to protect their aircraft, which took off and landed from any convenient field. Ivon-Jones, a passionate falconer, kept a sparrowhawk named Mrs Patton for some weeks, feeding her on birds and meat cut from dead cows. He and the other pilots flew perhaps four or five 40-minute sorties a day, ever

The British 17-pounder was the best Allied anti-tank gun of the war, capable of penetrating 149 mm of armour at 100 yards, 140 mm at 500 yards, 130 mm at 1,000 yards. In August 1944, small quantities of the new "Discarding Sabot" ammunition began to become available for the 17-pounder, dramatically increasing its hitting power. But throughout the campaign in north-west Europe, the Allies faced the problem that the strategic onus for attack lay upon themselves, and towed anti-tank guns were of limited value – except against German armoured counter-attacks, in which the 17-pounder proved its outstanding quality.

watchful for German fighters. Some Allied fliers became so accustomed to regarding every aircraft as friendly that the Luftwaffe could spring lethal surprises. "What are those, Geordie?" Captain Harry Bordon asked his observer. "Spitfires, sir," came the cheerful reply, seconds before five Me 109s shot them down.

Beyond the obvious dangers of enemy action, an extraordinary number of men were injured in accidents, or shot up by their own guns or aircraft. Padre Lovegrove was well behind the lines, looking for dead men of his unit from an earlier battle, when he stooped to pick up a man's web equipment, hoping to find his service number, and trod on a mine. John Price of the Ox & Bucks watched a man shake with fear when he was called for a reconnaissance patrol, then sag with relief as he returned alive. He laid down his bren, and fell asleep beneath it. A passing soldier tripped on the gun. It fired, killing its owner instantly. Hundreds of men were run over by tanks or trucks. As Stephen Dyson's tank troop halted after disembarking, the waterproof sealing on another Churchill blew up without warning, taking off the hand of the gunner beside it before he had been in France five minutes. Lieutenant Arthur Heal, having survived the storming of "Hillman" with the Suffolks on D-Day, had to be evacuated after rupturing himself. His replacement was killed within 24 hours. Lieutenant-Colonel Eric Hay of the 5th/7th Gordons had already been injured in Sicily when his own intelligence officer dropped a sub-machine gun. Now, after surviving six weeks in the Orne bridgehead, he was travelling in a staff car miles behind the forward positions when a single German shell exploded without warning alongside, wounding him badly in the head. Hundreds of soldiers paid the price of recklessly ignoring warnings about German booby-traps, failing to see tripwires between hedges, or charges linked to tempting booty on abandoned farmhouse tables.

With the coming of night, men lay down to sleep beneath the stars, wrapped in a blanket in their foxholes or the nearest ditch. Most tank crews stretched out a tarpaulin from the hulls of their vehicles and slept beneath it. Some felt safer lying under the tank itself, although enthusiasm for this practice diminished when the bad weather came and a number of men were found in the morning crushed by the vast weight of steel subsiding into the soft ground as they slept. The mosquitos plagued them, and seemed quite immune to the cream issued for their suppression. There were other natural miseries: swarms of flies and wasps; the dysentery from which so many men suffered despite the heavy use of chlorine in the water; and the lice.

We had been spared by the felt lice but their brothers, the lovely white ones, defeated us [wrote an SS trooper, Sadi Schneid]. As if the Allied invasion was not enough! I escaped from them only when I became an American prisoner six months later. I could never understand why the Germans with all their excellent chemists could not find something effective against this plague. The only thing available was Lysol, which had no effect, and cleaning our clothes in steam baths. The result was that we had permanent lice, and our leather equipment became stiff from steam. Our pullovers were so crawling with lice that we could not bear to put them on. Those Norman civilians who found underwear missing from their cupboards must forgive me for helping myself, but the constant torture of lice was sometimes worse than the fighter-bomber attacks.[15]

With hundreds of thousands of vehicles crammed into a narrow beachhead, movement by day was hampered by constant traffic jams. In darkness it became a nightmare: columns of tanks and trucks crawled nose to tail, guided solely by a pinpoint red lamp on the tail of each one, to reach their destinations only after interminable detours and delays. The vital role of the military police in making movement to any battlefield possible in Europe in 1944 has not been sufficiently recognized, nor the dangers that they faced in doing so from the shelling of crossroads as well as chronic traffic accidents.

242

Each side bombarded the other with propaganda of varying effectiveness. Allied leaflets promised German soldiers who surrendered a life of comfort and safety, evidenced by photographs of grinning Wehrmacht prisoners. One German leaflet was headed, CAUGHT LIKE FOXES IN A TRAP. It demanded:

English and American soldiers! Why has Jerry waited so long after the landings to use his so called secret weapons behind your back? Doesn't that strike you as queer? It looks very much as though after waiting for you to cross the Channel, he has set a TRAP for you. You're fighting at present on a very narrow strip of coast, the extent of which has been so far regulated by the Germans. You are using up an enormous number of men and huge quantities of material. Meanwhile the robot planes scatter over London and Southern England explosives, the power and incendiary efficiency of which are without precedent. They are cutting the bridge to your bases.

A more succinct document addressed to Bradley's men demanded: "American soldier! Are you on the wrong side of the street?" By far the most effective propaganda organ was Radio Calais, the British-run station which reached half the German army, who listened intently for the lists of prisoners which were regularly read over the air.

Although the Luftwaffe possessed no power to impede Allied operations seriously, it was still capable of causing considerable irritation, and even acute fear among men living and working on its principal targets, the beaches. Each night, up to 50 Luftwaffe aircraft droned overhead, bombing almost at random, yet with the near certainty of hitting something in the crowded perimeter. The Americans called the night visitation "Bedcheck Charlie". The men behind the beaches – a great army of support and supply troops, inevitably not the most highly-trained or best-equipped to withstand bombardment – dug themselves deeper and deeper into the dunes. "We were terrified by the bombing," said an NCO who had landed with a port construction company on 6 June, expecting to proceed immediately to Caen to reopen its facilities. Instead he and his comrades were stranded for weeks behind the beaches in bewilderment and misery. "We were so frightened, so glad to be alive every morning. We hadn't expected to be in anything like that." Each night they lay down in their gas masks, as protection from the great smokescreeen that was ignited to shroud the piers from enemy bomb aimers. "Golden City", the German pilots called the invasion coast, because of the dazzling array of tracer lacing the darkness offshore. The bald statistics of ships lost to German mines and one-man submarines in the Channel, dumps blown up by air attack, and men killed by brief strafing attacks make the Luftwaffe and German navy's impact upon the Allied build-up seem slight. But for those who were on hand to suffer these small disasters, they seemed very terrible indeed.

The great majority of Allied soldiers who went to Normandy had never before seen action. Many thousands of British troops, especially, had lingered at home through two, three, four years of training and routine. They approached the campaign with an eagerness that promised much to their commanders. "We were all very scared, but glad that we were now going into battle," said Lieutenant Andrew Wilson of The Buffs. "We had been frightened that the war would end before we were really in it. People had no great urge to kill, but they wanted to face the challenge to their manhood of being in danger."[16] Major William Whitelaw and his brother officers of the Scots Guards tank battalion were "thrilled that we were actually going to do something. We had been terrified that we weren't going to get there, and worried how we should answer that question about 'What did you do in the war, daddy?' "[17]

The first shock of battle, the first losses, however severe, did not entirely destroy the sense of wonder, exhilaration and fulfilment that was created by the consummation of months and years of training. A British infantryman wrote of the period following his first action in another theatre at this time:

We had been in some bloody fighting and lost many men. but the sense of nastiness had been overlaid, even at the time, by an exhilarating aura of adventure. I did not of course then realise that that sense of adventure, with its supercharged impulses of curiosity and excitement, was one of the few advantages that the infantryman new to battle enjoyed over the veteran; and that it would, alas, gradually fade away. Thereafter we would become much better soldiers, hardened and more expert. But we would also, to that end, have to draw more deeply on our innermost resources of discipline, comradeship, endurance and fortitude.[18]

After the enormous initial excitement of the landings, the quick capture of Bayeux, and the dramatic American seizure of Cherbourg and clearance of the northern peninsula, the mood among the men of the Allied armies slowly changed, stiffened as the line of battle congealed. They learned the cost of digging slit-trenches beneath trees if these were struck by shellfire, the vital importance of oiling rifles to protect them from the ravages of rust that set in almost overnight, the price of leaving magazines filled too long so that in action their springs would no longer feed the weapon chambers. As most soldiers on most days found themselves holding fixed positions among the nettles and cow parsley of the hedgerows, at risk principally from mortar and artillery harassing fire, they dug deeper and adjusted to a routine of war: dawn stand-to; breakfast of tea, coffee or self-heating soup in their observation positions or foxholes or tank harbours; then the daily grind of infantry patrolling or tank deployments – for the Allied armour almost invariably withdrew from the front line during the hours of darkness. There were map shoots by the gunners or local attacks to adjust a salient or clear a start-line for major operations to come. Among the greatest strains on all the armies in Normandy was the sheer length of the summer day – from 4.45 a.m. to 11.15 p.m. in the first weeks of June. This bore especially heavily on commanders and staff officers, who were compelled to continue writing reports and issuing orders when they returned to their headquarters from the front with the coming of the brief darkness. Most commanding officers found that they could remain on their feet only by sleeping a little during the day. It was difficult to remain undisturbed. One British colonel posted a sign outside his CP: "HAVE YOU HAD YOUR ORGANIZED REST TODAY? I AM HAVING MINE NOW."[19] Men discovered that they could sleep on their feet, under bombardment, in their tanks, on the march. Fatigue, and the struggle to overcome it, ruled their lives.

For the tank crews, even in battle, there were hours sitting motionless, closed down beneath their hatches, firing an occasional shell merely to provide a receptacle into which to urinate. Inside their hulls, they were vulnerable only to direct hits from artillery or mortar fire, but they were often more ignorant than the infantry of what was taking place around them. During the critical battle for Villers-Bocage, Trooper Denis Huett of 5th RTR never saw a German. Scout cars radioed that enemy tanks were approaching, "and stuff started flying about". They once traversed their turret violently to meet an oncoming tank, to discover just in time that it was one of their own. A nearby battery of 25-pounders was firing over open sights. Three of the crew of a neighbouring Cromwell, who lost patience with all the hanging about, dismounted for a private reconnaissance beyond the hedge and did not return, for they walked 100 yards to a barn and found themselves staring into the muzzle of a

German tank commander's Schmeisser. In an uncommon moment of humanity, when he learnt that it was the lap gunner's 21st birthday, he produced a bottle of wine in celebration before sending the prisoners to the rear.

All one night and through the next day, Huett and the other crews remained in their tanks, periodically starting the petrol engines to charge the batteries, acutely watchful when darkness came and they were no longer able to pull back to harbour: "Oh gawd, we thought, and every time we saw a shadow we were sure something was out there." Somebody said that they were surrounded. They were deeply relieved on the night of 15 June when at last they retired, exhausted infantry clinging to their hulls. But of who had gone where, who had gained or lost what, they understood little. There was only the vague ranker's awareness, communicated to Corporal Topper Brown, that, "the Germans had chewed us all for arsepaper, hadn't they?"[20]

The tankmen pitied the infantry, their bodies naked to every form of high explosive, just as most foot soldiers preferred the comfort of their slit trenches to facing the enemy in a vast, noisy steel box which seemed to ignite instantly when hit. Tank crews could carry all manner of private comforts and extra rations with them, and despite strict orders against cooking inside the tanks in action, all of them did so, brewing up on the floors of the turrets. The chief handicap was the poor visibility through their periscopes with the hatches closed. Many of the best tank commanders were killed by small arms, standing up in their turrets for a wider view of the battlefield. Their greatest fear was of breakdown or throwing a track under fire, which would compel them to dismount. Corporal Bill Preston of the U.S. 743rd Battalion had been in action for 32 days when his crew came upon another Sherman bogged down in a hedgerow ditch. He was peering out of the turret watching his commander and wireless operator hitch a cable to the casualty when two German mortar rounds dropped in their midst. Of the two men on the ground, one was killed and the other wounded. Preston himself fell to the bottom of the turret paralyzed – his neck broken by a hit in the spine. "Dad's not going to like this," he thought through his coma. He spent the next six months in hospitals, and reflected more pragmatically: "Thank God I'm out of it."[21]

Every forward unit suffered a steady drain of casualties from snipers, mortaring and artillery fire, which both sides employed daily to maintain pressure upon each other, the Allies in greater volume since they possessed greater firepower. 2nd Panzer reported in July that they were receiving an average of 4,000 incoming artillery and 5,000 mortar rounds a day on their front, rising dramatically during British attacks to a total of 3,500 rounds in two hours on one occasion. It is important to remember that throughout the campaign, even in sectors where neither side was carrying out a major offensive, there were constant local attacks. To emphasize the staggering weight of firepower that the Allies employed in support of their movements, it is worth citing the example of a minor operation near Cristot on 16 June. Throughout the night of the 15th, the German positions to be attacked were subjected to harassing fire. In the early morning of the 16th, from H–35 to H–20, naval guns on the objectives. From H–15 to H-Hour, Typhoons rocketed and strafed them. A squadron of tanks provided covering fire for the assault from a hull-down position on the flank. An entire armoured regiment carried out a diversionary manoeuvre just north of the intended thrust. A company of heavy 4.2-inch mortars stonked selected German positions from H–15 to H-Hour. The operation itself was supported by seven field regiments of 25-pounders, and four regiments of medium guns. At H-Hour, noon on the 16th, the battalion of 49th Division making the attack advanced two companies forward, at the normal infantry assault pace of 25 yards a minute; a troop of tanks accompanied each company. The tanks led across the open fields beyond the start-line, then, as they approached an orchard, allowed the infantry to overtake them and sweep it for anti-tank guns, before the tanks once again took over. At 1.15 p.m. the battalion passed through Cristot, where it reorganized. They found 17 German dead in the village and two armoured cars and one soft-skinned vehicle destroyed. The British had lost three killed and 24 wounded, almost all by enemy mortars. A few hundred yards of fields and ruins had been gained, at uncommonly small cost in British life. But the extraordinary firepower that had been deployed to make this possible readily explains why the Allies in Normandy suffered chronic shortages of artillery ammunition.[22]

Every German unit reported ceaselessly on the agonizing difficulties caused by constant Allied air surveillance, even when there were no incoming air strikes. The mere presence in the sky of Allied spotting aircraft frequently reduced every nearby German gun to silence. Anti-aircraft fire was discouraged by bringing down an immediate Allied barrage upon his source.

Snipers were detested and feared as much for the strain that they caused to men's routine movements in forward areas as for the casualties that they inflicted. Their activities provoked as much irrational resentment as the killing of baled-out tank crews or parachutists in mid-descent. Both sides habitually shot snipers who were taken prisoner. "Brad says he will not take any action against anyone that decides to treat snipers a little more roughly than they are being treated at present," wrote the First Army commander's ADC in his diary: "A sniper cannot sit around and shoot and then capture when you close in on him. That's not the way to play the game."[23] It is important to distinguish here between the work of the specially-trained, superbly-camouflaged marksmen who worked with telescopic-sighted rifles between the lines during periods of static warfare, and the universal habit of describing any man hit by a small-arms round as "shot by a sniper".

One of the chronic preoccupations of Allied commanders in Normandy was the need to persuade attacking infantry to keep moving, not to cause incessant delays by taking cover whenever small-arms fire was heard in their area. For most infantrymen, when a shot came from an unseen gun – and almost every gun fired in Normandy was unseen – it was a reflex action to seek cover until the danger had been pinpointed. No habit caused greater difficulties and delays to Allied movement, nor proved more difficult to overcome when those junior leaders who resisted it and pressed on were so frequently killed. "It is a natural tendency for inexperienced troops to think that every bullet that comes over their heads is fired from about a hundred yards away," stated an acerbic British report after the early fighting in France, "whereas in fact it is probably fired from a much greater range."[24] Many units in defensive positions habitually sprayed the surrounding area – above all, nearby woods – with random gunfire at dawn to shake out any enemy who had infiltrated during the night. Commanders sought in vain to discourage this practice, which almost invariably provoked an unwanted exchange of shooting.

Casualties

There was a brutally self-evident hierarchy of risk among the

248

armies: naturally this was lowest among lines-of-communication troops and heavy artillery, rising through field artillery and armoured units and engineers, to reach a pinnacle among infantry. Of the British forces in Normandy by August 1944, 56 per cent were classified as fighting troops rather than service elements. Just 14 per cent were infantrymen, against 18 per cent gunners, 13 per cent engineers, 6 per cent tank crews, 5 per cent signallers. Even within an infantry battalion, a man serving heavy weapons with the support company possessed a markedly greater chance of survival than his counterpart in a rifle company. It was here that the losses, turnover of officers and men, became appalling, far more serious than the planners had allowed for, and eventually reached crisis proportions in Normandy for the American, German and British armies. Before D-Day, the American logisticians had expected 70.3 per cent of their casualties to be among infantry. Yet in the event, of 100,000 American casualties in June and July, 85 per cent were infantry, 63 per cent riflemen. The British forecast casualties on the basis of staff tables known as the Evetts' Rates, which categorized levels of action as "Intense", "Normal" and "Quiet". After the army's early experiences in Normandy, it was found necessary to introduce a new scale to cover heavy fighting: "Double Intense".

Vision, for the men in the front line, narrowed to encompass only the immediate experience of life and death. "One was emotionally absorbed by the question: 'Am I going to get through tomorrow?' " said Lieutenant Andrew Wilson of The Buffs. "I really believed each time I went into action that I was going to get killed." For all his fear, Wilson was one of those young Englishmen who found the experience of war deeply fulfilling:

I had the delayed adolescence of so many English public schoolboys. Everything I learned about things such as how not to get a girl pregnant, I learned from my tank crew. In the truest sense, I developed a love of other men such as is not possible in Anglo-saxon society in peacetime. In some ways, our emotional capability developed beyond our years at this time. But in others, in our knowledge of life outside the battlefield, we were retarded.[25]

A close friend of Wilson's, commanding another flame-throwing tank troop, was shot along with his crew when he was captured because the Germans considered that the Crocodile somehow transcended the legitimate horrors of battle. Much has been made of the shooting of prisoners – most notoriously, Canadian prisoners – by 12th SS Panzer and other German units in Normandy. Yet it must be said that propaganda has distorted the balance of guilt. Among scores of Allied witnesses interviewed for this narrative, almost every one had direct knowledge or even experience of the shooting of German prisoners during the campaign. In the heat of battle, in the wake of seeing comrades die, many men found it intolerable to send prisoners to the rear knowing that they would thus survive the war, while they themselves seemed to have little prospect of doing so. Many British and American units shot SS prisoners routinely, which explained, as much as the fanatical resistance that the SS so often offered, why so few appeared in POW cages. The 6th KOSB never forgave or forgot the action of a wounded SS soldier to whom Major John Ogilvie leaned down to give water. The German drank, then shot the British officer.

German treatment of prisoners was as erratic as that of the Allies. Sergeant Heinz Hickmann of the Luftwaffe Parachute Division was holding a crossroads with a 12-man rearguard early one morning, when he was nudged out of a doze by an urgent whisper: "Tommy's here!" They shot up the lead jeep of a convoy of 12 lorries, from which a procession of rudely-awakened British supply personnel tumbled out with their hands up. Embarrassed by the burden of 34 prisoners, Hickmann had them locked in a nearby barn, and left them there when his squad pulled out: "In Russia, we would have shot them." Some men had special reasons for fearing capture: Private Abraham Arditti of the U.S. 101st Airborne could never forget the H for Hebrew imprinted on his dogtags. But although there were well-documented instances of SS units murdering their captives, overall it seems doubtful whether this was done on a greater scale by one side than the other. Lieutenant Philip Reisler of the U.S. 2nd Armored watched infantrymen of the 4th Division carelessly shoot three wounded Germans. One of his fellow officers echoed a common sentiment in the unit: "Anything you do to the kraut is okay because they should have given up in Africa. All of this is just wasted motion." Patton described how a German soldier blew a bridge, killing several GIs after their leading elements had passed: "He then put up his hands . . . The Americans took him prisoner, which I considered the height of folly." Lindley Higgins of the U.S. 4th saw a lieutenant shout impatiently to a soldier moving off with a prisoner: "You going to take that man to the rear?", and simply pull out his pistol to shoot the German in the head. Once a definable atrocity had been discovered – as with the bodies of the Canadians killed by 12th SS Panzer – and the conscious decision taken to respond in kind, it is difficult with hindsight to draw a meaningful moral distinction between the behaviour of one side and the other on the battlefield.

Corporal Topper Brown of the 5th RTR never even knew where his tank was hit when his squadron commander in the turret said quietly: "Bale out." He found himself alone in a ditch with his mate Dodger Smith, the gunner. They could hear the Germans digging in quite close to hand, and saw some tracer overhead. But they felt desperately tired, and after lying listening for a time, fell asleep. They woke in bright sunshine to hear only birdsong around them. Cautiously they explored, and found an abandoned Cromwell. They climbed onto the hull to find it commander dead inside, and tried in vain to use the radio to contact their own unit. Then they began to walk up the road until they heard voices, and found themselves face to face with a file of Germans. They put up their hands: "We couldn't have got them no higher." Even when shells began to land nearby and the Germans took cover, the frightened young Londoners remained standing in the road with their hands in the air.

At last they were stripped of their revolvers and watches and marched to a farmhouse, where they marvelled at the superbly-camouflaged Tiger tank dug in outside. They were led down to a cellar where they were sharply questioned by an English-speaking German who said finally: "You aren't very intelligent for a British NCO, are you? You know you're not going to win, don't you?" Then they were marched round a hedge in front of their escort. Brown said nervously, "They're going to shoot us, Dodge." A moment later, overcome with relief, they saw a lorry filled with men of the Queen's and the DCLI, shouting cheerfully: "Come on, you silly buggers!" and they were driven away into captivity. Brown thought a little about escaping, but he did not feel inclined to try it alone. Most of the others seemed to take the view: "Well, that's me f——ing finished, then", without great remorse. He remained in a POW camp until 1945.

Beyond those who left the battlefield as prisoners, or never left it alive at all, hundreds of thousands of men were more or less seriously wounded. Indeed, it became an exceptional achievement for an infantryman who had landed on D-Day to remain with his unit uninjured until July. The doctors and medical teams, who handled hundreds of cases each day – aided by facilities of unprecedented quality, and above all by the miracle of penicillin – found that many lightly-wounded men were deeply relieved to have escaped the battlefield with honour. "No *Heim ins Reich* for you, Langangke," sympathized the German doctor who patched up an SS panzer lieutenant after a shell fragment had hit him in the forearm – the wound was not sufficiently serious to give him the coveted ticket home. When Corporal Bill Preston was evacuated with serious wounds, his principal sensation was relief that he had done his job without disgracing himself. For most men, the need to continue the job, to sustain their own self-respect, was the principal motive force upon the battlefield.

John Price, a medical orderly with the British 2nd Ox & Bucks, was moved to discover how desperately men wished to be reassured that they would survive, how much words meant to them even when they were suffering the most terrible injuries. For all the wealth of facilities that the Allies possessed, there was seldom a short-cut from pain. One day in the farmyard in the Orne bridgehead where he was based, Price was appalled to see a young lieutenant drive up in a jeep, shouting with the pain of terrible bowel wounds. They laid him on a stretcher on the bonnet, and Price sat beside him as they drove for the casualty clearing station, holding his hand until he died. When Robin Hastings, CO of the Green Howards, was at last wounded by mortar fragments on 27 June, Padre Lovegrove was touched that a man of such courage and forcefulness suddenly showed fearful shock at his own vulnerability, and begged the orderlies who were tending him: "Don't hurt me." Hastings's temper was not improved when he met his detested brigadier as he was being driven to the rear by jeep. The senior officer demanded furiously: "What are you doing back here? I think you're perfectly fit," which, as Hastings remarked acidly afterwards, "showed what a bloody old fool he was."

In the field hospitals, doctors and nurses toiled over the procession of ruined men laid before them in the tents, cutting away mudstained battledress and bloody boots to reveal the interminable tragedies beneath.

Stepping over splinted limbs and stretcher handles [wrote Sister Brenda McBryde] we moved to the next man, a penetrating wound of the chest, needing a large firm dressing to contain those ominous sucking noises and another pillow to keep him upright. Lieutenant-Colonel Harding, one stretcher ahead with Audrey Dare, kept up a running commentary. "Stomach here. Put him number one. Quarter of morphia, Sister. Straight away. Two pints of blood, one of plasma . . ." Gunshot, mortar blasts, mines, incendaries. Limbs, eyes, abdomen, chest. He chewed his pencil. Who had priority? Of all these desperately wounded men, whose need was the most urgent?

. . . Men brought to Resus were always in a serious condition, some of them *in extremis*, past meaningful speech or any sustained communication. Each man was an island in his own desperation, unaware of other men on other stretchers, but their utterances were all the same. There were no impassioned calls to God, no harking back to mother, only an infinitely sad "Oh dear", from colonels and corporals alike. Strangely and mercifully, I have forgotten the deaths, although one bright face I do remember. He was brought into our tent with eyes wide open, looking about him, still remembering to be polite. "I've often wondered what you sisters got up to," he said, with a brave, cheeky smile. Then a sudden look of surprise opened his eyes very wide, and he was dead, still with the smile on his lips. A captain of the Coldstream Guards, the same age as myself, he was caught unawares by death. With part of a shell buried in his back, he had suddenly tweaked his spinal cord and, in one astonished moment, he was gone.[1]

The family of a wounded British soldier received a simple roneoed sheet from the Army Records Office at Ashford. For example, a Mr Griffin of 28 Dean Drive, Stanmore, Middlesex, was addressed:

Sir,
  I am directed to inform you, with regret, that a report has been received from the War Office stating that No . . . *6216504 . . . Private George Edward Griffin, the Middlesex Regiment . . .* was wounded in the north west Europe theatre of War on *3rd August 1944*. The report also states that he sustained . . . *shrapnel wound right buttock . . .* Please accept my sympathy in your anxiety, I am, Sir,
                                        Your obedient servant
                                        Major, for officer i/c Infantry Records[2]

It is a measure of the relative severity of the Normandy fighting, compared with later battles, that hospital admissions as a result of enemy action comprised 9.7 per cent of British soldiers engaged in the first three months following the invasion, falling to 2.6 per cent in the autumn quarter. Accidental injuries attained a remarkable 13.2 per cent in the wake of D-Day, although many of these were very slight. Psychiatric casualtie. reached a high of 14 per 1,000 among the British in the same period, falling to 11 per 1,000 by winter. Although "battle fatigue" never reached epidemic proportions in the British army, every unit in Normandy suffered its share of men who found themselves utterly unwilling to endure more. One morning, as Charles Mundy and his fellow troop commanders of the 22nd Dragoon Guards stood in their turrets on the start-line before an attack, they were startled by a brief burst of sten gun fire. A man had simply shot himself in the foot rather than endure the assault. An American company commander in Major Randall Bryant's battalion reported to him to declare flatly: "I've had it. You can do anything you want, but I won't go back." Men seldom despised or scorned those who were driven to these acts – they merely pitied them, and prayed that they themselves might not be reduced to such extremities. Major Bryant was only roused to real anger years later, when the ex-company commander showed himself at a veterans' reunion.

One morning, Captain Anthony Babington of the Dorsets heard the call "Stretcher bearer!" in the midst of an incoming barrage, and was surprised to see no reaction from the medical orderly's slit trench, for the man had hitherto been uncommonly quick to reach any wounded soldier. Running across, he found the orderly lying in the bottom of the trench, crying and shaking. He asked if the man was wounded, and received no reply. When the shelling stopped, he told his CO about the stretcher bearer. "Oh, send him back with an NCO and we'll find him a job in the rear," said the colonel. All of them understood, in the Second War, something which had not been contemplated in the First – that each man possessed a limit beyond which he could not be forced. It was merely vital to ensure that such problems did not become epidemic.

A few men deliberately recoiled in disgust from the labour of destruction upon which they were engaged. Lieutenant William Douglas-Home, who was to become a distinguished British playwright and was the brother of a future Prime Minister, had told his fellow-officers for years that if he disapproved of something that was done on the battlefield, he would say so. They did not believe him. Now, in France as a Crocodile troop commander, he was appalled by the impending massed air bombardment of a town to induce its garrison to surrender. He set out on his own initiative to attempt to parley the Germans into giving up, declining to have anything to do with the attack himself. He was stopped, court-martialled, and served a term of imprisonment in Wormwood Scrubs. When it was learned that he had been

254

threatening for months to make a gesture of this sort, his commanding officer was also sacked.

Each night, one of the most painful tasks for the commanding officer of every unit was to write to the families of his men who had died. Most widows and mothers bore the news with pathetic resignation. A few were bitter. On the way home from the Mediterranean, Padre Lovegrove of the Green Howards had listened for hours to an officer talking about the little daughter he looked forward so much to seeing. When they docked, he learnt that she had died while he was on passage. In the following months the officer suffered great strain comforting his wife. In Normandy, he too was killed. Lovegrove received a tragic, savage letter from the man's wife, demanding to know how the padre could pretend that there could be a loving God, who allowed such unspeakable miseries to occur.

That summer, there was no more pitiful measure of the enormity of what was taking place in Normandy than the death announcements in the newspapers of Britain and America: "Died of wounds", "Killed while leading his wing over Normandy", "Killed in action June 1944, aged 23". The London *Times* for 2 July reported on its news pages that "General Eisenhower may . . . look forward to the early use of a port of entry into France following the capture of Cherbourg," while "the time may be approaching when General Montgomery will be strong enough to march boldly inland." But among the columns of announcements on the front page, there were scores like this:

HORLEY – Killed in action in June 1944, Lt. Montague Bernard Horley, RTR Notts Yeomanry, elder son of the Rev. C. M. Horley, The Rectory, Bisley, Surrey, and brother of Sgt. John Midwood Horley, RAFVR, missing presumed killed in January 1942.

On the battlefield, men were reluctantly fascinated by the look of the dead. Lieutenant Wilson of The Buffs gazed down on a cluster of SS infantry, and was impressed by their physical splendour even as they lay lifeless. He was struck by the contrast between these young Nazi supermen and the usual British infantry platoon, "with all its mixtures which were a sergeant-major's nightmare – the tall and short, bandy-legged and lanky, heavy-limbed countrymen and scruffy, swarthy Brummagem boys with eternally undone gaiters."[3] How can we defeat men like these, he wondered, gazing down at the German bodies?

"To me, Normandy will always mean death," said Lindley Higgins, "that yellow-green, waxy look of corpses' hands. Anything that personalized death was upsetting, like seeing a 4th Division flash on a body's helmet."[4]

Keith Douglas, who was killed in Normandy, wrote:

Remember me when I am dead
and simplify me when I'm dead.

As the processes of earth
strip off the colour and the skin
take the brown hair and blue eye

and leave me simpler than at birth,
when hairless I came howling in
as the moon entered the cold sky.

Of my skeleton perhaps,
so stripped, a learned man will say
"He was of such a type and intelligence",
                              no more.

Some soldiers were supersititious about picking up a dead man's weapon, although few were above looting a German luger pistol if they found one. Almost every man had his private equivalent of touching wood, his secret luck charm. Trooper Steve Dyson of the 107th RAC, a Catholic, carried a little statuette of the Virgin in his tank, wedged between the smoke bombs. Philip Reisler's 2nd Armored tank gunner, a Polish boy from Michigan, convinced himself that he would be hit if he failed to write up his diary each night. Three times in the war when he did not do so, he was wounded. Coming out of action, the whole crew invariably sang over the intercom:

I'm going home where I came from,
where the mocking bird's sitting
on the lilac tree . . .

Men were frequently shocked by the speed at which an entire unit could be transformed into a ruin on the battlefield. One morning in mid-July, the 2nd KRRC were waiting in their half-tracks, on the reverse slope of a hill in the approved manner, to follow up the 43rd Wessex Division in an operation towards Evrecy. Lieutenant Edwin Bramall had just joined the other platoon commanders for a company Orders Group when they came under devastating fire from German self-propelled guns which had worked around to overlook them from high ground on

Defeat: a prisoner being searched by a British military policeman.
BBC Hulton Picture Library

(TOP LEFT) Digging: literally a matter of life and death, as so many troops discovered at terrible cost. *BBC Hulton Picture Library*

(TOP RIGHT) Exhaustion: a British doctor pauses between operations at a forward dressing station. *BBC Hulton Picture Library*

(ABOVE) Normandy was above all a battlefield of hedges and ditches, a succession of dashes between islands of cover, each one intensely dangerous for those making the movements. *BBC Hulton Picture Library*

(OPPOSITE) A British sniper pulls through while a young soldier grasps the most precious possession on the battlefield: sleep. *BBC Hulton Picture Library*

Behind the lines: Tommies make themselves at home in a Norman farmyard.
BBC Hulton Picture Library

The image of defeat: captured Germans and fallen horses. Note the pathetic attempt to camouflage the cart. *BBC Hulton Picture Library*

(RIGHT) Brutal encounter between a Norman shopkeeper and an abandoned Mk IV tank. *BBC Hulton Picture Library*

Glimpses in Normandy of "the most professionally skilful army of modern times" as a distinguished American historian has recently described the Wehrmacht: (OPPOSITE TOP LEFT) rearming a Panther; (BOTTOM) self-propelled *Nebelwerfers* – of all German weapons, those most detested by Allied soldiers; (THIS PAGE TOP) with *Panzerfaust*, their formidable close-quarter anti-tank weapon. OPPOSITE TOP LEFT AND RIGHT: *ADN*; OTHERS AND OVERLEAF *Ullstein Bilderdienst*.

(TOP) A classic propaganda image of liberators and liberated; in fact, the attitude of most Norman civilians to the Allies ranged between numbed indifference and sullen hostility.

(ABOVE LEFT) Field Marshal von Kluge. (ABOVE RIGHT) Collins of U.S. VII Corps with von Schlieben, the captured commander of Cherbourg. *Imperial War Museum*

(BELOW) Devastation: a typical Norman street scene in the summer of 1944. *BBC Hulton Picture Library*

(TOP) German Volksgrenadier on the Western Front. *Ullstein Bilderdienst.*

(ABOVE) The battlefield: a striking view of the difficulty of movement among the closely-set farmyards of the Norman villages, ideal for defence. The bespectacled figure in the back of the bren-gun carrier is the author's father, war correspondent for *Picture Post. BBC Hulton Picture Library*

A classic portrait of the British infantryman in Normandy. *BBC Hulton Picture Library*

their flank. Bramall dived under a half-track and found himself lying next to his friend Bernard Jackson, a slightly-built Old Harrovian who was senior platoon commander. "Do you think we've had it?" Jackson asked him. A moment later there was a fierce explosion as a shell hit the half-track, and Jackson lay blackened and dead. Bramall emerged from cover to find "quite a *götterdämmerung* situation, with vehicles and motor-cycles on fire everywhere." He suddenly felt a burning sensation in his side, and threw himself to the ground to extinguish flames on his clothing – he had also been hit by a shell fragment. Somehow Bramall and the other surviving platoon commander managed to shepherd the remaining half-tracks into dead ground before he was evacuated to the Regimental Aid Post. When he returned to his unit just a month later, "I found a very different battalion. There had been no dramatic heavy fighting – just a lot of casualties and a lot of shell-shock cases."[5]

The Scots Guards Tank Battalion – which numbered among its officers a future British Home Secretary, a Moderator of the Church of Scotland and an Archbishop of Canterbury – went into its first action, in support of 43rd Wessex Division in July, with all the enthusiasm of novices. They gained their objective with the loss only of Major Whitelaw's tank blown up by a mine. But as they stood deployed on a ridge in the midst of virgin country they found, characteristically of many British armoured units, that they had far outstripped their infantry. The officers were assembling for an Orders Group in a wood when they heard a huge explosion and saw a pillar of smoke in the distance. The second-in-command, Major Sidney Cuthbert, said: "I'll go and see what's happening," and dashed across the ridge in his tank, followed by Whitelaw in a second. Suddenly, Whitelaw saw the turret of Cuthbert's Churchill lifted bodily into the air. In the flash of bewilderment so common to men in war, he thought: How odd that the turret should do that. In a few ruthless minutes of fire, a single German self-propelled 88 mm gun, which had stalked unseen behind the Guards' positions, destroyed six of their tanks and killed 15 men.[6]

Every infantryman feared falling victim to a TOT – Time On Target, an artillery shoot carefully synchronized to concentrate the fire of an entire battery or regiment at a precise moment. Major Randall Bryant of the U.S. 9th Division was walking across an orchard near St Lô to a battalion Order Group, his closest friend, Captain Charles Minton, beside him: "Suddenly everything was exploding. There was blood all over me, and a helmet on the ground with a head inside it. It was Minton's. Three young 2nd lieutenants had just joined us, straight from the beach and Fort Benning. I had told them to sit down and wait to be assigned to companies. They were dead, along with six others killed and 33 wounded in a shoot that lasted only a matter of seconds."

The ambitions of most men in Normandy were pathetically simple: to survive, to finish the job, and to go home. "Everything is okay here," wrote Private Verrier to his parents in Stoke Newington on 24 July:

and I hope the war news continues to be good. I wonder if anything very serious will come of this stir inside Germany. It may be the beginning of their collapse. I hope so. I would very much like to see this war finish much sooner than the critics estimate. I read so much in the papers, and I begin to think that Jerry is in a tough position, although he has many occupied countries in his hands. I'm quite content to sit and patiently wait for Jerry to collapse. I don't think it will be as easy as the newspapers try to make believe. Dead Germans are the best Germans, especially these fanatical Nazis about 18 to 20.

I also think it is time we were given a break considering the Allies' so-called overwhelming masses of men. Many rumours go round about being sent to a rest camp, letters from Monty congratulating the division on doing such a fine job, which you have probably read in the papers, all of which are hardly worth taking any notice of as we still sit in the front line, wet dugouts, dirty clothes, no bath and very little comfort, and I'm beginning to wonder if once again we have been forgotten. I suppose one day, certain people will realise that we are human beings and not machines of war.

Sam mentioned that he has applied to try to get posted to France. Gosh – if I had his opportunity now to stop in England, I know what I would do with voluntary applications. He would be crazy to come out here, with Lily expecting a baby so soon, and the flying bomb raids at home. Surely he wil not be upgraded to A1. If he does come I sincerely hope he gets a job with a GHQ well behind the line . . .[7]

Early in August, John Hein of the U.S. 1st Divison came upon three unposted letters written by German soldiers in Normandy. He never knew which unit their authors came from, what rank they held, what fate overtook them. But the densely penned scrawls seem to reflect the equally simple, troubled emotions of all but the fanatical SS, now losing ground in Normandy against appalling odds.

My Irmi-love,

. . . It doesn't look very good, that would be saying too much, but nonetheless there is no reason to paint too black a picture. You know the high spirits with which I face things, which allow me to stroll through difficult situations with some optimism and a lot of luck. Above all there are so many good and elite divisions in our near-encirclement that we must get through somehow. The most difficult thing has been and remains the enemy air force . . . it is there at dawn, all day, at night, dominating the roads. Sadly my dog was pinched yesterday by soldiers passing through. I should so like to have taken him back to Germany, but it was not to be. The last three days we have had the most wonderful summer weather – sun, warmth, blue skies – so utterly in contrast to everything else around us. Ah well, it must turn out alright in the end. Don't lose heart, I'll get through this somehow as I always do. A thousand loving kisses to you and the children, your FERD.

My darling wife,

Yet another day. Nowadays I am grateful to the good Lord for every dawn he lets me wake. When I listen to the guns at night, my thoughts wander back home to you, my dearest, and I wonder whether I shall ever see you again. You will have to be prepared not to receive any letters from me for some time. I shall have to cope with great difficulties. May the good Lord be always with me as he has been! I long for you all! How much I would now like to look at your dear pictures, but my kit is far away and I am unlikely to get it back. Should I not return home then you, my treasure, will have to bear this lot too with courage. I leave you our dear boys, in them you will have me too. Your dear little Ortwin and our little Wilfried will be your dear Karl to you. I would so like to go with you after our victory into a lovely and happy future. Many thousands of loving greetings and kisses to you, my dear, good, loyal little wife and to my dear children from your dear Daddy! Farewell! God bless you! KARL

My dear Heather-love,

Do my letters still reach you? Nonetheless I will talk to you rather than mourn to you. One day the light of truth and clarity will shine over this time of humiliation. I just went for a walk in the hot sun to Bagnoles. I did not get there. On the way, I picked a sprig of heather and wore it on my breast. All nature's creatures were out – how high and low the bees, bumblebees, insects hummed, just like in 1926. Today there is another accompaniment as well, spreading death and destruction. I am constantly surprised how calmly I take it all. Is it because of the rocklike certainty of your love? I have written a letter which you should open later, if I don't return. I don't know if it will reach you. But you know what I have to say to you and the children. I have left my affairs in order. What love can express I have already done. The children are on their way, already independent, and will find a path through whatever befalls

259

them. It will not be easy in this chaos, but life is never handed to us on a plate.

Last night we had a little "soldier's hour" and sang our soldiers' and folk songs into the night. What would a German be without a song? The evening sky glowed with fire and explosions. One always thinks the earth brings forth new life, but now it is death. What new order will emerge from this devil's symphony? Can a vision, strong in faith, be born into a new world? The social order rooted in National Socialism cannot be delayed for ever.

Enough of that . . . What remains is great love and loyalty, the acknowledgement of the eternal source of life. I take you and the girls in my arms in gratitude for all you have given me, your FRITZ.

"It was quite against logic to suppose that you were destined to survive the war," wrote Andrew Wilson. "All the appearance of things was against it. You saw a pair of boots sticking out from a blanket, and they looked exactly like your own; there was no ground for thinking that the thing that had come to the owner of these boots was not going to come just as casually to you . . . So before going into action he would utter a phrase articulately beneath his breath: 'Today I may die.' I was a kind of propitation; and yet he could never quite believe in it, because that would have defeated its purpose . . ."[8]

260

8 Crisis of confidence

The fall of Caen

By early July, the struggle for Normandy was inflicting almost equal misery upon the German, British and American armies – the first having by far greater cause for it. The defenders knew that their forces were being inexorably ground down, and that they could not hope for tolerable replacements. Many of their difficulties of manpower, armour, supplies and ammunition were known to the Allies through Ultra. Yet it was small comfort to read the Germans' gloomy signals about their predicament when, on the battlefield, the force and effectiveness of their resistance seemed quite undiminished. Meanwhile, the men of the invading army were growing weary. The summer was slipping away, and the disturbing prospect of autumn weather in the Channel lay ahead. The safe refuge of the Brittany ports still seemed many miles and many battles away. What if FORTITUDE abruptly collapsed, and Rommel brought down powerful reinforcements from Fifteenth Army? What if the German flying bomb campaign, already causing so much alarm in England, intensified and gave way to new and more deadly secret weapons? The problem of infantry casualties, a matter of concern to the Americans, had become a crisis for the British. Sir Ronald Adam, the Adjutant-General, paid a personal visit to Montgomery to warn him about the shortage of replacements. Already battalions had been broken up to fill the ranks of others in the line; now came the possibility that entire divisions might have to be disbanded.

After the excitement of the capture of Cherbourg and the northern Cotentin, on 3 July the American VIII Corps, along with a division from VII Corps, began a new southward offensive in driving rain, mist and low cloud. Within the first days, it became bogged down in the mire of now-familiar difficulties: green formations, and stubborn defensive tactics which destroyed momentum. If British commanders were too slow to sack incompetent subordinates, their American counterparts were almost too swift. Now, there was a new spate of dismissals of divisional and regimental commanders in Bradley's army. The Americans were to discover in north-west Europe that it was easier to remove officers than to find more effective newcomers to replace them. As the months went by, their enthusiasm for purges declined, and they concluded that it was more profitable to give commanders time to settle down and learn their business than to remove them immediately after their formation's first failure. Eisenhower wrote to Marshall about the stagnation of First Army's push south: "The going is extremely tough, with three main causes responsible. The first of these, as always, is the fighting quality of the German soldier."[1] The others he identified as the terrain and the weather, which was hampering air support.

Meanwhile, on the eastern flank, Second Army was fighting the tough, slow-moving battle that at last gained its men a large part of the ruins of Caen. For almost a month since the landings, the British and Canadian 3rd Divisions had endured the frustrations of static warfare around Cambes wood, Carpiquet and other landmarks that they first beheld on 6 or 7 June. On the night of 7 July, 450 heavy aircraft of Bomber Command attacked Caen, principally with delayed-action bombs, in an operation designed to clear the way for an assault by I Corps the following morning. Hundreds of thousands of men of Second Army watched in awe as the waves of bombers droned steadily over the city, letting loose their loads and turning away, some bleeding smoke and flame as they slipped from the sky. Amid the rumble of constant explosions from the city, a great pall of smoke and dust rose upwards, shrouding the houses and factories. The use of the heavy bombers reflected the belief of Montgomery and the Allied high command that they must now resort to desperate measures to pave the way for a ground assault. Afterwards, this action came to be regarded as one of the most futile air attacks of the war. Through no fault of their own, the airmen bombed well back from the forward line to avoid the risk of hitting British troops, and inflicted negligible damage upon the German defences. Only the old city of Caen paid the full price.

About a quarter of the citizens of Caen had departed before the bombers came, urged by both the Germans and the local prefect. Many more remained, fearful for their homes and possessions, and arguing that "to evacuate is only to escape Germans to meet other Germans, to avoid bombs and shells to meet other bombs and shells."[2] Nothing had prepared them to expect the devastating rain of explosives from the massed air attack. As the sound of the bombers faded, "a great silence fell over the town, broken only by the cries of the wounded and the sound of falling masonry from burning buildings."[3] The *Palais de l'Université* was in flames, the initial fires in its chemistry department having spread in minutes to other parts of the building. Hopeless little groups of firemen struggled to draw water from the Odon, since the mains had been blasted in a hundred places. 38 civilians died in one cellar, 50 were killed and wounded in a single street. The survivors were so terrorized by the destruction around them that, even as the Germans at last began to withdraw through the streets, most inhabitants clung to the shelter of their cellars.

When I Corps jumped off on Operation CHARNWOOD the next morning, the troops were heartened by the memory of the air attack. But they quickly discovered that the Germans were resisting as tenaciously as ever. Meyer's men of 12th SS Panzer remained the core of the defence, apparently indestructible even though their ranks had been decimated by weeks of heavy fighting without replacements. Two days of desperate battle cost some British infantry battalions 25 per cent of their strength. They won through to the northern bank of the Orne, in the middle of the utterly desolated city, but could go no further. The Germans still held the critical high ground of the Bourgébus Ridge to the south and, nearer at hand, the steelworks of Colombelles, from which their observation posts could mark every British movement. Too much blood had been shed and too many weeks had elapsed for possession of the shattered ruins to offer any more to most thoughtful British commanders than a ghastly echo of other ruins, other empty victories, almost 30 years before. From CHARNWOOD, there was not even the compensation of having "written down" significant German forces.

While the British and Canadian 3rd Divisions painfully battered their way into Caen, further west 43rd Wessex and its supporting armour suffered 2,000 casualties in two days of renewed fighting for Hill 112, the commanding position beyond the Odon which had been lost in the last stages of EPSOM. Once again, the formidable fighting power of 12th SS Panzer forced Thomas's men into bloody difficulties. Like so many other

British assaults, that of 10 July began well in the wake of the huge bombardment, with the leading units reaching Eterville and well up the slopes of 112 by 8.00 a.m. Corporal Chris Portway was a 21-year-old section commander in the 4th Dorsets: "They plod along and do the job – not death or glory boys like the paratroops," the sort of comment which might be made about many solidly dependable British county regiments. Urged on by their colonel's hunting horn, they reached Eterville without serious casualties. Portway fought a fierce little private battle in its churchyard, pursuing two Germans between the gravestones until he reached them with a grenade in the church itself. He was dismayed to meet his commanding officer among the ruins, asking helplessly: "What's happening, corporal?" The colonel appeared to have lost all grip on events. But the day's work had been done at tolerable cost. They were digging in around Eterville, pleased to find themselves alongside a château painted with huge red crosses, "because the Germans were usually quite good about trying not to hit hospitals,"[4] when they were suddenly summoned to a new Orders Group and told that they must press on to the next village, Maltot.

Without enthusiasm, but also without knowledge of what lay ahead except that a battalion of the Hampshires was in trouble, they advanced in extended line through the cornfields towards the village. They reached an orchard, and suddenly found themselves under intense German DF[5] fire. With flame and smoke all around them, they pressed on, to meet machine-gun and tank fire from a screen of Tigers dug into pits covering Maltot. "They knocked us down in lines . . ." Portway and other survivors took shelter for a moment in an empty tank pit, and saw a German glance over the rim and reach back to throw a grenade down on them before a quick-thinking Dorset shot him. They ran from the hole to a house in which they hastily cleared a field of fire. The corporal felt a moment of revulsion about bringing the battle into some unknown family's home: "There we were, wrecking this house, and I suddenly thought – 'How would I feel if this was mine?'" Then a more pressing problem intervened. A noise upstairs showed that they were not alone. There was a fierce exchange of grenades and small-arms fire with the Germans above. They fought from house to house for some time until, without warning, a devastating artillery barrage began to fall among them. Portway learned later that it came from British guns. The order had been given for the brigade to withdraw from

Maltot, but it never reached the survivors of the Dorsets. Portway threw himself into a ditch, and a handful of others fell in on top of him. When the guns at last stopped, he wondered why nobody rose. He heard German voices, and lay motionless until he found one of the men above him being moved, and looked up into the face of the enemy. All the others on top of him in the ditch were dead. He felt a sense of unreality: "You imagine being wounded, being killed. But you never think of being captured. You think that when you've had a chat, they'll let you go home. I couldn't believe that I'd never see the unit again." The SS treated Portway unusually well, "much better than we did German prisoners. It was when one got further back that the nastiness started."

Portway's experience was almost precisely mirrored by that of Private Zimmer of 12th SS Panzer who was in Eterville the same day. Zimmer, as his narrative makes clear, was cast in a somewhat less heroic mould than some of his colleagues:

From 6.30 to 8.00 a.m. again heavy machine-gun fire. Then Tommy attacks with great masses of infantry and many tanks. We fight as long as possible but we realize we are in a losing position. By the time the survivors try to pull back, we realize that we are surrounded. In our sector, we had driven back the British infantry attack, but they had bypassed us to left and right. I moved back as fast as I could under the continuous firing. Others who tried to do the same failed. When the small-arms fire stopped our own guns got going. I lay there in the midst of it all. I still cannot understand how I escaped, with shelling falling two or three metres away, splinters tearing around my ears. By now I had worked my way to within 200 metres of our own lines. It was hard work, always on my stomach, only occasionally up on hands and knees. The small-arms fire began again, and the English infantry renewed their attack. My hopes dwindled. The advancing Tommies passed five or six paces away without noticing me in the high corn. I was almost at the end of the my tether, my feet and elbows in agony, my throat parched. Suddenly the cover thinned out and I had to cross an open field. In the midst of this, wounded Englishmen passed within ten metres without seeing me. Now I had to hurry. There were only ten metres to go to the next belt of corn. Suddenly three Tommies appeared and took me prisoner. Immediately I was given a drink and a cigarette. At the concentration point for prisoners I met my *unterscharführer* and other comrades of my company . . .[6]

It was a battle of shattering intensity even by the standards of Normandy. Brigadier Michael Carver, who had taken over 4th Armoured Brigade at half an hour's notice a few days earlier,

The 88 mm dual-purpose gun was the decisive force in the German destruction of many Allied tank attacks in Normandy, above all in the open country on the British flank, where its long reach could be exploited to best effect. It was, quite simply, the best gun produced by any combatant nation in the war, with a formidable killing power against all Allied tanks.

found himself compelled to draw his revolver to halt fleeing infantrymen, including an officer. Amid the blackened, leafless trees on the slopes of Hill 112 itself, the 5th Duke of Cornwall's Light Infantry attacked, two companies up, after the Somersets failed to gain the summit. Lieutenant David Priest's company commander had been killed shortly before, and he found himself leading his company forward. Their vehicles drove to the start-line over the bodies of British infantry spreadeagled across the road. They took a wrong turning and came under fire. The men dismounted and shook out for the advance. Priest had put his own platoon in the rear, but quickly found himself compelled to pass it forward when the point platoons were ravaged by mortar and machine-gun fire. Then he felt a blow. At first, it made him imagine that he had been struck with a pickaxe. Only after a few moment lying shocked on the grass did he understand that he had been hit in the chest by a machine-gun bullet. He felt somebody undoing his pouches and taking out his grenades. The he heard the acting battalion commander shouting, before he died, that he could not breathe. Priest lay gazing upwards, watching each side's mortar bombs soar unhurriedly across the sky. There was more fierce small-arms fire, and he was frightened of being hit again. When darkness cam he felt a little better. He managed to drag himself back towards the British line until he was challenged by a Somersets sentry.

Yet still the nightmare was not ended. That night, 12th SS Panzer counter-attacked. Priest was waiting at the rendezvous where the carriers picked up casualties, when a German tank suddenly crashed through the trees almost on top of him. Wounded men screamed as they were crushed beneath its tracks, and flares began to burst overhead as the defenders struggled to pinpoint the threat. The tank blundered away into the darkness, and the stretcher-bearers came. Priest learned that he had a clean entry and exit wound. He felt deeply grateful that he was not maimed or disfigured. Like every rifle company officer, he had long ago accepted the inevitability of being hit somewhere, at some time. It was six weeks before he walked again, and 1945 before he returned to his battalion.

The self-propelled 17-pounder M10s of E Troop, 129th Battery, left the start-line with the Hampshires and the supporting Churchill infantry tanks at 5.30 a.m. They had landed in France ten days before, and this was their first action of the war. German mortar and artillery fire began to fall amongst them soon after they set off, and the infantrymen of the Hampshires huddled behind the Churchills and E Troop's tank destroyers as they crawled forward through the barrage. Sergeant Burnell's gun was hit a few yards beyond Eterville by a mortar bomb which landed directly in its open turret; just two of the crew escaped wounded. The troop commander's gun received a direct hit from an 88 mm shell a few yards short of Maltot. Only he himself and an NCO were able to leap down and escape alive. A third gun's turret was jammed by fire and its aerial shot away. The crew baled out, expecting it to "brew up". When it failed to do so they remounted, with the exception of the wireless operator, who declined to leave the slit trench in which he had taken refuge. Then it became obvious that the attack had failed. The two surviving guns withdrew, bringing back the survivors of the other ruined M10. Of 20 men in the guns which had gone forward, six were dead, four wounded, one missing. Sergeant Jim Stephens, who had served with the battery since 1939, was heartbroken to have been left behind with the echelon, when the troop of which he was so proud went forward for the first time.

Now, he looked appalled at the return of the survivors, and the blank and shocked face of the young troop commander, Lieutenant Wimpey. The adjutant had recovered the gun whose turret had received a direct hit. Wimpey told Sergeant Stephens that they must bury its crew. Stephens never forgot the experience.

The explosion of the mortar in that confined space had devastated everything inside. The 17 pdr and .50 calibre ammunition had gone up. Lying on the floor of the turret was what was left of the crew, burnt to a cinder with their teeth bared in some kind of grin. I cried, having known them all for so long – Jimmy Burrell, a cockney whose wife had presented him with a baby a few weeks before D-Day, who used to hang a pair of bootees in the turret every time he went out; Dick Greenwood, no more than 5′ 2″, a Devonian from Newton Abbot who used to be E troop's storekeeper, but insisted on getting aboard an M10 as a gunner; Phillips, only 18, hardly knew what it was all about. I remember him being sick on one occasion after drinking too much, and me making him clear it all up. With some reverence Lt. Wimpey and I began to lift them out and place them in blankets. In some cases we had to use a shovel to get them off the floor, for so intense was the heat that they had become fused to it. We buried them at Marcelet, by the side of the Bayeux–Caen road. The regimental padre said a few words, the battery carpenter constructed wooden crosses, a few shots were fired, and so we left them.[7]

It was a little scene played out a hundred times daily on both sides of the Normandy line. Hill 112 was held briefly by Priest's shattered battalion of the Duke of Cornwall's Light Infantry, only to be lost to a German counter-attack.

Montgomery was now compelled to endure a crisis of confidence in his leadership which would have cracked the nerve of a more sensitive man. He had always been the object of animosity within the huge headquarters staff at SHAEF in England, and unloved by many of Bradley's Americans. The tensions now broke into open criticism. Commander Butcher, the embodiment of all gossip-ridden staff officers, wrote after his first visit to France on 1 July: "Some of the people I talked to venture that Monty has been too slow to attack and thus permitted the Germans to get set in fixed positions and to bring up reserves."[8] Patton, an unconcealed enemy, wrote venomously in his diary after a trip to Montgomery's Tactical Headquarters on 7 July: "Montgomery went to great lengths explaining why the British had done nothing." Eisenhower, himself under intense pressure from Washington and his own staff, frustrated by his own staff, frustrated by his own inability directly to influence the events for which he bore the huge responsibility, wrote an unhappy letter to the Commander-in-Chief of 21st Army Group that day expressing his concern about the German build-up: "It appears to me that we must use all possible energy in a determined effort to prevent the risk of a stalemate or of facing the necessity of fighting a major defensive battle with the slight depth we now have in the bridgehead . . . We have not yet attempted a major full-dress attack on the left flank supported by everything we could bring to bear . . ."[9]

The American press had become openly impatient with the lack of progress in France, causing a degree of concern in Washington that, as always, far outweighed the worry the British press could cause any British government. It was being suggested that the western Allies were content to mark time while the Russians did the hard fighting to defeat Hitler's armies. Even more dangerous to Montgomery's position was Churchill's growing impatience. The Prime Minister was at pains to remind Eisenhower, a few days after the landings, that the Supreme Commander had only to express his dissatisfaction with any British officer, "no matter what his rank", for him to be removed. Churchill had convinced himself that if there was no rapid breakthrough after D-Day, it might be a year or more before the Allies reached the Seine. His memory of Flanders haunted all his vision of the battle for France in 1944, especially as he read the infantry casualty lists. On the night of 6 July, Churchill furiously denounced Montgomery to Brooke. He had never warmed to his cold, awkward commander: now, remembering Montgomery's bold declarations at the St Paul's briefing about rapid armoured thrusts and the urgent need to "peg out claims inland", he felt that these intentions had been betrayed. Brooke was driven to defend his protégé with equal anger: "I flared up and asked him if he could not trust his generals for five minutes instead of continuously abusing them and belittling them."[10]

The air chiefs divided their ill-will between Montgomery and the hapless Leigh-Mallory. Tedder felt a persistent lack of confidence in the Commander-in-Chief of 21st Army Group, which he displayed with all the force of his personality. "It seemed clear to me that Montgomery did not attach sufficient importance to the pressing time factor. Few weeks of summer remained. Our urgent need was to get across the Seine."[11] Tedder was a man of genuine stature, and it is impossible to saddle him with the personal malice and small-mindedness that afflicted some of his subordinates. He sincerely believed that he possessed an understanding of the priorities of the land campaign which Montgomery lacked. But as Deputy Supreme Commander, he suffered all the handicaps and frustrations that are the lot of a second-in-command in any military organization: he was privy to all debate but lacked executive power. If Leigh-Mallory was not permitted to exercise executive authority, Tedder showed a marked reluctance to do so. He was invariably consulted and frequently intervened in the air debate, but he never accepted full responsibility for air operations. His intelligence and force of personality were not in doubt, but it is questionable whether he was able to employ these to best effect as Eisenhower's deputy, and whether his understanding of the ground campaign was sufficient to justify his chronic disloyalty to Montgomery, and his promise to Eisenhower of personal support if the Supreme Commander saw fit to sack his ground-force commander.

With all these dangerous currents swirling in his rear, Montgomery sat in the camouflaged caravans of his Tactical Headquarters, surrounded by his pet puppies and canaries, and pondered the course of the battle. One of his biographers, the war correspondent Alan Moorehead, wrote of his supposed conceit and gracelessness, then added that "these vices, if they existed in him, had also distilled a virtue which was regrettably lacking at times among the officers struggling up to a high command: he was nobody's sycophant, he could not be wined and dined into an amenable frame of mind, he could not be impressed by a show of authority nor were his wits clouded by ceremony."[12] Montgomery changed his plans in Normandy, but it cannot be proved that he did so because of the pressure of his enemies and rivals. If anything, the charge against him is that he became too isolated from the political and politico-military realities, too ready to absorb himself exclusively in the battle within the monastic loneliness of his Tactical Headquarters. His Chief of Staff talked freely to the Commander-in-Chief when he saw him, but there is no evidence that Montgomery unburdened himself of his innermost thoughts and hopes to de Guingand or any other man. Yet he possessed the great virtue of accepting the battle-field as he found it, and adjusting to its exigencies without complaint. He was seen to considerable advantage at a meeting of his commanders on 10 July, at which Bradley frankly admitted that the American attack southwards had failed.

Monty quietly replied: "Never mind. Take all the time you need, Brad." [Dempsey related later] Then he went on tactfully to say: "If I were you I think I should concentrate my forces a little more" – putting two fingers together on the map in his characteristic way. Then Monty turned to me and said: "Go on hitting: drawing the German strength, especially some of the armour, onto yourself – so as to ease the way for Brad."[13]

it seems significant that while Eisenhower became restless and unsympathetic to Montgomery as the Normandy battle developed – or rather, in the Supreme Commander's view, failed sufficiently to do so – Bradley did not complain about 21st Army Group's commander. Later, he would become one of Montgomery's most bitter critics. But "during these operations in the lodgement," Bradley wrote, "where Montgomery bossed the U.S. First Army as part of his 21st Army Group, he exercised his Allied authority with wisdom, forbearance, and restraint. At no time did he probe into First Army with the indulgent manner he sometimes displayed among those subordinates who were also his own countrymen."[14] Harmony between the two men at this stage may also have been assisted by Bradley's consciousness of the shortcomings of some of his own formations. It was only afterwards, when the Americans had carried out their sweeping dash through Brittany and across to Argentan, that exhilaration about their own achievement and British sensitivity about Second Army's painful march to Falaise fostered jealousies and resentments that persisted through the campaign.

GOODWOOD

On 7 July, the eve of CHARNWOOD, Montgomery's chief planner, Brigadier Charles Richardson, submitted a report on more far-reaching objectives than Caen. He argued, first, that it was necessary for Second Army to embark on a major offensive rather than merely to pursue a succession of limited operations; second, that in view of the desperate need to avoid heavy infantry casualties, the obvious course was to embark upon an armoured assault. Tanks were one commodity with which the British were amply provided. Indeed, there was scarcely sufficient fighting room within the beachhead for the proper employment of all the armour they possessed. At that date they outnumbered the Germans by four to one in tanks and two to one in infantry, while on the American front the ratios were eight to one and three to two. Bradley's men were holding a line 108,000 yards long, compared with the 77,500 yards in the hands of the British. On 10 July, Dempsey outlined for Montgomery a plan to employ massed armour in an attempt to break through the German defences from the constricted Orne bridgehead, still little larger than that gained by 6th Airborne Division early in June. Montgomery approved. The details of Operation GOOD-WOOD were settled two days later: all three British armoured divisions would attack, under the command of General O'Connor's VIII Corps, along a corridor blasted open by massed bomber forces. The aim was to strike fast through the German defences while the enemy were still reeling from the air bombardment, seize the Bourgébus ridge in the first hours and thence race on across the great sweep of open country beyond. The tanks would drive headlong for Falaise. Meanwhile, Simonds' II Canadian Corps would attack south from the centre of Caen in an effort to secure the rest of the city. I and XII Corps would launch subsidiary infantry attacks, with support from the independent armoured brigades, on the flanks.

"The Second Army is now very strong," Montgomery wrote to Brooke on the 14th, "it has in fact reached its peak and can get no stronger. It will in fact get weaker as the manpower situation begins to hit us. Also, the casualties had affected the fighting efficiency of divisions; the original men were very well trained; reinforcements are not so well trained, and the fact is beginning to become apparent and will have repercussions on what we can do . . . So I have decided that the time has come to have a real 'showdown' on the eastern flank, and to loose a corps of three armoured divisions into the open country about the Caen-Falaise road."[1] Eisenhower wrote to Montgomery of the GOODWOOD plan: "I am confident that it will reap a harvest from all the sowing you have been doing during the past weeks. With our whole front acting aggressively against the enemy so that he is pinned to the ground, O'Connor's plunge into his vitals will be decisive . . . I am viewing the prospects with the most tremendous optimism and enthusiasm. I would not be at all surprised to see you gaining a victory that will make some of the 'old classics' look like a skirmish between patrols."[2] It is interesting and important to notice that after the war Bradley, the most unlikely man to provide spurious alibis for

272

Montgomery, declared that he had never expected GOOD-WOOD to be anything other than a supporting operation for the American COBRA, which was originally scheduled to jump off at much the same time. Yet if Montgomery's hopes and objectives were really so limited, it was politically suicidal for him to allow Eisenhower, Tedder and even Brooke to be deluded about them. There was a perfectly sound military argument for the British to mount only a limited offensive. But there is no hint of evidence that Montgomery sought to explain GOODWOOD in these terms to any of his patrons in England, above all Brooke.

Every previous operation that Montgomery had mounted in Normandy was skilfully conceived, soundly based, offering a real prospect of success at its H-Hour. By the time GOODWOOD was launched, for political and moral reasons he was more seriously in need of a victory than at any time since D-Day. Yet from its inception the operation was flawed. It relied heavily upon surprise to gain the high ground which dominated the British line of advance, yet called for the movement of 8,000 tanks and armoured vehicles across the Orne to the assembly points. Until the armour had cleared the start-line, the artillery could not deploy to provide the massive bombardment which was such an important asset to any operation. Days before GOODWOOD was set in motion, 51st Highland Division's engineers had sown new minefield to cover their own positions, which could not now be properly cleared for the armoured advance. Only narrow corridors would be available through which the tanks could progress. Most damning of all, the Germans were expecting them. Sepp Dietrich claimed after the war that he had heard the British tanks coming by using an old trick he had learned in Russia, of putting his ear to the ground. Perhaps he did. But long before the tanks began to roll from the start-line, German intelligence had achieved one of its few important battlefield successes in Normandy, by alerting Rommel to the imminent British move against Bourgébus. General Eberbach of Panzer Group West reacted by adopting perhaps the most formidable defensive deployments of the entire campaign: five lines of tanks and anti-tanks guns, directly confronting VIII Corps' axis of advance. 36 hours before GOODWOOD was set in motion, Ultra interceptions revealed to the British that Field-Marshal Hugo Sperrle of Luftflotte 3 had signalled a forecast of a major British attack, "to take place south-eastwards from Caen about the night of 17–18th".

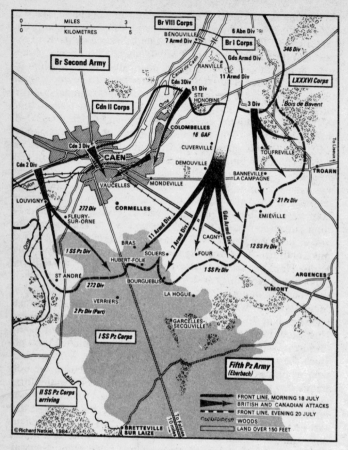

Operation GOODWOOD: 18–20 July

In Montgomery's directive to Dempsey before the battle, all mention of Falaise as an objective had vanished; a sudden onset of caution seemed to have overcome him. But Dempsey himself was still full of brilliant hopes as he transferred his Tactical HQ to a position alongside that of O'Connor, where he could oversee the battle at close quarters. "What I had in mind was to seize all the crossings of the Orne from Caen to Argentan," Second Army's commander said after the war.[3]

Carlo D'Este, the author of an important recent study of the Normandy battle, pays tribute to General O'Connor's understanding of the vital need for close armoured–infantry co-operation in GOODWOOD. O'Connor sought to employ some of the gunners' self-propelled chassis as infantry personnel carriers for the battle, and was much vexed by Dempsey's refusal to let them be used. Yet General "Pip" Roberts of 11th Armoured, probably the ablest British divisional commander in Normandy, suffered deep misgivings when he studied O'Connor's plan for GOODWOOD, and discovered that the armour and infantry had been given separate objectives. He felt so strongly about the error of this decision that he recorded his view in writing, which cause O'Connor to reply that if Roberts lacked the conviction to lead the attack according to his plan, one of the other armoured divisions could relieve the 11th as spearhead. Robert reluctantly acquiesced. But he believed that O'Connor did not understand the proper handling of armour on a European battlefield.[4] Other senior officers echoed Roberts' lack of confidence not only in the corps commander himself, but also in his staff.

Between 5.30 and 8.30 a.m. on the morning of 18 July, one of the greatest-ever air bombardments of ground forces was unleashed upon Panzer Group West by heavy and medium bombers of the RAF and USAAF. In three waves they attacked the German positions confronting O'Connor's armoured divisions: tanks were hurled bodily into the air or buried by earth and rubble; men were deafened and stunned for days or blasted into fragments; guns were wrecked and twisted on their mountings; fuel and ammunition exploded. Shortly after H-Hour, a scout car of the Inns of Court Regiment reported exultantly that it was well on the way to 11th Armoured's objectives, and could see no evidence of opposition. "I said 'Jolly good show' and didn't believe a word of it," said Roberts tersely.[5] His scepticism was rapidly justified.

One of the great surprises of warfare in the twentieth century has been the power of soldiers to survive what would seem to be overwhelming concentrations of high explosive, and emerge to fight with skill and determination. So it was now with the men of Panzer Group West. The leading units of 11th Armoured Division jumped off promptly at 7.30 a.m. and made rapid progress for the first two hours, before meeting heavy and stiffening resistance. Around the village of Cagny, just four 88 mm flak guns of the 16th Luftwaffe Field Division had escaped the air bombardment. At pistol point, Colonel Hans von Luck of 21st Panzer Division compelled their commander to abandon his delusions about his anti-aircraft role, and to engage the advancing British tanks at once. 16 of 11th Armoured's Shermans fell to these guns alone. It was 4.00 p.m. before the Guards Armoured Division entered Cagny. As other British units crossed the Caen-Vimont railway embankment and attempted to push on towards Bourgébus, they met ruthless German tank and anti-tank fire. The vehicle carrying 11th Armoured's sole RAF Forward Air Controller was knocked out in the first two hours, with the result that close air support for the advance was lost. Meanwhile, in the rear, the Guards Armoured and 7th Armoured Divisions had been seriously delayed by the huge traffic jam of vehicles moving along the corridors through British minefields. Without support, the British spearhead of 29th Armoured Brigade was already in serious trouble, only 12,000 yards from its start-line and scarcely through the crust of the deep defences. Trooper John Brown was driving a 17-pounder Sherman Firefly of the 2nd Fife and Forfar Yeomanry. He and his crew left the start-line in a mood of excited optimism, after watching the vast air bombardment, convinced that no German position could have survived such appalling punishment.

It was not long after the earlier euphoria that we realised what was in store for us – 13 tanks, one of our squadrons knocked out, some burning and what remained of their crews either walking or crawling back from the front. Our tanks reached the Caen–Vimont railway close beside a level crossing in the Cagny area. From our position we knocked out two, probably three German tanks, but it was difficult to recognise this in the carnage. We were shooting over the rear of the tank when fire broke out and the order was given to bale out. I tried my hatch but was unable to get it open. Lying on my back over the ammunition in the co-driver's position, a space of about eighteen inches between the shells and the hatch which I was able to open, I pulled myself out, falling to the ground. Lying beside the tank, we realised that it was only our equipment and bedding on the hull which was burning. Pulling this off, I said I would get back into the tank and bring it into the shelter of the house at the level crossing. I had got in and started the engine when suddenly a horrible eruption of molten metal came in through the side immediately behind the ammunitions. This was like an acetylene cutter in action. Fortunately I was able to bale out faster than the first time. From there my crewmates and I made our way back to rear echelon in the glider landing fields near Ranville.[6]

276

Soon after noon, bitterly conscious that his attack was running out of steam, O'Connor organized a new two-pronged thrust to be carried out by 11th Armoured on the right, 7th Armoured's Cromwells on the left.

We moved well for a while [wrote a British reconnaissance vehicle commander, Corporal Peter Roach], until we came to another flat stretch littered with knocked-out Cromwell tanks extending right away to the ridge in front. Delay, frustration, ignorance of what was happening . . . Some shells landed nearby; violent black smoke with a brilliant red centre and large jagged pieces of metal tearing at the unwary. The tank I was following stopped and the commander jumped down swearing. The driver, who had his head out, was hit. I got the lead from his headphones under his arms and we tugged him through the small hatch opening, floppy and inert. Our hands were wet with blood; we laid him on the ground; from his head oozed blood and sticky brains; he quivered and made quacking noises, and then mercifully died. The officer was crying . . .

The light was going slowly and the air warm. I sat on the top of the tank as we ate cold rice pudding from a tin. I looked at my hands gory with dried blood and brains. Nearby two flail tanks were talking on the radios and coming through on my set. The commanders were tired and their nerves were frayed. I could hear the scorn in the voice of A and the almost pleading voice of B as he complained bitterly that A had "pissed off without warning". It was frightening to hear men so open in their dislike on the one hand and dependence on the other. UJ came up on the air, asking my position and then querying my reference. I too was frayed, so I asked if he thought I couldn't read a map or didn't know where I was.[7]

The only regiment of 7th Armoured to approach its point of attack, after escaping the chaos around the Orne, did not reach 29th Brigade's battered squadrons until 5.00 p.m. by which time the latter had suffered 50 per cent tank losses, 11th Armoured losing a total of 126 tanks during the day. Guards Armoured Division lost 60 tanks in this, its first battle. Roberts' foreboding about O'Connor's separation of tanks and infantry had been entirely justified: his armour received no infantry support until 5.00 p.m. Although many officers liked O'Connor, and to this day there are energetic defenders of his conduct of the battles in Normandy, the evidence suggests that he never achieved the "grip" of VIII Corps which had so distinguished his command in the desert. Montgomery's public modifications of his ambitions for GOODWOOD can hardly have critically influenced O'Connor's conduct, when Dempsey declared his own hope that VIII

Corps would get to Falaise. Colonel Brian Wyldbore-Smith, GSO I of 11th Armoured, said flatly of GOODWOOD: "We really did think that this was to be the breakout."[8] Brigadier Richardson, 21st Army Group's BGS Plans, said that "at the time, I thought Goodwood had been a tremendous flop."[9] He subsequently modified his view in the light of post-war evidence that Montgomery only sought to maintain pressure on the eastern flank. But it seems absurd to suppose that GOODWOOD could have been secretly transformed into a limited operation without the acquiescence of Dempsey, the army commander, or the knowledge of the senior staff officers charged with carrying it out.

It becomes even more difficult to believe this in the light of Montgomery's behaviour at the time. In an extraordinary moment of optimism that afternoon – of the kind that did so much to damage his credibility with less sympathetic recipients – Montgomery signalled Brooke: "Operations this morning a complete success . . . The effect of the air bombing was decisive and the spectacle terrific . . . situation very promising and it is difficult to see what the enemy can do just at present."[10] Far more serious, he read to the assembled press corps a disastrously optimistic bulletin about the progress of the attack. Brigadier Williams remembered seeing on Alan Moorehead's face "this wonderful Australian disbelief". Yet in consequence of Montgomery's remarks, on 19 July *The Times* carried the headline, "Second Army breaks through", and quoted the communiqué's assertion that "early this morning British and Canadian troops of the Second Army attacked and broke through into the area east of the Orne and south-east of Caen." Another headline read, "British army in full cry", followed the next day by "Wide corridor through German front". A "Special Correspondent" was "at pains to rebut suggestions of 'setbacks' ".

In reality, the Canadians had gained most of Caen, but the Germans remained in absolute control of the Bourgébus Ridge, which they reinforced strongly during the night. Crerar's men were perhaps more angry and bitter about the disappointments of the battle than O'Connor's patient and long-suffering British troops. "Goodwood had been sold to us as a big deal," said Corporal Dick Raymond of 3rd Canadian Division. "To see those Shermans puffing into black smoke gave us a sick feeling in the stomach. It seemed a futile, clumsy thing." ATLANTIC, the Canadian operation on the GOODWOOD flank, cost Crerar's men 1,965 casualties. Two infantry battalions alone bore the brunt of these – the South Saskatchewans, who lost 215 men, and the Essex Scottish, losing 244. Two days later, after further brutal fighting, 7th Armoured Division had gained part of the ridge, but in the heavy rain and mud which now made the closure of the operation inevitable, the German line was still unbroken. The British had suffered 5,537 casualties and lost 400 tanks, 36 per cent of their armoured strength in France, of which only a proportion could be recovered and repaired. So prodigious were Allied reserves of *matériel* that replacements reached almost every armoured division within 36 hours. The restoration of Montgomery's prestige would take a great deal longer.

In the post-mortems in the wake of GOODWOOD, all manner of suggestions were made about what had gone wrong and what could have been done better. Since the assembly of such a vast force had proved impossible to keep secret, could more have been gained by opening the attack in darkness? Would a shorter interval between the end of the air bombardment and the British approach to the German positions have been decisive? Was the Guards Armoured Division briefed to expect too easy an assault in this, its first battle, and were its units thus too readily overcome by the unexpected strength of the opposition? Could O'Connor have pushed 7th Armoured Division forward faster? Why was there still such lamentable cohesion between tanks and infantry?

The answers to all these questions partially explain the British misfortunes. Yet none of them can mask the bald truth that Second Army sought to attack powerful and skilfully-directed German defences. Major changes of British tactics would have been necessary to bring about a different outcome. A daylight infantry attack across open ground would have been cut to pieces, but a carefully-planned night assault might have yielded dramatic dividends. The airmen were vociferous in their anger about the army's failure to gain a decisive result after calling upon a vast bomber force in support. Nothing, except their own parochialism, could justify such an attitude. Even if the air attack on Caen earlier in the month was misconceived, there were major enemy concentrations to be bombed on the Bourgébus ridge, and substantial damage was inflicted upon these, moral as much as material. The GOODWOOD experience showed the limitations of massive air attack, but it also revealed its value. Only the airmen's obsessive belief that all their squadrons could meanwhile have been better employed over Germany justified their furious reaction.

In the years since the revelation of the Allies' breaking of German ciphers in the Second World War, it has sometimes been assumed that Ultra provided the Allies with absolute knowledge of enemy deployments and capabilities. This is a travesty of the truth. Ultra was of immense value, but its reliability and comprehensiveness varied greatly from day to day, according to luck, the extent to which local German units were signalling by radio rather than using land-lines, and the speed of the decrypters at Bletchley Park. O'Connor's forces embarked upon GOODWOOD with no concept of the strength of the German defences they were to engage, while the Germans had been using observation posts, prisoner interrogation and aerial reconnaissance to powerful effect. This was the first and last occasion of the Normandy campaign on which von Kluge's men were able to fight a battle on terms that suited them, albeit at a cost which they could much less well afford than the Allies.

The British were attacking across more open country than in any battle of the campaign thus far. So much has been said about the difficulties of fighting amid the hedges of the *bocage*, that it seems worth emphasizing the equal difficulties of advancing against powerful defences over an unbroken field of fire. Tanks could use open country to great advantage if they could manoeuvre around enemy positions. But where they were confronted by a continuous line of defences, even a small number of well-handled German tanks and guns could do enormous execution. Here, perhaps more than in any other battle in north-west Europe, the British paid the price for their lack of a survivable battle tank; armour of the weight of the German Tigers and Panthers might have been battered a path up the Bourgébus ridge – a feat that the Shermans and Cromwells were too frail to achieve.

It has been suggested above that blame for the failure of some of Montgomery's June battles in Normandy lay more with those charged with directing and fighting them than with the planners who conceived them. Yet GOODWOOD failed because the concept, the plan, the preparations were unsound. The British were sometimes accused of being unimaginative in their use of armoured forces by comparison with the Americans. Below Bourgébus ridge in July, they attempted an extraordinarily ambitious massed tank operation which, had it succeeded, might have rivalled that of Patton a few weeks later. But there was an important difference between the British and later American operations: in the first, the German defence was unbroken: the old military axiom about the hazards of employing unsupported cavalry against an unbroken square still held good. Colonel Brian Wyldbore-Smith, GSO I of 11th Armoured, argued convincingly that it was a great mistake to launch the attack with massed tanks: "One squadron per infantry battalion would have been ample. More than that simply confused the issue." Here he touched upon the very heart of the GOODWOOD failure. The forces assembled for the operation were not those judged necessary to meet the ground or the nature of the defences, but those which the British then felt willing to expend – their tanks. The critical problem of manpower and infantry casualties thus directly influenced an important tactical decision.

As a result of GOODWOOD, Montgomery's prestige within the Allied high command suffered damage from which it never recovered. Eisenhower was disappointed and angered by the gulf between Second Army's promise and performance. His staff became genuinely concerned about the rise in the Supreme Commander's blood pressure. Butcher wrote on the 19th, referring to the tragic sudden death in France of 4th Division's deputy commander: "What a blow it would be to the world, not mentioning that to his personal followers, if he [Eisenhower] should pull a Teddy Roosevelt!"[11]

Tedder's animosity was redoubled. He considered that the air forces had been the victim of a deliberate deception by Montgomery, who had exaggerated his expectations merely to ensure that he received the support of the strategic bombers. Tedder told Eisenhower baldly: "Your own people are thinking you have sold them to the British if you continue to support Montgomery without protest." Of all the criticism heaped upon Montgomery in the course of the war, that following his handling of GOODWOOD is the most difficult to refute. He sent a limited directive to Dempsey before the battle,[12] a copy of which never reached SHAEF, who thus continued to expect more from GOODWOOD than 21st Army Group; this matter has been the subject of much speculation. Yet, directive or no directive, Montgomery could not escape the consequences of other grandiloquent declarations of expectation and achievement before and during the battle. Whatever written insurance policies he took out before 18 July, it is impossible to doubt that when he launched his three-corps attack, he hoped desperately to reach Falaise. He and his staff must have been aware of the expectations they had raised in London and Washington, and therefore of the inescapable cost of failing to meet these. After GOODWOOD, said Brigadier Richardson, 21st Army Group's BGS Plans, "we were distinctly worried. We knew Monty put on this impenetrable act of confidence, whatever was happening. But below Freddy de Guingand's level, it was difficult to judge whether this confidence was soundly based. My feeling was that we were getting into a bigger jam than he was prepared to admit."[13]

Montgomery admitted in his memoirs that he had overdone his public comment, and been "too exultant at the press conference I gave during the Goodwood battle. I realise that now – in fact, I realised it pretty quickly afterwards. Basically the trouble was this – both Bradley and I agreed that we could not possibly tell the Press the true strategy which formed the basis of all our plans. As Bradley said, 'We must grin and bear it.' It became increasingly difficult to grin."[14] It is almost tragic to behold a man of Montgomery's stature so far diminishing himself as to write such nonsense. GOODWOOD rendered great service to the American flank and to the Allied cause by maintaining pressure and by "writing down" irreplaceable German forces. But to demand that history should accept that this alone was the sum of British ambitions is to suggest that a man sows wheat to harvest straw. Montgomery, under all the pressures building up around him since early July, must have known that, had the British embarked upon an operation with such limited objectives as he afterwards attributed to GOODWOOD, the anger and impatience of the Americans towards their British allies would have become uncontainable. The truth, which he never avowed even to Brooke, yet which seems self-evident from the course of events, was that in GOODWOOD, and throughout the rest of the campaign, Montgomery sought major ground gains for Second Army if these could be achieved at acceptable cost. He forsook them whenever casualties rose unacceptably. This occurred painfully often.

When Montgomery and Eisenhower met privately on the afternoon of 20 July – one of their nine personal encounters during the campaign – it seems clear that the Supreme Commander vented his distress. It is possible, even probable, that Montgomery emphasized to Eisenhower his concern over British manpower and casualties, and said something of the Americans' greater ability to overcome these problems. For in Eisenhower's subsequent letter to his Commander-in-Chief, written the following day, he reminded Montgomery sharply that "eventually the American ground strength will necessarily be much greater than the British. But while we have equality in size we must go forward shoulder to shoulder, with honors and sacrifices equally shared."[15] Confidence in Montgomery, and in the performance of the British Second Army, had reached the lowest point of the campaign in north-west Europe among the Americans, among the airmen, and even among some of the British, including their Prime Minister. "Whatever hopes he [Montgomery] had of remaining overall ground commander died with Goodwood," Bradley believed. [16] He afterwards asserted his conviction that Eisenhower would have sacked the British general, had he felt able to do so.

Montgomery's behaviour throughout this period seems dominated by the belief that he could afford to spurn Eisenhower, whose unfittedness for field command was so apparent to every senior officer. It is undoubtedly true that even Bradley, the most loyal and patient of men, was irked by Eisenhower's inability to "read" the battle that was taking place in Normandy. As early as 7 June, Bradley was irritated by Eisenhower's sudden appearance aboard the *Augusta* in mid-Channel: "On the whole Ike's visit had been perhaps necessary for his own personal satisfaction, but from my point of view it was a pointless interruption and annoyance."[17] The First Army commander, both then and later, acknowledged the justice of Montgomery's claim that Eisenhower never understood the Allied plan in Normandy. The Supreme Commander laboured under a misapprehension that he himself could best serve the Allied cause by touring the touchline like a football coach, urging all his generals to keep attacking more or less simultaneously. Eisenhower's personal life-style, journeying between fronts with a ragbag of sycophantic staff officers, his Irish driver and mistress, occasionally his newly-commissioned son and cosseted pet dog, was more suggestive of an eighteenth-century European monarch going to war than a twentieth-century general.

Yet Dwight Eisenhower was the Supreme Commander of the Allied armies, upon whom hung the fervent hopes of two governments for the unity and triumph of their armies. His charm and statesmanship deeply impressed, even moved, all those who worked closely with him. Montgomery's inability to establish a personal relationship with the American, to confide to Eisenhower his own private hopes and fears for the battle, cost him dear. 21st Army Group's Commander-in-Chief made the immense error of believing that the Supreme Commander could be side-stepped, deluded, soft-talked into leaving himself, Montgomery, the supreme professional, to fight the war. He might indeed have been successful in this had his armies on the battlefield fulfilled his early hopes in Normandy. But when they did not, it was Eisenhower, fretting impotently in England, who bore the impatience of the American press, the doubts and fears of the politicians, the charges of failure of generalship which the ignorant associated with himself. Eisenhower might have been willing to ride passively upon a tide of success created by Montgomery. He was quite unwilling idly to accept responsibility for apparent failure and stagnation. At the time and for some years after the war, the extent of the breakdown of relations between Montgomery and Eisenhower was concealed. Today there is no doubt that by late July 1944, the American was weary to death of his ground-force commander.

Brooke urgently warned Montgomery on 19 July to drop his objections to a prime-ministerial visit to Normandy, and use the opportunity to rebuild a little of Churchill's flagging faith. The CIGS warned his friend "of the tendency of the PM to listen to suggestions that Monty played for safety and was not prepared to take risks." Brooke wrote in his diary:

Winston had never been very fond of Monty; when things went well he put up with him, when they did not he at once became "your Monty". Just at this time Eisenhower had been expressing displeasure and accusing Monty of being sticky, of not pushing sufficiently on the Caen front with the British while he made the Americans do the attacking on the right. Winston was inclined to listen to these complaints.[18]

Brigadier Richardson said that "in strategic terms, things were going according to plan. In tactical terms, they were not." It is much easier to understand the criticisms made of Montgomery by the Americans than those made by his fellow-countrymen. Until the very end of the war, the British demanded that they should be treated as equal partners in the alliance with the United States, and vied for a lion's share of Allied command positions. They could scarcely be surprised if the Americans

284

showed resentment when the British flinched before heavy casualties, and fought on the eastern flank with less apparent determination and will for sacrifice than the American army in the west. Whatever the Americans' weaknesses of command and tactics, their willingness to expend men to gain an objective was never in doubt. "On the whole, they were prepared to go at it more toughly than we were," said Brigadier Carver of 4th Armoured Brigade.[19]

Montgomery, however, was never allowed to forget that he was charged with responsibility for Britain's last great army, her final reserves of manpower in a struggle that had drained these to the limit. With the constant admonitions reaching him from England about casualties, he would have faced bitter criticism – from Churchill as much as any man – had losses risen steeply. It is indisputable that this knowledge bore hard upon the British conduct of operations in Normandy, from the summit to the base of the command structure. Butcher wrote on 24 July, after visiting Southwick House for an hour when Eisenhower drove there to see de Guingand:

Bill Culver, de Guingand's American aide, in response to my pointed question as to what really stopped Monty's attack, said he felt that Monty, his British Army commander Dempsey, the British corps commanders and even those of the divisions are so conscious of Britain's ebbing manpower that they hesitate to commit an attack where a division may be lost. When it's lost, it's done and finished . . . The Commanders feel the blood of the British Empire, and hence its future, are too precious for dash in battle.[20]

With hindsight it may be easy to suggest that a more ruthless determination to break through on the British front earlier in the campaign would, in the end, have cost fewer lives. Tedder's allegation that Second Army was not trying hard enough had some foundation, but it was much easier to take this sanguine view from the distance of SHAEF – or from the perspective of history – than for Montgomery and his commanders in Normandy, who had to watch their precious army take persistent punishment. Tedder's attitude proved his claim to be an outstanding Alliance commander, with a truly Anglo-American perspective, but it showed little sympathy for valid but more parochial British sensitivities. If the British army was to achieve major ground gains on the eastern flank against the powerful German forces deployed before it, the evidence suggested that the cost would be terrible.

Montgomery is entitled to the gratitude of his country, as well as of his soldiers, for declining to yield to the temptation to mount a ruthlessly costly attack merely to stave off the political demands made upon him. He judged, correctly, that if the Allies persisted with their existing plan for pressure in the east and breakthrough in the west, the Germans would eventually crack without a British bloodbath. Yet in July as in June, he denied himself the goodwill of either Americans or British sceptics by creating a smokescreen of distortion and untruth to conceal his disappointment with the failure of Second Army to gain ground at acceptable cost. It is a measure of the criticism now directed against him, and of the political pressure within the Alliance, that as late as 28 July, when the American breakout was already making good progress, Brooke was writing to him:

Now, as a result of all this talking and the actual situation on your front, I feel personally quite certain that Dempsey must attack *at the earliest possible moment* [emphasis in original] on a large scale. We must not allow German forces to move from his front to Bradley's front or we shall give more cause than ever for criticism.[21]

It is impossible to imagine that Montgomery could have been sacked – with whatever Tedder's delusion on that count – without inflicting an intolerable blow to British national confidence. He whom propaganda has made mighty, no man may readily cast aside, as Portal was compelled to acknowledge a few months later in his difficulties with "Bomber" Harris. But it is difficult to guess what new pressures and directives might have been forced upon the Commander-in-Chief of 21st Army Group had not the perspective of the Normandy campaign now been entirely transformed by the American Operation COBRA.

9 The breakout

Throughout the first half of July, while the British and Canadians were fighting their bitter battles around Caen, the Americans were enduring equal pain and frustration in their efforts to disentangle themselves from the clinging misery of the *bocage*. On 3 July, Middleton's VIII Corps attacked south towards Coutances–St Lô–Caumont. The corps commander himself was one of the most experienced fighting soldiers in the American army, having led a regiment in France in the First World War, and more recently a division in Italy. But Middleton was now seriously troubled and weakened by the pain of an arthritic knee, and his staff were conscious that this reduced his ability to concentrate upon the battle. Not that it was likely that the outcome of the early fighting would have been different had be been fit. By far the toughest initial objective was the 300-foot height of Mont Castre, dominating the Cotentin plain. After heavy fighting the superb 82nd Airborne Division, halved in strength by weeks in action, gained the hill and proved what a first-class formation could achieve even against dogged opposition. Elsewhere on the front, however, matters went much less happily. The accident-prone 90th Division made no headway, and Bradley prepared to sack yet another of its commanders, Landrum. The 79th Division suffered 2,000 casualties in the next five days to crawl forward a little over three miles. There was nothing to suggest that these difficulties were caused by command shortcomings, for when VII Corps joined the attack on 4 July under the dynamic Collins, they too found themselves rapidly bogged down. On the 7th, XIX Corps was thrown in, although Corlett, its corps commander, like Middleton was in visibly poor health, and even when fit had never been considered a driver of men. Hodges described him at the time as possessing "that hospital look".[1] Scenes of near-farce ensued when advancing elements of 30th Division became entangled with the tanks of 3rd Armored, creating terrible congestion. There was a furious confrontation between Generals Bohn and Hobbs about whose fault this was, which ended in the sacking of Bohn, the junior officer, but a tough old veteran who had started as a private soldier and risen through the ranks of the American army.

After 12 days of battle, VIII Corps had suffered 10,000 casualties to advance some seven miles. Corlett's and Collins' men had fared no better. "Thus my breakout and dreams of a blitz to Avranches failed badly," wrote Bradley, "a crushing disappointment to me personally."[2] The principal American achievement was the defeat of a counter-attack by Panzer Lehr towards St Jean-de-Daye on 11 July, which 9th and 30th Divisions threw back causing the loss of 25 per cent of the Germans' strength. Once again, it had been demonstrated that movement by either army was the crucial difficulty in the *bocage*, and that in defence American troops could hammer the Germans as hard as Hausser's men of Seventh Army had hit the Americans when they were defending.

Enduring the pain of their own difficulties, the Americans sometimes forgot the scale of suffering that they were inflicting upon the Germans. Sergeant Helmut Gunther, of 17th Panzergrenadiers, each day watched his company of the reconnaissance battalion whittled away without hope of replacements: Hahnel, who was killed by small-arms fire in their first battle; Heinrich, his veteran chess partner, who died on the Carentan road; Dobler, who took over a platoon when its commander was killed and was shot in the head as he jumped from the ditch to lead a counter-attack. All these old friends and many more were gone: "I used to think – 'What a poor pig I am, fighting here with my back to the wall.' "[3] Yet Gunther's self-pity was mixed with astonishment that the survivors stood the strain and the losses so well, and fought on. He was astounded that the Americans did not break through their line in early July. His own company was reduced to 20 men out of 120, yet when he sought his CO's permission to withdraw 50 yards to a better tactical position, it was refused.

On 9 July, they were at last driven from their positions, and Gunther found himself staring at a Sherman tank bearing down upon him only yards away. He was working forward to throw a sticky bomb at it when a German voice called "Come back!", and he glanced round to see a German tank behind him. He stood confused and uncertain for a moment as the panzer commander shouted, "Get down, he's going to shoot!" and a shell from the Sherman blasted into the German tank, splinters ricocheting into Gunther's back. Characteristically, the panzer survived the encounter. The Sherman did not. Gunther was evacuated to hospital.

The defeat of the German counter-attacks was encouraging to the Americans, but provided little consolation for Bradley, wrestling with his fundamental problem of breaking through into Brittany. At the highest level, the Americans discussed with deep concern the problem of giving their infantry divisions something of the thrust and attacking power that so far seemed the monopoly of the Airborne. "We were flabbergasted by the *bocage*," said General Quesada of IXth Tactical Air Command, who was working daily alongside Bradley. "Our infantry had become paralysed. It has never been adequately described how immobilized they were by the sound of small-arms fire among the hedges."[4] Patton reminded an old French army friend of a remark that he had made in the First War: "He had said, 'The poorer the infantry the more artillery it needs; the American infantry needs all it can get.' He was right then, and still is."[5] First Army reported on "the urgent need for the development of an aggressive spirit by the infantry soldier . . . The outstanding impression gained from a review of battle experience is the importance of aggressive action and continuous energetic forward movement in order to gain ground and reduce casualties."[6]

It had become brutally apparent to every man in First Army that service in an infantry unit was an almost certain sentence to death or wounds. The top sergeant in Corporal George Small's anti-aircraft battalion routinely threatened jesters: "One more crack like that and you'll find yourself in the infantry."[7] The unfortunate 90th Division suffered replacement of 150 per cent of its officers and over 100 per cent of enlisted men in its first six weeks in action. Typical tank casualty figures showed that in June alone, the 712 Battalion lost 21 out of 74 in 16 days of action, the 746th 44 out of 51 in 23 days, the 747th 41 out of 61 in 10 days. In July, the 712th lost 21 out of 68 in 16 days, the 756th 51 out of 91 ins 29 days. Temporary or permanent losses from "battle fatigue" had reached an alarming 10,000 men since D-Day, around 20 per cent of all casualties. Between June and November 1944, a staggering 26 per cent of all American soldiers in combat divisions were treated for some form of battle fatigue; this was out of a total of 929,307 such cases in the U.S. Army in the Second World War. There was a real fear that "battle fatigue" was reaching epidemic proportions. The after-action medical report of First Army declared that:

. . . the rate of admission to the exhaustion centres . . . during the first weeks of operations was in accord with the estimates made previously, however, the rate thereafter increased to such proportions that it became necessary to reinforce each of the platoons operating the exhaustion centres . . . Reasons for this increase: a) addition of a number of divisions to the army in excess of original estimates, b) difficult terrain, mud, hedgerows etc, c) stiff resistance offered by the enemy in the La Haye du Puits, Carentan and St. Lô actions, d) troops remaining in combat for long periods.[8]

Every army in the Second World War recognized battle exhaustion or shell shock as a genuine, curable condition among soldiers under acute strain. But it was felt by many officers in 1944 that the U.S. Army had become too ready to allow its men to believe that battle exhaustion was an acceptable state. There is a narrow borderline between humanitarian concern and dangerous weakness. If Patton had been overharsh in his treatment of battle exhaustion in Sicily, there seemed grounds for believing that in Normandy, First Army moved too far in the opposite direction. Major Frank Colacicco of the 3rd/18th Infantry described how men appeared before him claiming battle fatigue and, if challenged, defied him to court-martial them. "What was five years in the brig? They knew that the U.S. government would fluke out." By July, the rear areas of all the Allied armies were generously populated with deserters, whom American units often treated with much greater forbearance than the British. Provost-Sergeant James Dobie of the British 5th King's Regiment was astonished to discover, when he returned two errant GIs to their unit, that "they were greeted like long-lost brothers instead of absentees." The German army's discipline was not based entirely upon natural loyalty. Between January and September 1944, the Wehrmacht executed almost 4,000 of its own men, 1,605 of these for desertion.

Some senior Americans regretted that their army had failed to adopt Montgomery's policy before D-day, of leavening untried divisions with key officers and NCOs who possessed battle experience at battalion level and below. There had also been a failure to make the men of First Army familiar with their leaders. An extraordinary number of Americans soldiers who fought in north-west Europe regarded the high command as

impossibly remote, and Eisenhower and Bradley as hardly comprehensible figures. A few divisional commanders – Huebner,
Cota, Barton, Rose, Eddy – became widely known and respected by their men. But the roll call of senior American officers
found wanting and sacked in Normandy was astonishing: two
successive commanders of 90th Division, Brown of 28th Division, McMahon of 8th (who told Bradley frankly, "Brad, I think
you are going to have to relieve me."),[9] Watson of 3rd Armored,
to name only the most prominent. Bradley found 83rd Division's
leadership "uncertain", and that of the 79th and 80th suspect. Of
the corps commanders, only Collins had distinguished himself.
The commander-designate of First Army, Courtney Hodges,
was considered by most of his peers to be an officer of limited
imagination and self-effacing personality. Bradley described him
as "one of the most skilled craftsmen under my entire command," but was constrained to add that he was also "essentially
a military technician . . . a spare, soft-voiced Georgian without
temper, drama, or visible emotion."[10]

If Bradley's personal modesty was one of his most engaging
characteristics, it contributed to the impersonality of his army.
Whatever men thought of Patton – and many scorned him – all of
them knew who he was. Most took a pride, then and later, in
serving with Patton's Army. As Montgomery understood so
well, the cult of personality can be immensely valuable in war.
The lack of it within the American army in Normandy – the
difficulty for most infantry replacements of identifying with a
man, a unit, anything human beyond their own squad save the
vast juggernaut of tanks and guns with which they rolled –
contributed significantly to the difficulties of the American army.
Where the German army did its utmost to maintain men in
regional formations, the Americans pursued a deliberate policy
of dividing men from the same town or state – a legacy of the
First War, when the pain of a local unit's destruction was thought
to have borne too heavily upon individual communities. But
even industrialized war on a vast scale needs its focus of identity,
its charismatic leaders. These were instinctive human necessities
that America's commanders seemed slow to understand.

Private Gerard Ascher, a 27-year-old New Yorker who
worked in the family business until he was drafted in 1943, was
one of countless thousands of infantry replacements shipped to
Normandy in June 1944 in anonymous packages of 250 men, to
be directed wherever casualties dictated. One of his group gazed

around at Normandy for a few minutes after their landing, then declared decisively: "This is no place for me," and vanished from their ken for ever. Ascher reached the 357th Infantry in darkness with an unknown young Mississippian, to be greeted by a lieutenant, who said simply: "You two stay in this hedgerow – the others are in that one." The New Yorker's memories of the campaign were above all of disorientation, of utter ignorance of their purpose: "I really couldn't fathom the whole thing – I couldn't understand what it was all about. I never remembered seeing the battalion commander except at ceremonies."[11] If all infantrymen in all armies share something of this feeling, and if Ascher was uncommonly unlucky to be sent to the 90th Division, his sentiments reflected a problem that afflicted much of the American army in north-west Europe. Very many soldiers respected their NCOs. But in sharp contrast to the British army, in which most men looked up to their officers, few American rankers admitted to thinking well of theirs. Corporal George Small wrote of "this nearly universal scorn of American soldiers for most officers".[12] Above all at platoon level, the "90-day wonders" – the young lieutenants upon whom so much junior leadership depended – seldom won the confidence and respect of their soldiers.

The men of Bradley's army might not be privy to "the big picture", but in early July 1944 they felt a deep sense that much was going wrong. "We were stuck," said Corporal Bill Preston of the 743rd Tank Battalion: "Something dreadful seemed to have happened in terms of the overall plan. Things were going very awry. The whole theory of mobility that we had been taught, of our racing across the battlefield, seemed to have gone up in smoke." Sergeant Bill Walsh of the 102nd Cavalry thought that the struggle between Germans and Americans resembled "a pro fighter taking on an amateur who didn't want to fight. None of those American infantry boys wanted to be over there." Lieutenant Philip Reisler of 2nd Armored felt that the campaign had become "like an interminable succession of Thermopylaes. In every engagement, we were only able to present one tiny unit to the enemy at a time."

Yet even as First Army's difficulties seemed at their greatest, the transformation of American fortunes was at hand. Together with General Collins of VII Corps, Bradley had conceived a new plan. To clear the way for a major offensive, Collins' men began

292

to push forward to the St Lô–Périers road. By 20 July, they had reached positions commanding it. On 18 July, at a cost of 3,000 casualties in the 29th Division and more than 2,000 in the 35th, the Americans gained the vital heights of St Lô. The battle for the shattered rubble of the town was one of First Army's outstanding feats of arms in the campaign, driving back General Eugene Meindl's II Parachute Corps yard by yard, despite constant casualties. The body of Major Thomas Howie, killed leading the 3rd/116th Infantry to the rescue of the 2nd Battalion on the outskirts of St Lô, was laid on a bier of rubble outside the church of Notre-Dame. Hill 122 joined a host of other Norman map references among the American army's battle honours. The German 352nd Division, whose presence had wrought such havoc with American plans on 6 June, was now in ruins. Even Meindl's paratroopers had cracked. The stage was set for the supreme American military achievement of the Normandy campaign, Operation COBRA.

It was symbolic of the contrasting approaches to war by the two principal Allies in Normandy that the British codenamed their greatest efforts after race meetings, while the Americans adopted a symbol of deadly killing power. Montgomery's official biographer has recently argued that it was the C-in-C of 21st Army Group who produced the essential framework for COBRA, in a declaration of future intentions dated 13 June. After discussing immediate objectives for that period, he continued:

f) to capture ST LO and then COUTANCES
g) to thrust southwards from CAUMONT towards VIRE and MOR-TAIN; and from ST LO towards VILLEDIEU and AVRANCHES
h) all the time to exert pressure towards LA HAYE DU PUITS and VOLOGNES, and to capture CHERBOURG.

"This was," declares Montgomery's biographer, *"town for town the layout for the American Operation 'Cobra'.*"[13] [emphasis in original] If this assertion arouses ire among the ghosts of the First Army, it is also true that, after the event, Americans were too eager to write into history the view that COBRA was expected from the outset to lead inexorably to Lorient, Le Mans and Argentan, and that from its launching the rest of the campaign was preordained. In reality, of course, it would have been extraordinary to plan it as anything of the sort. It was an ambitious, well-conceived blueprint for a major offensive. Considering the proven difficulties of wrestling ground from the Germans, and the earlier failure of many equally high hopes, it could never have begun as more than that. To suggest that the Americans now consciously embarked upon a completely new phase of the campaign – "the breakout" – is to pretend that they had not been trying desperately to escape from the *bocage* for many weeks already. What took place in late July on the American flank was that First Army launched an offensive that worked, assisted by the absence of most of the best of von Kluge's army, who were engaged with the British and Canadians in the east. They then pursued and exploited their success with dramatic energy.

No earlier statement of objectives by Montgomery can diminish the personal achievement of Bradley, whose plan COBRA was. During the weeks since 6 June, there had been a subtle but steady shift in the command relationship between 21st Army Group and the Americans, reflecting both the growing weight of U.S. strength now deployed in Normandy, and the shrinking confidence of First Army in Montgomery's superior wisdom and experience. There was still the closest consultation between the Allies, and great care was taken to mesh British and American plans. Montgomery confirmed American intentions in crisply-worded written orders. There is little doubt that his *negative* authority over First Army was undiminished: he could have prevented the Americans from embarking upon a course of which he disapproved. But he could no longer expect to exercise *positive* authority, to compel them to initiate operations for which they felt disinclined. A study of Montgomery's files for this period, his successive orders to the armies, might give a different impression. But in real terms, while the Americans accepted his co-ordinating authority, it would be inaccurate to describe him as their commander, in the sense that Bradley was commander of First Army.

The American Secretary for War, Henry Stimson, visited Bradley's headquarters on 17 July, and recorded in his notes: "Plan Cobra – attack by 2 infantry divisions (30th and 9th) followed by 1st Infantry and 2nd Armoured to the left. Break through and turn to right, enveloping 5 or 6 divisions. If successful would have easy going to the SW end of the *bocage*."[14] In the event, between Stimson's visit and the COBRA jump-off, the thrust of VII Corps south-westwards from the St Lô–Périers road towards Coutances was strengthened by the addition of the 4th Division in the centre. In contrast to the usual American prefer-

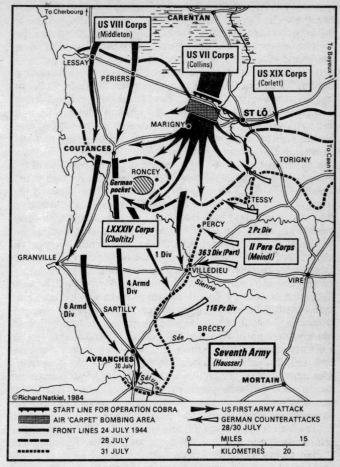

To Cherbourg ↑

US VIII Corps
(Middleton)

CARENTAN

US VII Corps
(Collins)

US XIX Corps
(Corlett)

To Bayeux →

LESSAY

PÉRIERS

ST LÔ

MARIGNY

COUTANCES

RONCEY

German
pocket

TORIGNY

To Caen →

TESSY

LXXXIV Corps
(Choltitz)

PERCY

2 Pz Div

363 Div (Part)

II Para Corps
(Meindl)

GRANVILLE

1 Div

VILLEDIEU

VIRE

4 Armd
Div

Sienne

6 Armd
Div

SARTILLY

116 Pz Div

BRÉCEY

Sée

Seventh Army
(Hausser)

AVRANCHES
30 July

Sélune

MORTAIN

©Richard Natkiel, 1984

START LINE FOR OPERATION COBRA	US FIRST ARMY ATTACK
AIR 'CARPET' BOMBING AREA	GERMAN COUNTERATTACKS
FRONT LINES 24 JULY 1944	28/30 JULY
28 JULY	
31 JULY	

MILES 0 — 15
KILOMETRES 0 — 20

Operation COBRA: 25 July–

ence for broad front assaults, this was to be a narrow, concentrated attack on a 7,000-yard front, immediately preceded by a
massive air bombardment. The fighter-bombers would concentrate on hitting forward German defences in a 250-yard belt
immediately south of the road. Spaatz's "heavies" would bomb

295

to a depth of 2,500 yards behind the German front, accompanied by the artillery fire of 1,000 guns.

The Americans' principal secret weapon for COBRA was the "Rhino" – a set of steel tusks welded onto the front of many of the Shermans, which so equipped had been found capable of battering a path through the Norman hedgerows in heartening fashion. Within weeks, the name of Sergeant Curtis G. Culin, of 2nd Armored's 102nd Cavalry Reconnaissance, echoed across America as the imaginative young American who had devised the battle-winner. The reality, as usual in these matters, was touchingly a little different. Every American armoured unit had been puzzling over the hedgerow problem, and one day Captain Jimmy de Pew of the 102nd summoned a "bull session" of his men to chew it over. A Tennessee hillbilly named Roberts asked slowly: "Why don't we get some saw teeth and put them on the front of the tank and cut through these hedges?" The crowd of men roared with laughter. But Sergeant Culin, a notably shrewd soldier known in the unit both as a chess player and a man impatient of army routines, said: "Hang on a minute, he's got an idea there." Culin it was who put Roberts' ill-articulated notion into effect, and directed the first demonstration: the tankers – and shortly afterwards General Bradley – watched in awe as a hedgerow exploded before their eyes to make way for the Sherman bursting through. In great secrecy, steel lengths stockpiled from the German beach obstacles were salvaged and used to modify hundreds of First Army's tanks. It is difficult to overstate the importance of the "Rhinos", as they were called, for they restored battlefield manoeuvrability to Bradley's armour. Henceforth, while the German tanks remained restricted to the roads, the Shermans possessed the power to outflank them across country. Culin was later summoned to appear before a press conference in Paris. An honest man, he tried hard to give some credit to Roberts. But the weight of the great propaganda and publicity machine was too much for him. He became a very American kind of national hero.[15]

Another kind of hero was lost to First Army on the very eve of COBRA – 54-year-old Colonel Paddy Flint, the hoary old commander of the 39th Infantry who had made himself legendary for the reckless courage which now killed him. Irritated by the slow progress of his 2nd Battalion approaching the COBRA start-line, he strode impatiently forward under heavy mortaring to galvanize them into life. He sent a message to his executive officer from the battalion CP: "Strangely quiet here. Could take nap. Have spotted pillbox. Will start them cooking." He reached the front line with his headquarters group to be greeted by a German with a machine pistol whose fire ripped Flint's trousers. Flint ordered a tank to move forward, and when its commander told him that he could not do so as he had turret trouble, Flint exploded: "It isn't often you'll have a colonel for a bodyguard!" The reluctant tank and a cluster of infantry advanced up the road with their colonel. At one point, when he was standing on the Sherman's hull directing the driver, German fire began to ricochet off the steel, and Flint was induced to step down into cover. The "bodyguard colonel" now advanced with his little group towards the Germans, disdaining their hand grenades: "I don't mind that – they can't hit me anyway." His driver was wounded, but while he was being taken to the rear Flint kept up heavy fire with the two carbines and M1 rifle with which he was now armed, and of which his unhappy staff officer sought to relieve him. The colonel was standing in a doorway lecturing a sergeant on infantry tactics when there was a single shot, and he pitched forward, hit in the head. The sergeant spotted the German sniper and worked forward until he shot him out of a tree. Flint was given morphia and a cigarette, and murmured as he lay: "You can't kill an Irishman, you only make him mad." He died in the field hospital. In one sense, Flint's performance was suicidal and wildly unsuited to the role of regimental commander. But in another, given the chronic difficulty of inducing the infantry to employ "Indian fighting", to get to close quarters with the enemy, it was a magnificent example. George Patton acted as one of Flint's pallbearers, and said with uncommon accuracy that he was sure that this was how his old friend would like to have gone. Flint was one of the great characters of First Army, cast in a mould of leadership that filled his men with immense pride.[16]

The launching of COBRA was delayed for some days by the same torrential rain and low cloud that sealed the fate of GOODWOOD. On 24 July, the order was given and 1,600 aircraft had already taken off for the preliminary air bombardment when the weather closed in again. Some were successfully recalled, or declined to risk bombing through the overcast atmosphere. But others again poured down explosives destined for the path of the American attack. The results were disastrously erratic. 25 Americans were killed and 131 wounded in the 30th Division, and the Germans were provided with final confirmation of the American intention to move on the St Lô–Périers front. Some enraged American units, such as the 2nd/120th Infantry, opened fire on their own aircraft, a not uncommon practice among all the armies in Normandy when suffering at the hands of their own pilots.

The next morning, the forecasters' promise of brighter weather was fulfilled. At 7.00 a.m., 901st Panzergrenadiers telephoned divisional headquarters to report: "American infantry in front of our trenches are abandoning their positions. They are withdrawing everywhere." As similar reports reached Bayerlein from all along the front, his operations officer, Kurt Kauffmann, said cheerfully: "Looks as if they've got cold feet. Perhaps Seventh Army is right after all." Hausser's staff had confidently predicted, despite every indication from Panzer Lehr to the contrary, that the major Allied attack would come south of Caen. Then the field telephones in Bayerlein's farmhouse at Canisy began to ring again, reporting: "Bombing attacks by endless waves of aircraft. Fighter-bomber attacks on bridges and artillery positions."[17] At 9.38 a.m., the fighter-bombers opened their first 20-minute assault on the German front line. Behind them, high above the dust and smoke, 1,800 heavy bombers of 8th Air Force droned slowly towards the target area, their glinting wings watched by thousands of expectant young Americans in their foxholes and tank turrets below, massed ready to move when the airmen had finished.

As we watched [wrote the war correspondent Ernie Pyle], there crept into our consciousness a realization that windrows of exploding bombs were easing back towards us, flight by flight, instead of gradually forward, as the plan called for. Then we were horrified by the suspicion that these machines, high in the sky and completely detached from us, were aiming their bombs at the smokeline on the ground, and a gentle breeze was drifting the smokeline back over us! An indescribable kind of panic comes over you at such times. We stood tensed in muscle and frozen in intellect, watching each flight approach and pass over us, feeling trapped and completely helpless.

Bradley had asked that the bombers attack east-west, out of the sun and parallel to the front on the St Lô–Périers road, to reduce the risk of "short bombing", or "creepback", as the British called it. The airmen, for their own reasons, came in north-south. Despite desperate efforts by the ground troops to identify their

298

positions with yellow panels and smoke markers, there was wild bombing by 8th Air Force, with appalling consequences for the men below. "The ground was shaken and rocked as if by a great earthquake," said Lieutenant-Colonel George Tuttle of the 30th Division. "The concussion, even underground, felt as if someone was beating you with a club."[18] Ernie Pyle wrote of "that awful rush of wind, like the rattling of seeds in a dry gourd." Lieutenant Sidney Eichen of the 120th Infantry had stood with his men watching the bombers approach with comfortable satisfaction: "We thought – 'How gorgeous.' Then it was – 'Goddamit, they're coming for us again!' My outfit was decimated, our anti-tank guns blown apart. I saw one of our truck drivers, Jesse Ivy, lying split down the middle. Captain Bell was buried in a crater with only his head visible. He suffocated before we could get him out."[19] 111 American were killed, including Lieutenant-General Lesley McNair, who had come forward to watch the attack, and 490 wounded. The entire command group of the 9th Division's 3rd/47th Infantry was wiped out. Maddened men were forcibly carried to the rear. Others merely ran blindly from the battlefield. Maimed men lay screaming for aid. Brigadier-General William Harrison of the 30th Division wrote savagely home that night: "When you read of all the great glamour of our flying friends, just remember that not all that glitters is gold!"[20] Harrison won a Distinguished Service Cross that day for his part in dragging men from their shock and paralysis, pulling together shattered units, and driving them forward to press on with the attack. He told the commanding officer of the 120th Infantry: "Colonel, the attack goes ahead as scheduled. Even if you have only two or three men, the attack is to be made." Eichen saw his regimental commander running from company to company shouting: "You've gotta get going, get going!" Eichen said: "Half-heartedly, we started to move."

General Courtney Hodges, commander-designate of First Army, visited 30th Division's command post to meet its enraged commander, Hobbs, who, "was naturally terribly upset by the air show . . . 'We're good soldiers, Courtney, I know, but there's absolutely no excuse, no excuse at all. I wish I could show some of those air boys, decorated with everything a man can be decorated with, some of our casualty clearing stations.' "[21]

Amid the shambles created by the bombing of their own forward areas, VII Corps' attack began hesitantly on the 25th, men moving slowly forward to discover, to their dismay, that the

Panzer Lehr division before them was battered but still unbroken. Some German troops had even moved rapidly forward to occupy ground evacuated by the Americans to provide an air safety zone – a technique they had also adopted on the 24th. Collins' troops were even more disheartened to meet fierce artillery fire, which they had confidently expected to find suppressed by the bombing. "It was hard to believe that any living thing could be left alive in front of our positions," said Colonel Tuttle. "However on moving to enemy-held territory, our men ran into some determined resistance."[22] Units found themselves entangled in protracted firefights against strongpoints and networks of foxholes held by the customary German mix of a handful of tanks, supporting infantry, and the inevitable 88 mm guns.

Bayerlein had personally ridden forward by motor-cycle to the 901st Regiment, whose commander, Colonel von Hausser, was sitting in a cellar beneath an old stone tower. Von Hausser declared gloomily that his entire front line had been devastated. Yet the survivors resisted with all their usual stubbornness. Colonel Hammonds Birks of 120th Infantry radioed to 30th Division that "the going was very slow . . . the boche had tanks dug in, hull down, and were shooting perhaps more artillery than they had ever previously used along any American sector." First Army's diary recorded bleakly: "This day, a day to remember for more than one reason, did not bring the breakthrough for which we had all hoped . . . There was no question but that the postponement of the attack from Monday to Tuesday, plus two successive days of bombing of our own troops. took the ginger out of several of the front-line elements."

Yet even in these first encounters, General Collins found cause for encouragement. While the German positions were resisting fiercely, they did not appear to form a continuous belt of defences. They could be outflanked, bypassed. In contrast to the meticulously-prepared succession of defensive positions in depth with which the Germans on the Bourgébus Ridge met GOODWOOD, below the St Lô–Périers road on 25 July, they retained only a crust. This, despite all the warning they had received of an impending American thrust. It was a tribute to the efforts of the British and Canadians that von Kluge's fears, as well as his principal forces, were still decisively fixed upon the eastern flank. That day, the 25th, the 2nd Canadian Corps launched a new attack towards Bourgébus which quickly broke

down and was counter-attacked by 9th SS Panzer. But, faced
with two heavy assaults, it was to the east that von Kluge chose
to go himself that day, to inspect the front. Against the 14 British
and Canadian divisions, the Germans still deployed 14 of their
own, including six panzer. The Americans faced only 11
seriously weakened enemy divisions, two of them armoured.
The old Panzer Lehr began the COBRA battle with a strength of
just 2,200 men and 45 operational armoured vehicles in the front
line. Against this weary gathering of German battle-groups and
depleted infantry formations, the full weight of 15 American
divisions would shortly be committed. Bayerlein was enraged to
receive a visit from a staff officer of von Kluge, conveying the
Field-Marshal's order that the St Lô–Périers line must be held:
not a single man must leave his position. A battalion of SS
Panthers was on its way to provide support. Bayerlein said flatly:
"Out in front every one is holding out. Every one. My grenadiers
and my engineers and my tank crews – they're all holding their
ground. Not a single man is leaving his post. They are lying silent
in their foxholes, for they are dead. You may report to the
Field-Marshal that the Panzer Lehr Division is annihilated."[23] In
keeping with the occasion, at that moment a vast ammunition
dump exploded nearby, hit by fighter-bombers. Bayerlein's
remarks were only slightly exaggerated.

On the afternoon of the 25th, Collins learned enough about
the vulnerability of the Germans to outflanking movements to
risk giving the order to his mobile columns to start moving. By
nightfall, elements of 1st Division were outside Marigny. The
next morning, across the entire VII Corps front, units began to
shake free from engagements with the defenders of Panzer Lehr
and move fast across country, reporting that resistance was
crumbling before them. The tank columns were slowed by the
need for the "Rhinos" to spend an average of two and a half
minutes cutting through each hedgerow. But delays of this order
were trifling by comparison with the hours of sluggish progress
under fire that had marked each battle in the *bocage* since
D-Day. The entire offensive was rapidly gaining momentum.
Pockets of resistance at crossroads halted the American tanks
only for such time as it took the infantry to jump down and pour
fire into them. Sergeant Hans Stober and his company of 17th SS
Panzergrenadiers had been ordered to hold their positions for 24
hours. "But we found that American units in company strength
had bypassed us. There was no choice but to order us to with-

draw."[24] So it was for thousands of German soldiers the length of the line. As darkness fell on the night of the 26th, the forceful Brigadier Maurice Rose of 2nd Armored's Combat Command A – the equivalent of a British brigade group – raced on. His men's progress had been dramatically rapid, a tribute to the careful training of his tank companies before the attack, alongside the foot soldiers of 22nd Infantry. At 3.00 a.m. the next morning, they had reached the first objective of COBRA, a road junction north of Le Mesnil-Herman. By noon on the 27th, 9th Division was also clear of all organized German resistance, and moving fast. Since the rear areas were alive with German stragglers and retreating units, it proved essential to provide armoured escorts for the American supply columns racing to follow the lead troops. Everywhere behind the front, they were now meeting the chaos of German defeat – fleeing men and vehicles, enemy columns searching desperately for a route of escape.

Lieutenant Philip Reisler of 2nd Armored was sitting dozing in the turret of his Sherman on a bend in a sunken road, his crew sleeping the sleep of utter exhaustion in the hull beneath him, when he heard an unfamiliar engine sound behind him, and turned to see a German half-track driving fast in his direction, the soldiers inside it laughing, oblivious of the Americans. The vehicle smashed full-tilt into the tank and stopped dead, its radiator hissing and steaming. The horrified German driver tore his gears in a desperate effort to reverse, while Reisler fumbled equally clumsily with his machine-gun, simultaneously kicking his gunner into life. A German machine-gunner began to fire wildly, and the half-track somehow swerved around the tank. Then the Americans slammed a 75 mm at point-blank range into its rear: it slewed across the road and began to burn. Reisler's coaxial machine-gun killed the crew as they leapt out of the flames. At that moment, a second half-track rounded the corner, steered around the tank, halted behind the flaming barricade and received another 75 mm shell which blew most of its occupants alive into the road. One German walked in a daze to the Sherman and leaned against it, shaking his head. Reisler pressed the trigger of his pistol. To his dismay nothing happened. The German, however, scrambled hastily up the bank into an orchard, and infuriated the American by turning back and grinning before he walked unhurriedly away through the trees. Three more Germans marched towards the tank, hands in the air. The tank crew chatted to them by the roadside. Reisler suggested to one that he should hide his wristwatch in his sock, for otherwise the MPs would surely take it.

A few minutes later, Reisler's battalion commander walked down the road and took over the Sherman's radio. His own tank, he said, had been hit. From the orchard came a burst of submachine gun fire. The colonel seized a Thompson gun and emptied clip after clip into the trees until, assuaged, he stepped down and walked forwards to the wreck of his own tank with Reisler. The lieutenant peered down into the driver's seat, and was appalled to find only the man's lower half remained. He looked upwards, and saw the remainder of the body hanging obscenely from the telephone wires, 20 feet above his head, one hand gently waving.

The flak battalion of the 17th SS was wiped out by air attack. "The troops had been trained to lose a battle quite calmly," said one of its survivors, Sergeant Stober, "we knew that the vital thing was to stick together. But we could see that the Americans had learnt how to break through, ignoring their flanks and pushing on to occupy crossroads and set up blocking positions so that our vehicles and heavy weapons could not get through. We lost vast quantities of *matériel*."

On 26 July, VIII Corps joined the offensive on the right. Middleton felt compelled to use the 8th and 90th Divisions to lead his attack, because their positions alone possessed clear paths in front through the floods and swamps. Both bitterly disappointed First Army by failing to gain ground. But the next morning, first light revealed that the Germans in front of them had gone, compelled to pull back because of their crumbling left flank, leaving only immense minefields to delay the advance of VIII Corps.

A sense of exhilaration such as they had not known since Cherbourg, perhaps not matched since 7 June, was now overtaking the Americans as they dashed through villages which welcomed them with all the warmth of civilians whose homes and possessions and livestock had not been destroyed. "This virtual road march was such as the American army was designed for," Russell Weigley has written, "especially the American armored divisions. Appealing also to the passion for moving on that is so much a part of the American character and heritage, it brought out the best in the troops, their energy and mechanical resourcefulness."[25] The infantry clung to the tank hulls and sat up in the trucks waving wildly to French onlookers as they raced south-westwards, blackened German vehicles by the roadside testifying to the achievement of the fighter-bombers in clearing the roads ahead of them. Despite stiffening resistance east of Coutances on the 28th, that evening the CC B of Middleton's 4th Armored swung up from the south to reach the town. "The highlight of the day", recorded First Army's diary of the 29th, "occurred when a considerable force of enemy tanks, vehicles and guns were bottled up on the Roncey–St Denis le Vêtu by-highways by elements of the 2nd and 3rd Armored Divs, and was pounded to bits by armor, artillery and aircraft." Lieutenant Eichen of the 120th Infantry said: "By now we were expecting to push them all the way through to Germany. You might come to a hill line or a road junction and find a few tanks or 88s firing from it, but for all the rest of that week it was just push and go."

The Americans destroyed two tanks within minutes of encountering Lieutenant Fritz Langangke's platoon of 2nd SS Panzer; a third bogged in a ditch. Langangke's driver, Zeeger, jumped down to fix a towing shackle to the hill of the cripple, and was immediately wounded badly in the face by shell fragments. Shocked, the man staggered into the undergrowth and vanished from sight. A retreating tank met him and got him away to the rear. Langangke leapt from his turret to the empty driving position and steered the Panther himself until, two hours later, a new driver was found for him. They all knew that the front was crumbling: "*Verloren!*"–lost!–was a word they heard much of that week.

Sergeant Helmut Gunther of 17th SS Panzergrenadiers had returned from hospital in Le Mans on the 14th after being wounded in the abortive American offensive in early July. The reconnaissance battalion with which he served was already reduced to two understrength companies, which were merged and placed under his command. They were sent together with the pioneer battalion to defend a supposedly quiet sector of the front. On the 23rd–24th, they heard the sound of fierce fighting on their right as a neighbouring paratroop unit held off a local American attack. Then, although they themselves were not in the direct path of VII Corps' assault, they were hastily ordered to fall back as the line around them cracked.

We were marching, marching back all the time. One morning we were ordered to keep a road open, but we found that the Americans had already blocked it. The roads were crowded with American vehicles, and all that we could do was to take to the fields on foot. On the fourth day, by sheer coincidence we ran into some of our own unit's vehicles, and kept going by road. But we were losing stragglers all the time – some of us later had letters from them from America. Once when we were moving to take up position an army staff car stopped beside us. I saluted. The officer in it asked me where we were going. "Have you gone crazy?" he said. "The Americans are there already." Then he drove on. In a ditch in a wood we met ten exhausted paratroopers who asked us for water. I suggested that they come with us, but they were reluctant. We moved off, and a while later heard shooting. One paratrooper caught up with us, and told us that all the rest were dead. They had tried to surrender, but it was too difficult.

We found a pig in a farm, killed it and cooked it. We took sheets from the farmhouse and laid them out on the table and prepared to eat. Suddenly a Luftwaffe man burst in shouting: "The Americans are right behind me." We grabbed the corners of the sheet with everything inside it, threw it in the back of a field car, and pulled out just as the first Sherman came in sight. Eventually we met up with our battalion head-quarters, who were expecting the enemy at any moment. From then on, I could not distinguish the days. I had seen the first retreat from Moscow, which was terrible enough, but at least units were still intact. Here, we had become a cluster of individuals. We were not a battleworthy company any longer. All that we had going for us was that we knew each other very well.[26]

The offensive now entered a new and bloodier phase. As the American columns lay strung out over miles of unfamiliar country, German units began to fight with all their customary ferocity to escape entrapment. There were elements of 2nd SS Panzer, 17th SS Panzergrenadiers and the 353rd Infantry Division seeking to break free, while von Kluge was at last moving reinforcements west – 2nd Panzer and 116th Panzer under the command of XLVII Panzer Corps. A single self-propelled 88 mm gun overran two American companies near Notre Dame de Cenilly until Sergeant Robert Lotz of 41st Armored Infantry shot out its periscope, then closed in to kill its commander. A fierce counter-attack was fought off by CC B of 2nd Armored and cost the Germans dearly when Quesada's fighter-bombers were vectored onto the scene. Americans came across abandoned German vehicles whose occupants had decided to flee on foot. On the night of 29 July, elements of 67th Armored Regiment and 41st Armored Infantry found themselves fighting for their lives against a column from 2nd SS Panzer and 17th SS who smashed through their lines in the darkness near St Denis-le-Gast. Most of the Germans eventually escaped, but they left behind 500 prisoners. Other elements of the same American units were attacked near Cambry the same night, and fought for six hours. But now the commanders of First Army knew that they were dominating the battlefield and that the German assaults reflected the thrashings of desperate men, rather than a genuine threat to the American front.

Lieutenant Fritz Langangke of 2nd SS Panzer was ordered to rendezvous with a paratroop unit at a crossroads which was to be held open until evening. He arrived to find no sign of the infantry, and was reinforced only by a single tank – that of his company commander. They camouflaged the Panthers and deployed to cover the road. Their engines were switched off as the first Sherman appeared, and although they struggled to hand crank the turret they were too slow. Their first round missed. While the American seemed to hesitate, Langangke roared hastily backwards, fired again and hit. The Sherman's commander was still standing uncertainly upright in his turret when his tank caught fire; the second Panther accounted for the next two Shermans. Mist, most unusual for the season, was drifting across the road. In its midst, Langangke was shocked to see Germans moving towards the Americans with their hands up. These were the infantry he had expected to meet: "They had taken their chance to finish the war."

There was a lull in the action. American artillery fire began to fall around the orchard, and the Germans took it in turns to doze. Then a solitary Sherman raced headlong towards them, and its gun began to traverse to meet that of the Panther. The German fired first. The American tank commander leapt from his burning turret and ran for cover. The heat in the Panther was becoming intolerable, and sweat was pouring down the crews' faces. There was another pause. Then came a sudden massive explosion against the hull, and they looked out to see American infantry all around them. To their astonishment, the tank responded when they roared into reverse. But now they were clearly visible, in the open, and a succession of American tank shells hit them. The driver shouted: "I can't see! The periscope's gone!" Langangke pushed up his head and directed the driver further back. Another shell sprang open the turret welding, and they could see daylight through the steel. The crew baled out, Langangke wrenching his neck as he jumped without removing his headset.

They left their company commander still in his tank, working on a jammed gun, and ran away down the road towards the main German positions. They were in open country when a passing fighter-bomber swooped upon them, and Langangke's gunner was killed by a cannon shell. Like all soldiers attacked by aircraft, they felt a passionate hatred for the pilot: "If we had had a chance to get that man, there would have been another war crime." They walked on until they reached the headquarters of one of the division's panzergrenadier regiments, and were eventually provided with a repaired tank from the workshops, in time for the Mortain counter-attack

Corlett had been pressing Bradley for a role for his XIX Corps in the offensive. Now he gained his point. As his men began to advance on the left of VII Corps, they encountered the first German reinforcements reaching the west. West of Tessy-sur-Vire, between the 28th and 31st, they collided with 2nd Panzer and then with the newly-arrived 116th Panzer in the fiercest fighting since COBRA began. On the 30th, Brigadier-General Rose's CC A of 2nd Armored, recently attached to Corlett's command, approached the town of Percy and was attacked in the rear by German tanks and infantry.

Percy lay in a hollow surrounded by hills. At about 4.30 p.m., a cluster of Rose's tank commanders and infantry officers were at the bottom of the hill preparing to advance, ignorant of the powerful opposition in the area. Some of the tank crews were out of their vehicles, cheerfully milking cows in a field. Men of 4th Infantry lay on their backs under a hedgerow, smoking. Without warning, the entire area erupted under German mortar fire. Wounded and dying GIs lay scattered in the grass as the Americans hastily deployed to move up the hill, the tanks crawling forward at walking pace to allow the infantry to keep with them. As they paused to breast a hedge, two tanks were hit and burst into flames. The gunners poured fire into every hedge in front of them, but from his Sherman Lieutenant Phil Reisler could see infantry dropping around him:

. . . like some terrible war film. I saw one tall, very thin man drop his rifle and start to run away down the hill. Then I caught sight of holes in his head, and he crashed full tilt into an apple tree. He was running dead, like a chicken. I'll never forget the dedication of those men of 4th Infantry walking up that hill over their dead buddies like British redcoats attacking in Revolutionary War days. It was magnificent. We got to the top with about ten tanks and about thirty-five foot soldiers.[27]

They placed two careful rounds through Percy clock tower and church and the mortaring stopped. But all that night they stood on the hill under heavy German fire, the tank crews listening unhappily to the moans and screams of wounded American infantrymen. The scene was lit by flames from the wrecked tanks, which burned through the darkness. On the radio net, they heard the infantry company commander asking repeatedly for medical support, until his unit ordered: "Quit calling. We can't get to you." At intervals, the little infantry medical corporal would run to Reisler and beg him to call through again for aid, and the tank officer pretended to do so, without pressing his transmission switch. Once the corporal laid a blanket over a man who had gone. A few hours later, the men on the hill were appalled to see the figure beneath it sit up and scream. In the morning, the six surviving American tanks out of the 15 that had driven up, together with what was left of the infantry, withdrew from the hill, the Shermans coasting in neutral so that the Germans would not know that they had gone. Later Figurski, the gunner, had to pull human remains from their bogie wheels. Reisler said: "We never did get to see any krauts. Only dead ones."

After more fierce fighting, Rose's men and the other divisions of XIX Corps threw back the Germans, inflicting heavy losses of men and tanks. Some Sherman crews kept their engines running almost continuously for seven days. In the course of the entire battle, from 26 July to 12 August, one tank battalion – the 2nd/66th – lost 51 per cent of its combat personnel and 70 per cent of its tank strength. By 31 July, after fighting off repeated German assaults, the 743rd Tank Battalion was reduced to 13 Shermans.

But the Americans could afford losses of this kind far better than 2nd and 116th Panzer. Colonel Heinz-Gunther Guderian, 116th's senior staff officer, described the desperate frustration of seeking to concentrate the division for its attack on 29 July amid incessant American fighter-bomber activity. They were expecting to go in with direct support from 2nd Panzer, but they did not receive this, for the other division had problems of its own. Their assault was postponed from the night of the 29th until the morning of the 30th, but they still had had no chance to probe the American front. On their left was relatively good tank going. Ignorant of this, they attacked with maximum weight on their right, and immediately found themselves plunged into thick *bocage*. All the frustrations that the Allies had endured in the

308

preceding weeks overtook 116th Panzer. Unable to move across country and largely restricted to the roads, their hesitant advance struck an enemy exhilarated by success, at last gaining confidence in his own powers on the battlefield. Only one German infantry company reached the St Lô road on the 30th, and the vital tanks were still struggling far behind. By noon that day, the Germans knew that their attack had failed. From the bus which served as divisional headquarters, Guderian and the staff struggled to switch the axis of advance to the west, but they were now informed that their tank battalions were being transferred elsewhere under the direct command of LXXXIV Corps. They were being pounded remorselessly by American air and artillery. The next morning, the 31st, they were not surprised when a renewed attack failed. Their only concern now was to disengage, as the Americans began to push forward again in front of them. On the night of 1 August, they were successful. Thereafter, reduced to little more than the effective strength of a battlegroup, they were moved south to support the sagging German left. Guderian confessed his own disappointment in the performance of some of the division throughout the battle: "Without proper artillery and armoured support, the panzergrenadiers would not hold. These were not the men of 1941–42."[28]

While 2nd Armored's CC A was fighting around Percy, the rest of Corlett's XIX Corps were struggling to gain ground further east. On 31 July, Sergeant Bill Walsh of 102nd Cavalry was with a mixed team of tanks and assault guns which fought a characteristic action to clear the bridge across the Vire and the high ground dominating it at the little town of Torigny, southeast of St Lô.

The American armour rattled up the ruined main street of Torigny, watched in silence by clusters of frightened French civilians, hugging their doorways. One out of three bridges across the river remained intact, and across this the vehicles rolled one by one, under fire from small arms and artillery from Germans on the ridge above, Hill 204. The Americans turned and began to advance steadily up the hill towards the enemy, dug in behind the inevitable hedgerow. To their horror, Walsh's crew found their assault gun sagging, losing grip and sinking sideways into a small swamp. They baled out hastily and ran for the shelter of a cluster of trees. As they caught their breath and watched shells bursting around the crippled gun, Walsh suggested to the driver that he might try again to unstick it. He declined. Walsh ran across, started the engines, accelerated and braked in vain for a moment or two, then fled back to the trees.

He heard an officer shout for all dismounted men to follow the tanks up the hill. He began to run with the infantry, clutching his carbine. Beside him a big, walrus-moustached mechanic called Cerbeck, who had joined the battle because he said that he wished to see what combat was like before he went home, was killed by small-arms fire along with the man beyond. Walsh made a desperate grab to clamber up on a Sherman as it paused, tracks grinding and throwing up clods of earth and stones, to smash a hedgerow with its "Rhino" prongs. He fell off as the tank broke through, and looking around saw that it was the only American vehicle to have survived the drive. Propped against the reverse bank of the hedge, he found a bareheaded German soldier sitting bleeding badly from a stomach wound, muttering feebly: "*Bitte, bitte.*"

Walsh now saw the solitary Sherman reversing hard through the hole that it had cut, evidently pulling back. He ran desperately alongside until infantrymen clinging to the hull dragged him up. They withdrew to a safer distance from the German positions, and lay down around the tank waiting for reinforcements. Walsh saw a little cluster of unhappy men gathered around a soldier he knew from B Troop, who was lying footless after stepping on a *Schuemine*. The doctor appeared and dressed the clean amputation while the others fed the man cigarettes and tried to force themselves to chat easily to him as he lay in the calm of acute shock. Exhausted and drained soldiers lay all along the hedgerow, roused to life only for a few moments of heavy firing when an officer shouted that some Germans were trying to counter-attack ahead. Then the battle seemed to peter out, the Germans disappearing beyond the reverse slope of the ridge. American vehicles clattered forward nose-to-tail across the bridge below, on the road to Vire, amid inefectual enemy artillery fire. The word came that the division had decided to bypass the Germans on the ridge rather than continue a direct assault upon them. Two days later, with the enemy long gone as the advance reached far ahead of their flanks, Walsh returned with an armoured recovery vehicle and rescued his abandoned gun. The sharp, bitter little afternoon at Torigny had cost the Americans 33 casualties, three tanks and a clutch of trucks and half-tracks.

The 82nd Reconnaissance Battalion of 2nd Armored suffered

a similar shock on the afternoon of 2 August, as it moved fast south-eastwards at the head of CC B. Led by a Sherman, its column drove up a steep winding hill through the thickly-wooded forest of St Sever towards the town of Calvados beyond. In their haste to reach their objectives, they had dispensed with infantry flank protection or advance patrols. As teh lead vehicle emerged from the wood, it was halted by a road block of trees felled across the road. The commander, a Pennsylvanian named Sergeant James Maser, dismounted to inspect the trees seconds before fire from two Tiger tanks, hull-down covering the road, destroyed his Sherman. German infantry in the woods began to bring down machine-gun and mortar fire the length of the column. Americans ran from their vehicles to try to pinpoint their attackers, but could see nothing through the trees and thick scrub. Within a few minutes, one of the survivors wrote, "it became a nightmare of embarrassing, disorganized rout." 25 Americans died in a few minutes of furious German firing, before the rest of the battalion could make their escape. Half their NCOs were lost, and two more became casualties in accidents in their assembly area that night. It was a brutal, stinging reminder of the punishment that the Germans could still inflict upon tactical carelessness. It was 7 August before 2nd Armored cleared St Sever and advanced to St Hilaire and Barenton.

As von Kluge's exhausted men at last recoiled further east, the Allies were pressing forward. On 30 July, the British VIII Corps launched Operation BLUECOAT south from Caumont towards Vire and Mont Pinçon, while the U.S. V Corps advanced on their right. V Corps' official task was merely to protect the flank of COBRA, but General Hodges told Gerow that there was nothing to stop him making all the ground that he could in the process. There was some confusion between the British and Americans about rights of access to roads, and mutual irritation when British reconnaissance vehicles found Vire empty and claimed its liberation, only to find the Americans occupying the town before British main elements could reach it. For the British, any satisfaction at the extraordinary loosening of the front that had now begun was soured by the discovery that, once again, XXX Corps and 7th Armoured Division were performing feebly. Montgomery's patience was finally exhausted: Bucknall and Erskine were sacked. The U.S. First Army's diary for 31 July reported:

Resistance in the XIX Corps sector continues to be rugged; the boche here shows no sign of demoralization, 30th division made only 300 yards, and the 29th were only able to make 800. V Corps had things a bit easier, the 2nd and 5th divisions making more than two miles, 35th div a mile. The Second British Army continued its drive, but met determined enemy resistance and consequently had to be content with a stalemate . . . Some 10,000 prisoners have been taken during the drive.

The disappointments on Gerow and Corlett's fronts could not mar the exhilaration of the vast success of COBRA to the west, the personal triumph of Collins, who played a pre-eminent role in the achievement. This passionate, intolerant, impatient soldier had once again demonstrated his outstanding qualities as a corps commander. All the American virtues of speed and energy had at last come into play on the battlefield. The plan and the army had found their moment. It is highly doubtful whether an operation resembling COBRA could have been launched earlier in the campaign. Its prerequisites were, first, a degree of battle wisdom that First Army only attained after weeks of painful experience; and second, an erosion of German strength that had taken much hard fighting to bring about. Against an army of such supreme professionalism, a premature American dash deep into the German front might have resulted in a crushing defeat for the attackers; the Allies needed first to cripple the fighting power of the enemy and crumble their resources. Having done so, they now reaped rich rewards.

At this pivotal moment in the Allies' fortunes, the long-scheduled shift in the American command structure took effect: Lieutenant-General Courtney Hodges assumed command of First Army; Patton's Third Army formally came into being; Bradley stepped up to exercise overall command of the American forces, now designated 12th Army Group. The stage was set for one of the most dramatic American strategic movements of the war.

The limits of air power

It has become an historical cliché of the Normandy campaign to assert that Allied air power was decisive in making victory possible. This is a half-truth. Overwhelming Allied air superiority enabled the ground troops to operate with almost total freedom from Luftwaffe interference. This was the battle chiefly won by

Spaatz's Mustang fighters in the sky over Germany during the first months of 1944, and maintained until the end of the war by the vast numbers of Allied interceptors over the battlefield. A second factor, of which more will be said below, was the fighter-bombers' ability to smash German attempts to concentrate for a decisive armoured thrust. Thanks to the bombing of communications and constant fighter-bomber sweeps over the German rear areas, German daylight movement became hazardous, and was often impossible. In the first weeks of the campaign, while the air forces' claims about the level of destruction that they had inflicted upon German units advancing to the front were exaggerated, the delay and anxiety that they caused were of critical importance. The infantry suffered much more than the armoured units, since they possessed few vehicles and were almost entirely dependent upon horses for divisional transport.

Yet in Normandy, the greatest concentration of air power ever assembled in support of ground operations also revealed its limitations. It was unable to inflict sufficient damage upon German defensive positions to offer the Allied armies anywhere an easy passage, despite Sir Arthur Harris' characteristically extravagant assertion in 1945 that the air forces had given the armies in north-west Europe "a walkover". The poor flying weather – which averaged one day in three through the summer – and the hours of darkness provided the Germans with sufficient respite from air attack to move their forces more or less where they wished, and to continue bringing forward a bare minimum of ammunition and supplies. Every captured German officer in 1944–45 complained bitterly about the difficulties caused to his unit by Allied aircraft and this, together with the exaggerated claims of the airmen, caused Allied intelligence to be too uncritical in its assessments of the material damage inflicted upon enemy formations in transit. Almost all were indeed seriously delayed by the wrecked river bridges and railways and the harassment upon the roads. But careful study of German records shows that only in a very few cases was the combat power of a unit seriously diminished by air attack on the journey to Normandy. Even allowing for the early morning cloud, it is remarkable that 21st Panzer's armoured regiments were able to reach the battlefield on D-Day from their harbours around Falaise with only minimal losses from air attack. Panzer Lehr's journey was fraught with frustration and harassment, but its order of battle was diminished by less than 10 per cent. Most Germans interviewed for this narrative recall the smashed railway junctions and bridges they passed on their way to the front, but very few remember their units suffering the actual loss of more than a few trucks. The allegedly appalling journey of the 2nd SS Panzer Division from Toulouse to Normandy has passed into the legend of the Second World War, and its arrival was certainly much delayed by encounters with the Resistance and Allied air forces. But its material losses of tanks and armoured vehicles were negligible.* The truth is that tactical air power began to inflict crippling damage upon enemy transport only in the later stages of the battle for Normandy, when difficulties on the ground compelled the Germans to move in daylight, and when techniques of forward air control, which should have been available from 6 June, were at last put into practice.

The fundamental difficulty overhanging all Allied air support of operations in Normandy was that, with two very honourable exceptions of whom more will be said below, senior Allied airmen remained obsessed with their conviction that it was not the major function of the air forces to serve as flying artillery for the army. This, of course, was precisely the role in which the Luftwaffe had achieved such remarkable results for the Wehrmacht in the first half of the war. In 1944 and in their own writings after the war, Allied airmen wrote with astonishing condescension about the diversion of their forces to support ground operations.[1] Vandenburg records a conversation with a colleague on 15 June about the army's demand for a massed bomber attack, "to blast the English army from in front of Caen . . . We both agreed that the use contemplated was not proper . . ."[2] Whatever Montgomery's shortcomings in other directions, he could never be accused of failing to understand the vital importance of air support. He harangued his officers again and again about the need to live and work in the closest proximity to the airmen. It was the airmen themselves, and Air-Marshal Coningham in particular, who resolutely refused to accept a close relationship with the soldiers. Coningham had been nettled by Montgomery's supposed failure to grant sufficient credit to the air forces under his command in the desert, and he never forgave him. He saw as little of the C-in-C of 21st Army Group as he could, and physically distanced himself from the ground

*For a detailed study of 2nd SS Panzer's terrible march, and the impact of the French Resistance upon the Normandy campaign, see the author's *Das Reich* (London and New York, 1981).

headquarters. It is remarkable that Coningham's attitude and behaviour was not rewarded with dismissal. But Tedder shared many of Coningham's views, and above all sympathized with his distate for Montgomery.

Tedder's high intelligence has often been praised by his colleagues, yet his arrogant self-assurance matched that of Montgomery. He shared the views of the "bomber barons" that air support by heavy aircraft for ground operations was a diversion from their war-winning role in attacking German industry: "I told Leigh-Mallory that he was in danger of leading the Army up the garden path with his sweeping assurances of help . . . I felt that the limitations of air support on the battlefield were not sufficiently understood; neither was the full scope of the role of air power outside the battle area sufficiently appreciated by the Army, or by Leigh-Mallory."[3]

Studying Tedder's writings, it is impossible to escape the conclusion that he suffered the same grievous handicap as most airmen of his generation – the inability to perceive that the war could only be won by the defeat of the German army upon the battlefield, an enormously difficult task to which all other operations by sea and air must be subordinated. There were grounds for much disappointment and sympathy over the failures of ground operations in Normandy in June and July. It has been suggested above that few of these were the fault of Montgomery's generalship. Yet Tedder's remorseless hostility to the Commander-in-Chief of 21st Army Group, his sniping and carping from SHAEF about the shortcomings of the soldiers, lessen his stature as a commander; although, of course, the anomaly of his position was that he could speak his mind in the highest places about any aspect of the campaign that he chose, but bore direct responsibility for none of it. Early in July, he was agreeing with Coningham "that the Army did not seem prepared to fight its own battles."[4] He persuaded Eisenhower to amend a draft letter to Montgomery promising that all the resources of the air would be available to support him: "I insisted that the Air could not, and must not, be turned on thus glibly and vaguely in support of the Army, which would never move unless prepared to fight its way with its own weapons."[5] He made common cause with two senior British officers at SHAEF known for their enmity to Montgomery – Morgan and Humphrey Gale – in discussing the possibility of removing the British general. On 20 July after GOODWOOD, "I spoke to Portal about the Army's

315

failure. We were agreed in regarding Montgomery as the cause. We also talked about the control of the Strategic Air Forces. Portal felt that the time was drawing near when their control could revert to the Combined Chiefs of Staff exercised through himself."[6] Yet it was Portal who, during the autumn and winter, would prove wholly incapable of controlling the British strategic bomber force, to the extent that he was obliged to confess his own inability to induce Sir Arthur Harris to conform to Air Staff policy.

The airmen considered that they were on most solid ground in their complaints against the army about heavy bomber operations. The soldiers repeatedly demanded and received the support of the "heavies" in a role for which the airmen insisted they were unsuitable. The soldiers were then surprised when the bombers failed to achieve the expected results, whether against coastal positions on D-Day or tank concentrations on the Bourgébus Ridge. The bombing of Caen had accomplished nothing but the levelling of a great Norman city. The bombing before GOODWOOD had been provided, the airmen claimed, only because the army insisted that it would pave the way for a major breakthrough. This it did not. On 21 July, somewhat obscurely, Tedder "saw the Supreme Commander at once and told him that Montgomery's failure to take action earlier had lost us the opportunity offered by the attempt on Hitler's life."[7] This comment appears to reflect the airman's wholly mistaken assumption that the German army was on the brink of internal collapse.

A SHAEF Operational Research report upon the benefits of heavy bombing in support of ground operations declared that "it is the provisional opinion of the investigators that the moral effects of the bombing upon the enemy and upon Allied troops far outweigh the very considerable material effects."[8] Quesada of IXth Air Force declared that he doubted whether the American bombing before the attack on Cherbourg had killed more than 10 Germans: "Of course, our army loved to see it before they went in. But it made me more sceptical about whether we should be using the air force as a USO show. I believed in attacking specific, identifiable targets that could be destroyed by aircraft."[9]

The airmen considered that the proven inability of heavy bombers to do crippling material damage to enemy ground forces was sufficient reason to confine them to assaults upon

Germany's cities and industrial plants. Yet if massed bomber attacks provided moral benefits in the greatest campaign of the western war – which all concerned on both sides agreed that they did – it seemed reasonable to suggest that the armies were entitled to them. It was also forgotten, amidst the recriminations about "short bombing" and ground force failures, that the use of the "heavies" had in fact inflicted immense damage upon the German defences before both COBRA and GOODWOOD, even if this was not conclusive. What was gravely needed, and never achieved as a result of the lack of sympathy between the personalities concerned, was improvement in the technique of co-ordinating heavy bomber operations with ground offensives. Vandenburg recorded sourly in his diary for 27 July: "Leaving for lunch with the C-in-C and Bedell Smith, I heard Beadle tell Jimmy [Doolittle] to the effect that what was needed to correct deficiencies in strategic bombers operating with ground forces was to get a commander who could view that support sympathetically."[10] As late as November 1944, a 21st Army Group report on air support lamented that "we have lacked and still do lack high-powered air staff officers at the Army Group HQ to be in on the initial stages of planning just as the gunners and sappers are."[11] This was surely a damning reflection on the gulf between the two services even in the last months of the war. All that summer of 1944, the feuds within the air forces, which had so disfigured the Allied high command in the spring, continued unabated. Vandenburg's diary for 23 June reports: "Lunched with General Spaatz at which time he cautioned me to be very careful not to create an incident which, in his opinion, was desired by the RAF to start the disintegration of this can of worms by 'the Tedder, Coningham, Harris clique'."[12] Brereton, commanding IXth Air Force, held a press conference following the COBRA short bombing tragedy, at which he blamed COBRA's slow start upon the sluggishness of the ground troops.

Yet the sluggishness with which ground–air co-operation techniques developed in Normandy must be attributed principally to the attitudes of the airmen. Air-Marshal "Mary" Coningham, commanding the British 2nd Tactical Air Force, was a bitter enemy of Montgomery and of Leigh-Mallory. Brigadier Charles Richardson, Montgomery's very able BGS Plans, worked closely with the airmen on ground support plans, and found Coningham to be "a prima donna. He seemed to have a glorified concept of his own position, and to be too remote from the battle."[13] For many weeks, Coningham continued to direct air support from Stanmore, outside London, on the grounds that communications in France were too poor for him to command his squadrons from a headquarters with the armies. While the wide-ranging fighter-bomber sweeps carried out every day over France by Allied aircraft created great difficulties for the Germans, it was Typhoons and Thunderbolts operating in close support of the ground troops and directed by a Forward Air Controller (FAC), which could play the critical role. Requests for air support channelled through a rear staff and then passed forward with merely a map reference to the squadrons did not produce rapid or precise results. There was no lack of communications technology for Forward Air Control. Yet above all in the early stages of the battle, there were nothing like enough FACs with the front-line troops. The destruction of a single RAF vehicle in the first hours of GOODWOOD wiped out Forward Air Control for the central axis of the offensive. "As a result of our inability to get together with the air in England," wrote Bradley, "we went into France almost totally untrained in air–ground co-operation."[14] Brigadier Richardson said: "In North Africa we seemed to have got the air business right, yet we had lost some of it in Normandy."[15]

Only two senior air force officers distinguished themselves by an absolute commitment to assisting the armies, undiminished by personal hostilities or jealousies. The first was British, Air Vice-Marshal Harry Broadhurst, working alongside Dempsey's Second Army as the RAF's AOC 83 Group. Broadhurst, a fighter pilot of great experience and a veteran of the desert, earned the affection and respect of all the soldiers with whom he worked. The second was the American General Elwood R. "Pete" Quesada, a pioneering airman of Spanish extraction, quick intelligence and easy charm who commanded IXth Tactical Air Command, responsible to Bradley for close air support of the American armies.

Quesada may claim to have done more than any other airman in the Allied ranks to originate and refine techniques of ground–air co-operation, and to put them into practice. "Unlike most airmen who viewed ground support as a bothersome diversion to war in the sky," wrote Bradley, "Quesada approached it as a vast new frontier waiting to be explored."[16] The American airman had served in North Africa, where he found that the prevailing USAAF attitude "was that air forces should take care of

318

themselves, with little consideration to the needs of the armies." Indeed, in 1943, it was Coningham – such a thorn in Montgomery's side in Europe in 1944 – to whom Quesada paid generous tribute, "for forcing the USAAF to participate in the ground battle". It was in North Africa that Quesada's undogmatic willingness to adjust command arrangements to the needs of the battle first caught the attention of Eisenhower. The airman handed over operational control of a B-24 anti-submarine wing to the navy rather than seeking to direct it himself through Casablanca, on the simple grounds that this scheme was likely to be more effective. Undramatic enough, perhaps, but his gesture should be seen in the context of a war in which most airmen fought tooth and nail to retain control of their squadrons rather than surrender direction to either of the other two services. Only 38 years old, unmarried, with a quaint enthusiasm for cabinetmaking in his off-duty hours, Quesada was the embodiment of the American "can do" spirit which so attracted all those Europeans of his generation who were not intractably prejudiced.

In France – "not until Normandy did the army air force become a real participant in the ground battle" – Quesada flew a Lightning into the beachhead on D+1 to establish his own headquarters alongside that of Bradley, with whom he established a close personal relationship. It was Quesada who first mounted aircraft radios in American tanks at the time of COBRA – it was a measure of the earlier suspicions between the two services that the airman was astonished when Bradley agreed to give them to him. Thus equipped, Forward Air Controllers could direct strikes from the very tip of the front. While on the British front the RAF jealously kept forward air control in the hands of its own personnel, among the Americans, specially-designed army officers with every unit were able to call down their own support.

Lieutenant Philip Reisler of the U.S. 2nd Armored Division had begun his career as a Forward Air Controller in Sicily, "where the bombing confusion was horrible", equipped only with red and green signal lights, which were quite invisible to the pilots, and yellow smoke canisters to reveal the Allied line. The limitations of these were still apparent in Normandy. Too many troops well behind the front fired smoke or laid out identification panels, only to expose the men ahead of them to a hail of bombs and rockets. In July, Reisler at last received a radio for his Sherman with which he could talk direct to the pilots, and operate directly under the orders of his Combat Command's brigadier. A glimpse of clear skies at dawn and the words, "it looks like we're going to have air today", became one of the great morale boosters on the unit radio net. CC A headqaurters would inform Reisler of fighter-bombers on the way, and at the scheduled hour he would seek contact: "Hello, Skudo leader" (or Red Flag or Back Door or whatever the air group's callsign), "this is Cutbreak. I am at co-ordinate 656474 south-east Vire." For the pilot above, conditions in the cockpit made map reading difficult, and as he reported to the soldier that he was approaching his area, Reisler would seek to call down a round or two of artillery or tank smoke to mark the target. Then he would hear the flight commander on the ground ordering his pilots in: "Jake, you go down first, Pete fly high cover . . ." As they bombed or rocketed, Reisler would correct their fire around the target. Within five minutes, the mission was over and the aircraft gone.

It was not unknown for the Germans to spot the planes and fire smoke onto the American positions, once obliging a desperate Reisler to yell, "Pull out! Pull out!" to a Thunderbolt pilot as he dived onto the Shermans. More often still, for reasons which the tank crews were never told, there was simply no air available to them. They had no power to command the presence of the fighter-bombers; they could only request them. When they did have support and it was obliged to turn home for lack of fuel, Riesler would sometimes get the planes to attack empty countryside simply to encourage the ground troops.[17] This was a practice that infuriated the pilots, for whom every ground-attack sorties was fraught with peril. If they were hit, they enjoyed very little hope of parachuting at low level. When a shortage of Typhoon pilots developed in 2nd Tactical Air Force, the RAF asked for volunteers to transfer from Spitfires. There were none. Men had to be drafted.

Quesada and Broadhurst were frequent visitors to forward areas to discover at first hand what their squadrons were achieving. One morning the American was riding a jeep in search of his old fellow pupil at the Command and General Staff School, Maurice Rose, now leading the CC A of 2nd Armored Division. Following the directions of a succession of tankers up a surprisingly silent road, 100 yards away he glimpsed a tank he took to be the brigadier's. He was driving towards it when a 75mm shell from its turret slammed into the jeep, smashing the vehicle into a ruin and wounding Quesada's driver. It was a Panther. The two men spent an uncomfortable twenty minutes crawling away under small-arms fire. Quesada was conscious that only the previous day he himself had laughed heartily as he heard a German corps commander's aide being interrogated about the whereabouts of his general. The aide answered: "The last time I saw him, he was crawling up a ditch." Now it was the American general's turn to crawl, and he was fortunate to escape alive. Few airmen of any nationality went to such lengths to keep in touch with the realities of the ground battle.

Conversely, Quesada worked hard to keep the ground commanders up to date with the air situation. The tiny handful of Luftwaffe aircraft that ventured over the Allied lines caused wholly disproportionate distress among the ground troops, and were sometimes used as an alibi by divisional commanders to explain difficulties and failures. One morning, Quesada was compelled to listen to complaints from Bradley that the 29th Division had been harassed by enemy air attack. The airman persuaded Bradley to ride with him to see the 29th Division's commander, the excitable Gerhardt, "more like a rooster than a divisional commanding officer," suggested Quesada wryly. He demanded to know precisely what the army was complaining about. After much prevarication and inquiries down the chain of command, it transpired that a regimental commander was fulminating about an attack by two German aircraft on his command post, which had set a half-track on fire and wounded his cook. Bradley drove back in silence, to compose a letter to all divisional commanders suggesting that they should not expect to be immune to air attack. On another occasion when a similar protest was made, Quesada sent reconnaisance aircraft up to provide Bradley with two sets of photographs of the battlefield. One showed the area behind the German lines, with its empty roads and utter absence of visible movement. The other showed the Allied zone, crawling with nose-to-tail armour and transport convoys, uncamouflaged dumps in the fields, shipping unloading off the beaches. Bradley took the point.

Another personal venture by Quesada was more controversial. During one of Eisenhower's visits to France in mid-June, the airman got up from a staff meeting, declaring that he was off on a fighter sweep. In an impulsive moment, the Supreme Commander asked boyishly: "Can I come?" Equally impulsive, Quesada agreed. Within the hour he took off in his Mustang with Eisenhower crammed behind his seat in place of a 70-gallon fuel

321

tank. "Once we were airborne, I began to realize, first, that he didn't fit – I told him that I would have to turn the plane over if we were hit – and then that perhaps this was wrong." A few miles over the lines, Quesada aborted the sweep and took the general home. This spared neither himself nor Eisenhower severe reprimands from Washington for the risk they had taken.

For aircraft, as for so much else among the Allied armies, the abundance of resources was staggering. Quesada controlled 37 squadrons of aircraft, with enough reserves to ensure that losses could be replaced immediately. He was irked to see six Lightnings on an airstrip one morning marked as unserviceable, because their canopies had been damaged by pilots forgetting to lock them down on take-off. It was the type of damage that could be repaired in hours by an air force in real need of fighters, "like putting an automobile on the junk pile with a flat tyre". Pilots flew three or four days a week, perhaps five missions a day that might be as brief as 20 minutes, living between sorties in much the same mud and discomfort as the ground forces. The Normandy dust contained a hard silicon-like material that played havoc with aircraft engines running up on improvised strips. Filters were hastily designed and fitted to cope with this. "I was never consciously short of pilots or aircraft," said Quesada. British fliers were acutely nervous of their eager but inexperienced American counterparts, who were prone to attack any aircraft in the sky that they could not immediately identify. RAF Typhoons found that being attacked by Mustangs or Thunderbolts was not an occasional freak, but an alarmingly regular occurrence. So too was being fired upon by the Royal Navy over the Channel.

Despite the resentment felt towards the air forces by those Allied units which had suffered from "short bombing", the pilots earned the respect of most troops who watched them in action. Well-controlled close air support became, by late summer, one of the most formidable weapons in the hands of a unit which found itself bogged down. Yet for the fliers, ground attack enjoyed none of the glamour of high-level fighter interception, and was infinitely more hazardous. Like all low-level flying, it required unrelenting concentration and precision. A New Zealand Typhoon pilot described a morning over Normandy:

Swirling clouds of yellow dust hung over the busy roads beneath us, and further to the south-east the battered city of Caen flickered and smouldered under a huge mushroom of pink and black smoke. Southwards, in the region of Villers-Bocage, a furious gun battle was taking place, and to the west, thin streams of coloured tracer spouted into the morning sky before falling away in chains of red-hot clusters. In the more open country the fields were strewn with the bloated carcasses of hundreds of tan and white cattle. Shell craters, bomb holes and burnt-out tanks littered the tortured countryside.

To the south of Potigny we began climbing but streams of light flak came racing towards us. So I hastily sank down again to the comparative safety of the taller trees and hedgerows . . . I caught sight of the object of our early-morning mission. The road was crammed with enemy vehicles – tanks, trucks, half-tracks, even horse-drawn wagons and ambulances, nose to tail, all pressing forward in a frantic bid to reach cover before the skies once more became alive with the winged death of 2nd Tactical Air Force. As I sped to the head of this mile-long column, hundreds of German troops began spilling out into the road to sprint for the open fields and hedgerows. I zoomed up sharply over a ploughed field where 20 or 30 Germans in close array were running hard for a clump of trees. They were promptly scythed down by a lone Mustang which appeared from nowhere. The convoy's lead vehicle was a large half-track. In my haste to cripple it and seal the road, I let fly with all eight rockets in a single salvo; I missed but hit the truck that was following. It was thrown into the air along with several bodies, and fell back on its side. Two other trucks in close attendance piled into it.

. . . Within seconds the whole stretch of road was bursting and blazing under streams of rocket and cannon fire. Ammunition wagons exploded like multi-coloured volcanoes. Several teams of horses stampeded and careered wildly across the fields, dragging their broken wagons behind them. Others fell in tangled heaps, or were caught up in the fences and hedges. It was an awesome sight: flames, smoke, bursting rockets and showers of coloured tracer – an army in retreat, trapped and without air protection.[18]

Quesada believed that his British counterparts never approached tactical air support with enough imagination; for instance, they did not follow the Americans in using radar for the navigational guidance of fighter squadrons rather than merely for defensive purposes. He felt that the RAF was hampered by the incubus of its immense force of Spitfires, superb aircraft for high-level interceptor work, of which there was now almost none, but unsuited to the ground-attack task because of their small 1,000-pound payload and lack of robustness. It was essential for any close-support aircraft to be able to withstand small-arms fire. The British Typhoon carried 2,000 pounds and was a sound ground-attack aircraft, but Quesada much preferred his own Thunderbolts and Mustangs, the former also carrying 2,000 pounds.

A close personal friend of both Spaatz and General Ira Eaker, Quesada would never acknowledge any lack of enthusiasm for the support of ground forces among his USAAF colleagues. Indeed, he argued that it was precisely because of their long term ambitions for their service that "Spaatz saw that it was vital that we should do whatever we could for the land battle – it was always on his mind that after the war we must have an independent air force. We were obsessed by proving our worth."

Nothing above diminishes the claims of the Allied air forces to have made a vital contribution to the Normandy campaign. The bombers' execution of the Transport Plan was central to ensuring that the invasion forces won the battle of the build-up. The fighter-bombers' low-level operations inflicted immense damage upon the German army, above all in the later stages of the campaign. The issue is simply whether, if the leading airmen of Britain and America had devoted themselves earlier and more wholeheartedly to the support of the armies, the air forces could have provided even more effective, perhaps decisive, direct support for the ground offensives. From 1940 to 1942, the humiliations of the British army were consistently attributed to the Luftwaffe's command of the air. Yet in 1944, when the Allies possessed air forces of a strength Goering's pilots had never dreamed of, the German army continued to mount a formidable resistance until broken in bloody ground action.

10 The open flank

By the last days of July 1944, the German army in Normandy had been reduced to such a condition that only a few fanatics of the SS still entertained hopes of avoiding defeat, far less of achieving victory. Any faint prospect of replacing the huge casualties in the west vanished in the wake of the Russian offensive against Army Group Centre, which had destroyed 28 German divisions in five weeks, a blow as shattering to Hitler as that which was now befalling him in Normandy. The Allies' intelligence reports of the German order of battle flattered their opponents – or perhaps themselves by detailing the divisions still before them: Panzer Lehr, 2nd SS Panzer, 12th SS Panzer and so on. In fact, these formations were shattered ruins of their old selves, sustained by a fraction of the men and a tiny fragment of the armour and gun power that they had carried into battle weeks before. Attrition, not manoeuvre, had been decisive in reducing von Kluge's formations to a state in which they could no longer sustain the sagging line. As the tide poured over the walls of their sandcastle from Bourgébus to Rennes, they lacked both the mobility to race the Allies to the breaches and the fighting power to seal the gaps, even where they could reach these. Von Kluge reported to Hitler:

Whether the enemy can still be stopped at this point is questionable. The enemy air superiority is terrific, and smothers almost every one of our movements . . . Losses in men and equipment are extraordinary. The morale of our troops has suffered very heavily under constant murderous enemy fire, especially since all infantry units consist only of haphazard groups which do not form a strongly coordinated force any longer. In the rear areas of the front terrorists, feeling the end approaching, grow steadily bolder. This fact, and the loss of numerous signal installations, makes an orderly command extremely difficult.[1]

Wholesale collapses in morale were resulting in the mass surrender of units swamped by the American advance. General Hausser of Seventh Army, a legendarily tough SS commander, reported that 10 of his divisions had disintegrated, leaving scattered bands of demoralized stragglers roaming north-west France without equipment or leadership. Sergeant Hans Stober admitted that even in 17th SS Panzergrenadiers, from mid-July shell-shock – hitherto an almost unrecognized condition in SS units – became a significant problem. "By this stage, the whole German army was deteriorating," said Lieutenant Langangke of 2nd SS Panzer. "We no longer had a chance to do anything big. We could only play foxes, do this or that in a small way. *Heim ins Reich* –Home to Germany– was the principal thought in many people's minds." It was astonishing that the German east–west front held together at all. Yet the surviving fragments of the old elite units still disputed the Allied advance at every stage.

The reverberations of the bomb explosion on 20 July at Hitler's headquarters echoed through the upper ranks of his army. "At one moment was to be seen a set of men and things which together formed a focal point of world events," wrote one of the survivors, Jodl's Deputy Walter Warlimont. "At the next, there was nothing but wounded men groaning, the acrid smell of burning and charred fragments of maps and papers fluttering in the wind."[2] Hitler's chronic mistrust and scorn for his generals became manic. Throughout the Normandy campaign, he had intervened in their decisions. Now he began to sweep aside the unanimous advice of men as unfailingly loyal to him in the past as Hausser, Eberbach, Dietrich, as well as the wavering von Kluge, and to direct the battle in a fashion that severed all contact with reason or reality. On 30 July Jodl placed before him an order "for possible withdrawal from the coastal sector", which was in effect a blueprint for the evacuation of France.[3] Hitler brushed this aside, saying that it was not at present necessary. Jodl anyway telephoned Blumentritt at von Kluge's headquarters and told him to be prepared to receive such an order when it came. Late on the night of 31 July, Hitler personally briefed Warlimont for the trip he was to make to France, declaring simply: "The object remains to keep the enemy confined to the bridgehead and there to inflict serious losses upon him in order to wear him down."[4] When Warlimont received his final orders at the midday conference the next morning, Hitler said irritably, "You tell Field-Marshal von Kluge to keep on looking to his front, to keep his eyes on the enemy and not to look over his shoulder."[5] Warlimont was to be Hitler's personal agent at von Kluge's headquarters, ensuring that the havering

Field-Marshal executed his orders precisely.

The Führer suffered increasingly from self-pity in the days following the assassination attempt. On hearing a recital of the sufferings of his soldiers and of the German people, he remarked crossly: "I think it's pretty obvious that this war is no fun for me. I've been cut off from the world for five years. I've not been to a theatre, a concert or a film . . ."[6] It was a remarkable irony that, at a time when his own faith in his army was crumbling, most of its officers and men in the field were shocked by news of the bomb plot, and were continuing to hold their positions despite intolerable difficulties. Colonel Heinz-Gunther Guderian of 116th Panzer was astonished and disgusted by the news from the rear: "We were not part of some South American military junta. We had the constant feeling that there were traitors in our midst." Captain Eberhard Wagemann of 21st Panzer staff had long ago concluded, in a discussion with an older officer of the division who was a personal friend of Count von Stauffenburg, that the war could not be won. But like many German officers, he felt that however hopeless the situation, "no officer, no soldier had any business to concern himself with treachery." Corporal Adolf Hohenstein of 276th Infantry retained no faith in victory, but was thoroughly dismayed by Stauffenburg's bomb. "It cost us thousands of lives at the front," he believed. A 21st Army Group intelligence report based upon prisoner interrogation following the bomb plot concluded: "The overall effect of the news on the men of fighting units was one of no excitement. One effort to end the war had been frustrated. Therefore everything was as before."[7] The same document came to the conclusion that only 5 per cent of German troops now believed in the possibility of final victory. 10th and 12th SS Panzer were the only divisions in which it could be said that morale was still high.

The principcal consequences of the bomb plot among the men in Normandy was to sow an almost poisonous mistrust within the officer corps. It was ironic that many officers whose confused sense of honour had convinced them that they should not be party to the bomb plot, now suffered bitter consequences because that same interpretation of honour had prevented them from betraying the plotters to Hitler. The Wehrmacht found itself deprived of all power or respect within the German state, subjected to the final humiliation of being compelled to adopt the Hitler salute. Relations between the SS and the *Heer* – the soldiers of the Wehrmacht – were normally good at field level.

Now a chasm widened between the fanatical loyalists and those despairing of victory and increasingly weary of defeat. In the hospital where Corporal Werner Kortenhaus of 21st Panzer was recovering from his wounds, a young soldier playing chess said as they talked about news of the bomb plot: "He'd be better dead." An SS NCO sprang to his feet and caught the speaker a furious slap across the face. Kortenhaus himself, along with most men of the *Heer*, had no illusions left: "We reckoned that the whole game was up." The SS were increasingly obsessed by the conviction that the anti-Hitler plotters were contributing directly to their misfortunes on the battlefield. "It was obvious to us that there was a lot of treachery," said Lieutenant Walter Kruger of 12th SS Panzer. Hitler raged that the lack of *Panzerfausten* in Normandy was clearly the consequence of sabotage by the Quartermaster-General, Wagner, one of the dead plotters.

After the war, when the names of those concerned with the plot were shown to include such men as Rommel's Chief of Staff, Hans Speidel, and Graf von Schwerin, commanding 116th Panzer, thousands of their former comrades sought to blame their treachery for the misfortunes that befell the German army in Normandy. Above all, they allowed themselves to be convinced that delays in moving units from the Pas de Calais and in getting ammunition and supplies to the front were the result of sabotage. There will never be conclusive evidence one way or the other. But it remains far more probable that the failures and difficulties were genuine accidents and errors of war. The plotters were guided by a desire to make peace on the best available terms with the western Allies. Nothing could have made this task more difficult than for Hitler's death to take place at a moment when the German army was in collapse after a shattering defeat. It was very much to the plotters' advantage that the line in Normandy should be stable when the Führer died. By July, some officers and men were giving less than their best efforts to the war because they were convinced of its futility. But there was a great gulf between passive defeatism of this kind, and an active attempt to sabotage the campaign. By early August, the German army in France was on the edge of catastrophe because of its ruin on the battlefield and the demented strategy of Hitler, not because it had been betrayed from within.

For the Allied armies, the battle now took on a new character. Hitherto, while generalship had naturally been important, the progress of the campaign depended above all upon the ability of

British, American and Canadian units to seize ground from their German opponents on the next ridge, in the next hedge, beyond the next road. Henceforth, while hard fighting still lay ahead, Normandy became a commanders' battle. It was the decisions of the generals that determined the manner in which events unfolded in August, their successes and failures which brought about the position that was achieved by September.

Of all the Allied movements of the campaign, few have evoked such widespread post-war criticism as the American "right turn" into Brittany at the beginning of August.[8] The German XXV Corps was known to be weak and lacking the mobility to create a major threat to Bradley's armies. Montgomery anticipated that no more than a single U.S. corps would press on west from Avranches towards Brest and the other Breton ports. In fact, two of Patton's three corps swept across the bridge at Pontaubault into Brittany, and Bradley was determined to embark on no reckless adventures south-eastwards unless he was certain of holding the Avranches "elbow" in their rear. "We can't risk a loose hinge," he said.[9] He feared a German counter-attack north-westwards, breaking through to the coast and cutting off Patton's armoured divisions from their fuel and supplies – with disastrous consequences. Bradley himself later accepted responsibility for the decision, for good or ill, to swing large American forces west into Brittany.

Patton won the admiration of the world for the energy and ruthlessness with which he forced his army through Avranches and into its dash across Brittany. "If the greatest study of mankind is man," he said, "surely the greatest study of war is the road net."[10] He wrote with justified pride of his own direction of the movement:

The passage of Third Army through the corridor at Avranches was an impossible operation. Two roads entered Avranches; only one left it over the bridge. We passed through this corridor 2 infantry and 2 armoured divisions in less than 24 hours. There was no plan because it was impossible to make a plan.[11]

Yet for all the verve and energy of Patton's movements, of which so many other American and British commanders were envious, there is considerable force in the remarks of those veterans exasperated by the Patton legend. They declare: "He didn't break out. He walked out."[12] Bradley had no patience with Patton, dismissing one of Montgomery's wilder flights of strategic fantasy with the adjectives, "militarily unsound, Pattonesque". He wrote of Third Army's great sweep in early August: "Patton blazed through Brittany with armored divisions and motorized infantry. He conquered a lot of real estate and made big headlines, but the Brittany campaign failed to achieve its primary objectives."[13] Bradley referred, of course, to the rapid seizure of the western ports in a usable condition. The true architects of Patton's rush through Brittany were Collins and the men of his VII Corps who had broken the German line in COBRA – and the British and Canadian armies still facing the bulk of von Kluge's effective formations. It is essential to emphasize that there was no German front in the west – merely a disorganized jumble of units retreating with all the speed that they could muster into the fortified ports where they were expected to make a stand. When Patton's army later met serious German resistance, the American divisions under his command fought no better and no worse with his leadership than under that of any other commander. At the beginning of August 1944, the posturing general was the man for the hour, performing feats of movement that probably no other Allied commander could have matched. But it would be absurd to suppose that he had discovered a key to the downfall of the German armies which had escaped his peers. It was they who had made possible the glory that he now reaped with such relish.

The fruits of the dash into Brittany were intoxicating for the men riding the tanks and trucks – an almost unopposed swing across country already largely in the hands of the French Resistance, gaining for Gerow's 6th Armored Divisions 4,000 prisoners at a cost of 130 killed, 400 wounded, 70 missing. Yet most of the Germans in the region were given time to withdraw into Brest, whose garrison swelled to 38,000 men, and whose defences held until 19 September. Far more seriously, the vital turn east towards Mayenne and Alençon, intended to initiate the rolling up of the main German front in Normandy, was delayed by days.

Major-General John "P" Wood of the 4th Armored Division was one of the outstanding American commanders of the campaign. On 2 August, having advanced over 50 miles in four days, Wood and his tanks stood west of Rennes, where he had shrewdly bypassed a 2,000-strong German garrison – too weak to present a serious threat, but possibly strong enough seriously to delay a direct assault. Wood perfectly grasped the urgency of turning east. Late on the afternoon of 3 August, his tanks were more than 30 miles south of Rennes, and had cut seven of the ten major roads to the city. Wood gave initial orders for a move south-east, on Châteaubriant. Then Middleton at VIII Corps intervened. First, he ordered that Wood must not merely cut off Rennes, but capture it. This Wood's 13th Infantry achieved with a bold push for the heart of the city which prompted the defenders to withdraw during the night of the 3rd. But Middleton's eyes were still fixed west towards the sea. Quiberon Bay had been a vital Allied objective since D-Day, the intended site of a major artificial port. VIII Corps' commander drove to see Wood and insist that, rather than pressing east, where the countryside yawned empty of all significant German forces, 4th Armored must make for the coast. Early on the morning of 4 August, Middleton found Wood standing by his vehicles in a field, stripped to the waist, gazing at the maps laid out before him on the grass.

He came over and threw his arms around me. I said, "What's the matter, John, you lost your division?" He said, "Heck no, we're winning this war the wrong way, we ought to be going toward Paris."[14]

"I protested long, loud and violently," Wood said later. He believed that he could have been in Chartres in two days. "But no! We were forced to adhere to the original plan – with the only armor available, and ready to cut the enemy to pieces. It was one of the colossally stupid decisions of the war."[15] But Middleton confirmed Wood's orders, and so also did Patton's Chief of Staff, Gaffey. Gaffey told Middleton that his general "assumes that in addition to locking the roads . . . you are pushing the bulk of the [4th Armored Division] to the west and south-west to the Quiberon area, in accordance with the army plan."[16] Patton, desperately anxious not to become entangled in a wrangle with Bradley when his own position remained that of probationer, had no intention of crossing his wished. 4th Armored spent 6–10 August standing before Lorient, attempting to induce the German garrison to surrender. It was 15 August before the division was once more pushing east.

There is little doubt that the commitment of major forces in Brittany was ill-judged, when resistance was so slight and – after the example of Cherbourg – the prospect so small of the port being in early use. Bradley lies open to the charge of lack of imagination in failing to adjust the original OVERLORD plan to meet the changed situation and the great new opportunity in the west. If the Germans had now behaved rationally, recognized the threat of envelopment to their entire front and begun a full-scale retreat east, then Bradley could indeed be accused of losing his armies a great prize. But, driven on by Hitler's delusions, they did nothing of the sort. They prepared a major counter-attack and, even when it failed, were so slow to begin pulling back that Bradley's divisions had all the time that they needed to reach around behind the German rear. The diversion into Brittany may have been poor strategy, a future source of grief to staff college students. But the ultimate prize at Falaise was as great as it was ever likely to be, whatever course the American had adopted. It is also useful to remember that, while the Channel ports were in Allied hands within a month, making those of Brittany largely unnecessary, Bradley still had too much respect for the German army at the beginning of August to be confident that its collapse was total. Almost every witness at American headquarters to the events of early August agrees that their finality only became apparent later. There was no immediate conviction that the end in France had come, that von Kluge was not merely defeated, but routed. Many officers still expected to be fighting around the Seine – if not further east – come September.

On the night of 6 August, von Funck's XLVII Panzer Corps launched a major attack against the positions of the 30th Division around Mortain, which had fallen to 1st Division on the 3rd. The Germans advanced without a preparatory artillery bombardment, for they still cherished the illusion of surprise. Armoured columns of 2nd SS Panzer and 17th SS pushed forward from north and south to seize the town, and by noon of the 7th were close to St Hilaire in the south-west. Von Luttwitz's 2nd Panzer overran two companies of the American 117th Infantry. Elements of 1st SS Panzer were also committed as they arrived on the battlefield. 116th Panzer's commander pleaded the difficulty of disengaging on his existing front to explain his own formation's absence from the start-line. But within a few hours, German units were within nine miles of Avranches. If they could break through to the coast, they might cut off the 12 American divisions south of the junction from their lifeline of fuel and supplies.

Yet from the moment on the night of 6 August that Ultra

provided a brief warning to Bradley's headquarters of the Mortain counter-attack, the Americans perfectly understood this as an opportunity, not a threat. The Germans had plunged enfeebled forces into battle against powerful American formations which were not not merely confident of withstanding them, but expected to destroy them. Bradley told the visiting Henry Morgenthau: "This an opportunity that comes to a commander not more than once in a century. We are about to destroy an entire German army."[17] The veteran U.S. 4th Division, in VII Corps reserve, was deployed to seal the German flanks while 3rd Armored's CC B went to the aid of the hard-pressed 30th Division. Haislip's XV Corps was ordered to press on with its push south to Le Pau, then swing north-east to Alençon and Argentan. Third Army's great sweep was not to be impeded by the Mortain battle. Collins' VII Corps would handle the business of repelling von Funck's panzers, with formidable assistance from the Allied air forces.

Hitler had personally dispatched to von Kluge detailed plans for the armoured attack, Operation LUTTICH. "We must strike like lightning," he declared. "When we reach the sea the American spearheads will be cut off. Obviously they are trying all-out for a major decision here, because otherwise they wouldn't have sent in their best general, Patton . . . We must wheel north like lightning and turn the entire enemy front from the rear."[18] It will remain one of the great enigmas of history, not that the German generals could have accepted the invasion of Poland or the mass murder of the Jews, but that so many sane men could have borne obediently with fantasy such as this. The Commander-in-Chief of Army Group B, too weak to reject the plan as absurd, determined that if it was to be launched at all, the armour must move immediately, before the American envelopment had rendered any move impossible. He could not wait, as Hitler demanded, for the full weight of panzer forces to be transferred westwards. Of 1,400 tanks committed to battle in Normandy, 750 had already been lost. The panzer divisions initially committed to the Mortain thrust – 2nd, 1st and 2nd SS – attacked with only 75 Mk IVs, 70 Mk Vs, and 32 self-propelled guns.

From the outset, they ran into difficulties. 2nd Panzer on the right left the start-line on time, at midnight on 6 August, but 1st SS Panzer's armour was seriously delayed by a fighter-bomber which crashed onto the leading tank in a sunken lane, creating an impassable road block. It was daylight before the SS tank crews

333

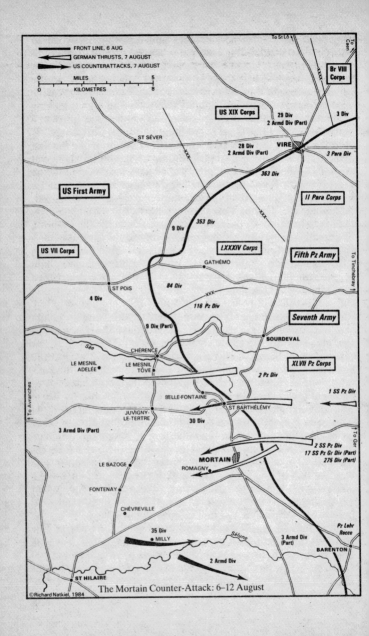

The Mortain Counter-Attack: 6–12 August

© Richard Natkiel, 1984

had reversed out of the shambles and found a new road to Mortain. After promising early gains beyond the little town of St Barthélémy, 1st SS met CC B of the U.S. 3rd Armored and were quickly in deep trouble. 116th Panzer, which appeared on the scene only late in the afternoon, was stopped dead by an American anti-tank screen. Only 2nd Panzer seemed to be making good progress. "Bad weather is what we need," said Luttwitz's operations officer. "Then everything will work out alright."[19] But as the early morning mist lifted, out of the sky came the first aircraft of the greatest concentration of fighter-bombers yet deployed in the west, Quesada's Thunderbolts supported by the RAF's rocket-firing Typhoons. They caught 2nd Panzer at Le Coudray. The promised Luftwaffe air cover never materialized. Almost every approaching German sortie was intercepted by Allied fighters. The ground attack, begun with little hope even among the most formidable remaining formations of the German army, foundered in disarray and destruction. Far from creating even temporary relief from the threat of encirclement, von Kluge's divisions had driven themselves deep into the destructive embrace of the Americans.

Yet for the men in the path of von Kluge's offensive that week in August, it was difficult to view the situation as enthusiastically as did Bradley's staff. Corporal George Small of 465th Anti-Aircraft Battalion, covering the Pontaubault bridges against the resurgence of Luftwaffe activity, was appalled to find his unit's triple AA guns being issued with armour-piercing ammunition: "Then we were really scared." The 30th Division bore the brunt of the German attack. Most men had been roused from their rest area on the night of the 6th, aware of a German attack but not of its details, and marched forward under the full moon to relieve infantry of the 1st Division. Guides showed them the foxholes and trenches that they were taking over. Then the men of "The Big Red One" padded away into the darkness, leaving the newcomers to meet the enemy, supported by a sprinkling of tanks and tank destroyers. On Hill 317 east of Mortain, 700 Americans of the 2nd/120th Infantry and K Company of the 3rd/120th fought surrounded for five days, supplied by erratic air drops, by the end losing 300 killed and wounded. The four rifle companies were reduced by repeated attacks to 8, 24, 18 and 100 men respectively. Men grubbed in the village gardens for radishes and potatoes when their rations were exhausted. By

3.07 p.m. on the afternoon of 7 August, the 120th's Regimental CP was reporting German tanks within 200 yards. One of them was knocked out with a bazooka by a telephone operator, Private Joe Shipley. A platoon commander of the 1st Battalion, Lieutenant Lowther, called to a driver from his company standing on the far side of a hedge to join him immediately. "I can't," the driver called back unhappily. "I'm captured." The 2nd Battalion's aid station was captured by the Germans on the night of the 8th. An SS officer carrying a white flag approached the Americans' positions on Hill 282 to demand their surrender – without success. Soon afterwards, they were called upon to withstand a fierce attack. Medical supplies were fired into the American positions by artillery shell. Brigadier-General William Harrison, deputy divisional commander, moved from battalion to battalion urging and encouraging his men as he had on the first morning of COBRA. To one of his officers, he seemed to possess "the radiant face of a confident shepherd, for that is what he was to us in those difficult, horrible days". The little stone farmhouse where he had his command post was known to the Americans as "Château *Nebelwerfer*".

At Abbaye Blanche, 150 men and the company mascot – a tiny dog named Mobile Reserve – held a junction where five roads converged. One private soldier, Robert Vollmer, used a bazooka to demolish in succession an armoured car, a motorcycle, another armoured car and a fuel truck. A soldier named Estervez was wounded by a grenade taking men to the rear in a jeep, but returned for a second journey on which he was killed. The defenders were disturbed to find small-arms fire rattling at them from the rear – a classic German infiltration movement. But they held their ground with the support of a steady trickle of stragglers who found their way into their lines. Some men found a rocky cave beside the road, and took refuge in it when the German shelling became intense. Sometimes as they lay in their foxholes they could hear the sound of German voices. Every few hours there was a grinding of tracks or wheels as a vehicle approached up the road, and a brief exchange of fire as an American tank destroyer or anti-tank gun engaged it – and almost invariably, destroyed it. One man somehow found the means to get himself hopelessly drunk. When another soldier declined to take up an exposed position, the drunk said promptly, "Sure, I'll go," and attempted to man a bazooka and a machine-gun simultaneously.

The American command handling of the battle suggested a new maturity and grip within Twelfth Army Group. From beginning to end of the German push, officers at every level responded with vigour and sureness. Hodges' First Army diary for 7 August reported: "The boche is attacking . . . The air went after the enemy armor with a vengeance . . . The general is not too worried over the situation, although there is admittedly the strongest kind of pressure." On 8 August, the diary first noted a visit from the actor Edward G. Robinson, then added: "The situation appears a bit better tonight . . . 9th Div repulsed several small local enemy counter-attacks . . . The 30th Div was heavily engaged . . . 35th Div advanced against very light resistance." Next day, Hodges was greeting Henry Morgenthau, then: "Tonight, as before, the General issued orders for all troops to 'button up tight' for the night, and be prepared for anything, although it appears to be the General's feeling that his [von Kluge's] main effort is over, and that it has been decisively broken."

On the night of 12 August, the 35th Division at last broke through to relieve the 120th. Lieutenant Sidney Eichen of the 2nd Battalion's anti-tank platoon felt overcome by a great surge of relief as the files of fresh troops marched through their positions: "What a sight they were, coming off the hill." War correspondents and photographers swarmed over the positions, eager to interview the tired survivors of the fine American stand. Around the road junction at Abbaye Blanche, they found 24 wrecked German vehicles. As the Americans cleared the Mortain battlefield, they counted over 100 abandoned German tanks.[20]

Hitler, with his unerring instinct for reinforcing failure, now did so yet again. In the south, where Haislip's XV Corps was hastening towards the Loire, for 100 miles from Domfront to Angers there was only one panzer and one infantry division in its path, along with a few security battalions. Yet Hitler ignored Hausser's vehement protests, and ordered the panzer division – 9th Panzer – shifted north for a renewed attack towards Avranches on the 10th. Hausser called this movement "A death blow not only to Seventh Army but also to the entire Wehrmacht in the west". Von Kluge said simply: "It is the Führer's order."[21] But as the new attack was about to be launched, the Caen front also began to buckle. The despairing von Kluge asked Hitler that the panzers might be "temporarily transferred from the Mortain area to . . . destroy the enemy spearheads thrusting north-wards."[22] Hitler gave his grudging assent on the 11th, but still declined to countenance any general withdrawal. Von Kluge's weekly situation report declared baldly: "The enemy's first main objective is to outflank and encircle the bulk of the 5th Panzer Army and 7th Army on two sides."[23] As late as 8 or 9 August, von Kluge could readily have executed the only sane movement open to him, a withdrawal to the Seine covered by a sacrificial rearguard. Hitler, and Hitler alone, closed this option to him and presented the Allies with their extraordinary opportunity. The climate within the German high command plumbled new depths of fantasy and grotesque comedy. The Luftwaffe had been lamentably directed for years by Goering, but at last its failure at Mortain drove Hitler to turn upon his old henchman.

"Goering! The Luftwaffe's doing nothing." [Guderian reported a confrontation that August] "It is no longer worthy to be an independent service. And that's your fault. You're lazy." When the portly Reichs-marschall heard these words, great tears trickled down his cheeks.[24]

Hitler placed the principal responsibility for failure at Mortain upon von Kluge's lack of will. Yet he seemed far more depressed by small personal tragedies, such as the death of his former SS orderly, Captain Hans Junge, who was killed by Allied strafing in France. He broke the news personally to the man's widow, his youngest secretary, Traudl Junge: "*Ach*, child, I am so sorry; your husband had a fine character."[25] When von Choltitz report-ed to Hitler fresh from the front, he was informed that the Führer was about to hurl the Allies into the sea. The general concluded that "the man was mad".[26]

On 11 August, with Haislip's XV Corps still pushing east around Alençon, it became Montgomery's responsibility to consider setting a new boundary between the American, British and Canadian forces, which expected to meet east of the German armies imminently. Despite the changed circumstances, he declined to alter the line he had set near Argentan on 6 August. He believed that XV Corps would meet slow going on its turn north, where it re-entered the *bocage*, which the Germans could exploit to their advantage. It seemed reasonable to assume that the Canadians, pushing south across reasonably open country, would be in Argentan before Haislip. The new boundary, the

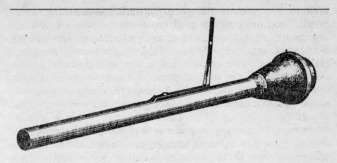

The German *Panzerfaust* was the best hand-held infantry anti-tank weapon of the war, exceptionally useful in Normandy, where the close country made it possible for its operators to reach Allied tanks at the very short ranges for which it was designed. It was a one-shot, throwaway weapon, weighing 11½ pounds. Its hollow charge could penetrate 200 mm of armour at 30 yards, and an improved version, introduced in the summer of 1944, possessed a higher velocity and was effective up to 80 yards. By contrast, the American 2.36 inch "bazooka" fired too light a projectile to be effective against the frontal armour of most German tanks. The British PIAT was moderately useful – it was effective up to 100 yards and could be used as a primitive mortar as well as against tanks. But it was twice as heavy as the *Panzerfaust*, cumbersome to carry, to cock and to fire.

point at which XV Corps would halt its advance, was therefore set just south of Argentan. Patton nonetheless warned Haislip to be ready to push up to Falaise, despite the corps commander's fears that his division would not prove strong enough to hold a trap closed in the face of the wholesale retreat of Army Group B. Patton urgently began to seek reinforcement from XX Corps and from Brittany. Just before midnight on the 12th, Haislip informed Third Army that his 5th Armored Division was just short of Argentan. Did Patton wish him to continue north to meet the Canadians? Patton now telephoned Bradley with his legendary demand: "We have elements in Argentan. Shall we continue and drive the British into the sea for another Dunkirk?"[27]

Despite Bradley's refusal, Patton anyway ordered Haislip to advance cautiously north of Argentan. Only at 2.15 p.m. on the 13th did XV Corps receive categoric orders to halt at Argentan and recall any units north of the town. Bradley's staff had consulted 21st Army Group about a possible boundary change, but were refused it. Patton wrangled with Bradley until at last, having taken care to ensure that the circumstances of the order to halt were made a matter of record, he acquiesced. Bradley was always at pains to make it clear that he himself opposed any further push north, irrespective of the opinions of Montgomery. He feared, as Haislip did, the danger of presenting a thin American front to German troops who would have no alternative but to seek to break through it. Throughout the days that followed, he resolutely refused to press Montgomery for a change in the boundaries.

On the ground, the situation was developing imperatives of its own as resistance stiffened in front of Haislip. 116th Panzer – with 15 surviving tanks – and elements of 1st SS and 2nd Panzer – with 55 tanks between them – were now deployed on his front. The Germans had still made no decision to attempt to flee the threat of encirclement. As mopping up around Mortain was concluded and forces of the U.S. First Army became available to move east, Collins' VII Corps began a rapid advance north-east from Mayenne on the 13th. At 10.00 a.m. that day, Collins telephoned First Army in a characteristically ebullient mood, asking for "more territory to take". First Army's diary recorded:

1st Div was, in some places, on the very boundary itself, and General Collins felt sure that he could take Falaise and Argentan, close the gap, and "do the job" before the British even started to move. General Hodges immediately called General Bradley, to ask officially for a change in boundaries, but the sad news came back that First Army was to go no further than at first designated, except that a small salient around Ranes would become ours.

Bradley, curiously enough, claimed now to be convinced that the importance of closing the trap at Falaise had diminished, because most of the Germans had already escaped eastwards, a view which neither Ultra nor air reconnaissance confirmed. For whatever reasons, he switched the focus of American strategic energy east, towards the Seine. Haislip, he told Patton, was to take two of his four divisions east, while the remainder, with VII Corps, remained at Argentan. It was almost as if Bradley had lost all interest in the "short envelopment" which he himself had proposed to Montgomery on 8 August. He now seemed determined instead to concentrate upon trapping the Germans against the Seine, the rejected "long envelopment". In these days, an uncharacteristic uncertainty of purpose, a lack of the instinct to deliver the killing stroke against von Kluge's armies, seemed to overtake Bradley. General Gerow of V Corps, sent to take

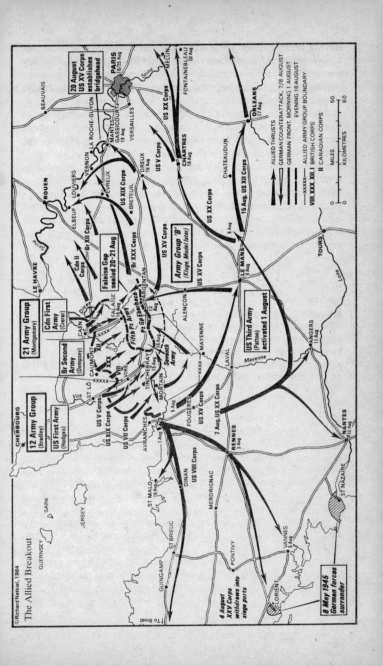

The Allied Breakout

© Richard Natkiel, 1984

21 Army Group (Montgomery)

Cdn First Army (Crerar)

Br Second Army (Dempsey)

12 Army Group (Bradley)

US First Army (Hodges)

US Third Army (Patton) activated 1 August

Army Group 'B' (Kluge, Model later)

20 August US XV Corps establishes bridgehead

PARIS 19/25 Aug

Falaise Gap sealed 20–21 Aug

8 May 1945 German forces surrender

4 August XXV Corps withdraws into siege ports

ALLIED THRUSTS

GERMAN COUNTERATTACK, 7/8 AUGUST

GERMAN FRONT, MORNING 1 AUGUST
EVENING 16 AUGUST

ALLIED ARMY GROUP BOUNDARY

VIII, XXX, XII, I   BRITISH CORPS

II   CANADIAN CORPS

0   50   MILES
0   80   KILOMETRES

CHERBOURG

GUERNSEY
SARK
JERSEY

LE HAVRE
ROUEN
BEAUVAIS

Seine

LOUVIERS
VERNON
LA ROCHE-GUYON 19 Aug
ELBEUF
EVREUX
BRETEUIL
DREUX 16 Aug

NANTES/GASSICOURT 19 Aug
VERSAILLES
MELUN
FONTAINEBLEAU 20 Aug

US XX Corps

US XIX Corps
Br XII Corps
Cdn II Corps

US V Corps

CHARTRES 16 Aug
CHATEAUDUN

ORLEANS 17 Aug

CAEN
CAUMONT
ST LO
Vire

FALAISE
ARGENTAN 13 Aug
Fifth Pz Army
Pz Gp Eberbach 13 Aug
ALENCON
MAYENNE
Seventh Army 16 Aug

Br XXX Corps
US XV Corps
US XV Corps

LE MANS 8 Aug

US XX Corps 15 Aug US XII Corps
6 Aug

Dives

TINCHEBRAI 16 Aug
MORTAIN 5 Aug
FOUGERES
AVRANCHES 1 Aug

US V Corps
US XIX Corps
US VII Corps

US VIII Corps
US XV Corps
7 Aug US XX Corps

LAVAL

Mayenne

ANGERS 11 Aug

TOURS

Loire

ST MALO 16 Aug
DINAN 16 Aug
MERDRIGNAC
ST BRIEUC
GUINGAMP
to Brest

PONTIVY
VANNES 5 Aug

RENNES 3 Aug

NANTES 8/10 Aug

ST NAZAIRE

LORIENT

charge of the situation at Argentan after Haislip's departure, found the command there almost completely ignorant of the whereabouts of the Germans, or even of his own men.

But now Montgomery and Bradley at last agreed that they would enlarge the scope of the pocket eastwards, and seek to bring about a junction of the Allied armies at Chambois. Their plans had thus evolved into a series of compromises: instead of the "short envelopment" through Argentan-Falaise, Haislip was launched upon the "long envelopment" to the river Seine, while Gerow and the Canadians in the north attempted to complete the trap along a line between them. On the night of 17 August, 90th Division attacked north-east to gain the Le Bourge–St Leonard ridge commanding the approach to Chambois. On their left, the raw 80th Division attempted to move into the centre of Argentan. The commanding officer of their 318th Infantry described his difficulties:

This was our first real fight and I had difficulty in getting the men to move forward. I had to literally kick the men from the ground in order to get the attack started, and to encourage the men I walked across the rd without any cover and showed them a way across. I received no fire from the enemy and it was big boost to the men. A tank, 400 yards to our front, started firing on us and I called up some bazookas to stalk him. However the men opened fire at the tank from too great a range and the tank merely moved to another position. I walked up and down the road about three times, finding crossings for my troops. We advanced about 100 yds across the rd and then the Germans opened up with what seemed like all the bullets and arty in the world. I call up my tanks . . . When my tanks came up we lost the first four with only eight shots from the Germans.[28]

The Germans held the 90th Division through the night of 18/19 August south of Chambois, and it was only in the morning that the first American elements reached the village. All the next day and night, the 90th's artillery pounded Germans fleeing east from encirclement. The 80th Division secured Argentan only on the 20th. Bradley's divisions had effectively stood behind the town for over a week.

Hundreds of thousands of Allied soldiers at this time hardly understood the enormity of the events unfolding around them. They knew that some days they had moved a little further, some days a little less; that some days they encountered fierce German resistance, and on others it seemed, incredibly, as if the enemy's will was fading. In a field near Aunay-sur-Odon in the British

342

sector on 14 August, a tank wireless-operator named Austin Baker was camped with his squadron of the 4th/7th Royal Dragoon Guards:

We hadn't been there more than a couple of hours when everybody in the regiment had to blanco up and go over by lorry to the 13/18th Hussars area to hear a lecture by General Horrocks, who had just taken over command of XXX Corps. He was very good, and made us feel quite cheerful. He told us about the Falaise pocket – how the German Seventh Army was practically encircled and how the RAF were beating up the fleeing columns on the roads. He said that very soon we should be breaking out of the bridgehead and swanning off across France. That seemed absolutely incredible to us. We all thought that we should have to fight for every field all the way to Germany. But Horrocks was right.[29]

11 The road to Falaise

Through most of the campaign in north-west Europe, while there were tensions between the American and British high commands and each army possessed a large stock of quizzical jokes about the other, there was no real ill-will between the soldiers. "We knew that they were the chaps that mattered," said Major John Warner of British 3rd Reconnaissance Regiment about the Americans. "We couldn't possibly win the war without them."[1] But during the weeks between the start of COBRA and the march to the Seine, many men of the British Second Army and the newly-operational Canadian First Army found the blaring headlines about the American breakout, their armoured parade through Brittany and down to the Loire, a bitter pill to swallow. Much more than most armies in most campaigns, they were very conscious of the press. They received newspapers from England only a day or two after publication, and studied avidly the accounts of their own doings in Normandy. They saw photographs of jubilant American infantry, helmets pushed back and weapons slung, waving as they rode their tanks through liberated villages alive with smiling civilians. They studied the sketch maps that revealed their allies controlling tracts of country far greater than their own overcrowded perimeter. Above all, they read of the light opposition that the advance was meeting. An NCO of 6th KOSB asked his commanding officer bitterly, "if it was the high command's intention to wipe out all the British and finish the war with the Americans."[2]

For throughout the weeks of COBRA, Brittany, Mortain, almost every day the British and Canadians were pushing slowly forward on their own front with much pain and at heavy cost. The British VIII and XXX Corps were attacking on an axis south-east from Caumont, while the Canadians moved directly south from Caen towards Falaise. Second Army was still in thick country, facing an unbroken German line with far greater armoured strength and *Nebelwerfer* support than anything the American Third Army encountered. Only immediately before the Mortain counter-attack did the weight of German armour begin to shift dramatically eastwards. Most of Dempsey's men were very tired by now, above all the infantrymen of 15th Scottish, 43rd Wessex and 50th Northumbrian divisions, who had borne so much of the heaviest fighting, and continued to do so. It was a matter of astonishment to officers of other units that 43rd Division still retained any morale at all. Its commander, Major-General G. I. Thomas, was a ruthless, driving soldier for whose determination Montgomery was grateful, but who had earned the nickname "Butcher" for his supposed insensitivity to losses. The purge in XXX Corps when Montgomery sacked Bucknall, together with Erskine and Hinde of 7th Armoured, dismayed many of the 7th's men, but did not produce a dramatic improvement in performance.

The episode that prompted the sackings, the fumbling of BLUECOAT, was characterized by many of the misfortunes that befell the British that summer, and deprived them in the eyes of the Americans of the credit that was justly theirs for bearing so thankless a burden on the eastern flank. It began with the usual confident, even cocky, letter from Montgomery to Eisenhower: "I have ordered Dempsey to throw all caution overboard and to take any risks he likes, and to accept any casualties, and to step on the gas for Vire."[3] On 30 July, O'Connor's VIII Corps drove hard for Le Bény Bocage and Vire along the boundary with the American XIX Corps, while on their left XXX Corps made for the 1,100-foot summit of Mont Pinçon. Roberts' 11th Armoured – by now established as the outstanding British tank division in Normandy – made fast going and seized the high ground of Le Bény Bocage, at the vulnerable junction between Panzer Group West and Seventh Army. Boundaries are critical weak points in all formations in all armies, the seams in the garment of defence. It has been suggested in recent years[4] that Montgomery missed a great opportunity by failing to push through here, seize Vire and roll up Seventh Army instead of leaving Vire to the American XIX Corps. When 11th Armoured approached the town before obeying orders to turn south-east on 2 August, it was virtually undefended. But by the time the Americans moved against it the Germans had rushed in troops to plug the gap, mounted vigorous counter-attacks, and were only finally dispossessed on the night of 6 August. Once again, the line had congealed.

But Montgomery and Dempsey's attention in the first days of August was focussed upon the new failure of 7th Armoured. Bucknall was warned to reach Aunay-sur-Odon quickly, or face the consequences. After two days of BLUECOAT he was still five miles short. Montgomery acted at last – belatedly, in the view of much of his staff, particularly his Chief of Staff, de Guingand, who was far more sensitive than his Commander-in-Chief to the prevailing scepticism about the British at SHAEF.

In the days that followed, Second Army continued to push forward south-east of Caumont, gaining a few miles a day by hard labour and hard fighting. Tank and infantry co-operation was now much improved, with the armoured divisions re-organized to integrate tanks and foot-soldiers within their brigades. Since GOODWOOD, it had at last become accepted tactical practice for infantry to ride forward clinging to the tanks when there was suitable opportunities for them to do so. If there was less of the flamboyant spirit of the landings, there was much more professionalism. Most of the Scottish units, which in June so eagerly sent forward their pipers to lead the men into battle, had long ago dispensed with such frivolities by August. Too many pipers would never play another pibroch.

But for the men among the corn and the hedges, each morning seemed to bring only another start-line, another tramp through incessant mortar and shellfire, coated in dust, to another ruined village from which the Germans had to be forced by nerve-racking house-clearing.

The war artist Thomas Hennell wrote late in July of "the sense-haunted ground" the armies left in their wake. "The shot-threshed foliage of the apple orchards was fading and just turning rusty, fruit glowed against the sky; there were ashes of burnt metal, yellow splintered wood and charred brown hedge among the shell pits; every few yards a sooty, disintegrated hulk . . ." The equipment in the hands of von Kluge's armies was perfectly suited to generating maximum firepower with minimum manpower. The multi-barrelled mortar, employed in powerful concentrations, was a devastating weapon against advancing infantry. By August, British artillery was making intense efforts to grapple with the problem by creating specialist counter-mortar teams. The surviving German tanks were as resistant as ever to Allied penetration. A sergeant-major of the KOSB received a well-earned Military Cross for knocking out an

346

enemy Panther which endured six hits from his PIAT before succumbing. The fields at evening were landmarked with up-turned rifles jammed in the earth to mark the dead. The tank crews cursed the ripened apples that cascaded into their turrets as they crashed through orchards, jamming the traverses, while the shock of repeated impacts on banks and ditches threw their radios off net. The Germans had lost none of their skill in rushing forward improvised battle-groups to fill sudden weak-nesses that were exposed. Again and again, British scout cars or tanks reported an apparent gap which might be exploited, only to find it filled before an advance in strength could be made. 15th Scottish Division signalled one of its battalions one evening that Guards Armoured had reported a withdrawal by the enemy on their front. The infantry must ensure that they patrolled to avoid losing contact. An acerbic message came back from the company commander on the front line, that since he was at that moment engaged in a fierce close-quarter grenade battle, there was scant need for patrolling to discover where the enemy was. But another German skill, much in evidence in those days, was that of disengagement: fighting hard for a position until the last possible moment, then breaking away through the countryside to create another line a mile or two back, presenting the British yet again with the interminable problems of ground and momentum.

You turn off the main road to Vire at Point 218 and go down a side road to the top of a ridge [Lieutenant Richard Mosse, commanding 1st Welsh Guards Anti-Tank Platoon, described his battalion's position on 8 August]. "Dust means shells" notices were in great evidence. It was the worst place I have ever been in. Numerous bodies of our predecessors lay in the fields between the companies, with about 25 knocked out vehicles, mostly British. A thick dust covered everything, and over it all hung that sweet sickly smell of death. By day we could not move as we were under observed mortar fire, and going up to the forward companies under machine-gun fire at times . . . August 12 brought news that our guns had opened short again, and Sgt. Lentle and one other had been killed and several wounded. Sgt. Lentle I could ill afford to lose. He was a steady, sensible man. He would not take risks, he had a wife and two boys he adored, but he would obey any order however dangerous. I could always rely on him . . . David Rhys, the mortar platoon comman-der, was wounded. Hugh, Fred and I were all that was left in the company, so we helped hold a bit of the line. We had advanced some half a mile; our casualties were 122, 35 killed . . . As long as I live that word *bocage* will haunt me, with memories of ruined countryside, dust, orchards, sunken lanes and the silly little shoots that were all I could find for the guns.

Mosse's description of his battalion's predicament is a sober corrective for those who suppose that by the middle days of August, with the German army in Normandy within a week of collapse, the pressure upon their opponents was easing. The pain and the constant drain of losses persisted to the bitter end.

On the night of 7 August, preceded by a massive air attack by Bomber Command, Lieutenant-General Guy Simonds launched his II Canadian Corps on a renewed offensive southwards towards Falaise: Operation TOTALIZE. Simonds, who had commanded a division in Sicily, was to prove one of the outstanding Allied corps commanders in Europe, a dour, direct officer who brought unusual imagination to bear on every operational plan for which he was responsible. It was Simonds who now decided to make his attack across open country in darkness, to use 76 converted self-propelled gun-mountings to move his lead infantry, and to employ a sophisticated range of electronics and illuminants to guide his men to their objectives through the night. There was to be no delay in following up the bombers.

Even as the planning for TOTALIZE was being carried out, von Kluge's redeployment for Mortain was taking place. 9th SS Panzer retired from the British front on 1 August, followed by 1st SS Panzer on the night of the 4th, to be relieved by 89th Infantry. A Yugoslav deserter from the 89th reached the Canadian lines almost immediately, bringing this information to Simonds. For the first time since 7 June, the weight of the German army had been lifted from the eastern flank. On Crerar's right, 43rd Division had at last cleared the heights of Mont Pinçon in a fine action on 6/7 August, and the 59th Division was across the Orne north of Thury–Harcourt. The Germans' left front was thus already under heavy pressure when the Canadians moved.

At 11.30 p.m. on 7 August, the assault forces crossed the start-line, led by navigating tanks and flails. They rumbled forward, in four columns of four vehicles abreast, into the great dust cloud raised by the bombing. Bomber Command had done its job, guided by coloured marker shells, with astonishing accuracy – there were no casualties among Allied troops and 3,462 tons of bombs had fallen on the villages in the path of the attack. There was no preliminary artillery bombardment. For the men on the ground, the spectacle was astonishing, with searchlights directed towards the clouds – "Monty moonlight" –

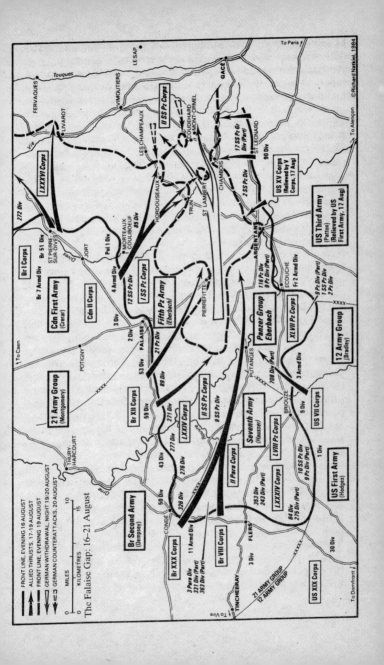

The Falaise Gap: 16–21 August

being used to improve visibility, and bofors guns firing tracer to mark the axes of advance. Their early progress was encouraging. Despite collisions and navigation errors, the early objectives had fallen by first light. 51st Highland Division on the left were making good ground, leaving much mopping-up to the follow-up units. German counter-attacks were repulsed, and 2nd TAF's Typhoons were out in strength, aided by Mustangs and Spitfires flying sweeps over German approach roads. At about 12.50 p.m., the first of 492 Fortresses of 8th Air Force began to launch a new wave of support attacks. The bombing was wild. The Canadians, British and Poles beneath suffered over 300 casualties. The men below on the ground were enraged. "We asked – how the hell could they fail to read a map on a clear day like this?" said Corporal Dick Raymond of 3rd Canadian Division. "A lot of our guns opened up on the Fortresses. When they hit one, everybody cheered."

Now came the familiar, depressing indications of an offensive losing steam. Tilly-la-Campagne still held. As so often throughout the campaign, German positions which had been bypassed, and which it was assumed would quickly collapse when they found themselves cut off, continued to resist fiercely. II Canadian Corps had advanced more than six miles, but Falaise still lay 12 miles ahead. Night attacks by Canadian battle-groups were driven back with substantial loss. The familiar screens of 88mm guns inflicted punishing losses upon advancing armour. Meyer's battered units of 12th SS Panzer had been under orders to move westwards when TOTALIZE was launched, but were thrown quickly into the line to support 89th Infantry. 12th SS still possessed 48 tanks of its own, and also had 19 Tigers of 101st SS Heavy Tank Battalion under its command. Although his formation was out of the line when the Canadian attack began, Meyer had left liaison officers at the front who were able to report to him immediately. Early on 8 August, battle-groups Waldmuller and Krause of 12th SS Panzer – the latter hastily switched from the Thury–Harcourt front – drove into action around the Falaise road. It was in the fierce fighting which now developed that Michael Wittman, the German hero of Villers-Bocage and the greatest tank ace of the war, at last met his end amid concentrated fire from Shermans of 'A' squadron, Northamptonshire Yeomanry.

Both the Polish and Canadian armoured divisions spearheading the Allied attacks were in action for the first time, and this undoubtedly worsened their difficulties and hesitations. On the night of 8 August, Simonds ordered the tanks to press on with operations through the darkness. Many units simply ignored him, and withdrew to night harbours in the manner to which they were accustomed. The few elements which pressed on regardless found themselves isolated and unsupported, and were destroyed by the German 88mm guns. On 9 August, Simonds' staff were exasperated by the persistent delays that appeared to afflict almost every unit movement, the repeated episodes of troops and tanks firing on each other, the difficulty of getting accurate reports from the front about what was taking place. A fierce German counter-attack by a battle-group of 12th SS Panzer completed the chaos. The British Columbia Regiment lost almost its entire strength, 47 tanks in the day, together with 112 casualties. The infantry of the Algonquins, who had been with them, lost 128. The Poles on the left made some progress, getting through to St Sylvain. On the night of the 9th the Canadian 10th Brigade made good progress further west. But after accomplishing little during the day of 10 August, a major night attack on Quesnay woods by 3rd Canadian Division ended in its withdrawal early the following morning.

The Canadians' enthusiasm was obviously waning; difficulties at higher headquarters compounded uncertainty on the ground. Montgomery had always lacked confidence in Crerar, the Canadian army commander, and much upset the Canadians at the outset of this, their first battle as an army, by sending his own staff officers from 21st Army Group to Canadian headquarters to oversee their performance. Crerar became locked in dispute with the rugged Crocker, the British I Corps commander, whom he attempted to sack on the spot. An impatient Montgomery sought to persuade both men to focus their animosity upon the enemy. "The basic cause was Harry. I fear he thinks he is a great soldier, and he was determined to show it the moment he took over command at 1200 on 23 July. He made his first mistake at 1205; and his second after lunch . . ."[5] It is an astounding reflection upon the relative weight of forces engaged north of Falaise that by the night of 10 August, the German tank strength was reduced to 35 (15 Mk IV, five Panther, 15 Tiger), while the Canadian II Corps, even after losses, mustered around 700. Yet on 10 August, with some German reinforcements moving onto the front, it was decided that nothing less than a full-scale, set-piece attack with massed bomber preparation would break the Canadians through to Falaise. The defenders had shown their usual skill in shifting such armour and anti-tank guns as they possessed quickly from threatened point to point, presenting strong resistance to each successive Canadian push. It was also evident that the Canadians were not performing well. Because their government, until very late in the war, would ask only volunteers to serve overseas, it had great difficulty in maintaining First Canadian Army at anything like its establishment level. Many men on the battlefield were embittered by the feeling that the Canadian nation as a whole was not sharing their sacrifice. The best of Crerar's troops were very good indeed. But his army was handicapped by its undermanning, and chronically troubled by leadership problems, which were also the cause of the notorious indiscipline of Canadian aircrew. Even the Canadian official historian ventured the opinion that their army suffered from:

. . . possessing a proportion of regimental officers whose attitude towards training was casual and haphazard rather than urgent and scientific. Analysis of the operations in Normandy seems to support this opinion. Regimental officers of this type, where they existed, were probably the weakest element in the Army. At the top of the command pyramid, Canadian generalship in Normandy does not suffer by comparison with those of the other Allies engaged . . . The Canadian regimental officer at his best . . . had no superior . . . There still remained, however, that proportion of officers who were not fully competent for their appointments, and whose inadequacy appeared in action and sometimes had serious consequences.[6]

On 11 August, Simonds ordered his armoured divisions to pull out of the line, to be relieved by infantry formations. On the 12th, the U.S. First Army's diarist recorded sardonically: "The British are making some gains, none of them sizeable or of break-through proportions." In Paris, the press was reporting triumphant German claims to have destroyed 278 Allied tanks, and Berlin's assertion that "each foot of ground gained is being paid for with enormous losses of men and equipment."

For Montgomery, the breakdown of TOTALIZE was a disappointment, but there is no evidence that he yet perceived it as a long term threat to his hopes. It still appeared incredible to many officers that von Kluge could commit such an act of madness as to leave his forces in the closing Allied noose. There remained ample time and space for the Germans to retreat eastwards. Montgomery had always planned to swing the Canadians and the British left from Falaise across to the Seine, while the American Third Army blocked the so-called Paris–Orleans gap between the Loire and the Seine. This was what was known as the "long envelopment", designed to entrap the entire surviving German forces in western France within its grasp. But when Eisenhower telephoned Montgomery from Bradley's headquarters on the afternoon of 8 August to discuss American proposals for a "short hook", with the arms of Third Army and the Canadians and British meeting somewhere around Argentan to create a much smaller noose, Montgomery was receptive. He signalled to Brooke the next day: "There are great possibilities in the present situation. If we can get to Alençon, Argentan and Falaise fairly quickly, we have a good chance of closing the ring around the main German forces, and I am making all plans to drop an airborne division at Gacé about 15 miles east of Argentan in order to complete the block."[7] Montgomery retained some reservations about the "short hook", which were shared, unusually enough, by Patton. Both men feared that too many Germans might escape a trap closed at Argentan. They were attracted by the much more dramatic gains of ground and prisoners that might result from encircling the greater area towards Paris and Orleans. But Montgomery was uncharacteristically indecisive, and Bradley was absolutely determined on Argentan. The British general acceded. He told Brooke: "Should the Germans escape us here I shall proceed quickly with the plan outlined in M517"[8] – the "long envelopment".

It was now, on 11 August, with the Canadians bogged down north of Falaise, that Montgomery missed probably his last opportunity to conduct a major switch of forces in time to hasten the closing of the German pocket. Had he recognized that the Canadians' difficulties reflected fundamental shortcomings in unit leadership and fighting power, he might have rushed tested British formations south-eastwards to support them, or even to take over the lead. But this was not Montgomery's way. Such a course would have been exceedingly "untidy" – the word he most detested in military operations – and would have created genuine, though not insuperable, problems of movement, control and supply. It may also be that he was reluctant to impose new strains upon British divisions which had already suffered so much; or even that he doubted whether they would do any better than the Canadians. For whatever reasons, he merely ordered Dempsey's Second Army to continue pushing south-east. He left the vital operation – the drive to meet the Americans at

Argentan – entirely in the hands of Crerar's Canadian Army, which had graphically demonstrated its shortcomings in the past four days. From that moment, all that followed on the British-Canadian front was preordained.

Beyond a limited operation by 2nd Canadian Division down the Laize valley on the 12th and 13th, those days were passed entirely in preparations for another big set-piece attack on Falaise, Operation TRACTABLE. It is easy to understand the impatience of the Americans, so conscious of time slipping away. TRACTABLE at last jumped off at 11.42 a.m. on the morning of the 14th, shielded by a smokescreen which Simonds on this occasion substituted for the darkness of TOTALIZE. With the smoke compounded by the great dust cloud thrown up by the advancing armour, the Canadians found navigation difficult. The brigade commander of their leading tanks was mortally wounded in the first hour, causing acute control problems in the actions that followed. More seriously, the Germans had found a copy of Simond's orders on the body of a scout car commander killed the day before. They redeployed with exact knowledge of the Canadian lines of advance.

Most of the attack's early problems resulted from difficulties in finding paths across the little stream of the Laison, which proved a much more formidable anti-tank obstacle than had been expected. More disruptive still, "short bombing" by the RAF's Bomber Command – much of it, ironically enough, by Canadian squadrons – caused more than 300 casualties among the assault troops. By a tragic error, some ground units ignited their usual yellow identifying smoke, while Bomber Command was employing yellow target indicators. All this seemed to be yet more poisoned fruit of the lack of close liaison and staff planning between the army and the air forces. The Canadians declared that the bombing disaster had a severe effect upon the morale and determination of the troops embarking upon TRACTABLE.

On 15 August, the renewed advance still made poor progress. 4th Armoured Brigade's chaotic operations broke down after their leading units met a German anti-tank screen. 3rd Canadian Division made some headway, but lost the village of Soulangy to a counter-attack. That evening, 2nd Division reached positions a mile from the edge of Falaise only after the Germans had disengaged and pulled back in front of them. The Canadian and Polish armoured divisions were now ordered to push south-eastwards for Trun, hooking beyond the original "Falaise gap". Meanwhile, 2nd Infantry Division drove on into the shattered town, which they cleared only on the 17th. Some 50 Hitler Jugend fought to the last in the *Ecole Supérieure*. Only four were reported to have escaped from the blazing building. Two, chosen by lot from among the defenders, had slipped out the previous night to report the situation to Meyer. None surrendered. In many parts of the town, surrounded by rubble, the Canadians found it difficult to judge where the streets had run. It was hours before the bulldozers could clear a path for vehicles.

It was now, for the first time, that large elements of the German army began to retire eastwards out of the shrinking pocket. On the 16th, von Kluge at last issued the order for a full-scale retreat. It was his last act as Commander-in-Chief, almost the last of his life. On the 15th, his car had been shot up by Allied fighter-bombers, his wireless destroyed, and he was cut off from all contact with OKW or with his own forces for some hours. Hitler was convinced, fallaciously, that during his absence the Field-Marshal had been attempting to open negotiations with the Allies. At midday on the 16th, von Kluge declined to execute an order from OKW for a counter-attack, which he declared was utterly impossible. Although a withdrawal was at last authorized by order of the Führer later that afternoon, on the evening of the 17th von Kluge was relieved. On his way back to Germany to explain himself to Hitler, he killed himself. He left behind an extraordinary letter affirming his undying devotion to the Führer, a final testimony to the German officer corps' obsession with loyalty, its utter inability to grapple with any greater issues of morality, humanity, or the historic interests of the German people. Suicide, for an astonishing procession of German senior officers who failed in Normandy, became the final expression of their own retreat from reason. Von Kluge was succeeded by Field-Marshal Walter Model. The supply of senior officers willing to attempt to implement their master's deranged will seemed limitless. Model's first act was to order the immediate escape of Seventh Army and Panzer Group Eberbach, while II SS Panzer Corps (the ruins of 2nd SS, 9th SS, 12th SS and 21st Panzer) held the north against the British and Canadians, and XLVII Panzer Corps (2nd and 116th Panzer) the south against the Americans.

For the Allies, time had now become the critical factor in blocking the German army's escape. Yet while the Americans stood at

Argentan, the Canadian armour edged south towards Trun with agonizing sluggishness. Their 4th Division reach Louvières, two miles north of the village, on the evening of the 17th after delays caused as much by traffic problems in narrow village streets and at little rustic stone bridges across trickling streams, as by enemy action. At 2.45 p.m. that day, Montgomery himself telephoned Crerar's Chief of Staff to press the urgency of the situation upon him: "It is absolutely essential that both the Armoured Divs of 2 Cdn Corps close the gap between First Cdn Army and Third U.S. Army. I Polish Armoured Div must thrust on past Trun to Chambois at all costs, and as quickly as possible."[9]

Yet the Poles, too, were slow to move. Their 2nd Armoured Regiment was ordered on the evening of the 17th to push immediately for Chambois, but instead departed only early on the 18th for Les Champeaux, possibly as a result of a misunderstanding with their local French guide, who shortly afterwards disappeared. The gap through which German vehicles and infantry were pouring in headlong retreat had now narrowed to a few thousand yards. Yet the principal labour of destroying the forces within it was being borne by the Allied air force. The fighter-bombers, flying 2–3,000 sorties a day throughout this period, inflicted massive losses. There were still serious problems with identification of ground troops. The British 51st Highland Division reported 40 separate incidents of accidental air attack for 18 August alone, costing its units 51 casualties and 25 vehicles. The Poles, who had lost scores of men in the "short bombing" of the 8th and 14th, the same day lost half their petrol supplies to Allied air attack.

On the morning of the 19th, Simonds spoke personally to his four divisional commanders at the headquarters of the 4th east of Morteaux-Couliboeuf. He emphasized that their objective was to ensure that no Germans escaped from the pocket. There was fierce fighting that day in the village of St Lambert, where two Canadian infantry companies fought all morning to gain a foothold in the village, then found themselves unable to go further. They dug in, and for the rest of the day fought off successive counter-attacks as German troops struggled to hold open the road east. Extraordinary sacrificial efforts by Meindl's survivors of 3rd Parachute Division defended the path east for thousands of their comrades. Canadian units blocked enemy attempts to escape through Trun. Artillery forward observers on the high ground overlooking the gap were calling down massive fire upon

The German *Nebelwerfer* multi-barrelled mortar was one of the most formidable weapons in Normandy, the object of bitter hatred and cause of a remarkable proportion of casualties among Allied troops – some estimates attributed 75 per cent of infantry losses to German mortaring, even if many of the wounds were slight. In the last phase of the war, the Germans concentrated more and more attention upon the massed use of mortars in preference to artillery, and the *Nebelwerfer* – or "moaning minnie" as the Allies called it – proved outstandingly useful in generating defensive fire when the shortage of German infantry and guns had become a chronic problem.

every column of vehicles and infantry on the roads and in the fields. The evening, Polish and American units met in Chambois.

Yet still the gap was not closed. Both the Poles and the Canadian 4th Armoured were under ferocious pressure from elements of 2nd SS Panzer, fighting westwards to hold open the retreat of Seventh Army. 1,500 Poles and 80 tanks were cut off from their lines of communication, unable to evacuate their wounded, perilously short of fuel and ammunition. Their battle was fought out with a fury uncommon even by the standards of Normandy. Poles and Germans detested each other with real passion, and each believed that they had much to avenge, the Poles with better reason. Now, from the heights of Mont Ormel, their tank machine-gunners raking the Germans below them, they called down artillery fire on every passing column of vehicles. From their wooded ridge, they could view the battle-field for miles. Meanwhile, the Canadian 4th Armoured Division's war diary recorded: "Due to the heavy fighting, Germans attacking from both the east and the west and the numerous calls made on the div to seal off any German escape routes, the units are all mixed up and it is difficult to define any particular brigade areas."[10] The Canadians merely poured fire into German elements wherever they encountered them. "Until about 0800," (on the 21st) wrote an officer of the Cameron Highlanders of Ottawa, "the machine-gunners fired at whatever they could see. During this time a host of white flags appeared and hundreds of the enemy crowded in to surrender. Many others were unable to give up, for every move towards our lines brought bursts of fire from certain SS troops patrolling the low ground behind them in an armoured half-track."[11] Corporal Dick Raymond, one of the Camerons' Vickers gunners, said: "It was the first time we had ever seen the German army out in the open. We would see a group trying to run across a field from one wood to another, and watch some fall, some run on, some lie moaning in front of us. It was more of an execution than a battle. I remember feeling puzzled that it didn't upset me more."

Yet the pocket at Falaise was being closed too late to prevent the escape of a formidable cadre of the German army, including some of its most skilled and dedicated officers, who lived to lead men through many more battles. It was only the most determined who still possessed the will to try the gap. Few, even within the Canadians' own ranks, disputed that the principal cause of this Allied failure was the feeble performance of First Canadian Army. Characteristically, the British official history describes the advance to Falaise in terms of hard fighting, "a gruelling day for the Canadians . . . Germans fighting strongly . . . dogged resistance." All this is perfectly true, but it evades the central fact that the ragged remains of two German divisions and a handful of tanks held all Crerar's army for 13 days, from the opening of TOTALIZE to the closing of the gap at Chambois, a distance of barely 30 miles. The Canadian official historian is far more frank than his British counterpart: "A German force far smaller than our own, taking advantage of strong ground and prepared positions, was able to slow our advance to the point where considerable German forces made their escape."[12] General Foulkes of the Canadian 2nd Division said: "When we went into battle at Falaise and Caen, we found that when we bumped into battle-experienced German troops, we were no match for them. We would not have been successful had it not been for our air and artillery support."[13] The Canadians had already recognized their difficulties by replacing a long succession of officers commanding brigades and battalions since 6 June. On 21 August, Crerar sacked the commander of his 4th Armoured Division, Major-General Kitching, a ritual sacrifice to his formation's failure.

The focus of the struggle now concentrated upon a few square miles of fields and little villages in which the wreckage of a half-million-strong army was fighting for survival. Command and control by signal had been almost entirely lost. Such direction as existed was provided by German officers to whatever men they chanced to find around them. Blackened vehicles, blackened corpses, blackened buildings and hedgerows scarred every acre over which the fighter-bombers had passed. The wounded were merely gathered where they might be tended by their captors when the Allies reached them – there were no more drugs and few enough doctors. Men ate what they could find in shattered vehicles or farmhouses – every surviving building was crowded with stragglers hunting food or seeking shelter from the shelling and bombing, or merely rest from the interminable march among the dead. The Allied cordon was a swollen, bulging sac against the walls of which thousands of men were pressing and forcing their bodies in a hundred places, seeking escape and often dying to find it. Amongst a vast mass of despondent Germans who sought only to surrender, there were still some thousands who fought at Falaise with desperate courage, hurling themselves again and again against Allied positions despite ferocious artillery fire and concentrated machine-guns.

Montgomery issued a directive on 20 August urging his forces to greater efforts: "There is no time to relax, or to sit back and congratulate ourselves. I call on all commanders for a great effort. Let us finish the business in record time . . . The first task of Canadian army is to keep the Normandy 'bottle' securely corked."[14] On the 22nd, it was concluded that all significant German forces west of the Allied lines were dead or in captivity. The "cork", it was concluded, could be removed from the empty bottle. The Allied armies could make free with the ruins of St Lambert and Coudehard, Chambois and Trun, the ghastly killing ground of the Falaise Gap.

12 The Gap

Some men had already been fortunate enough to achieve their *Heim ins Reich* before the collapse in Normandy came. Corporal Schickner of 2nd Panzer was in hospital in Germany recovering from a head wound inflicted by an American sniper in July. Lieutenant Schaaf and his gunners of the 1716th Artillery had been sent back to re-equip with new guns when those which they had fired since 6 June were worn out from ceaseless use. Corporal Kortenhaus of 21st Panzer was still in hospital after catching his foot in his tank track. Captain Wagemann of 21st Panzer staff had been posted back to Germany at the end of July. But the mass of the German army in Normandy remained, to endure one of the great nightmares of military history in the Falaise Gap. Pounded by shells from north and south and fighter-bomber strikes from first light to dusk, the long columns of men, horse-drawn carts and the few surviving tanks and vehicles struggled slowly eastwards, past their unburied dead by the roads and in the fields, the stinking carcasses of countless hundreds of horses and cattle, the ruins of Panthers and half-tracks, field cars and trucks, the last hopes of Hitler's armies in France.

20 August was a beautiful summer's day. To the straggling clusters and columns of Germans moving painfully eastwards, the weather mocked them as shells searched the roads and tracks, and tore open the meadows in which so many sought safety. The detested Piper Cubs droned busily overhead, directing their destruction. Colonel Heinz-Gunther Guderian sent two officers forward to St Lambert to reconnoitre a route for the vestiges of his division. With the coming of darkness, at the head of a column of 300 men, 50 vehicles and a battery of guns, they edged cautiously forward beneath the Allied positions, moving 100 yards at a time, then halting in silence to listen, then slipping forward again. At last, after hours of desperate tension, they met panzergrenadiers of 2nd SS Panzer holding the eastern line. Guderian and his men sank wearily into sleep by the roadside,

and slept all through the day that followed. Yet his glimpse of safety was illusory. The next morning, he was ordered to take the remnants of the formation south, to stiffen the tenuous line against American pressure. On the road in his Volkswagen field car, he was caught by an Allied fighter-bomber diving out of the sun. Guderian, hit in the shoulder, was still in the vehicle when the petrol tank exploded. He never fought again in France.

Lieutenant Walter Kruger, signals officer of 12th SS Panzer, was wounded by shrapnel as he sat in his truck in a great unmoving press of transport on the Falaise road. "Then I saw that the whole column was on fire. Everybody was running." He walked for three days, then sat by the roadside near Breteuil among the endless lines of filthy, bloody, exhausted men passing east, looking for survivors of his own unit and collecting them to continue the retreat. His divisional commander, Kurt "Panzer" Meyer, outstanding combat commander and fanatical Nazi, escaped according to his own account "guided by a French civilian". It is not difficult to picture the means of persuasion Meyer brought to bear. Yet even the iron Meyer described later how he climbed out of his vehicle amid the shambles of the Gap, "my knees trembling, the sweat pouring down my face, my clothes soaked in perspiration."[1] He and his men represented, at one level, the utmost perversion of national socialism. Yet at another, they command reluctant respect. No formation caused the Allies such deep trouble in Normandy until the end as 12th SS Panzer.

Sergeant Hans Stober of 17th SS Panzergrenadiers encountered no difficulties driving east until he and his handful of surviving men reached the Dives. There they became entangled in the chaos of the retreat. By ruthless determination they forced a way through and found a track north of Mont Ormel that remained open, and slipped past the silent Canadian army positions in darkness, with the men and even a few vehicles. "The Poles never closed that pocket for anybody who really wanted to get through," claimed Stober scornfully. Eventually they reached a reporting station near Paris, which had been set up to gather and reorganize men arriving from the west. Ten days after passing Mont Ormel they reached the Saar area, where they spent three days resting and regrouping. Then they were sent back into action with the remains of 116th Panzer in *Kampfen-gruppe Fick*.

General Eugene Meindl of II Parachute Corps spent two

hours hidden beneath a wrecked Polish Sherman within yards of the Allied lines, waiting for a moment to make his escape from the pocket. Like so many men in those days of turmoil, he had a succession of extraordinary personal encounters: with his own son; with a general named Eric Straube whom he was disgusted to find bivouacked in comfort with his staff, well supplied with food and wine; with a corps commander whom he did not identify, sitting weeping alone by the roadside. Meindl finally fought his way out at the head of a few score paratroopers and three tanks of 2nd SS Panzer.[2] General Hausser of Seventh Army was wounded by shrapnel as he marched amongst his men, and was carried out upon the back of a tank of 1st SS Panzer.

Lieutenant Fritz Langangke of 2nd SS Panzer had been driving since the beginning of August in a hastily-repaired tank with chronic overheating problems. Its collapse on the start-line for the Mortain counter-attack probably saved his life, and the same Panther carried him eastwards as the line crumbled, sustained by petrol drained into a canvas bucket from abandoned vehicles. In the final days of the pocket, the Panther's engine caught fire for the last time. The crew blew it up and started walking: "We just kept going along with the rest of the German army." They rejoined the remains of the division around Mont Ormel, finding their tank regiment now under the command of Major Enzerling. Their old commander, the bullet-headed Colonel Tyschen, an officer in the mould of "Panzer" Meyer, had died in the Mortain battle. The spirit of absolute doom was abroad. Enzerling solemnly visited his tank crews to say farewell to each man personally. Just west of the Seine, they were finally compelled to abandon all their vehicles, and each man to seek salvation as best he might. Langangke and eight others reached the river at Elbeuf to find French resistants already all over the town, waving tricolours and shooting at German stragglers. The lieutenant and his group hid in a house, considering their next move. There was no choice open to them save to cross the river. Neither his gunner nor his loader could swim, but they had to try. They drowned. Langangke himself reached the eastern bank clinging to the bloated body of a dead cow which was floating downriver amidst a host of other hapless animals and debris from the battlefield. He rejoined his unit at Huy-on-the-Maas, whence they were withdrawn to retrain and re-equip.

The SS and those men of the German army still determined to fight on were enraged by the wholesale collapse of will that they

The Hawker Typhoon – the 'Tiffy' to all its pilots – was a big, heavy, rugged fighter-bomber which bore the brunt of the RAF's low-level ground-attack tasks over Normandy, carrying eight 50-pound rockets or 2,000 rounds of bombs. Handling a rocket-equipped Typhoon was a delicate art, since the rails reduced its speed and affected its handling. It was necessary to attack either at very low level – risking heavy punishment from ground fire – or almost vertically, as most pilots preferred. Typhoons were the principal destructors of the retreating German army at Falaise, and became legendary in the last nine months of the war for their effectiveness in the "cab rank" role, circling over advancing troops until directed onto a target by a forward air controller.

saw around them in those days. Lieutenant Ernst Krag of 2nd SS Panzer's assault gun battalion came upon a group of Wehrmacht armoured crews intent upon blowing up a company of new Panthers which they had just brought forward from Germany as replacements. The furious Krag ordered them to hand over the tanks intact to his own men, and they salvaged five. "What do you do," he demanded bitterly, "if even your commanders have begun to work according to the principle of *Heim ins Reich*?" Colonel Kurt Kauffmann, the operations officer of Panzer Lehr, who had contributed so much to the recapture of Villers-Bocage in June, walked out of the pocket in the clothes he stood up in, the entire divisional headquarters and its documents having been lost in the American breakthrough. He was posted to the eastern front for speaking openly about the hopelessness of the military situation.

Corporal Adolf Hohenstein of 276th Infantry marched eastward out of the pocket with a handful of men, having lost all contact with his unit. A general passed along the column of slow-moving soldiers, telling them that it was every man for himself – they were now encircled. Hohenstein said that this did not trouble him as much as it might, "for in Russia we had been surrounded again and again." He was one of the few who had escaped from the Sixth Army's disaster at Stalingrad, clinging to the hull of a tank. Now they came upon a château, where they paused to gaze sadly upon the wonderful library, torn open to the elements by shellfire. Around noon on 20 August, they were lying in a field wondering desperately how to cross the flat ground ahead, littered with dead horses, burning vehicles, wounded men, and still under furious shellfire. Suddenly the firing stopped. There was a rumour, probably unfounded, that a local truce had been declared while a German hospital was handed over to the Allies. They seized their moment, and hastened through the smoking chaos, wading the Dives to reach St Lambert. Many men, said Hohenstein, were no longer seeking to escape, but merely lingering in the hope of making a safe surrender. The houses of St Lambert were crowded with Wehrmacht fugitives who had abandoned their weapons and clutched only sheets to assist their efforts to give themselves up. Men said that it was no longer possible to get through to the east.

In the church, Hohenstein found scores of wounded being treated with such pathetic resources as the doctors still possessed, and a cluster of generals. The corporal met a colonel who said that he was going to take a tank through, and if the soldier wished, he could follow with his men. That night, when darkness came, they fell in behind the tank, moving eastwards. But they were deeply uneasy, travelling with the squealing monster that now seemed more a source of danger than security. They decided to separate from it and make their way alone. It started to rain, and the corporal had only a feeble torch to check their bearings. At 5.00 a.m. on the 21st, they approached the village of Coudehard, its houses burning quietly in the early morning light. They heard voices. They strained to discover from the shelter of the trees to which army the men belonged. At last they moved cautiously forward until an unmistakably German accent called "Halt!" They had reached the lines of 10th SS Panzer.

They struggled on eastwards in the days that followed, hastening to remain ahead of the Allies. In the little village of Le Sap near Vimoutiers, they found the entire population gathered around tables laid out with food and wine to greet their liberators. The exhausted, desperate Germans seized what provisions they could carry. Wary of a sudden attack by local *résistants*, Hohenstein told the frightened Frenchmen: "Me and my men just want to get through here in one piece. In a few hours you'll have a chance to find out if the other army treats you any better than ours." They marched the mayor and the curé at pistol point in front of them through the town until they were safe on the road beyond. On 25 August, they crossed the Seine at Elbeuf, sitting on a tank which was carried across on the sole surviving ferry, already under artillery fire. "After Normandy," said Hohenstein, "we had no illusions any more. We knew that we stood with our backs to the wall."

As the first Allied forces moved into the pocket, gathering up prisoners in their thousands, they were awed by the spectacle that they discovered:

The roads were choked with wreckage and the swollen bodies of men and horses [wrote Group-Captain Desmond Scott]. Bits of uniform were plastered to shattered tanks and trucks and human remains hung in grotesque shapes on the blackened hedgerows. Corpses lay in pools of dried blood, staring into space and as if their eyes were being forced from their sockets. Two grey-clad bodies. both minus their legs, leaned against a clay bank as if in prayer. I stumbled over a typewriter. Paper was scattered around where several mailbags had exploded. I picked up a photograph of a smiling young German recruit standing between his parents, two solemn peasants who stared back at me in accusation . . . Strangely enough it was the fate of the horses that upset me most. Harnessed as they were, it had been impossible for them to escape, and they lay dead in tangled heaps, their large wide eyes crying out to me in anguish. It was a sight that pierced the soul, and I felt as if my heart would burst. We did not linger, but hurried back to the sanctity of our busy airfield near Bayeux.[3]

Men moved among the bloated bodies firing bursts of sten-gun rounds to empty them of their ghastly gasses before they were burned. "Falaise was not the most frightening sight, but the most disgusting of the war," said Private Alfred Lee of the Middlesex Regiment. "The bodies crawled with blue-grey maggots. The spectacle was unspeakable when tanks drove over them. Many men had to put on their gas masks to endure getting through it." With the great burden of fear lifted from them, French civilians began to show much greater warmth and kindness to their deliverers. Trooper Dyson of the RAC, collecting replacement tanks from a depot near Villers-Bocage, was wined and dined with his mate by a French family: "They treated us like kings.

That village made us feel that we had liberated France all on our own." The last shell fell on Caen as late as 17 August. Nicole Ferté, having endured weeks as a refugee in a convent crowded with terrified and wounded civilians, had at last been forced out into countryside along with thousands of others late in July. She was living with a group of 30 in a barn, and was out scavenging for food one morning when she saw American tanks rolling down the road towards her. A GI sitting on the hull of the leading Sherman leapt down and kissed her, declaring in one of the phrases that the period of Liberation made immortal: "You look just like my girlfriend!" Ironically, on that very day of liberation, the girl was wounded in the foot by shrapnel. But she recovered to work as interpreter to the Town Major of Caen, and to experience the extraordinary life of France amid the Allied armies that summer. She said sardonically: "All the Americans thought that everybody would go with them because they had the cigarettes, the stockings, the money." Many did.

In a village south of Caen, a platoon commander of 15th Scottish Division sat with his men in their trucks:

An enormous convoy crammed with dishevelled, dusty Wehrmacht prisoners rolls in the opposite direction: "The bastards!", wrenches out my truck driver with a sudden rush of feeling; while a great bearded Frenchman, like a ferocious dog, stands alone in the desolation of a village square, shaking his fist at the vast POW convoy and yelling after them as though his heart would break: "Kaput! . . . Kaput! . . ."[4]

Most Allied soldiers found that now, for the first time in the wake of their own crushing victory, they could spare pity for the defeated enemy. Trooper Dyson watched the lines of prisoners shuffling through the forward area, "some of them old men wearing overcoats down to their ankles." Like so many Allied soldiers, he took a German's belt for its eagle buckle, then felt ashamed because the man's trousers fell down. "I looked at them all, and somehow it seemed unbelievable that they were the Germans, the enemy – some mother's sons." Jerry Komareks's battalion of the U.S. 2nd Armored adopted a little blond 14-year-old Russian prisoner as a unit mascot. Pedro, as they called him, was given cut-down American fatigues and a pistol, then rode with them all the way to Berlin. There they were compelled to surrender him, crying bitterly, to the Russians. Presumably he was shot, like so many thousands of others turned over to the Red Army.[5]

It was only on 21 August that the Falaise Gap could properly be accounted closed, as tanks of the Canadian 4th Armoured Division linked with the Poles at Coudehard, and the Canadian 3rd and 4th Divisions secured St Lambert and the northern passage to Chambois. 344 tanks and self-propelled guns, 2,447 soft-skinned vehicles and 252 guns were counted abandoned or destroyed in the northern sector of the pocket alone. The battle for Normandy had cost the German army a total of 1,500 tanks, 3,500 guns and 20,000 vehicles. They had lost around 450,000 men, 240,000 of these killed or wounded. On 22/23 August, Army Group B reported the state of its eight surviving armoured divisions:

2 Pz: 1 infantry battalion, no tanks, no artillery
21 Pz: 4 weak infantry battalions, 10 tanks, artillery unknown
116 Pz: 1 infantry battalion, 12 tanks, approx. two artillery batteries
1st SS Pz: weak infantry elements, no tanks, no artillery
2nd SS Pz: 450 men, 15 tanks, 6 guns
9th SS Pz: 460 men, 20–25 tanks, 20 guns
10th SS Pz: 4 weak infantry battalions, no tanks, no artillery
12th SS Pz: 300 men, 10 tanks, no artillery.

Meyer's division alone had driven into Normandy with over 20,000 men and 150 tanks. Panzer Lehr had ceased to exist as a formation after COBRA, 9th Panzer was wiped out in the Mortain battle. Of the 100,000 men of First Army, facing the Bay of Biscay, who had been ordered to retire east, some 65,000 crossed the Seine, having lost most of their equipment. Only what was left of Fifteenth Army in the Pas de Calais, and Nineteenth Army, retiring north in the face of the American landings in the south of France which began on 15 August, still possessed any semblance of organization and cohesion. More than 40 German divisions had been destroyed. The Allies had achieved this at a cost of 209,672 casualties, 36,976 of these killed. British and Canadian losses amounted to two-thirds those suffered by the Americans. Some 28,000 Allied aircrew were also lost either over Normandy, during the vast campaign of preparatory bombing of communications and coastal installations, or the execution during 1943–44 of the POINTBLANK programme designed to pave the way for OVERLORD.

Few episodes in the Normandy campaign have provoked such a torrent of words since the war as the Allied failure to close the gap south of Falaise more speedily,[6] permitting the escape of a significant fragment of the German army which seemed doomed to absolute destruction, given the military situation around 7 August. Before considering the reasons for the Allied fumbling – if fumbling it was – it seems worth emphasizing that the portion of the German forces which got away was tiny by comparison with that which was destroyed. Only 24 tanks and 60 guns were ferried east across the Seine. Something over 20,000 Germans escaped the pocket, with only the clothes on their backs and personal weapons. Events around the Falaise Gap between the opening of TOTALIZE and 22 August became a source of anger and controversy much more because it appeared that Allied operations had been clumsily handled, than because any such failure cost Montgomery and Bradley important fruits of victory. The Americans were bitter because they considered that, once again, Montgomery had promised to achieve an objective on the battlefield, and failed: namely, to get the Canadians to Argentan before the Germans began to escape east. Montgomery himself implicitly acknowledged the importance of the Canadian failure to reach Falaise in time on 16 August, when he directed elements of the Canadian First Army to bend sharply south-east to Trun and Chambois, and asked Bradley to push American forces there to meet them. He hoped that by creating a wider noose the Germans could still be held within it.

A number of recent writers, including Martin Blumenson and Carlo D'Este, have noted the absurd over-simplification by critics who suggest that if Bradley's men had been set free to push north to Falaise, they would have closed the gap days earlier.[6] In reality, an American south-north line around 17 or 18 August would almost certainly have been broken by the Germans, fighting with the desperation they revealed everywhere at this period. The U.S. division which finally closed the gap at Chambois, the 90th, had shown itself to be one of the least effective formations among the Allied armies in Normandy. Meindl's paratroopers, and the survivors of 2nd SS and 12th SS Panzer, would almost certainly have cracked the 90th, inflicting an embarrassing and gratuitous setback upon the Americans. This prospect and danger must have occupied Bradley's thoughts when he declined to allow the move north, and declared that he preferred "the strong shoulder" at Argentan to "a broken neck at Falaise".[7] Bradley knew that the fleeing German army was already being devastated by air attack and pounded by artillery. His avowed reason for failing to close the gap – fear of a collision between the Allied armies – scarcely merits serious examination.

It seems far more probable that he saw a situation in which the enemy was being mauled almost to death without significant risk to the Allied armies; to slam the trap precipitately shut with ground forces and to close for a death-grapple with the desperate men fighting eastwards, offered a risk of humiliation which could not be justified by any possible tactical or strategic gain. If the man outside the thicket knows that the wounded tiger within it is bleeding to death, he would be foolish to step inside merely to hasten collection of the trophy. If this was indeed Bradley's reasoning, he was almost certainly correct.

Far too much of the controversy and criticism surrounding the Falaise Gap and other Normandy battles has focussed solely upon the generals, as if their making of a decision ensured its effective execution.[8] It seems equally important to consider whether a given option was feasible *within the limits of the capabilities of the forces concerned*. It has been the central theme of this book that the inescapable reality of the battle for Normandy was that when Allied troops met Germans on anything like equal terms, the Germans almost always prevailed. If the campaign is studied as an abstract military exercise, then all manner of possibilities become acceptable: the British could and should have got men into Caen on D-Day; they could and should have broken through at Villers-Bocage on 13 June; EPSOM and GOODWOOD should have led to decisive advances and the collapse of the German defences. As it happened, of course, nowhere did the Allies achieve decisive penetrations against high-quality German formations until these had been worn down by attrition and ruined by air attack. COBRA was a superb example of American dash and movement, but the vast American attacking force met only the shattered remains of Panzer Lehr and a few flanking battle-groups. Even these gave Collins' men a hard time on the first day. The British began to make significant ground gains in August only when the Germans in front of them were greatly outnumbered and reduced to a few score tanks and guns. It may be argued that any Allied attempt at envelopment before the German forces had been brought to the brink of destruction by attrition would have cost the attackers dear. A British or American breakthrough southwards in June might have been very heavily punished by German counter-attack.

It has become commonplace to assert that the Allies' basic difficulty was that they devoted too much thought and energy before the landings to the problems of getting ashore, not enough to what must happen thereafter. There is an element of truth in this, applicable to events on the afternoon of D-Day and on 7 and 8 June. Thereafter, however, the Allies' difficulties lay not in any lack of planning, but in the difference in fighting ability between the opposing forces on the battlefield.

The Allies in Normandy faced the finest fighting army of the war, one of the greatest that the world has ever seen. This is a simple truth that some soldiers and writers have been reluctant to acknowledge, partly for reasons of nationalistic pride, partly because it is a painful concession when the Wehrmacht and SS were fighting for one of the most obnoxious regimes of all time. The quality of the Germans' weapons – above all tanks – was of immense importance. Their tactics were masterly: stubborn defence; concentrated local firepower from mortars and machine-guns; quick counter-attacks to recover lost ground. Units often fought on even when cut off, which was not a mark of fanaticism, but of sound tactical discipline, when such resistance in the rear did much to reduce the momentum of Allied advances, as in GOODWOOD. German attacks were markedly less skilful, even clumsy. But they adapted at once to the need for infiltration in the *bocage*, a skill of which few Allied units proved capable, even at the end. Their junior leadership was much superior to that of the Americans, perhaps also to that of the British.

Few American infantry units arrived in Normandy with a grasp of basic tactics – a failure for which many men paid with their lives. The American airborne units showed what was possible on the battlefield, what the American soldier at his best could achieve. But only a handful of other formations proved capable of emulating the 82nd and 101st. The belief that firepower could ultimately save the infantry from the task of hard fighting underlay many difficulties and failures on the ground. It is interesting that Lieutenant Andrew Wilson, who fought as a British tank officer in north-west Europe and worked on occasion with American infantry, visited Vietnam a quarter of a century later as a correspondent, and noted the same carelessness on the battlefield that he had observed in 1944–45. Some more dedicated and skilful infantry fighting earlier in the Normandy campaign might, in the end, have saved a great many American lives. Both British and American commanders sometimes seemed to search for scapegoats rather than causes of poor performance by their men on the battlefield. Some of the generals sacked in Normandy (and elsewhere) were incompetent. But there was a limit to what a corps or divisional commander could achieve with the material he was given. It is striking that when Patton or Collins were given poor-qualitjy divisions with which to gain an objective, they could extract no better performance from these than less competent commanders. The same was true of the British 7th Armoured – none of its successive commanders in north-west Europe could make anything of it. The problems, where there were problems, often descended to regimental and battalion level. There were not nearly sufficient able field officers for any solution to be found in wholesale sackings.

The British were superior to the Americans in regimental leadership and staffwork. But they proved unable to generate the weight of fighting power – combat power, as the Americans call it – to smash through unweakened German defences. Germans who fought in the desert often expressed their surprise at the willingness of the British soldier to do what he believed was expected of him, and then to stop – even to surrender – when ammunition ran low, petrol ran out or he found himself encircled or deprived of officer leadership. Again and again in Normandy, British units fought superbly, with great bravery, only to lack the last ounce of drive or follow-through necessary to carry an objective or withstand a counter-attack. The inexperience of American, British and Canadian formations must be measured against the performance of 12th SS Panzer. This, too, was a "green" division, which had never fought a battle before 7 June. The Canadian official historian wrote: "One suspects that the Germans contrived to get more out of their training than we did. Perhaps their attitude towards such matters was less casual than ours."[9]

An ethos, a mood, pervades all armies at all times about what is and is not acceptable, what is expected. Within the Allied armies in Normandy in 1944–45, the ethos was that of men committed to doing an unwelcome but necessary job for the cause of democracy. The ethos of the German army, profoundly influenced by the threat from the east, was of a society fighting to the last to escape *götterdämmerung*. Lieutenant Langangke was perhaps not exaggerating when he said that as he sat in his Panther, knocking out Shermans one after the other, he felt like Siegfried. Mercifully for the future of western civilization, few men in the Allied armies ever believed for a moment that they were anyone other than Lindley Higgins from Riverdale in the Bronx, or Corporal Brown from Tonbridge. Montgomery wrote to Brooke from the desert: "The trouble with our British lads is that they are not killers by nature." Each man knew that he was a small cog in the great juggernaut of armed democracy, whose eventual victory was certain. Suicidal, sacrificial acts of courage were admired when performed by individuals and rewarded with decorations. But they were not *demanded* of whole Allied formations as they were of so many of Hitler's armies. Even Corporal Hohenstein of that very moderate organization, the 276th Infantry, never allowed himself to be troubled by encirclement because this was an experience that he, like so many others, had often overcome in Russia: they were merely expected to break out of it. The attitude of most Allied soldiers was much influenced by the belief, conscious or unconscious, that they possessed the means to dispense with anything resembling personal fanaticism on the battlefield: their huge weight of firepower. This view was not unjustified. Artillery and air power accomplished much of the killing of Germans that had to be done sooner or later to make a breakthrough possible. But it could not do all of this. It is not that the Allied armies in Normandy were seriously incompetent, merely that the margin of German professional superiority was sufficient to cause them very great difficulties.

All this Montgomery and Bradley understood perfectly well, and they shaped their plans and expectations accordingly. They had not been sent to Normandy to demonstrate the superiority of their fighting men to those of Hitler, but to win the war at tolerable cost – a subtly but importantly different objective. Their business and their difficulty, while acknowledging the difference in mood and spirit between their own soldiers and those of Hitler, was to persuade their armies to do enough – albeit, just enough – to prevail on a given battlefield and in a given action. This they were at last able to do, inflicting an absolute defeat upon their enemies. Overall, it may be said that Montgomery accomplished as much in Normandy as he could with the forces available to him. He is owed a greater debt for his performance than has been recognized in recent years, when his own untruths and boastfulness have been allowed to confuse the issue; and when the root problem of the limited abilities of his troops, and the dynamism of the Germans, has often been ignored.

Much of the criticism emanating from SHAEF, the airmen and Washington was based upon the inability of men lacking direct contact with the battlefield to grasp painful truths. The American and British public had been fed for years upon a necessary diet of propaganda about the superiority of their fighting men to those of the enemy. Even some senior service officers could not now understand the difficulty of fighting the German army. Brooke did, and his awareness lay at the heart of many of his fears about OVERLORD and about the course of the campaign on the continent. He was too big a man to continue to support Montgomery blindly, merely because the Commander-in-Chief of 21st Army Group was his protégé. He backed Montgomery and sympathized with his disappointments and failures because he understood, perhaps better than any man outside France, the difficulty of arranging matters so that British and American soldiers could defeat German soldiers on the ground. Brooke knew – as surely also did Montgomery in his secret thoughts – that it was the Allies' superiority of *matériel* that enabled them to prevail at the last, assisted by competent generalship and a solid performance by most of their men on the battlefield. Patton's headlong rush around western France was a far less impressive command achievement than the cool, professional response of Bradley and his corps commanders to the Mortain counter-attack. By that first week of August, the balance of psychological advantage had at last shifted decisively. The German thrust lacked conviction – even formations such as 2nd SS Panzer fought half-heartedly. Meanwhile, the Americans had gained a new confidence in their own powers Isolated infantry units held their ground; headquarters staffs kept their nerve; the American forces dispatched to meet the Germans – with the possible exception of the 35th Division, which seemed slow to achieve the relief of the 30th – drove hard and sure to throw back the panzers.

Normandy was a campaign which perfectly exemplified the strengths and weaknesses of the democracies. The invasion was a product of dazzling organization and staffwork, and marvellous technical ingenuity. Once the armies were ashore, there was no firework display of military brilliance. Instead, for the armies, there was a steady, sometimes clumsy learning process. Each operation profited from the mistakes of the last, used massed firepower to wear down the Germans, absorbed disappointments without trauma. This last was a true reflection of the nature of the struggle: most German commanders, amidst the insuperable difficulties of grappling both with Hitler and the Allies, declined towards a state bordering on hysteria. Among the Allied armies, however, there was sometimes gloom, but never real alarm or nervousness. These symptoms were more in evidence at SHAEF, where the role of impotent spectator taxed some men, even the highest, beyond endurance. Montgomery and Bradley and their staffs and corps commanders merely fought, reconsidered, and fought again until at last their resources granted them victory. Armchair strategists and military historians can find much to look back upon and criticize in Normandy. On 22 August 1944, it is doubtful whether many regrets troubled the Allied army commanders in France.

One lesson from the fighting in Normandy seems important for any future battle that the armies of democracy might be called upon to fight. If a Soviet invasion force swept across Europe from the east, it would be unhelpful if contemporary British or American soldiers were trained and conditioned to believe that the level of endurance and sacrifice displayed by the Allies in Normandy would suffice to defeat the invaders. For an example to follow in the event of a future European battle, it will be necessary to look to the German army; and to the extraordinary defence that its men conducted in Europe in the face of all the odds against them, and in spite of their own demented Führer.

Liddell Hart described Normandy as "an operation that eventually went according to plan, but not according to timetable."[10] A good case can be made that the Allies' disappointments and delays in gaining ground eventually worked to their advantage. Just as in Tunisia, more than a year earlier, Hitler's obsessive reinforcement of failure caused him to thrust division after division into the cauldron for destruction. By the time the breakout came, no significant forces lay in front of the Allies before the German border. Paris fell on 25 August, Patton crossed the Meuse on 31 August, and was at Metz on the Moselle the next day. The Guards Armoured Division reached Brussels on 3 September, after advancing 75 miles in a single day. 11th Armoured reached Antwerp on the 4th, to find the port intact.

On 1 September, Eisenhower assumed direct control of the Allied armies in the field – to Montgomery's bitter frustration, disappointment and chagrin. The Commander-in-Chief himself was the only man at 21st Army Group unable to understand the imperative by which American dominance among the armies demanded American command in the field. Williams and de Guingand attempted to explain this reality to him, and the fact that his loss of control was inevitable, "even if the Americans thought you the greatest general in the world – which they do not."[11]

At this juncture, there were perhaps 100 German tanks on the entire western front against over 2,000 in the Allied spearheads; 570 Luftwaffe aircraft against the Allies' 14,000. By yet another herculean feat of organization, Student mobilized 8,000 men of First Parachute Army to cover a 100-mile chasm in the front. The Allies paused to regroup and resolve their immense logistical problems. By mid-September, the German line was thickening everywhere. "I left France almost convinced that Germany was through and that the war would end in 1944," wrote Gavin of the 82nd Airborne. "But many in the division felt more cautious, since the fighting at times had proved to be far more difficult and costly than we had anticipated."[12] The battles in Holland and along the German border so often seem to belong to a different age from those of Normandy that it is startling to reflect that Arnhem was fought less than a month after Falaise; that within weeks of suffering one of the greatest catastrophes of modern war, the Germans found the strength to halt the drive of Horrocks' XXX Corps in its tracks, and to prolong the war until May 1945. But if this phenomenon reveals the same staggering qualities in Hitler's armies which had caused the Allies such grief in Normandy, it is also another story.

Notes and references

All quotations in the text based upon the author's interviews with individuals are given specific references on the subject's first mention, but not thereafter unless there are grounds for confusion between personal interview quotations and those not listed in the bibliography.

FOREWORD
1   *Lessons Of Normandy*, Liddell Hart; essay in LH papers, King's College, London

PROLOGUE
1   This narrative is based entirely upon an interview with Lt-Col. John Warner, 16.vi.83

CHAPTER 1
1   Fraser, *Alanbrooke*, p. 397
2   Bryant, *Triumph in the West,* p. 205
3   Howard, *Grand Strategy* vol. iv, p. 252
4   Harrison, *Cross Channel Attack*, p. 10
5   Ehrman, *Grand Strategy*, vol. v, p. 108
6   *ibid*, p. 109
7   *ibid*, p. 109 *et seq.*
8   U.S. CoS papers, ABC 384, Europe: 5.viii.43
9   Ehrman, *Grand Strategy*, p. 43
10 Portal Papers, Christchurch College, Oxford, File 2, 2g
11 Howard (op. cit.), p. 249
12 For instance, see Grigg, *1943: The Victory that Never Was*, Walter Scott Dunn, *Second Front Now – 1943*
13 See Nigel Nicolson, *Alexander*, p. 211
14 Bryant (op. cit.), p. 160
15 Public Record Office WO205/33
16 PRO WO205/2
17 *ibid*
18 *ibid*
19 PRO WO205/33
20 *ibid*
21 Fraser (op. cit.), p. 421
22 Eisenhower, diary

23 For an extreme example, see Irving, *The War Between The Generals* (London, 1981), which highlights the squabbles within the Allied high command and the personal vices of its commanders to a degree which obscures the extraordinary co-operation on the military issues that mattered.

24 Eisenhower, diary

CHAPTER 2

COMMANDERS

1 Omar Bradley, *A Soldier's Story*, p 171
2 *ibid*, p. 176
3 Interview with the author, vi.83
4 Ronald Lewin, *Wavell: The Chief* (London, 1980)
5 Russell Weigley, *Eisenhower's Lieutenants*, p. 37
6 Quoted in Hamilton, *Montgomery: Master of the Battlefield*, p. 513
7 Palmer, Wiley & Keast, *Procurement and Training of Ground Combat Troops*, p. 258
8 Ehrman, *Grand Strategy*, p. 50
9 PRO WO205/118
10 Williams, interview with the author, 14.vi.83
11 PRO WO205/118
12 *ibid*
13 Interview with the author
14 PRO WO232/1
15 Some special forces, above all the U.S. Rangers and the French SAS parachuted into Brittany, made a notable contribution on D-Day and in the weeks that followed. But their story has been repeated so often in earlier narratives of OVERLORD that it seems redundant to retrace the story in detail here.
16 Quoted in Hamilton (op. cit.), p. 562 *et seq.*
17 *ibid*
18 See Aron, *De Gaulle Before Paris*; François Kersaudy, *Churchill and De Gaulle* (London, 1981). None of the parties concerned emerge with great credit from the pre-D-Day struggle concerning the future administration of liberated France, the Americans showing extraordinary insensitivity by their determination to treat her as if she were bankrupt stock purchased in blood from some global liquidator, rather than one of the great nations of the world.

AIRMEN

1 Harris quoted in Hastings, *Bomber Command*, p. 257
2 Craven & Cate, *The U.S. Army Air Forces in World War II*, vol. ii, p. 735
3 Hastings (op. cit.), p. 275
4 Carl F. Spaatz, diary, 21.i.44, in Spaatz papers, Box 15, Library of Congress

5   Spaatz papers, Box 14 (loc. cit.)
6   Quesada, interview with the author, 5.vii.83
7   *ibid*
8   Gavin, interview with the author, 8.vii.83
9   Vandenberg, diary, 24.iii.83, MS Division, Library of Congress
10 PRO WO216/139

INVADERS
1   Wilson, interview with the author, 20.vi.83
2   *ibid*
3   Gosling, interview with the author, 21.vi.83
4   Richardson, interview with the author, 21.vii.83
5   Priest, interview with the author (pseudonym at subject's request), 14.vi.83
6   Portway, interview with the author, 13.vii.83
7   Heal, interview with the author, 27.vi.83
8   Bramall, interview with the author, 28.vi.83
9   PRO WO216/101
10 Bach, interview with the author, 30.vi.83
11 Weigley, *Eisenhower's Lieutenants*, p.31
12 Patton, *War as I Knew it*, p.336
13 Butcher, diary, unexpurgated MS, Eisenhower Library
14 *et seq.* Higgins, interview with the author, 3.vii.83
15 *et seq.* Herman, interview with the author, 3.vii.83
16 Pre-war American tactical doctrine dictated that forces advance with the weight of their fighting power centred in valleys, their flanks on hilltops. This proved absurd in the face of German defenders who invariably concentrated their strength on available high ground.
17 Colacicco, interview with the author, 6.vii.83
18 Bradley (op. cit.), p.226–7
19 Marshall, on sacking corps commanders
20 Colacicco, interview with the author (loc. cit.)
21 Herman, interview with the author (loc. cit.)
22 Walsh, interview with the author, 1.vii.83
23 *et seq.* Raymond, interview with the author, 2.vii.83
24 Svboda, interview with the author, 3.vii.83
25 Papers of Admiral Allen G. Kirk, U.S. Navy Archives, Washington DC
26 Original letter in possession of Herman
27 Quoted in Hamilton (op. cit.), p.570
28 Bradley (op. cit.), p.223
29 *inter alia* Gavin, interview with the author (loc. cit.)
30 Bradley (op. cit.), p.209
31 *et seq.* Reisler, interview with the author, 5.vii.83

DEFENDERS

1   Warlimont, *Inside Hitler's Headquarters*, p. 403
2   Ehrman (op. cit.), p. 108
3   *ibid*, p. 406–7
4   *ibid*
5   To the Dominions Secretary; *Churchill*, vol. v (op. cit.), p. 602
6   Cruickshank, *Deception in World War II*, p. 186
7   German forecasting was drastically impeded by the loss of their outlying weather stations. Their blindness in meteorology, as in military intelligence, contributed directly to the German high command's unpreparedness on D-Day. Where Group-Captain Stagg and his colleagues had predicted the "window" of reasonable weather which would follow the poor conditions prevailing in the Channel on 5 June, their German counterparts had not.
8   In the British press, drawing entirely unwarranted conclusions from material contained in West, *MI6: British Secret Intelligence Service Operations 1909–45*.
9   To the author, 25.ix.83
10 Most sensationally, Irving, *The Trail Of The Fox*; Cave-Brown, *Bodyguard Of Lies*
11 Cruickshank (op. cit.), p. 213
12 To the author, 14.vi.83
13 Irving, *Trail Of The Fox*, p. 320
14 Interview with the author, 3.v.83
15 Schaaf, interview with the author, 4.v.83
16 *ibid*
17 Interview with the author, 2.v.83
18 Guderian, *Panzer Leader*, p. 332
19 Interview with the author, 6.v.83

CHAPTER 3

OVERTURE

1   Quoted in Harrison, *Cross Channel Attack*, p. 274
2   Combat narrative from Cota papers in Eisenhower Library
3   Letter to the author, 16.iii.82
4   This, and all subsequent F. O. Richardson quotations, from unpublished narrative loaned to the author, or interview of 2.vii.83
5   Quoted in Hamilton, *Montgomery: Master of the Battlefield*, p. 561
6   See note 7 to Chapter 2, DEFENDERS
7   For instance, Cooper, *The German Army: Its Political and Military Failure 1933–45*, p. 502
8   Interview with the author, 6.viii.83
9   Gosset & Lecomte, *Caen Pendant La Bataille*, p. 26
10 Extract loaned to the author
11 Barrett, privately printed narrative on *The First Ship Sunk On D-Day*, loaned to the author

12 *ibid*
13 Diary loaned to the author
14 Williams, interview with the author (loc. cit.)
15 Fraser, *Alanbrooke*, p. 423
16 Interview with the author, 4.vii.83

THE AMERICAN BEACHES

1 Quoted in Carell, *Invasion – They're Coming*, p. 49 *et seq.*
2 *ibid*, p. 80 *et seq.*
3 Bradley (op. cit.), p. 270
4 *ibid*
5 Interview with the author, 3.vii.83
6 Interview with the author, 1.vii.83
7 Letter to the author
8 Rehm, interview with the author, 3.vii.83
9 Cota papers, combat narrative (op. cit.)
10 *ibid*
11 For example, see Wilmot, *Struggle for Europe*; Howarth, *Dawn of D-Day*
12 Wilmot, *Struggle for Europe*, p. 253 *et seq.*

THE BRITISH BEACHES

1 Unpublished narrative loaned to the author
2 Unpublished narrative loaned to the author

INLAND

1 Warlimont, *Inside Hitler's Headquarters*, p. 431
2 Narrative published in the regimental magazine of the King's Own Shropshire Light Infantry
3 I Corps operational order in PRO WO171/258
4 Carell (op. cit.), p. 106
5 Diary loaned to the author
6 Bradley, *A General's Life*, p. 253
7 Craven & Cate, *The U.S. Army Air Forces in World War II*, vol. iii, p. 181

CHAPTER 4

CLOSING THE LINES

1 Quoted in Brett-Smith, *Hitler's Generals*, p. 162
2 Schaaf, interview with the author (loc. cit.)
3 Stacey, *The Victory Campaign*, vol. iii, p. 133
4 *ibid*, p. 137
5 Raymond, interview with the author, 30.vi.83
6 Hamilton, *Montgomery: Master of the Battlefield*, p. 631
7 *ibid*, p. 596
8 Williams, interview with the author (loc. cit.)
9 Wilson, *Flamethrower*, pp. 74–5

VILLERS-BOCAGE

1   Author's interview with 7th Armoured eye-witness
2   Fergusson, *The Black Watch and the King's Enemies*, p. 206
3   Salmud, *History of the 51st Highland Division* (Edinburgh, 1953), p. 144
4   Kortenhaus, interview with the author, 6.iv.83
5   Hamilton (op. cit.), p. 649
6   Carell (op. cit.), p. 169
7   Peter Roach, *The 8.15 To War* (London, 1982), p. 138–9
8   Lockwood, interview with the author, 9.xi.82
9   Carver, interview with the author, 22.vi.83
10 Dempsey, interview with Chester Wilmot, Liddell Hart papers, King's College, London

EPSOM

1   Woollcombe, *Lion Rampant*, p. 49
2   Bramall, interview with the author, 28.vi.83
3   Woollcombe (op. cit.), p. 60
4   Baker, unpublished narrative loaned to the author
5   Richardson, interview with the author, 21.vii.83
6   Dyson, interview with the author, 28.i.83
7   Wilson, interview with the author, 14.ii.83
8   Priest, interview with the author (loc. cit.)
9   Montgomery, interview with Wilmot, Liddell Hart papers, King's College, London
10 For instance, Hamilton (op. cit.)
11 *ibid*, p. 580
12 Quoted in Ellis, *Normandy*, p. 261
13 Leigh-Mallory, diary, PRO AIR 37
14 Brooke, diary, 31.iii.43; Bryant (op. cit.), p. 297
15 PRO CAB106/1092, 15.vii.44
16 Quoted in Hamilton (op. cit.), p. 714–5
17 War Office, *Current Reports From Overseas*, 8.vii.44, Staff College Library
18 *ibid*, no. 44
19 Interview with the author, 24.vi.83
20 PRO WO205/118
21 C-in-C's order quoted in *Current Reports from Overseas* (op. cit.)
22 *ibid*, no. 54
23 PRO WO208/3193
24 *Current Reports* (op. cit.), no. 58
25 PRO WO208/393. For a further fascinating, damning but unbiased view of British tactics and of the British army's general performance in Normandy, see the notes of Brigadier James Hargest, New Zealand observer with XXX Corps in PRO CAB 106/1060
26 Richardson, interview with the author (loc. cit.)
27 Grigg papers, Churchill College, Cambridge. The name of the com-

manding officer concerned is given in the document, but is omitted here to spare personal embarrassment.

28 *ibid*
29 *Lessons of Normandy*, Liddell Hart papers, King's College, London
30 Williams, interview with the author (loc. cit.)

CHAPTER 5

THE *BOCAGE*
1 Gavin, *On to Berlin*, p. 121
2 Bradley (op. cit.), p. 280
3 Cota papers, Combat narrative (loc. cit.)
4 Bradley (op. cit.), p. 295
5 *ibid*, p. 283
6 Richardson, narrative (loc. cit.)
7 *ibid*
8 Eichen, interview with the author, 7.vii.83
9 Cota (op. cit.)
10 *ibid*
11 Cota (loc. cit.)
12 Herman, unpublished narrative loaned to the author
13 *ibid*
14 Bryant, interview with the author, 9.vii.83
15 First Army diary, copy held in DDE Library
16 It is an apparent paradox that while all the combatants in Normandy agreed upon the prodigious scale of Allied resources, the Allied high command complained of constant difficulties with supplies, above all artillery ammunition. Many observers both at the time and since have suggested that the ammunition shortages could readily have been remedied had the vast shipments of rations, equipment, vehicles been moderated somewhat, especially on the American flank. But the scale of supplies provided for the Allied forces reflected a philosophy determined many months before D-Day.
17 Preston, interview with the author (loc. cit.)
18 Collins, *Lightning Joe*, p. 220
19 First Army diary

THE BATTLE FOR CHERBOURG
1 Carell, *Invasion – They're Coming*, p. 194
2 Herman, narrative (loc. cit.)
3 Bryant, interview with the author (loc. cit.)
4 Hughes, diary
5 Palmer, Wiley & Keast, *The Procurement and Training of Ground Combat Troops*, p. 1
6 First U.S. Army Report of Operations, p. 117
7 PRO WO205/401
8 PRO WO232/17

9   Gavin (op. cit.), p. 71
10 Interview with the author, iv.83
11 Gavin (op. cit.), p. 71
12 Weigley, *Eisenhower's Lieutenants*, p. 45

CHAPTER 6

SOLDIERS
1   PRO219/1908
2   Schickner, interview with the author, 3.iv.83
3   Harrison, *Cross Channel Attack*, p. 374
4   Kruger, interview with the author, 30.iv.83
5   PRO WO219/1908
6   Bradley (op. cit.), p. 292
7   Quoted in Irving, *Trail Of The Fox*, p. 340
8   *ibid*, p. 343
9   *ibid*
10 PRO WO205/1021 (Dietrich interrogation)
11 Kauffmann, interview with the author, 4.v.83
12 Irving (op. cit.), p. 346
13 *ibid*, p. 351
14 *ibid*, p. 353
15 *ibid*, p. 363–4
16 PRO WO205/1022 (von Rundstedt interrogation)
17 Irving (op. cit.), p. 74
18 Ruge, quoted in Irving (op. cit.), p.375
19 *ibid*
20 *ibid*, p. 376
21 Williams, interview with the author (loc. cit.)
22 Hellmuth Lang, interview with the author, 6.v.83
23 For instance, Cave Brown and Irving (op. cit.)
24 Kauffmann, interview with the author (loc. cit.)
25 Kruger, interview with the author (loc. cit.)
26 Guderian, interview with the author, 4.v.83
27 Williams, interview with the author (loc. cit.)
28 Quesada, interview with the author (loc. cit.)
29 PRO WO219/1908
30 Dupuy, *A Genius for War*, pp. 253–4
31 Bradley (op. cit.), p. 357

WEAPONS
1   PRO WO205/5b
2   Quoted in Hamilton, *Montgomery: Master of the Battlefield*, pp. 713–4
3   Kay Summersby, diary, 2.vii.83
4   Gavin, *On to Berlin*, p. 51
5   Discarding sabot was a formidable British innovation in armour-

piercing ammunition. The casing of the shell was shed after leaving the gun-barrel, and only a slender bolt of hardened steel continued to the target at very high velocity, generating unprecedented power of penetration. Discarding-sabot ammunition had been available for some time for 6-pounder guns, but became available for 17-pounders only in the summer of 1944. It has been one of the principal forms of anti-armour projectile ever since.

6 Wilson, *Flamethrower*, p. 54
7 Ross, *The Business of Tanks*, p. 153
8 *ibid*
9 *ibid*, p. 263
10 ORS reports nos. 12 & 17, Staff College Library
11 Ross (op. cit.), p. 275
12 Bradley (op. cit.), p. 320
13 *et seq*. Hansard
14 Ross (op. cit.), p. 316–17

CHAPTER 7

FROM THE BEACHHEAD TO THE FRONT

1 Letter loaned to the author by Mr James Verrier
2 See, for instance, Dunn, *Second Front Now*; Hartcup, *Code Name Mulberry*
3 *ibid*
4 See Fergusson, *The Watery Maze*
5 Patton, *War as I Knew It*, p. 101
6 Baldwin, MS (op. cit.)
7 Lee, interview with the author, 4.iii.83
8 Hein, interview with the author, 1.vii.83
9 Zimmer, diary from Hoover Institute, S644D/1.5.202
10 Gunther, interview (loc. cit.)
11 Gosset & Lecomte, *Caen Pendant la Bataille*, p. 51
12 Quesada, interview (loc. cit.)
13 Ratliff, interview with the author, 3.vii.83
14 Ivon-Jones, interview with the author, 4.ii.83
15 Sadi Schneid, *Beutesdeutscher*, p. 119
16 Wilson, interview (loc. cit.)
17 Whitelaw, interview with the author, 27.vii.83
18 Sir David Cole, *Rough Road to Rome* (London, 1982), p. 82
19 *Current Notes* (op. cit.), no. 44
20 Brown, interview with the author, 18.ii.83
21 Preston, interview (loc. cit.)
22 *Current Notes* (op. cit.) for 8.vii.44
23 Hansen, diary, U.S. Army Military History Institute
24 *Current Notes* (op. cit.), no. 54
25 Wilson, interview with the author (loc. cit.)

CASUALTIES

1   Brenda McBryde, *A Nurse's War* (London, 1979), p. 86–7
2   Copy loaned to the author
3   Wilson, *Flamethrower*, p. 70
4   Higgins, interview (loc. cit.)
5   Bramall, interview (loc. cit.)
6   Whitelaw, interview (loc. cit.)
7   Letter loaned to the author by Mr James Verrier
8   Wilson (op. cit.), p. 71

CHAPTER 8

THE FALL OF CAEN

1   Quoted in Wilmot, *The Struggle For Europe*, p. 338
2   Gosset & Lecomte, *Caen Pendant La Bataille*, p. 37
3   *ibid*
4   Portway. interview with the author, 16.v.83
5   DF: Defensive Fire – a standard gunnery technique whereby bat-
    teries designate certain likely lines of enemy attack by code
    numbers, and range in upon them in advance. Then, when an attack
    develops, men in the forward positions can summon immediate
    artillery support at a threatened point by radioing simply to the guns
    for "DF63" or "DF14", rather than having to waste precious
    minutes correcting the gunners' aim onto map coordinates from
    scratch.
6   Zimmer, diary (loc. cit.)
7   Stephens, unpublished MS loaned to author
8   Butcher, diary, DDE Library
9   *Eisenhower Papers*, vol. iii, p. 1982
10 Bryant (op. cit.), p. 229
11 Tedder, *With Prejudice*, p. 555
12 *Colliers' Magazine*, 5.x.46
13 Note of 18.iii.52 in Dempsey file, Liddell Hart papers (loc. cit.)
14 Bradley (op. cit.) p. 319

GOODWOOD

1   Montgomery to Brooke, M511
2   Quoted in Pogue, *The Supreme Command*, p. 188
3   Dempsey, notes in Liddell Hart papers, "The aims of Operation
    Goodwood"
4   Roberts, interview with the author, 17.vi.83
5   *ibid*
6   Brown, unpublished MS loaned to the author
7   Roach, *The 8.15 to War*, p. 144–6
8   Wyldbore-Smith, interview with the author, 13.vi.83
9   Richardson, interview with the author, 21.vii.83
10 Quoted in Ellis (op. cit.), pp. 344–5

11   Butcher, diary (op. cit.)
12   Most recently by Hamilton, *Montgomery: Master of the Battlefield*, and Carlo D'Este, *Decision in Normandy*
13   Richardson, interview with the author (loc. cit.)
14   *The Memoirs of Field-Marshal Lord Montgomery*, p. 257
15   *Eisenhower Papers* (op. cit.), p. 2018–9
16   Bradley, *A General's Life*, p. 274
17   *ibid*, p. 257
18   Bryant (op. cit.), p. 235
19   Carver, interview with the author (loc. cit.)
20   Butcher, diary, DDE Library
21   Bryant (op. cit.), p. 245

CHAPTER 9

COBRA
1   First Army diary, 7.vii.44
2   Bradley (op. cit.), p. 271
3   Gunther, interview with the author (loc. cit.)
4   Quesada, interview with the author (loc. cit.)
5   Blumenson, *The Patton Papers*, vol. ii, p. 521
6   First U.S. Army report (loc. cit.)
7   Interview with the author, 2.vii.83
8   First U.S. Army report (loc. cit.)
9   Bradley (op. cit.), p. 270
10   Bradley, *A Soldier's Story*, p. 226
11   Ascher, interview with the author, 5.vii.83
12   In a letter to the author, 3.viii.82
13   Hamilton (op. cit.), p. 650
14   Stimson papers, Yale University
15   This account is derived from information provided by another NCO of 102nd Cavalry Reconnaissance, Bill Walsh.
16   Contemporary narrative by Flint's executive officer, in DDE papers no. 84, Patton G. no. 2.
17   Carell, *Invasion – They're Coming*, p. 257 *et seq.*
18   *History of the 120th Infantry Regiment* by Officers of the Regiment (Washington Infantry Journal Press, 1947)
19   Eichen, interview with the author, 26.vi.83
20   Quoted in D. Bruce Lockerbie, *A Man Under Orders*, p. 79
21   First U.S. Army diary (loc. cit.)
22   *History of the 120th* (op. cit.), p. 133
23   Carell (op. cit.), p. 259
24   Stober, interview with the author, 6.v.83
25   Weigley, *Eisenhower's Lieutenants*, p. 157
26   Gunther, interview with the author (loc. cit.)
27   Reisler, interview with the author, 4.vii.83
28   Guderian, interview with the author (loc. cit.)

1 For instance, see Tedder, *With Prejudice*; Harris, *Bomber Offensive*; and the memoirs of other more junior air force officers who wrote in a fashion that suggested it was an indulgence on the part of their service to accept any responsibility for direct support of the armies
2 Vandenberg, diary, MS Division Library of Congress
3 Tedder (op. cit.), p. 559–60
4 *ibid*, p. 557
5 *ibid*, p. 557–8
6 *ibid*, p. 562
7 *ibid*, p. 565
8 PRO WO232/51
9 Quesada, interview with the author (loc. cit.)
10 Vandenberg, diary.(loc. cit.)
11 PRO WO232/51
12 Vandenberg, diary (loc. cit.)
13 Richardson, interview with the author (loc. cit.)
14 Bradley, *A Soldier's Story*, p. 249
15 Richardson, interview with the author (loc. cit.)
16 Bradley (op. cit.), p. 249
17 Account based upon Reisler interview (loc. cit.)
18 Scott, *Typhoon Pilot*, p. 120

CHAPTER 10
1 Liddell Hart papers, translations of Army Group B and C-in-C West reports, quoted in Cooper, *The German Army*, p. 507
2 Warlimont, *Inside Hitler's Headquarters*, p. 442
3 *ibid*, p. 445
4 *ibid*
5 *ibid*
6 *ibid*, p. 453
7 PRO WO219/1908
8 Among the strategic theories, most authoritatively from Basil Liddell Hart, but also from some serving U.S. commanders, such as John "P" Wood (see text below)
9 Hansen, diary, U.S. Army Military History Institute
10 Patton, *War as I Knew It*, p. 92
11 *ibid*, p. 382
12 A remark repeatedly made to me in interviews with veterans of the U.S. First Army of all ranks.
13 Bradley, *A General's Life*, p. 285
14 Frank Price, *Middleton* (Louisiana State University, 1974), p. 188
15 *ibid*
16 Blumenson, *Breakout and Pursuit*, p. 463
17 Bradley, *A Soldier's Story*, p. 367
18 Irving, *Hitler's War*, pp. 683–4

19 Carell, *Invasion – They're Coming*, p. 278
20 The above account is compiled from the *History of the 120th
    Infantry* (op. cit.), interview with Sidney Eichen (loc. cit.), First
    Army diary (op. cit.).
21 Quoted in Wilmot, *The Struggle for Europe*, p. 404
22 *ibid*, p. 416
23 Liddell Hart papers, translations of Army Group B reports (loc.
    cit.) quoted in Cooper, p. 510
24 Guderian, *Panzer Leader* (op. cit.), p. 445
25 Irving (op. cit.), p. 686
26 Warlimont (op. cit.), p. 451
27 Bradley (op. cit.), p. 376
28 Blumenson, *Patton Papers* (op. cit.), vol ii, p. 521
29 Baker MS (op. cit.)

CHAPTER 11
 1 Warner, interview with the author (loc. cit.)
 2 Richardson, interview with the author (loc. cit.)
 3 Signal M69, Montgomery papers, quoted in Hamilton, *Mont-
    gomery: Master of the Battlefield*, p. 768
 4 See How, *Normandy: The British Breakout*
 5 Letter to Brooke, 26.vii.83, quoted in Hamilton (op. cit.), p. 780
 6 Stacey, *The Canadian Army in World War II*, vol. iii, p. 275
 7 Hamilton (op. cit.), p. 779
 8 *ibid*
 9 Stacey (op. cit.), p. 252
10 *ibid*, p. 263
11 *ibid*
12 *ibid*, p. 276
13 *ibid*
14 *ibid*, p. 266

CHAPTER 12
 1 PRO WO205/1021 (Interrogation of Meyer)
 2 *ibid* (Interrogation of Meindl)
 3 Scott (op. cit.), p. 129
 4 Woollcombe (op. cit.), p. 107
 5 Komarek, unpublished MS loaned to the author
 6 For an extreme and extraordinary example of fanciful thinking
    about the failure wholly to destroy the German army at Falaise, see
    Richard Rohmer, *Patton's Gap* (London, 1981).
 7 Bradley (op. cit.), p. 337
 8 It is odd that while Chester Wilmot wrote with great frankness in
    1952 about the difficulties and shortcomings of the Allied armies in
    north-west Europe, in more recent years most narratives have
    focussed overwhelmingly upon the alleged virtues and vices of the
    commanders on both sides, and lapsed into comfortable platitudes

when discussing the relative fighting performance of the armies engaged.

9   Stacey, *The Canadian Army in World War II*, vol. iii, p. 275
10 Liddell Hart, *History of The Second World War*, p. 543
11 Williams, interview with the author (loc. cit.)
12 Gavin, *On to Berlin*, p. 121

Appendix I

Glossary

ADGB	Air Defence of Great Britain
ANVIL	Codename for the Allied invasion of southern France, later designated DRAGOON
AOC	Air Officer Commanding
AVRE	Armoured Vehicle Royal Engineers — Churchill tank mounted with Petard short-range heavy mortar, and various devices for bridging and ditching
BAR	Browning Automatic Rifle — American squad light machine-gun
Battalion	Basic infantry unit of 600–1,000 men in all armies in Normandy, sub-divided into four rifle companies and a support company of 100-plus men each, with organic anti-tank guns, heavy machine-guns and mortars. Companies were divided into platoons of three or four rifle squads, each commanded by a corporal — or an NCO in the Germany army.
Bazooka	American infantry anti-tank rocket-projector
BEF	British Expeditionary Force
BGS	Brigadier General Staff
Bren	.303 British squad light machine-gun
Brigade	British nomenclature for a formation normally composed of three infantry or tank battalions — roughly equivalent in strength to a German or American regiment
CC	Combat Command
CIGS	Chief of the Imperial General Staff
COBRA	American breakout operation, 25–29 July
Corps	A group of divisions assembled under the command of a lieutenant-general, their number and identity varying constantly according to the task for which the corps is being employed.
COSSAC	Chief of Staff to the Supreme Allied Commander
CP	Command post
CSM	Company Sergeant-Major
DCLI	Duke of Cornwall's Light Infantry
DD	Duplex-Drive amphibious Sherman tank
DF	Defensive fire

Division	The basic formation through which all armies are controlled, commanded by a major-general and comprising 12–18,000 men. A British armoured division in Normandy normally comprised two tank brigades, one infantry. The Americans preferred to divide the armoured division into two "Combat Commands" (CC), A and B, each in the hands of a brigadier-general.
DUKW	Duplex-Drive amphibious truck
EPSOM	2nd Army's attacks to the Orne and beyond, 26 June to 1 July
Flail	Tank mounted with chains on a revolving drum for minesweeping
FORTITUDE	Allied deception plan for OVERLORD
FUSAG	First U.S. Army Group — the fictitious army commanded by Patton, whose supposed threat to the Pas de Calais was central to FORTITUDE
GOODWOOD	British attack on the Bourgébus ridge, 18–21 July
GSO	General Staff Officer (grades I, II or III)
HE	High Explosive
Kangaroo	Canadian infantry armoured personnel carrier improvised from self-propelled gun mountings
KOSB	King's Own Scottish Borderers
KRRC	King's Royal Rifle Corps
KSLI	King's Own Shropshire Light Infantry
LCA	Landing Craft Assault
LCI	Landing Craft Infantry
LCT	Landing Craft Tank
LCVP	Landing Craft Vehicle and Personnel
LST	Landing Ship Tank
ML	Motor launch
NCO	Non-commissioned officer
NEPTUNE	Naval assault phase of OVERLORD
ODs	American army combat clothing
OKW	*Oberkommando der Wehrmacht* — high command of the German armed forces
OP	Observation post
OSS	Office of Strategic Services, the American wartime foreign intelligence service
Panzerfaust	German hand-held infantry anti-tank weapon
Petard	Short-range tank-mounted heavy mortar
PIAT	Projector Infantry Anti-Tank — British hand-held platoon anti-tank weapon
POINTBLANK	Pre-OVERLORD strategic bombing of Germany
Priest	British self-propelled mounting for 25-pounder
PT	Patrol Torpedo boat
RAC	Royal Armoured Corps

RAOC	Royal Army Ordnance Corps
Regiment	American or German equivalent of a British brigade, normally composed of three battalions, commanded by an American brigadier-general or German colonel
REME	Royal Electrical and Mechanical Engineers
ROUNDUP	Plan for an Allied invasion of Europe in 1943, superseded by OVERLORD
RTR	Royal Tank Regiment
SAS	Special Air Service
SHAEF	Supreme Headquarters Allied Expeditionary Force
SOE	Special Operations Executive
Spandau	Allied shorthand for German MG 34 or MG 42 machine-guns
TOT	Time On Target concentrated artillery, a speciality of American gunners, although practised by all armies
TOTALIZE	Canadian army attack towards Falaise, 8–11 August
TRACTABLE	Canadian attack towards Falaise, 14–16 August
Vickers	British .303 water-cooled heavy machine-gun — the infantry battalion support weapon

Appendix II

Chronology of the Normandy Campaign

13 MARCH 1943	Lt-Gen. F. E. Morgan appointed COSSAC — Chief of Staff to the Supreme Commander (designate)
23 JANUARY 1944	Eisenhower approves Montgomery's plan for the landings in Normandy
7—8 APRIL	Montgomery presents the OVERLORD plan at St Paul's, and presides over Exercise THUNDERCLAP with subordinate commanders
15 MAY	Montgomery's final presentation at St Paul's
3 JUNE	D-Day postponed from 5 June to 6 June
4 JUNE	D-Day ordered for 6 June
6 JUNE	Allied landings in Normandy
7 JUNE	Bayeux falls
8 JUNE	U.S. First and British Second Armies link near Port-en-Bessin
12 JUNE	Omaha and Utah beachheads united
13 JUNE	British 7th Armoured Division checked and repelled at Villers-Bocage
	Germans open V-I flying bomb offensive against Britain
18–21 JUNE	The "great storm" in the Channel
18 JUNE	U.S. VII Corps reach west coast Cherbourg peninsula at Barneville
19 JUNE	Americans take Montebourg
22 JUNE	Russians open their summer offensive against Army Group Centre with 146 infantry divisions and 43 tank brigades attacking on a 300-mile front
25 JUNE	British Operation EPSOM south-west of Caen
26 JUNE	Americans in Cherbourg
27 JUNE	Resistance in Cherbourg ends
29 JUNE	British break off EPSOM
1 JULY	Geyr von Schweppenburg sacked and replaced by Eberbach
	Americans secure Cap de la Hague
2 JULY	Von Rundstedt sacked and replaced by von Kluge
6 JULY	Flotilla of *biber* one-man submarines attack Allied shipping off the beachhead, sinking three minesweepers and damaging a Polish cruiser for the loss of seven German craft

8 JULY	British attack Caen, Americans seize La Haye-du-Puits
10 JULY	British occupy Caen
17 JULY	Rommel wounded and replaced as C-in-C Army Group B by von Kluge
18 JULY	British Operation GOODWOOD east of Caen
	Americans take St Lô
20 JULY	Hitler wounded by bomb at his headquarters, abortive conspiracy and its aftermath rocks the Third Reich
25 JULY	American Operation COBRA launched west of St Lô
30 JULY	British Operation BLUECOAT launched south-east of Caumont
	Americans "turn the corner" at Avranches
31 JULY	Russians within 10 miles of Warsaw. Uprising begins
1 AUGUST	Hodges assumes command U.S. First Army, Patton's Third Army activated, Bradley becomes C-in-C U.S. Twelfth Army Group
7 AUGUST	Germans launch Mortain counter-attack
	Canadian Operation TOTALIZE launched towards Falaise
10 AUGUST	TOTALIZE broken off
12 AUGUST	U.S. XV Corps takes Alençon
14 AUGUST	Canadian Operation TRACTABLE launched towards Falaise
	DRAGOON landings in southern France
17 AUGUST	Model assumes command German armies, orders full retreat east from Allied pocket
	Falaise falls
19 AUGUST	Polish Armoured Division and U.S. 90th Division reach Chambois
21 AUGUST	Falaise Gap closed
25 AUGUST	Paris falls
1 SEPTEMBER	Eisenhower assumes direct command Allied ground forces
	Montgomery promoted Field-Marshal
2 SEPTEMBER	U.S. First and Third Armies ordered to halt by Eisenhower in view of huge fuel and supply problems
3 SEPTEMBER	Brussels falls
16 SEPTEMBER	U.S. First Army units cross the German border near Aachen
17 SEPTEMBER	Operation Market Garden launched against Arnhem and the Maas and Waal bridges

Appendix III

PART A

Allied order of battle

SUPREME HEADQUARTERS ALLIED EXPEDITIONARY FORCE

Supreme Allied Commander
General Dwight D. Eisenhower

Chief of Staff
General Walter Bedell Smith

TWENTY–FIRST ARMY GROUP
General Sir Bernard L. Montgomery
Commander-in-Chief
Major-General Sir Francis W. de Guingand
Chief of Staff

G.H.Q. AND ARMY TROOPS

79th Armoured Division
Major-General Sir Percy C. S. Hobard

30th Armoured Brigade	*1st Tank Brigade*
22nd Dragoons	11th, 42nd and 49th Battalions
1st Lothians and Border Horse	R.T.R.
2nd County of London Yeomanry	
(Westminster Dragoons)	*1st Assault Brigade R.E.*
141st Regiment R.A.C.	5th, 6th and 42nd Assault
	Regiments R.E.

79th Armoured Divisional Signals
1st Canadian Armoured Personnel Carrier Regiment

4th Armoured Brigade
The Royal Scots Greys
3rd County of London Yeomanry (Sharpshooters) (to 28.7.44)
3rd/4th County of London Yeomanry (Sharpshooters) (from 29.7.44)
44th Battalion R.T.R.
2nd Battalion The King's Royal Rifle Corps (Motor)

8th Armoured Brigade
4th/7th Royal Dragoon Guards
24th Lancers (to 29.7.44)
The Nottinghamshire Yeomanry
13th/18th Royal Hussars (from 29.7.44)
12th Battalion The King's Royal Rifle Corps (Motor)

31st Tank Brigade
7th Battalion R.T.R. (to 17.8.44)
9th Battalion R.T.R. (to 31.8.44)
144th Regiment R.A.C. (23–31.8.44)

34th Tank Brigade
107th and 147th Regiments R.A.C.
153rd Regiment R.A.C. (to 24.8.44)

6th Guards Tank Brigade
4th Tank Battalion Grenadier Guards
4th Tank Battalion Coldstream Guards
3rd Tank Battalion Scots Guards

27th Armoured Brigade
(to 29.7.44)
13th/18th Royal Hussars
1st East Riding Yeomanry
The Staffordshire Yeomanry

33rd Armoured Brigade
1st Northamptonshire Yeomanry
144th Regiment R.A.C. (to 22.8.44)
148th Regiment R.A.C. (to 16.8.44)
1st East Riding Yeomanry (from 16.8.44)

2nd Canadian Armoured Brigade
6th Armoured Regiment (1st Hussars)
10th Armoured Regiment (The Fort Garry Horse)
27th Armoured Regiment (The Sherbrooke Fusiliers Regiment)

H.Q. Anti-Aircraft Brigades
74th, 76th, 80th, 100th, 101st, 105th, 106th and 107th

Heavy Anti-Aircraft Regiments
60th, 86th, 90th, 99th, 103rd, 105th, 107th, 108th, 109th, 112th, 113th, 115th, 116th, 121st, 146th, 165th and 174th; 2nd Canadian

Light Anti-Aircraft Regiments
20th, 27th, 32nd, 54th, 71st, 73rd, 93rd, 109th, 112th, 113th, 114th, 120th, 121st, 123rd, 124th, 125th, 126th, 127th, 133rd, 139th and 149th

Searchlight Regiments
41st

56th Infantry Brigade
(Became integral part of the 49th
Division from 20.8.44)
2nd Battalion The South Wales
Borderers
2nd Battalion The Gloucestershire
Regiment
2nd Battalion The Essex
Regiment

1st Special Service Brigade
Nos. 3, 4 and 6 Commandos
No. 45 (Royal Marine)
Commando

47th Special Service Brigade
Nos. 41, 46, 47 and 48 (Royal
Marine) Commandos

OTHER FORMATIONS AND UNITS

Armoured
G.H.Q. Liaison Regiment R.A.C.
('Phantom')
2nd Armoured Replacement
Group
2nd Armoured Delivery Regiment
25th Canadian Armoured
Delivery Regiment (The Elgin
Regiment)

Artillery
*H.Q. Army Groups Royal
Artillery:* 3rd, 4th, 5th, 8th and
9th; 2nd Canadian

Heavy Regiments: 1st, 51st,
52nd, 53rd and 59th

Medium Regiments: 7th, 9th,
10th, 11th, 13th, 15th, 53rd,
59th, 61st, 63rd, 64th, 65th,
67th, 68th, 72nd, 77th, 79th,
84th, 107th, 121st and 146th;
3rd, 4th and 7th Canadian

Field Regiments: 4th R.H.A.,
6th, 25th, 86th, 147th, 150th and
191st; 19th Canadian

Engineer
*H.Q. Army Groups Royal
Engineers:* 10th, 11th, 12th,
13th and 14th; 1st Canadian

G.H.Q. Troops Engineers: 4th,
7th, 8th, 13th, 15th, 18th, 48th
and 59th

Airfield Construction Groups:
13th, 16th, 23rd, 24th and 25th

Army Troops Engineers: 2nd,
6th and 7th; 1st and 2nd
Canadian
2nd and 3rd Battalions Royal
Canadian Engineers

Signal

Twenty-First Army Group Headquarters Signals
Second Army Headquarters Signals
First Canadian Army Headquarters Signals
Air Formation Signals, Nos. 11, 12, 13, 16, 17 and 18
1st Special Wireless Group

Infantry

4th Battalion The Royal Northumberland Fusiliers (Machine Gun)
First Canadian Army Headquarters Defence Battalion (Royal Montreal Regiment)

Royal Marine

Armoured Support Group: 1st and 2nd Royal Marine Armoured Support Regiments

Army Air Corps

Glider Pilot Regiment: 1st and 2nd Glider Pilot Wings

Special Air Service

1st and 2nd Special Air Service Regiments
3rd and 4th French Parachute Battalions

European Allies

1st Belgian Infantry Brigade
Royal Netherlands Brigade (Princess Irene's)

ARMIES, CORPS AND DIVISIONS

Second Army

Lieutenant-General Sir Miles C. Dempsey
General Officer Commanding-in-Chief
Brigadier M. S. Chilton
Chief of Staff

First Canadian Army

Lieutenant-General H. D. G. Crerar
General Officer Commanding-in-Chief
Brigadier C. C. Mann
Chief of Staff

I Corps

Lieutenant-General J. T. Crocker
The Inns of Court Regiment R.A.C. (Armoured Car)
62nd Anti-Tank, 102nd Light Anti-Aircraft, 9th Survey Regiments R.A.
1 Corps Troops Engineers   I Corps Signals

VIII Corps

Lieutenant-General Sir Richard N. O'Connor
2nd Household Cavalry Regiment (Armoured Car)
91st Anti-Tank, 121st Light Anti-Aircraft, 10th Survey Regiments R.A.
VIII Corps Troops Engineers   VIII Corps Signals

Lieutenant-General N. M. Ritchie
1st The Royal Dragoons (Armoured Car)
86th Anti-Tank, 112th Light Anti-Aircraft, 7th Survey Regiments R.A.
XII Corps Troops Engineers   XII Corps Signals

XXX Corps
Lieutenant-General G. C. Bucknall (to 3.8.44)
Lieutenant-General B. G. Horrocks (from 4.8.44)
11th Hussars (Armoured Car)
73rd Anti-Tank, 27th Light Anti-Aircraft, 4th Survey Regiments R.A.
XXX Corps Troops Engineers   XXX Corps Signals

II Canadian Corps
Lieutenant-General G. G. Simonds
18th Armoured Car Regiment (12th Manitoba Dragoons)
6th Anti-Tank, 6th Light Anti-Aircraft, 2nd Survey Regiments R.C.A.
II Canadian Corps Troops   II Canadian Corps Signals
  Engineers

Guards Armoured Division
Major-General A. H. S. Adair

5th Guards Armoured Brigade	*32rd Guards Brigade*
2nd (Armoured) Battalion Grenadier Guards	5th Battalion Coldstream Guards
1st (Armoured) Battalion Coldstream Guards	3rd Battalion Irish Guards
2nd (Armoured) Battalion Irish Guards	1st Battalion Welsh Guards
1st (Motor) Battalion Grenadier Guards	

Divisional Troops

2nd Armoured Reconnaissance Battalion Welsh Guards	55th and 153rd Field, 21st Anti-Tank and 94th Light Anti-Aircraft Regiments R.A.
Guards Armoured Divisional Engineers	Guards Armoured Divisional Signals

7th Armoured Division
Major-General G. W. E. J. Erskine (to 3.8.44)
Major-General G. L. Verney (from 4.8.44)

22nd Armoured Brigade
4th County of London Yeomanry
  (Sharpshooters) (to 29.7.44)
1st and 5th Battalions R.T.R.
5th Royal Inniskilling Dragoon
  Guards (from 29.7.44)
1st Battalion The Rifle Brigade
  (Motor)

131st Infantry Brigade
1/5th, 1/6th and 1/7th Battalions
  The Queen's Royal Regiment

Divisional Troops
8th King's Royal Irish Hussars
7th Armoured Divisional
  Engineers
7th Armoured Divisional Signals

3rd and 5th Regiments R.H.A.;
  6th Anti-Tank and 15th Light
  Anti-Aircraft Regiments R.A.

11th Armoured Division
Major-General G. P. B. Roberts

29th Armoured Brigade
23rd Hussars
2nd Fife and Forfar Yeomanry
3rd Battalion R.T.R.
8th Battalion The Rifle Brigade
  (Motor)

159th Infantry Brigade
3rd Battalion The Monmouthshire
  Regiment
4th Battalion The King's
  Shropshire Light Infantry
1st Battalion The Herefordshire
  Regiment

Divisional Troops
2nd Northamptonshire Yeomanry
  (to 17.8.44)
15th/19th The King's Royal
  Hussars (from 17.8.44)
11th Armoured Divisional
  Engineers

13th Regiment R.H.A.; 151st
  Field, 75th Anti-Tank and 58th
  Light Anti-Aircraft Regiments
  R.A.
11th Armoured Divisional Signals

3rd Division
Major-General T. G. Rennie (to 13.6.44)
Brigadier E. E. E. Cass (acting)
Major-General L. G. Whistler (from 23.6.44)

8th Brigade
1st Battalion The Suffolk
  Regiment
2nd Battalion The East Yorkshire
  Regiment
1st Battalion The South
  Lancashire Regiment

9th Brigade
2nd Battalion The Lincolnshire
  Regiment
1st Battalion The King's Own
  Scottish Borderers
2nd Battalion The Royal Ulster
  Rifles

185th Brigade
2nd Battalion The Royal Warwickshire Regiment
1st Battalion The Royal Norfolk Regiment
2nd Battalion The King's Shropshire Light Infantry

Divisional Troops

3rd Reconnaissance Regiment R.A.C.	7th, 33rd and 76th Field, 20th Anti-Tank and 92nd Light Anti-Aircraft Regiments R.A.
3rd Divisional Engineers	2nd Battalion The Middlesex Regiment (Machine Gun)
3rd Divisional Signals	

6th Airborne Division
Major-General R. N. Gale

3rd Parachute Brigade
8th and 9th Battalions The Parachute Regiment
1st Canadian Parachute Battalion

5th Parachute Brigade
7th, 12th and 13th Battalions The Parachute Regiment

6th Airlanding Brigade
12th Battalion The Devonshire Regiment
2nd Battalion The Oxfordshire and Buckinghamshire Light Infantry
1st Battalion The Royal Ulster Rifles

Divisional Troops

6th Airborne Armoured Reconnaissance Regiment R.A.C.	53rd Airlanding Light Regiment R.A.
6th Airborne Divisional Engineers	6th Airborne Divisional Signals

15th (Scottish) Division
Major-General G. H. A. MacMillan (to 2.8.44)
Major-General C. M. Barber (from 3.8.44)

44th (Lowland) Brigade
8th Battalion The Royal Scots
6th Battalion The Royal Scots Fusiliers
6th Battalion The King's Own Scottish Borderers

46th (Highland) Brigade
9th Battalion The Cameronians
2nd Battalion The Glasgow Highlanders
7th Battalion The Seaforth Highlanders

227th (Highland) Brigade
10th Battalion The Highland Light Infantry
2nd Battalion The Gordon Highlanders
2nd Battalion The Argyll and Sutherland Highlanders

Divisional Troops

15th Reconnaissance Regiment
R.A.C.
15th Divisional Engineers
15th Divisional Signals

131st, 181st and 190th Field, 97th
Anti-Tank and 119th Light
Anti-Aircraft Regiments R.A.
1st Battalion The Middlesex
Regiment (Machine Gun)

43rd (Wessex) Division
Major-General G. I. Thomas

129th Brigade
4th Battalion The Somerset Light
Infantry
4th and 5th Battalions The
Wiltshire Regiment

130th Brigade
7th Battalion The Hampshire
Regiment
4th and 5th Battalions The
Dorsetshire Regiment

214th Brigade
7th Battalion The Somerset Light Infantry
1st Battalion The Worcestershire Regiment
5th Battalion The Duke of Cornwall's Light Infantry

Divisional Troops

43rd Reconnaissance Regiment
R.A.C.
43rd Divisional Engineers
43rd Divisional Signals

94th, 112th and 179th Field, 59th
Anti-Tank and 110th Light
Anti-Aircraft Regiments R.A.
8th Battalion The Middlesex
Regiment (Machine Gun)

49th (West Riding) Division
Major-General E. H. Barker

70th Brigade (to 20.8.44)
10th and 11th Battalions The
Durham Light Infantry
1st Battalion The Tyneside
Scottish

146th Brigade
4th Battalion The Lincolnshire
Regiment
1/4th Battalion The King's Own
Yorkshire Light Infantry
Hallamshire Battalion The York
and Lancaster Regiment

147th Brigade

11th Battalion The Royal Scots Fusiliers

6th Battalion The Duke of Wellington's Regiment (to 6.7.44)

7th Battalion The Duke of Wellington's Regiment

1st Battalion The Leicestershire Regiment (from 6.7.44)

56th Brigade (from 20.8.44)

See under GHQ

Divisional Troops

49th Reconnaissance Regiment R.A.C.

49th Divisional Engineers

49th Divisional Signals

69th, 143rd and 185th Field, 55th Anti-Tank and 89th Light Anti-Aircraft Regiments R.A.

2nd Princess Louise's Kensington Regiment (Machine Gun)

50th (Northumbrian) Division
Major-General D. A. H. Graham

69th Brigade

5th Battalion The East Yorkshire Regiment

6th and 7th Battalions The Green Howards

151st Brigade

6th, 8th and 9th Battalions The Durham Light Infantry

231st Brigade

2nd Battalion The Devonshire Regiment

1st Battalion The Hampshire Regiment

1st Battalion The Dorsetshire Regiment

Divisional Troops

61st Reconnaissance Regiment R.A.C.

50th Divisional Engineers

50th Divisional Signals

74th, 90th and 124th Field, 102nd Anti-Tank and 25th Light Anti-Aircraft Regiments R.A.

2nd Battalion The Cheshire Regiment (Machine Gun)

51st (Highland) Division
Major-General D. C. Bullen-Smith (to 26.7.44)
Major-General T. G. Rennie (from 27.7.44)

152nd Brigade

2nd and 5th Battalions The Seaforth Highlanders

5th Battalion The Queen's Own Cameron Highlanders

153rd Brigade

5th Battalion The Black Watch

1st and 5th/7th Battalions The Gordon Highlanders

154th Brigade
1st and 7th Battalions The Black Watch
7th Battalion The Argyll and Sutherland Highlanders

Divisional Troops

2nd Derbyshire Yeomanry R.A.C.
51st Divisional Engineers
51st Divisional Signals

126th, 127th and 128th Field, 61st Anti-Tank and 40th Light Anti-Aircraft Regiments R.A.
1/7th Battalion The Middlesex Regiment (Machine Gun)

53rd (Welsh) Division
Major-General R. K. Ross

71st Brigade
1st Battalion The East Lancashire Regiment (to 3.8.44)
1st Battalion The Oxfordshire and Buckinghamshire Light Infantry
1st Battalion The Highland Light Infantry
4th Battalion The Royal Welch Fusiliers (from 5.8.44)

158th Brigade
4th and 6th Battalions The Royal Welch Fusiliers (to 3.8.44)
7th Battalion The Royal Welch Fusiliers
1st Battalion The East Lancashire Regiment (from 4.8.44)
1/5th Battalion The Welch Regiment (from 4.8.44)

160th Brigade
2nd Battalion The Monmouthshire Regiment
4th Battalion The Welch Regiment
1/5th Battalion The Welch Regiment (to 3.8.44)
6th Battalion The Royal Welch Fusiliers (from 4.8.44)

Divisional Troops

53rd Reconnaissance Regiment R.A.C.
53rd Divisional Engineers
53rd Divisional Signals

81st, 83rd and 133rd Field, 71st Anti-Tank and 116th Light Anti-Aircraft Regiments R.A.
1st Battalion The Manchester Regiment (Machine Gun)

59th (Staffordshire) Division
Major-General L. O. Lyne

176th Brigade (to 26.8.44)
7th Battalion The Royal Norfolk Regiment
7th Battalion The South Staffordshire Regiment
6th Battalion The North Staffordshire Regiment

177th Brigade (to 26.8.44)
5th, 1/6th and 2/6th Battalions The South Staffordshire Regiment

(to 26.8.44)
1/7th Battalion The Royal Warwickshire Regiment
2/5th Battalion The Lancashire Fusiliers
5th Battalion The East Lancashire Regiment

Divisional Troops

59th Reconnaissance Regiment R.A.C. (to 31.8.44)
59th Divisional Engineers
59th Divisional Signals

61st, 110th and 116th Field (to 31.8.44), 68th Anti-Tank (to 26.8.44) and 68th Light Anti-Aircraft (to 22.8.44) Regiments R.A.
7th Battalion The Royal Northumberland Fusiliers (Machine Gun) (to 24.8.44)

4th Canadian Armoured Division
Major-General G. Kitching (to 21.8.44)
Major-General H. W. Foster (from 22.8.44)

4th Armoured Brigade

21st Armoured Regiment (The Governor General's Foot Guards)
22nd Armoured Regiment (The Canadian Grenadier Guards)
28th Armoured Regiment (The British Columbia Regiment)
The Lake Superior Regiment (Motor)

10th Infantry Brigade

The Lincoln and Welland Regiment
The Algonquin Regiment
The Argyll and Sutherland Highlanders of Canada (Princess Louise's)

Divisional Troops

29th Reconnaissance Regiment (The South Alberta Regiment)
4th Canadian Armoured Divisional Engineers

15th and 23rd Field, 5th Anti-Tank and 8th Light Anti-Aircraft Regiments R.C.A.
4th Canadian Armoured Divisional Signals

2nd Canadian Division
Major-General C. Foulkes

4th Brigade

The Royal Regiment of Canada
The Royal Hamilton Light Infantry
The Essex Scottish Regiment

5th Brigade

The Black Watch (Royal Highland Regiment) of Canada
Le Régiment de Maisonneuve
The Calgary Highlanders

6th Brigade
Les Fusiliers Mont-Royal
The Queen's Own Cameron Highlanders of Canada
The South Saskatchewan Regiment

Divisional Troops

8th Reconnaissance Regiment
(14th Canadian Hussars)
2nd Canadian Divisional
Engineers
2nd Canadian Divisional Signals

4th, 5th and 6th Field, 2nd Anti-
Tank and 3rd Light Anti-
Aircraft Regiments R.C.A.
The Toronto Scottish Regiment
(Machine Gun)

3rd Canadian Division
Major-General R. F. L. Keller (to 8.8.44)
Major-General D. C. Spry (from 18.8.44)

7th Brigade
The Royal Winnipeg Rifles
The Regina Rifle Regiment
1st Battalion The Canadian
Scottish Regiment

8th Brigade
The Queen's Own Rifles of
Canada
Le Régiment de la Chaudière
The North Shore (New
Brunswick) Regiment

9th Brigade
The Highland Light Infantry of Canada
The Stormont, Dundas and Glengarry Highlanders
The North Nova Scotia Highlanders

Divisional Troops

7th Reconnaissance Regiment
(17th Duke of York's Royal
Canadian Hussars)
3rd Canadian Divisional
Engineers
3rd Canadian Divisional Signals

12th, 13th and 14th Field, 3rd
Anti-Tank and 4th Light Anti-
Aircraft Regiments R.C.A.
The Cameron Highlanders of
Ottawa (Machine Gun)

1st Polish Armoured Division
Major-General S. Maczek

10th Polish Armoured Brigade
1st Polish Armoured Regiment
2nd Polish Armoured Regiment
24th Polish Armoured (Lancer)
Regiment
10th Polish Motor Battalion

3rd Polish Infantry Brigade
1st Polish (Highland) Battalion
8th Polish Battalion
9th Polish Battalion

10th Polish Mounted Rifle
   Regiment
1st Polish Armoured Divisional
   Engineers
1st and 2nd Polish Field, 1st Polish
   Anti-Tank and 1st Polish Light
   Anti-Aircraft Regiments
1st Polish Armoured Divisional
   Signals

LINES OF COMMUNICATION AND REAR MAINTENANCE AREA

Headquarters Lines of Communication
Major-General R. F. B. Naylor
Nos. 11 and 12 Lines of
   Communication Areas
Nos. 4, 5 and 6 Lines of
   Communication Sub-Areas
Nos. 7 and 8 Base Sub-Areas
Nos. 101, 102 and 104 Beach Sub-
   Areas
Nos. 10 and 11 Garrison

Engineers
Nos. 2, 3, 5 and 6 Railway
   Construction and Maintenance
   Groups
No. 3 Railway Operating Group
No. 1 Canadian Railway
   Operating Group
No. 1 Railway Workshop Group
Nos. 2, 6, 8, 9, 10 and 11 Port
   Operating Groups
Nos. 1, 2, 4 and 5 Port
   Construction and Repair
   Groups
Nos. 3 and 4 Inland Water
   Transport Groups
No. 2 Mechanical Equipment
   (Transportation) Unit

Signals
Nos. 2 and 12 Lines of
   Communication Headquarters
   Signals
No. 1 Canadian Lines of
   Communication Headquarters
   Signals

Infantry
5th and 8th Battalions The King's
   Regiment
7th Battalion The East Yorkshire
   Regiment
2nd Battalion The Hertfordshire
   Regiment
6th Battalion The Border Regiment
1st Buckinghamshire Battalion
   The Oxfordshire and
   Buckinghamshire Light Infantry
5th Battalion The Royal Berkshire
   Regiment
18th Battalion The Durham Light
   Infantry

UNITED STATES TWELFTH ARMY GROUP

Lieutenant-General Omar N. Bradley
Commanding General
Major-General Leven C. Allen
Chief of Staff

First Army
Lieutenant-General Courtney H.
Hodges
Commanding General
(Succeeded General Bradley from
1.8.44)
Major-General William B. Keen
Chief of Staff

Third Army
Lieutenant-General George S.
Patton, Jr
Commanding General
Major-General Hugh J. Gaffey
Chief of Staff

Corps

V.   Major-General Leonard T.
Gerow

VII.   Major-General J. Lawton
Collins

VIII. Major-General Troy H.
Middleton

XII.   Major-General Gilbert R.
Cook (to 18.8.44)
Major-General Manton S.
Eddy (from 19.8.44)

XV.   Major-General Wade H.
Haislip

XIX. Major-General Charles H.
Corlett

XX.   Major-General Walton H.
Walker

Divisions

Armored: 2nd, 3rd, 4th, 5th, 6th
and 7th; 2nd French

Infantry: 1st, 2nd, 4th, 5th, 8th,
9th, 28th, 29th, 30th, 35th, 79th,
80th, 83rd and 90th

Airborne: 82nd and 101st

Forces available in ETO for Operation "Overlord" "D" Day – 6 June 1944

PART I: LAND FORCE DIVISIONS

	INFANTRY	ARMOURED	AIRBORNE	TOTAL
United States	13	5	2	20
British	8	4	2	14
Canadian	2	1	–	3
French	–	1	–	1
Polish	–	1	–	1
TOTAL	23	12	4	39

PART II: AIR FORCES
A/C on Operational Combat Stations

A. *Summary by Types*:

		OPER & NON O	OPERAT'L	EFFECTIVE STRENGTH*
Heavy	Bombers	3,958	3,455	3,130
Med & Lt	Bombers	1,234	989	933
Ftrs & Ftrs	Bombers	4,709	3,824	3,711
	TOTAL	9,901	8,268	7,774

B. *Summary by Command*:

		OPER & NON O	OPERAT'L	EFFECTIVE STRENGTH*
VIII A/F	Hvy Bomb	2,578	2,243	1,947
	Fighters	1,144	961	961
IX A/F	Med Bomb	624	513	467
	Lt Bomb	228	165	156
	Fighters	1,487	1,132	1,123
		5,061		
BOMB CMD	Hvy Bomb	1,380	1,212	1,183
	Lt Bomb	134	98	97
2ND TAF	Med Bomb	88	67	67
	Lt Bomb	160	146	146
	Fighters	1,006	856	831
ADGB	Fighters	1,072	875	796
	TOTAL	9,901	8,268	7,774
		5,061		
		4,940		

* Operational aircraft with crews available.

PART III: NAVAL FORCES

A. *Major Combat Vessels*:

Battleships	7
Monitors	2
Cruisers	23
Gunboats	2
Destroyers	93
Sloops	15
Escorts	142
TOTAL	284

B. *Landing Craft and Ships*:

LST & LST (2)	233	
LST (1)	3	
LCT (A)	48	
LCT (R)	36	
LCT (64 flotillas)	768	
LCT (CB)	5	
LCT (HE)	16	
XAP	3	873
APA	7	
LSI (L)	18	
LSI (M)	3	
LSI (H)	18	
LSI (S)	6	
LSH (L)	5	
LSH (S)	9	
LSD	3	
LCI (L)	208	
LCI (S)	39	
LCH	18	
LCF	29	
LCA	486	
LCC	9	
LCG (L)	25	
LCE	6	

LCP (L) smoke	144
LCA (HR)	45
LCS (L) (2)	10
LCS (L) (1)	4
LCS (M)	26
LCS (S)	36
LCVP	839
LCM (1)	128
LCM (3)	358
LBF	15
LBV (2)	228
LBO	100
LBE	60
LBW	20
LBK	10
TOTAL	4024
	284
	4308

C. *Special Type Equipment*:

LVTs	470
DD Tanks	514
DUKWs	2583
TOTAL	3567

PART IV: STRENGTHS*

A. *Totals*: (Officers and Men)

Air	659,554
Land	1,931,885
Sea	285,000
TOTAL	2,876,439

* Officers and Men

Appendix IV

German land forces encountered by the Allies in Normandy

The composition of German armies and corps varied constantly during the campaign, but at different times part or all of the following were engaged:

Seventh, Fifteenth, Fifth Panzer (formerly Panzer Group West) and First Armies, embracing the following 13 corps and 15 divisions:

Panzer Corps: I SS, II SS, XLVII, LVIII
Infantry Corps: II Parachute, XXV, LXVII, LXXIV, LXXX, LXXXI, LXXXII, LXXXIV, LXXXVI
Panzer Divisions: 1st SS, 2nd SS, 2nd, 9th, 9th SS, 10th SS, 12th SS, 21st, 116th, Panzer Lehr
Panzergrenadier divisions: 3rd, 15th, 17th SS
Infantry Divisions: 2nd, 3rd, 5th and 6th Parachute; 16th, 17th, 18th Luftwaffe Field; 47th, 48th, 49th, 77th, 84th, 85th, 89th, 91st Airlanding, 226th, 243rd, 245th, 265th, 266th, 271st, 272nd, 275th, 276th, 277th, 326th, 331st, 343rd, 344th, 346th, 348th, 352nd, 353rd, 363rd, 708th, 709th, 711th, 716th

SS Panzer divisions were substantially larger and better-equipped than their Wehrmacht counterparts. All panzer divisions normally contained an armoured regiment of two battalions — one equipped with Mark IV tanks, the other with Panthers. Army panzer divisions also contained two infantry regiments, each of two battalions, but SS divisions mustered six infantry battalions. The average panzer division went into Normandy with 160 tanks, 700 machine-guns, 70 mortars, 37 infantry guns, 40 field and medium guns, 33 anti-tank guns and over 100 anti-aircraft guns. Each division's vehicle establishment was around 3,000. Wehrmacht divisions mustered almost 15,000 men at full strength, SS divisions up to 20,000.

Panzergrenadier divisions possessed no tanks but their infantry were fully motorized, and supported by a battalion of 45 self-propelled guns.

Of the 38 German infantry divisions that fought in Normandy, five were "static" formations comprising nine battalions, the same organization as the parachute units. The other 30 were on "1944 establishment" of six infantry battalions, with a fusilier reconnaissance battalion, often bicycle-mounted. Each division mustered, on average, 650 machine-guns, 76 mortars, 24 infantry guns and howitzers, 31 anti-tank guns and 48 medium and field guns. Transport was provided by 615 motor vehicles and 1,450 horse-drawn vehicles.

GHQ and army troops included III Flak Corps' 160 88 mm guns in a dual-purpose role facing the British front. There were three heavy tank battalions, each containing up to 45 Tigers; two battalions of *Jagdpanthers,* 88 mm tank-killing self-propelled guns; several independent towed 88 mm gun battalions and 75 mm-mounted self-propelled gun battalions. The Germans possessed relatively few field or medium guns, and only one heavy regiment of 170 mm guns.

Appendix V

Some British administrative statistics

Units	
1 New Units formed in theatre	756
2 Existing Units reorganised, including 50 Div	634
3 Units disbanded	177
4 Units placed in suspended animation	33
5 Unit designation changed	270

Courts Martial Held		
Type of Offence	In respect of Officers	Other Ranks
1 Absence and Desertion	4	7,018
2 Other offences	59	3,628
3 TOTAL ALL OFFENCES	63	10,646

Admissions to Mil Prisons, Detention Barracks and Field Punishment Camps (5 May 45)	
Type of Sentence	Other Ranks
4 Penal Servitude and Imprisonment	4,032
5 Other Sentences	4,421
6 TOTAL ALL TYPES OF SENTENCES	8,453

Leave (excluding Personnel in 2 TAF)

	Type of Leave	No. of leaves granted to All Ranks
7	Privilege Leave in UK	472,000
8	Short Leave on the Continent	468,000
9	Compassionate Leave	23,600
10	TOTAL ALL TYPES OF LEAVE GRANTED	963,600

Marriages approved between British subjects and aliens 398

BATTLE CASUALTIES

As known at 2nd Echelon 12 May 45 which approximates to the situation on 30 Apr 45

		British	Canadian	Allied
1	Killed	30,289	9,872	1,421
2	Wounded	97,947	30,072	4,662
3	Missing and prisoners	15,485	2,137	418
4	TOTAL	143,721	42,081	6,501

STRENGTHS

		Strength 6 Jun 44		Strength 30 Apr 45	
		Offrs	ORs	Offrs	ORs
1	Total strength of force	37,937	680,021	46,138	792,722
2	Second Army	15,808	300,392	14,333	280,934
3	Airborne Troops	1,798	26,987	1,644	25,612
4	Allied forces under comd 21 A Gp	1,332	21,400	1,814	32,905

1	AFs B115 (Declaration of illegal absence)	3,030
2	AFs B252 (Charge Sheets—Summary Disposal)	140,508
3	AFs A3104 (Review of Sentences awarded by Courts Martial)	16,779

4	AFs A2 (Courts of inquiry re Accidental Injuries)	4,565
5	AFs B117 (Reports on Accidental Injuries)	29,613
6	Intimation received of personnel granted compassionate leave	7,270
7	Intimation received of extension of compassionate leave and extension of privilege leave granted on compassionate grounds	20,794
8	Notification to soldiers of casualties affecting their families	9,498
9	Welfare enquiries re soldiers made by their relatives	1,558
10	Marriages (abroad) registered (First ceremony conducted 3 Oct 44)	280

CHAPLAINS

Battle Casualties

	Type of Casualty	Number of Chaplains
1	Killed in action	10
2	Died of wounds	7
3	Missing	11

Religious Offices

4	Soldiers baptised	22
5	Soldiers confirmed	443
6	Soldiers admitted to the Free Churches	4
7	Soldiers seeking ordination	300
8	Marriages performed between British subjects	56

Number of New Testaments distributed	30,000

General Medical Statistics

1	Casualties cleared from Army Areas to Base Hospitals by air	36,000
2	Cases admitted to Medical Units:	
	Battle	181,695
	Non-Battle	224,393
3	Cases evacuated to UK by air	77,174
4	Cases evacuated to UK by sea	70,466
5	Attendances for dental treatment	674,958
6	New dentures supplied	29,111
7	Dentures repaired	30,458

Specialised Treatment to Casualties

8	Pints of whole blood given	85,000
9	Pints of other intravenous fluid given	165,000
10	Millions of units of penicillin used for wounded	65,000
11	Morphine—doses given	470,000
12	Bandages used (32,000,000 yards)	8,000,000
13	X-ray plates used	250,000

Incidence of Disease—Mean Monthly Rate per 1,000 Strength

	Disease	First World War 1914–1918	Second Word War Jun 44–May 45
14	Venereal Disease	2.474	2.116
15	Enteric	1.525	0.006
16	Dysentery	0.466	0.314
17	Pneumonia	0.419	0.066
18	Meningitis	0.026	0.007
19	Influenza	0.890	0.231
20	Trench Foot	0.503	0.039

	Sick and Accidentally Injured	First World War 1914–1918	Second World War Jun 44–May 45
21	Sick and accidentally injured admitted to Medical Units (per month, per 1,000 strength)	53.9	23.2

GENERAL NOTES:

(a) The use of penicillin, combined with close liaison between surgeons, physicians and pathologists, has been a large factor in producing a recovery rate of over 93% of all casualties who reach the Medical Unit.

(b) Psychiatry has been extensively used in combating cases of exhaustion and treatment of cases in Forward Areas, and also in selection of personnel for suitable employment.

(c) Preventive inoculations and the standard of Unit hygiene have been responsible for an almost complete absence of major infectious diseases.

PAY

1 Commencing on D+2 Field Cash Offices and Forward Base Pay Offices landed on D+6 with 6,500 million French francs weighing 120 tons. Not one franc was lost in transit.

2 Although only five currencies are current in the theatre, work has involved almost every currency in world circulation. Average weekly advances of pay to Officers and Other Ranks in these currencies approximated in sterling value one million pounds, whilst 100,000 currency exchange have been carried out weekly.

3 Impounded from enemy Prisoners of War:
    12 million Francs
    $5\frac{1}{2}$ million Reichmarks
    $\frac{1}{2}$ million Guilders

4 20,000 British Commonwealth ex-Prisoners of War have been given advances of pay.

5 The Pay Service has been responsible for supplying cash to 5,000 British Army Imprest Holders.

PROVOST

1	Length of routes signposted in British sector—miles	4,000
2	Military police signs erected	141,800
3	Information posts manned by CMP	370
4	Arrests made of Military Personnel	2,335
5	Total arrests made	7,875
6	Summaries of charges preferred by CMP (to 31 Mar)	36,366
7	Total Special Investigation Branch cases:	
	reported	6,404
	completed	5,880
8	Specimen traffic density test—Number of vehicles which passed a CMP post in 24 hours at Antwerp	41,679
9	Value of property recovered by Provost (SIB)	£384,454

EDUCATION

1	Army Study Centres and Libraries formed	12
2	Mobile Libraries circulated among forward troops	7
3	Formation newspapers published daily	30

The first Formation newspaper was published on D+3, entitled
"Triangle". The paper "Pegasus" was delivered to airborne troops east of
the Rhine within 20 hours of the airborne landing.

WELFARE

1	Number of clubs opened	316
2	Personnel CVWW (British Voluntary Organisation)	584
	Personnel Voluntary Workers (Belgian Red Cross canteens)	893
3	Average daily number of men served by these clubs	420,000
4	Mobile canteens	374
	Whole-time entertainment parties:	
5	ENSA	57
6	Army	32
	Entertainment and Welfare equipment issued:	
7	Musical Instruments	10,000
8	Gramophones	500
9	Gramophone Records	35,600
10	Wireless Sets	13,600
11	Books	1,185,000
12	Magazines	4,000,000
13	Dart Sets	225,000

420

14	Cigarettes	41,000,000
15	Value of sales in Brussels and Bruges gift shops—Belgian francs	22,723,000
16	Cases now in hand in three Legal Aid Sections	7,000
	Army Kinema Services:	
17	Number of sections operating	20
18	Average performance per week	3,700
19	Average audiences per week	400,000
20	Public kinemas put into operation	74

TONNAGE OF STORES
landed by commodities 6 Jun 44–8 May 45

		Total Tonnage	Daily Average	Daily Average per Equivalent Div
		tons	tons	tons
1	AMN (excl. RAF)	951,865	2,825	155
2	POL (Army) (excl. bul)	632,500	1,877	103
3	POL (RAF) (excl. bulk)	92,184	274	15
4	SUPS	875,308	2,597	142
5	RE	767,383	2,277	125
6	ORD	494,853	1,468	80
7	CA (incl. wheat, edible oils)	518,041	1,537	84
8	MISC (incl. coal, RAF amn)	814,220	2,416	132
9	TOTAL	5,146,354	15,271	836

ENGINEER WORKS

1	Tons of timber felled by Forestry Coys (this does not include civilian production, captures or imports. A fifth of this was used for pitprops)	250,000
2	Miles of hutting erected (equivalent 20 ft span)	180
3	Miles of hutting manufactured locally	30
4	Tons of stone quarried	2,000,000
5	Oil: High pressure pumps installed	330
6	Tons of bulk storage in 110 tanks	101,000
7	Total pipes laid—miles	1,200
8	Total weight of equipment—tons	97,000
9	Tons of Engineer Stores imported	750,000
10	Items of Engineer Plant and Machinery imported	25,000

11	Sterling value of local production of equipment	£3,250,000
12	Electric Generators installed (this represents 10,000 horse power)	420
13	Miles of overhead electric cable erected	280
14	Miles of insulated cable installed	3,000
15	Airfields constructed or repaired (this represents an equivalent of 2,020 miles of roadway, 20 ft wide)	125
16	No. of Bailey Bridges built (8% were cl. 70, 80% cl. 40, 12% less than cl. 40)	1,350
17	Miles of Bailey Bridges built	29
18	No. of FBE bridges built (cl. 9)	80
19	Miles of FBE bridges built	3

AIR FREIGHT

		tons
1	Total tonnage flown into theatre between 6 June 44 and 8 May 45	35,174

Consisting of:

Mail	1,043 tons
Newspapers	946 „
Blood	308 „
Ord stores	6,362 „
Engr stores	480 „
Currency	46 „
Maps	419 „
Airfield Track	2,421 „
Amn	10,397 „
Pet	11,612 „
Rations	539 „
Med stores	90 „
Other stores	511 „
	35,174 tons

Excluding 9,017 tons of food for HOLLAND flown by Bomber Comd and VIII USAAF between 29 Apr and 8 May 45

2	Average daily lift	107
3	Largest special lifts:	
	(a) Food for HOLLAND 7 May 45	1,151
	(b) 882 tons POL and 178 tons Amn for SECOND ARMY 29 Sep 44	1,060

SUPPLIES AND TRANSPORT
(To 8 May 45)

Transport

1	Tonnage capacity of RASC task vehicles in theatre	148,252
2	Tonnage lifted from ship to shore by DUKWs	414,509
3	Mileage run by bulk petroleum vehicles	12,831,484

Number of RASC task vehicles at 8 May 1945

4	Lorries 3–6 ton	20,788
5	Lorries 10 ton	2,959
6	DUKWs	228
7	Tippers	1,181
8	Tank Transporters	1,089
9	Troop-carrying vehicles	693
10	Tankers 800–2000 galls	981
11	Total	27,919

Supplies

12	Tonnage of supplies landed	810,305
13	Tonnage of supplies procured locally	32,500
14	Average daily feeding strength (including PW and civil mobile labour)	1,127,915
15	Maximum feeding strength (including PW and civil mobile labour)	2,113,962
16	Reserve of supplies on 1 May 45 in rations	70,145,265
17 (a)	Number of different ration scales for British Personnel	8
17 (b)	Number of different ration scales for PW and Civilian Internees	5
17 (c)	Number of different ration scales for animals	8
17 (d)	Number of different ration scales for civilian labour	2
17 (e)	Scale of provision of miscellaneous and disinfectant items	1
17 (f)	Average nett weight of rations per head Field Service Scale Fresh Items	70 ozs
17 (g)	Average nett weight of rations per head Field Service Scale tinned equivalents	50 ozs
17 (h)	Calorific value of Field Service Ration (male personnel)	3,900
17 (i)	Calorific value of Field Service Ration (women's services)	3,400

			2,000
17 (*j*)	Calorific value of Ration Scale for European PW and Civil Internees		2,000
17 (*k*)	Calorific value of Ration Scale for civilian labour (Enrolled)		3,400
17 (*l*)	Calorific value of Ration Scale for midday meal for casual labour		800

POL

		Tons	Equivalent Gallons
18	Bulk POL imported through ports	1,020,927	306,278,100
19	Bulk POL imported through pipeline	313,596	94,078,800
20	Packed POL imported through ports	612,786	141,467,782
21	POL pumped through pipeline	746,075	223,522,500
21a	Average daily rate of construction of 6-in Victaulic pipeline	3,2 miles	
21b	Total length of pipeline laid	1,125 miles	
22	POL filled into containers by Mobile Petrol Filling Centres	549,695	164,908,500
23	Average daily issues of POL (including civil requirements but excluding aviation spirit for RAF)	4,459	1,029,392
24	Reserve of POL on 1 May 45	242,968	65,177,837
25	Average daily POL import	6,000	
26	Number of jerricans imported	15,580,000	

POL was being landed in bulk D+13. Pipeline finally ran from UK to
BOCHOLT (GERMANY).

ORDNANCE
Vehicles—Total Numbers Landed

1	By Units	231,000
2	Reserve "A" Vehicles	23,000
3	Reserve "B" Vehicles	70,000
4	TOTAL VEHICLES LANDED	324,000

Ammunition

5	Total tons landed	942,562
6	Total tons expended	722,546

Ordnance Stores

7	Total tons landed	486,650
8	Average tons issued daily	1,140

Nature / Month	7.2 in How HE	155 mm Gun HE	5.5 in Gun HE	4.5 in Gun HE	25 pr all types	95 mm	77 mm
1944							
Jun (from 12th)	6166	11058	101453	20746	516400		
Jul	23547	31612	448057	23686	1934002		
Aug	12788	19510	348580	24953	1660137		
Sep	4619	9160	125444	5369	751374		
Oct	23411	24236	337155	37411	1800871		
Nov	8650	11864	202655	16787	768560		
Dec	5421	3144	60126	4150	314681		
1945							
Jan	5205	6743	169838	10849	802855	1906	
Feb	23957	7966	334985	29485	1751557	1542	661
Mar	31485	13251	328278	50864	2127072	682	
Apr	12031	8314	140386	38736	1277696	9181	298
May (to 8th)	2618	1815	10190	4743	123754	423	
Total	159898	148673	2610747	267779	13828959	13734	959

Nature / Month	7.2 in How HE	155 mm Gun HE	5.5 in Gun HE	25 pr HE	95 mm	77 mm	76 mm
1944							
Jun (from 12th)	15.1	27.1	35.2	46.3			
Jul	20	26.9	45.7	70.6			
Aug	10.3	15.7	30.6	49.3			
Sep	3.8	7.6	11.4	21.7			
Oct	18.9	19.5	30.5	48.6			
Nov	7.2	9.9	19.5	20.4			
Dec	4.4	2.5	5.7	9			
1945							
Jan	4.2	5.4	16.3	21	0.6		0.4
Feb	21.4	7.1	35.6	53.5	0.5	0.3	0.5
Mar	25.4	10.7	32.9	59.5	0.2		1.2
Apr	8.1	5.6	13.1	30.6	2.4		0.1
May (to 8th)	5.8	4.1	3.5	11	0.4		0.1
Total	12.1	11.2	23.6	36.8	0.9	0.1	0.5

PER MONTH

76 mm	75 mm	17 pr	6 pr	All types 3.7 in AA	40 mm	4.2 in Mortar	3 in Mortar	Vickers .303 VIII Z
	22261	2858	7925	37588	64170	16867	224977	
	35558	6426	9735	98381	157747	131283	192881	
	58495	9288	8005	56291	54428	106943	118169	
	35827	6668	4966	35415	64183	34729	64974	
	41962	8695	8759	86019	117609	126735	148115	
	49509	7853	9884	64237	76933	87385	106057	
	29011	7360	2319	62855	79012	55375	62610	
1542	91970	14658	2192	103894	119759	73626	160251	3071354
2119	51313	20562	4016	194353	121621	75329	121647	7389561
5057	199295	18862	2526	180959	279876	76694	79159	5929800
365	139121	27389	11390	109216	187934	70268	150149	6821174
64	19345	2008	695	18194	15587	6578	6417	125750
9147	773667	132627	72412	1057402	1338899	861812	1435406	23337629

PER DAY (AVERAGE)

75 mm	17 pr	6 pr	3.7 AA HE	40 mm HE	4.2 in Mortar HE	3 in Mortar	Vickers .303 VIII Z	4.5 in Gun HE
0.7	0.3	0.5	10.5	4.0	7.5	16.9		68.2
0.5	0.3	0.3	12.7	4.0	24.9	6.7		47.8
0.9	0.3	0.2	5.1	1.1	19.8	4.1		50.3
0.6	0.3	0.2	2.2	1.5	7.1	3.2		11.2
0.6	0.3	0.3	4.8	2.4	24.8	6.5		41
0.8	0.3	0.3	3.6	1.4	16.2	4.7		17.5
0.5	0.2	0.1	3.3	1.4	10.8	2.8		4.2
1.4	0.4	0.1	4	2.2	13.4	6.4	305.8	10.9
0.8	0.7	0.1	7.4	2.5	16	5.5	814.5	32.9
3.4	0.6	0.1	6.8	5.1	14.4	3.4	589	34.9
2	0.6	0.3	5.8	3.5	10.8	5.3	596.5	16.8
1.1	0.2	0.1	5.2	1.2	3.6	0.8	38.9	6.3
1.1	0.4	0.2	5.3	2.5	15.1	5.4	532.2	24.3

REME
Repairs and Maintenance (excluding Work in LADs)

1	"A" Vehicles	40,000
2	"B" Vehicles	205,000
3	Wireless and Radar equipment	90,000
4	Small Arms and Machine Guns	650,000
5	Artillery equipment	18,500
6	TOTAL NUMBER OF EQUIPMENTS	1,003,500

LABOUR
Total effective personnel incl. train guards but excl. adm personnel and cadres

	Numbers employed	Military Labour	Civil Labour	PW Labour	Total
1	D Day	6,500	—	—	6,500
2	20 Jun 44	27,000	700	—	27,700
3	8 Sep 44	43,000	6,000	8,000	57,000
4	1 May 45	56,000 incl. Allied Pnr Coys	175,000	15,000	246,000

POSTAL

1	First delivery of inward mail made D+1	
	Daily average delivery of letters:	
2	Inward	1,000,000
3	Outward	800,000
4	Daily tonnage of parcels received	100

VETERINARY and REMOUNT SERVICES

1	Number of horses used between 6 June 44 and 8 May 45	913

These animals were all draft horses. They were used principally at ANTWERP docks and in certain depots in the Advanced Base. Initially V and RS personnel were in charge. Later RASC personnel took over the supervising duties, with civilian labour working the horses.

2	Number of horses captured in FRANCE	6,000
3	Number of horses captured in BELGIUM and the NETHERLANDS	4,000
4	Number of horses captured in GERMANY	794
5	Total number of horses captured	10,794

The animals captured in FRANCE, BELGIUM and the NETHER-LANDS were all disposed of to farmers with the exception of those horses retained for work.

FIRE

1	Fires caused by enemy action	340
2	Fires by other causes	1,451
3	TOTAL FIRES DEALT WITH BY AFS	1,791

Q (MOVEMENTS AND TRANSPORTATION)

PORTS

Mulberry (Opened 12 Jun 44. Closed 28 Nov 44)

	Amount of traffic during period:	
1	Personnel	231,315
2	Vehicles	45,181
3	Tons of stores	628,000

Ports (Other than Mulberry)

	Port	Date Opened	Date Closed	Daily Average Tons of Stores
		1944		
4	Beaches	6 Jun	Jul–Aug 44	13,392
5	Port en Bessin	8 Jun	25 Sep 44	869
6	Caen	31 Aug	12 Mar 45	782
7	Dieppe	8 Sep	28 Dec 44	3,768
8	Ostend	26 Sep	—	2,908
9	Boulogne	13 Oct	8 Jan 45	1,422
10	Calais	6 Dec	—	156
11	Antwerp	27 Nov	—	10,203
12	Ghent	23 Feb	22 Apr 45	4,464

13	Peak day traffic of stores discharged through MULBERRY and over beaches	17,000
14	Average tons through Ports	20,517
15	Total tons through Ports (including Grain and POL)	6,720,695
16	Area dredged to open Ports—cubic yards	2,800,000

INLAND WATER TRANSPORT

1	Miles of waterways opened for traffic (this is equal to one-third of canal mileage in UK)	870
2	Average tons carried daily	8,528
3	Tons carried during peak month (Apr 45) (this is equal to more than a quarter of average monthly lift on canals in UK)	400,000
4	Number of barges brought into service	4,230

RAILWAYS

1	Number of track miles opened	7,000
2	Route miles of L of C railways at peak period	2,000
3	Present daily average personnel moving by rail	30,000
4	Total personnel carried by rail	1,750,000
	Daily average tons of stores carried:	
5	Aug 44	5,000
6	Apr 45	25,000
7	Peak period—tons of stores carried in one day	70,000
8	Tons of military stores (less coal) carried	4,500,000
9	Tons of coal carried	2,500,000
10	Tons of military stores and coal carried	7,000,000

11	Locomotives imported	1,076
12	Locomotives repaired	2,745
13	Wagons imported	3,200
14	Wagons erected	1,700
15	Wagons repaired	4,200
16	Ambulance trains imported	11
17	Bridges rebuilt	91
18	Total length of bridgework—miles	3
19	Bridges at present under construction	17

Bibliography and a note on sources

The literature of the north-west Europe campaign in general and of Normandy in particular is vast. I have omitted many battlefield reminiscences, together with the invaluable regimental and divisional histories which are available for almost every British and American formation mentioned in the text. I have also left out a number of books whose accuracy has been the subject of such severe strictures as to make them of doubtful value to students of the period. I am deeply indebted to all those men, British, American and German, who have lent me contemporary letters, diaries, and narratives.

I have learned much about contemporary attitudes to the campaign from the files of *The Times,* the *New York Times,* the *Daily Express* and *Picture Post,* for whom my father served as war correspondent in Normandy. For this as for other books of mine, I must acknowledge the generosity of David Irving in lending documents and files he had assembled for his own researches. Among original sources which have proved especially valuable, I must mention *Current Notes From Overseas,* the weekly British tactical pamphlet circulated to unit commanding officers; the diaries of General Carl Spaatz, General Hoyt Vandenburg, Captain H. C. Butcher; the papers of Sir John Grigg; copies of papers pertaining to General Walter Bedell Smith, General Everett Hughes, Air-Marshal J. M. Robb, General George Patton, General Raymond Barker held in the Eisenhower Library; the personal diary of Brigadier N. Elliott Rodger, Chief of Staff II (Canadian) Corps; the superb after-action reports of U.S. units in France; and of course, the SHAEF, War Office and War Department files in the U.S. National Archive and the Public Records Office in London.

AMBROSE, Stephen, *The Supreme Commander,* New York, 1970.
ARON, Robert, *De Gaulle Before Paris*, New York, 1962;
    De Gaulle Triumphant, New York, 1964.
BATCHELOR & HOGG, *Artillery,* New York, 1973.
BELCHEM, David, *All in a Day's March,* London, 1967.
———, *Victory in Normandy*, London, 1981.
BENNETT, Ralph, *Ultra in the West,* London, 1979.
BLUMENSON, Martin, *Breakout and Pursuit*, Washington, 1961.
BRADLEY, Omar, *A Soldier's Story,* London, 1952
———, *A General's Life*, New York, 1982.

BRYANT, Arthur, *The Turn of the Tide*, London, 1957
———, *Triumph in the West*, London, 1959.
BUTCHER, Captain H. C., *My Three Years with Eisenhower*, London, 1946.
BUTLER, J. R. M., & GWYER, M. A., *Grand Stategy*, vol. iii, London, 1964.
CARELL, Paul, *Invasion — They're Coming*, London, 1962.
CHALFONT, Alun, *Montgomery of Alamein*, London, 1976.
CHURCHILL, Winston, *Triumph and Tragedy*, London, 1954.
COLLINS, J. Lawton, *Lightning Joe*, Louisiana, 1979.
COOPER, Matthew, *The German Army: Its Political and Military Failure*, London, 1978.
CRAVEN & CATE, *The U.S. Army Air Forces in World War II*, Chicago, 1951.
CRUIKSHANK, Charles, *Deception in World War II*, Oxford, 1979.
De GUINGAND, Frederick, *Operation Victory*, London, 1960.
D'ESTE, Carlo, *Decision in Normandy*, London, 1983.
DUNN, Walter Scott, *Second Front Now — 1943*, Alabama, 1980.
DUPUY, Colonel T. N., *A Genius for War*, London, 1977.
EHREMAN, John, *Grand Strategy*, vol. v, London, 1956.
EISENHOWER, Dwight, *Crusade in Europe*, New York, 1948.
———, *Papers*, vol. iii, Baltimore, 1970.
ELLIS, Major L. F., *Victory in the West*, vol. i, London, 1962.
FARAGO, Ladislas, *Patton: Ordeal and Triumph*, New York, 1963.
FARRAR-HOCKLEY, Anthony, *Infantry Tactics 1939–45*, London, 1976.
FERGUSSON, Bernard, *The Black Watch and The King's Enemies*, London, 1950.
———, *The Watery Maze*, London, 1961.
FOOT, M. R. D., *SOE in France*, London, 1966.
FRASER, Sir David, *And We Shall Shock Them*, London, 1983.
———, *Alanbrooke*, London, 1982.
GAVIN, James, *On To Berlin*, London, 1978.
GOLLEY, John, *The Big Drop*, London, 1982.
GOSSET & LECOMTE, *Caen Pendant La Bataille*, Caen, 1946.
GREENFIELD, PALMER & WILEY, *The U.S. Army in World War II: The Organization of Ground Combat Troops*, Washington, 1946.
GRIGG, John, *1943: The Victory that Never Was*, London, 1980.
GUDERIAN, Heinz, *Panzer Leader*, London, 1952.
HAMILTON, Nigel, *Montgomery: The Making of a General*, London, 1981.
———, *Montgomery: Master of a Battlefield*, London, 1983.
HARRISON, Gordon, *Cross Channel Attack*, Washington, 1951.
HASTINGS, Max, *Bomber Command*, London, 1979.
———, *Das Reich*, London, 1982.
HASWELL, J. *The Intelligence and Deception of the D-Day Landings*, London, 1979.
HINSLEY, Prof. F. H. & others, *British Intelligence in the Second World War*, vol. ii, London, 1981.

433

How, J. J., *Normandy: The British Breakout*, London, 1981.

Howard, Michael, *Grand Strategy*, vol. iv, London, 1972.

Howarth, David, *Dawn of D-Day*, London, 1959.

Irving, David, *Hitler's War*, London & New York, 1979.

———, *The Trail of the Fox*, London & New York, 1977.

———, *The Rise and Fall of the Luftwaffe*, Boston, 1973.

Ismay, Lord, *Memoirs*, London, 1960.

Joly, Cyril, *Take These Men*, London, 1955.

Jonson, G., & Dunphie, C., *Brightly Shone the Dawn*, London, 1980.

Keegan, John, *Six Armies in Normandy*, London, 1982.

Kohn & Harahan (eds), *Air Superiority in World War II and Korea*, Washington, 1983.

Lamb, Richard, *Montgomery in Europe*, London, 1983.

Lane, Ronald L., *Rudder's Rangers*, Manassas, 1979.

Lewin, Ronald, *Montgomery as Military Commander*, London, 1971.

———, *Ultra Goes to War*, London, 1978.

Liddell Hart. Basil, *The Other Side of the Hill*, London, 1951.

———, *The Second World War*, London, 1970.

Lovat, Lord, *March Past*, London, 1978.

Lucas, J., & Barker, J. *The Killing Ground*, London, 1978.

Macksey, Kenneth, *Armoured Crusader*, London, 1967.

Maule, Henry, *Caen: The Brutal Battle and the Break-out from Normandy*, London, 1976.

Marshall, S. L. A., *Night Drop*, London, 1962.

McBryde, Brenda, *A Nurse's War*, London, 1979.

McKee, Alexander, *Caen, Anvil of Victory*, London, 1964.

Montgomery, Earl, *The Memoirs of Field-Marshal Montgomery*, London, 1958.

———, *Normandy to the Baltic*, London, 1947.

Moorehead, Alan, *Montgomery*, London, 1947.

Morgan, F. E., *Overture to Overlord*, London, 1950.

Nelson, *Second Front Now — 1943*, Alabama, 1980.

Palmer, Wiley & Keast, *The U.S. Army in World War II: The Procurement and Training of Ground Combat Troops*, Washington, 1948.

Patton, George S., *War as I Knew it*, Boston, 1947.

Pogue, Forrest C., *George C. Marshall,* vols ii & iii, New York, 1965, 1973.

Roach, Peter, *The 8.15 to War*, London, 1982.

Rohmer, Richard, *Patton's Gap*, London, 1981.

Ross, George MacLeod, *The Business of Tanks*, London (privately printed), 1976.

Ruge, Frederich, *Rommel in Normandy*, London, 1979.

Ruppenthal, Ronald G., *The U.S. Army In World War II: Logistical Support of the Armies*, Washington, 1966.

Ryan, Cornelius, *The Longest Day*, London & New York, 1959.

Scarfe, Norman, *Assault Division*, London, 1947.

SCOTT, Desmond, *Typhoon Pilot*, London, 1982.

SEATON, Albert, *The Fall of Fortress Europe 1943–45*, London, 1981.

———, *The German Army*, London, 1982.

SHULMAN, Milton, *Defeat in the West*, London, 1948.

SPEIDEL, Hans, *We Defended Normandy*, London, 1951.

STACEY, C. P., *The Canadian Army in the Second World War*, vol. iii, Ottawa, 1960.

STRONG, Kenneth, *Intelligence at the Top*, London, 1968.

TEDDER, Lord, *With Prejudice*, London, 1966.

VAN CREVELD, Martin, *Supplying War*, London, 1978.

———, *Fighting Power: German Military Performance 1914–45*, Washington, 1980.

WARLIMONT, Walter, *Inside Hitler's Headquarters*, London, 1962.

WEBSTER & FRANKLAND, *The Strategic Air Offensive Against Germany*, vol. iii, London, 1961.

WEIGHLEY, Russell F., *Eisenhower's Lieutenants*, London & New York, 1980.

WELLER, Jac, *Weapons and Tactics: Hastings to Berlin*, New York, 1966.

WEST, Nigel, *MI6: British Secret Intelligence Service Operations 1909–45*, London, 1983.

WESTPHAL, S., *The Germany Army in the West*, London, 1951.

WILMOT, Chester, *The Struggle for Europe*, London, 1952.

WILSON, Andrew, *Flamethrower*, London, 1974.

WOOLLCOMBE, Robert, *Lion Rampant*, London, 1970.

Acknowledgements

Then men who fought in Normandy are today 40 years older than they were in 1944, but it is astonishing how vividly retentive are their memories. All those listed below — American, British, German, French — contributed to the narrative above, either through personal interviews, diaries, contemporary letters, or correspondence. I have omitted their ranks and decorations, which would otherwise overwhelm these pages. To each of them I offer my gratitude, and my admiration for what they endured.

L. W. Ainslie 5th Kings Regiment, W. Anderson 5th Battalion, Abraham Arditti 101st Airborne Div., D. W. Armstrong REME, R. A. H. Arnold 3rd Infantry Div., G. Ascher 357th Infantry, A. Ashley 3rd Infantry Div., T. K. Atherton 93rd LAA Regt., Julian Bach, Charles F. Baldwin, S. Bamber RAMC, Alan Barber RAF, G. Barden Armoured Div. Guards, D. Barker 6th Airborne Div., C. Barnby 1st Royal Norfolks, Mrs N. F. Barnes 6th Airborne Div., H. T. W. Barter 49th Div., Bill Bartlett USAAF, Hubert S. Bass 82nd Airborne Div., T. R. Beason RE, Chris Belcher 2nd Armored Div., William T. Belvin 2nd Infantry Div., M. Bennett Royal Navy, Arthur Berry, R. L. Beverley RAF, Richard Bills U.S. Navy, D. G. Bion 5th RTR, Peter Birkett Tyneside Scottish, Norman Bishop U.S. Navy, Edward J. Bisso Jr, A. Blooman RAOC, B. Boden, Robert Bogart 1st Infantry Div., J. Bond RASC, G. A. Bone RAF, Frank Booth RASC, L. Bour 1st Infantry Div., G. A. D. Bourne Royal Navy, R. I. M. Bowen RAF, G. Braysford Royal Engineers, Dr Warren E. Breniman, C. Brewer No. 12 Field Surgical Unit, G. Brice 246th Coy RE, A. Briggs, A. D. Briggs RE, D. Brinkman, D. G. Brown 5th RTR, J. Brown 11th Armoured Div., A. J. Brown 3rd Infantry Div., John Brown 11th Armoured Div., W. Brown 3rd Canadian Div., H. Brown, G. Bruce Royal Engineers, Randall Bryant 9th Infantry Div., Mrs Jean Buck, B. E. Buck REME, Eric Bulman, M. A. Burgess, James N. Burt 2nd Armoured Div., Jesse T. Butler 9th Infantry Div., R. W. Campbell 6th Airborne Div., W. A. Carter, Arthur L. Chaitt 1st Infantry Div., Mrs M. Chandler, O. H. Clark, Roy Clark Royal Navy, S. R. Cockaday 3rd Div. Provost Coy, Al Cohn U.S. Navy, W. A. Coke Royal Marines, Frank Colacicco 1st Infantry Div., Harry Collins 6th Airborne Div., Robert L. Conway 5th Engineer Special Brigade, James William Cook Royal Navy, Leo Cooper, John Purley Cooper Jr. 29th Div., Paul W. Corrigan 3rd Armored Div., John Craig, E. A. Crofts, R. B. Crosby Essex Yeomanry, Robert Michael Crossley, Rupert Curtis Royal Navy, Milton Dank, Mrs Margaret Darley-Bentley, W. Davies RAF, Harold Davies 7th Armoured Div., William E. Davis Royal Artillery, Frederick Davis RE, E. Dearsley, Bernard W. Deehan 2nd Armoured Div., M. Delaney Armoured Div., Ronald C. Denhand RAF, James Dobie The Kings Regiment, George W. Dohmann 9th Infantry Div., H. H. Downs RAF, F. G. Dubber 165th HAA Regt. RA, G. T. Duckworth RAF, Hayes W.

Dugan 3rd Armored Div., Martin Dumoch U.S. Navy, Steve Dyson 5th RTR, C. J. Eason 2nd Lincolnshires, J. Eccles, Alec Ecclestone Royal Navy, J. Edmondson 2nd Armoured Guards Div., J. E. Edney 7th Armoured Div., Sidney Eichen 30th Infantry Div., William J. Eisemann U.S. Navy, J. H. Ellis 1st Ox & Bucks, F. K. Faulkner REME, K du B. Ferguson RAF, W. M. H. Flory RAF, Mrs M. Floyd-Norris QAIMNS/R, A. H. Forrest RASC, J. S. Forster Royal Signals, E. A. Fowles RAF, Edward T. Francis 47th Anti-Aircraft Brigade, Jerrold Freeman RAF, W. M. Frick 79th Infantry Division, R. Frith Royal Navy, Robert Frost Royal Navy, Col. William B. Gara 1st Infantry Div., Wayne Garrets 90th Infantry Div., G. George 6th Airborne Div., E. H. Gibbs 9th Beach Group, A. C. Gigg 50th Infantry Div., J. A. Gill 2nd Infantry Div., A. F. Gillespie RASC, L. C. Gimbert RASC, Doug Ginder 3rd Div., Joe Glavan 35th Infantry Div., J. G. Glixby Royal Tank Regiment, Don Gordon Royal Engineers, Richard Gosling Essex Yeomanry, J. W. Goulder Royal Navy, Henry Grant 3rd Canadian Division, Mrs M. Z. Gray, J. Greenfield 116th HAA Regt., N. Griffin Royal Signals, G. Griffin 43rd Infantry Div., L. Griffiths 2nd Army HQ, Heinz Gunther Guderian 116 Panzer Div., Helmut Gunther 17 SS Panzergren. Div., William I. Hahn U.S. Navy, L. Haines 2nd/60th Rifles, J. G. Hanson RAF, Mrs Edward W. Harrison, Robin Hastings 6th Green Howards, R. E. Hauchan Royal Navy, J. A. Hawkes Royal Marines, S. D. Hayden 49th Div., A. Heal Royal Engineers, Richard Heap, John Hein 1st Infantry Div., Pamela Hensy QAIMNS/R, Harry Herman 9th Infantry Div., Andrew Hertz 834th Engineer Aviation Battalion, Heinz Hickmann Luftwaffe Parachute Div., Lindley R. Higgins 12th Infantry Rgt., H. Highwood Queens Regiment, George Hird RAOC, R. A. Hoar Royal Artillery, H. W. S. Hodd, Dr Adolf Hohenstein 276th Infantry Div., Alan W. Holmes RASC, F. A. Honey Royal Engineers, G. B. Honour Royal Navy, S. Hooker 6th Airborne Div., Charles T. Horner, H. Horsfield Royal Marines, James Houston Royal Navy, R. A. Howard Army Air Corps, W. T. Hoy REME, D. J. Hudson ACC, B. Hudson Staffordshire Yeomanry, D. S. Huett Armoured Div., J. A. Hughes Royal Marines, G. E. Humnas RAOC, S. F. Humphrey 344th Indep. Searchlight Battery RA, J. H. Humphries 50th Div., Mrs N. S. Hyde-Ferte, H. M. Irwin, J. L. Irwin 45th RM Commando, Jackson 50th Division, Harolds L. Jett U.S. Navy, Frank A. Jobson 6th Airborne Division, Mrs Susan Johnson ATS, A. E. Johnson 4th/7th Royal Dragoon Guards, R. Johnson 24 Base Section Royal Signals, A. Johnson Durham Light Infantry, G. R. Johnson 5th RTR, Carl R. Jones USAAF, Albert M. Jordan 2nd Armored Div., T. Josephs 29th Infantry Div., Kurt Kauffman Panzer Lehr, J. E. Kean 3rd Recce Regiment, R. O. Keeffe RASC, G. Keighley Sussex & Surrey Yeomanry, Dennis Kelley 9th Infantry Div., Lt. H. G. Kenyon Royal Navy, Henry W. Kilburg 875th Ordnance Battalion, R. R. Killona 237th Engineer Combat Battalion, Jerry W. Komarek 2nd Armored Div., Vincent A. Kordack 6th Beach Battalion, U.S. Navy, Warner Kortenhaus 21st Panzer Div., Hal Kosut 979th Batt., Edward B. Kovar 110th AAA Batt., Walter Kruger 12th SS Panzer Div., D. Lancaster, Mrs J. Lang WAAF, Helmut Lang Army Group B Headquarters, Fritz Langangke 2nd SS Panzer Div., T. Langston RA, Bruce A. Larose 1st Infantry Div., J. Law 147th Regiment RAC, P. Lawton 49th West Riding Div., J. E. Leather 4th Ox & Bucks, R. D. Lee 1st Ox & Bucks, A. Lee 1st Middlesex, J. M. Leggate FRCS 46th Field Surgical Unit, Edward M. Leitch 2nd Army Troop, Andrew J. Lento 4th Infantry Div., P. Leslie 79th Armoured Div., Arthur Lester, J. Leverett 6th Airborne Div., C. T. Lightman 11th Royal Scots Fusiliers, Mrs R. Lindner QAIMNS/R, Theodore S. Liska 4th Infantry Div., Dominic J. LoPiccolo 2nd Engineer Combat Battalion, S. Lockwood 4th CLY, Donald E. Loker US Navy, Len Lomell, J. S. Longster Suffolk Regt., A. V. Looker 1st KOSB, Rev. T. H. Lovegrove 6th Green Howards, W. W. Lund 6th

Airborne Div., R. Lyon REME, P. R. MacIver 8th Armoured Brigade, James G. Macpherson Merchant Navy, Maj. Gen. John J. Maginnis, J. S. Malkin 7th Field Reg. RA, G. C. Mantripp Royal Navy, Arlo J. Markestad 29th Infantry Div., P. Marshall 78th Coy. Royal Engineers, E. A. Martin 3rd Infantry Div., W. Martin, S. B. Mason, L. F. Matthews Royal Navy, John P. McGirr 65th Armored Field Artillery Batt., John A. McAllister 29th Infantry Div., Robert McCosh, Andrew McFadzean 29th Infantry Division, Dr Marie McHugh, L. J. McLaughlin 9th Infantry Div., Alan W. McQuillin RAF, S. Mills Royal Marines, James H. Moninger, Jr. 79th Infantry Div., Bidwell Moore 1st Infantry Div., G. Moore Royal Engineers, David Morgan REME., W. T. Morgan REME, Ted Morris, H. J. Morris Jones 746th Tank Batt., G. W. Moses, R. Mosse Guards Armoured Div., Anthony Mott 500th Div. RHR, F. L. Muttor 1st Infantry Div., Lt. Gen. Samuel L. Myers, Philip D. Myers 78th Armored Field Artillery Batt., W. E. Needler, A. L. Neely, Albert E. Nelson RCAF, D. C. Newton 6th Airborne Div., Ralph A. Nichols U.S. Navy, A. E. Nicholson RAMC, Ronald N. Palmer RMAS, J. Parkinson Royal Engineers, L. S. Parnell RAOC, A. Pascarell 487th Bomb Troop, Lt. Brewster G. Pattyson U.S. Coast Guard, Joseph K. Perkins 29th Infantry Div., R. Perkins, G. J. Peters 2nd Warwicks, N. C. Phillips, James Taillie Phillips U.S. Navy Minesweep-Unit 9, M. A. Philip Royal Signals, A. G. Pickely, H. A. Pickering 3rd Infantry Div., C. Piercy-Hughes 6th Airborne Div., Brig. Gen. Allan G. Pixton 5th Engineer Special Brigade, C. J. Potter, Bill Preston 29th Div., J. K. Price 2nd Ox & Bucks, Carl D. Proffitt DSC 29th Infantry Div., Clay Purvis 29th Infantry Div., Paul J. Quaiver 326th Engineer Batt., Lt. Gen. E. R. Quesada, Daniel Quinn 9th Infantry Div., G. T. Radmore 6th Airborne Div., G. L. Ramage, George L. Ramage Royal Engineers, Edward Rapp 4th Armored Div., Mrs Margaret R. Rathbone WRNS, Floyd Ratliff 30th Artillery., Ken Rawlings 35th Infantry Div., Dick Raymond 3rd Canadian Div., Mr & Mrs L. R. Reed, Philip B. Reisler 2nd Armored Div., A. J. Rennie KOSB, L. Reynolds 6th Airborne Div., Eric Richards, A. Richardson 43rd Infantry Div., F. O. Richardson 82nd Airborne Div., Robert L. Riggs 82nd Airborne Div., G. H. Robinson 5th Dorsets, Walter Rodman 102nd Cavalry Recon., A. Rolph 50th Div., George Rosie 101st Airborne Div., S. 'Rossant 2nd Welsh Guards, H. Rowe Pioneer Corps, E. Royle Royal Highland Reg. of Canada, G. E. M. Ruffee 14th Field Reg. Canadian Royal Artillery, K. M. Rugman 6th Airborne Div., R. R. Rylands KSLI, A. W. Sadler RASC, Charles Salt 4th Armoured Brig., H. L. Salter, Alvin Sapinsley U.S. Army Signals Corps, Richard W. Sargent 2nd Infantry Div., Rudolf Schaaf 716th Infantry Div., R. Schafer 9th Infantry Div., Wilhelm Schickner 2nd Panzer Div., Kevin Sharkey, Carl R. Sherrets, W. P. Shines Kings' Regiment, C. Shread 69 Field Coy (RE), E. F. Siderits U.S. Navy, Frank L. Sills RAF, Lawrence Silverman 5th Amphibious Engineer Special Brigade, P. Silverman 35th Infantry Div., W. J. Skittrall Essex Regiment, George L. Small 35th Infantry Div., Lt. Col. A. T. Smith 1st Infantry Div., Henry Smith Armored Div., Anthony M. Smith 819th Av. Engineers, J. R. Smith 141st Regt. RAC, Roy Smith 4th Airborne Div., J. F. Smyth Royal Navy, Mrs Robert F. Snetzer, Henry D. Soderberg 507th Military Police Batt., Sid Solomon, Saul Solow 30th Infantry Div., Mrs A. Sowerby, E. F. Spottiswoode REME, Vernon C. Squires 81st Construction Batt., A. Stackpole, William Stelling 29th Infantry Div., J. W. Stephens 86th Anti-Tank Reg. RA, Hans Stober 17th SS Panzergren. Div., W. L. Stray KSLI, Wallace C. Strobel 101st Airborne Div., D. J. Studdard 2nd Army HQ Troops, Edward Sullivan, William A. Sutton, G. R. Tait 3rd Div., D. A. Tait 101st Airborne Div., Peter Terry 47 Commando, Peter J. Terry, Hans Teske, O. H. Thomas 5th Beach Group, G. W. Thomas RAF, Charles H. Thomas 1st Div., David E. Thomas 82nd AB Div., G. Thorn Royal Marines, John M. Thorpe 11th Armoured Div., Matt N. Touchton

U.S. Navy, Major F. B. Upfold REME, E. H. Upward Royal Navy, L. J. Verier Home Guard, Dr. Eberhard Wagemann 21st Panzer Div., P. Wagg RE, Bill Walsh 102nd Cavalry, Edward Warman, John Warner 3rd Recce Regt., Geoffrey L. Way, A. C. Webb REME, Reg. A. F. Weigall, J. M. Welch 4th Infantry Div., A. H. Wells RE, Mrs Doreen Westaway QAIMNS, John A. Wheeldon 11th Armoured Div., F. W. White 51st Highland Div., Mrs H. G. White RE, Jack D. Whiteley 9th Infantry Div., A Whittenbury RE, Dr. John S. Wier 2nd Armored Div., K. M. Wilford RAF, Cyril Wilkins Royal Navy, Harold Wilkinson 3rd Infantry Div., Col. J. B. Wilks, Mary Williams WAAF, C. A. Williams Royal Navy, J. Williamson 3rd Scots Guards Tank Batt., Col. John Williamson 1st Infantry Div., S. E. Willis Royal Navy Commandos, F. V. Wilson Royal Navy, Thomas G. Wilson Merchant Navy, George R. Wilson Royal Navy, P. C. Wixey KRRC, N. C. Wood Military Police, A. S. Woods RAF, D. A. Woods Royal Navy, T. Woodward 3rd Infantry Div., R. Wright, H. Yarwood, A. E. Younger RAF.

Index

448

459

Max Hastings
Das Reich £2.50

June 1944: within days of the D-Day landings, the 'Das Reich' Panzer Division marched north through France to reinforce the defenders of Hitler's Fortress Europe. They were veterans of the bloody fighting of the Russian front, 15,000 men, hounded for every mile of their march by saboteurs of the Resistance and agents of the Allied Special Forces. Along their route they took reprisals so savage they will live for ever in the chronicles of war atrocity.

'My literary VC goes without doubt to Max Hastings for his *Das Reich* ... the story of a march that left behind a trail of blood and death, torture and heroism' SUNDAY TELEGRAPH

Bomber Command £2.95

Winner of the W. Somerset Maugham Award for Non-Fiction 1980 ... Bomber Command's offensive against the cities of Germany was one of the last war's epic campaigns. Hamburg, Berlin, Dresden – the author traces the development of area bombing, using a wealth of documents, letters, diaries and interviews.

'Probably the most brilliant use of anecdotal material that has so far come out of the Second World War ... brilliant' THE TIMES LITERARY SUPPLEMENT

'The most critical book yet written about Bomber Command ... also far and away the best' ECONOMIST

Max Hastings and Simon Jenkins
The Battle for the Falklands £2.95

This is the book on the Falklands war that serious readers have been waiting for. Max Hastings' reports from the battlefront for the *Standard* made him Journalist of the Year. Simon Jenkins, *Economist* political editor, offers a cogent analysis of the war's political and diplomatic background. At once a vivid chronicle of a feat of arms and a thoughtful and informed analysis of an astonishing historical chapter – the definitive account of the war.

H. R. Trevor-Roper
The Last Days of Hitler £1.95

'An incomparable book, by far the best written on any aspect of the
second German war: a book sound in its scholarship, brilliant in its
presentation, a delight for historians and laymen alike.' A. J. P. TAYLOR

'Absolutely enthralling . . . It is all there, the fantastic comings and
goings, Hitler's last-minute marriage to Eva Braun and the supposed
suicide and ritual burning of the corpse.' DAILY WORKER

William L. Schirer
The Rise and Fall of the Third Reich £4.95

The world-famous history of Nazi Germany.

'A magnificent work . . . documented, reasoned, objective and never dull
. . . the standard, indeed the classic, history of Nazism' HUGH TREVOR-
ROPER, SUNDAY TIMES

'I can think of no book I would rather put into the hands of anyone who
wanted to find out what happened in Germany between 1930 and 1945'
ALAN BULLOCK, GUARDIAN

You can buy these and other Pan books from booksellers and newsagents; or
direct from the following address:
CS Department, Pan Books Ltd, PO Box 40, Basingstoke, Hants
Send purchase price plus 35p for the first book and 15p for each additional book,
to allow for postage and packing
Prices quoted are applicable in the UK

While every effort is made to keep prices low, it is sometimes necessary to
increase prices at short notice. Pan Books reserve the right to show on covers and
charge new retail prices which may differ from those advertised in the text or
elsewhere